"High and Mighty Queens" of Early Modern England

"High and Mighty Queens" of Early Modern England: Realities and Representations

CO-EDITED BY

Carole Levin, Jo Eldridge Carney, and
Debra Barrett-Graves

HIGH AND MIGHTY QUEENS OF EARLY MODERN ENGLAND
© Carole Levin, Jo Eldridge Carney, Debra Barrett-Graves, 2003

All rights reserved. No part of this book may be used or reproduced in any manner whatsoever without written permission except in the case of brief quotations embodied in critical articles or reviews.

First published 2003 by
PALGRAVE MACMILLAN™
175 Fifth Avenue, New York, N.Y. 10010 and
Houndmills, Basingstoke, Hampshire, England RG21 6XS.
Companies and representatives throughout the world.

PALGRAVE MACMILLAN is the global academic imprint of the Palgrave Macmillan division of St. Martin's Press, LLC and of Palgrave Macmillan Ltd. Macmillan® is a registered trademark in the United States, United Kingdom and other countries. Palgrave is a registered trademark in the European Union and other countries.

ISBN 1–4039–6088–7 hardback

Library of Congress Cataloging-in-Publication Data

"High and mighty queens" of early modern England: realities and representations/co-edited by Carole Levin, Jo Eldridge Carney, and Debra Barrett-Graves.
   p. cm.
   Includes bibliographical references and index.
   ISBN 1–4039–6088–7
   1. English literature—Early modern, 1500–1700—History and criticism. 2. Queens in literature. 3. Women and literature—Great Britain—History—16th century. 4. Women and literature—Great Britain—History—17th century. 5. Queens—Great Britain—Biography—History and criticism. 7. Women in literature. I. Levin, Carole, 1948– II. Carney, Jo Eldridge, 1954– III. Barrett-Graves, Debra, 1953–

PR428.Q44 H54 2003
820.9′352351—dc21   2002032205

A catalogue record for this book is available from the British Library.

Design by Newgen Imaging Systems (P) Ltd., Chennai, India.

First edition: April, 2003
10 9 8 7 6 5 4 3 2 1

Printed in the United States of America.

"Say she shall be a high and mighty queen"
The Tragedy of King Richard III

For Joan, John, and Lillian, with much love
Debra

For my dear friends, Laurie, Kelly, Carron, and Cathy
Jo

For Michael Altschul, Margaret Hannay, Howard Solomon,
Gerald Sorin, and Retha Warnicke,
as a token of my gratitude for all the loving support
throughout my career
Carole

Contents

Acknowledgments xi

List of Illustrations xii

Introduction 1
Carole Levin, Jo Eldridge Carney, and Debra Barrett-Graves

Part I The Nature of Renaissance Queens 9

1. *Timothy G. Elston*, Transformation or Continuity? Sixteenth-Century Education and the Legacy of Catherine of Aragon, Mary I, and Juan Luis Vives 11

2. *Judith M. Richards*, Mary Tudor: Renaissance Queen of England 27

3. *Louis H. Roper*, Unmasquing the Connections between Jacobean Politics and Policy: The Circle of Anna of Denmark and the Beginning of the English Empire, 1614–18 45

4. *Karen L. Nelson*, Negotiating Exile: Henrietta Maria, Elizabeth of Bohemia, and the Court of Charles I 61

Part II Imaging Renaissance Queens and Power 77

5. *Matthew C. Hansen*, "And a Queen of England, Too": The 'Englishing' of Catherine of Aragon in Sixteenth-Century English Literary and Chronicle History 79

6. *Susan Dunn-Hensley*, Whore Queens: The Sexualized Female Body and the State 101

7. *Jo Eldridge Carney*, "Honoured Hippolyta, Most Dreaded Amazonian": The Amazon Queen in the Works of Shakespeare and Fletcher 117

8. *Sid Ray*, "No head eminent above the rest": Female Authority in *Othello* and *The Tempest* 133

9. *Kirilka Stavreva*, "There's magic in thy majesty": Queenship and Witch-Speak in Jacobean Shakespeare 151

Part III Cultural Anxieties and Historical Echoes of Renaissance Queens **169**

10. *Carole Levin*, The Taming of the Queen: Foxe's Katherine and Shakespeare's Kate 171

11. *Joy Currie*, Mary Queen of Scots as Suffering Woman: Representations by Mary Stuart and William Wordsworth 187

12. *Georgianna Ziegler*, Re-imagining a Renaissance Queen: Catherine of Aragon among the Victorians 203

13. *Elaine Kruse*, The Woman in Black: The Image of Catherine de Medici from Marlowe to *Queen Margot* 223

14. *Retha M. Warnicke*, Anne Boleyn in History, Drama, and Film 239

Notes on Contributors 257

Index 261

Acknowledgments

The beginning of this collection of essays was a seminar for the Shakespeare Association of America that met in Montreal in 2000. Our thanks to the SAA and Lena Orlin, Executive Director, all of the participants and the commentators, Ilona Bell, and Steven May. As well as the essays that came out of the seminar, several of the essays in this collection were presented under the auspices of the Society for the Study of Early Modern Women at the Sixteenth Century Studies Conference in Denver 2001. We very much appreciate the help of R. Emmet McLaughlin, President of the Sixteenth Century Studies Conference for that year, and Ronald Fritze, Secretary of the organization, for their help in scheduling these sessions. The editors at Palgrave were wonderful people with whom to work. We are most appreciative of Rohana Kenin for her work on the index.

Carole wishes to express her deep appreciation for the Humanities Program and the UCARE program at the University of Nebraska for their generous support. She would also like to thank the graduate students at the University of Nebraska in her queenship seminar for their valuable perspectives and suggestive discussions. Carolyn Biltoft, Jarrod Brand, Christine Couvillon, Timothy Elston, and Teri Imus were most helpful in providing research support. She also greatly appreciates the expert and thoughtful help of the librarians at Love Library at the University of Nebraska, especially Gretchen Holten Poppler and Kathy Johnson, and in Special Collections, Mary Ellen Ducey and Carmella Garman Orosco. She was delighted with the opportunity to work again with her wonderful colleagues and co-editors, Debra and Jo.

Jo is most grateful to The College of New Jersey for released time to work on this project. She also very much appreciates the support of her family—Sandy, Alex, Julie, and Annie. Debra is most appreciative of the support of the College of Santa Fe, where she taught previously, and to the faculty and staff at Fogelson Library at the College of Santa Fe, particularly Matthew Clinton, Allison Aran, Peggy Rudberg, R. David Myers, Margaret Johnson, Rebecca Schwilling, Daria Carson, and Harriet Meiklejohn.

Illustrations

Uxoria Virtues from Geffrey Whitney, *A Choice of Emblems*
Reprinted by permission of the Newberry Library   79

Sir John Mandeville, *Travels* (1574)
Reprinted by permission of the Houghton Library,
Harvard University   134

Henry VIII and Catherine Parr
1868 engraving from the painting by R. Smirke   172

Mary Queen of Scots
From S. Griswold Goodrich, *Lives of Celebrated Women*
New York: John Allen (1844)   188

Henry VIII, Act IV, scene 2 in Cassell's *Illustrated Shakespeare*
Reprinted by permission of the Folger Shakespeare Library   204

Anne Boleyn by an unknown artist
Reprinted by courtesy of the National Portrait Gallery   240

Introduction

*Carole Levin, Jo Eldridge Carney, and
Debra Barrett-Graves*

> Now say, have women worth? or have they none?
> Or had they some, but with our Queen is't gone?
> Nay Masculines, you have thus taxt us long,
> But she, though dead, will vindicate our wrong.
> Let such as say our sex is void of Reason,
> Know tis a slander now, but once was treason.[1]

Though Anne Bradstreet was not born until almost a decade after the death of Queen Elizabeth I in 1603, the tremendous impact of having a queen on the throne of England for much of the latter part of the sixteenth century was such that it was part of women's cultural memory. Yet, Elizabeth was not the only significant queen in the early modern period; there were a number of others, queen regnants, queen consorts, and queen mothers, who are well worth studying. Moreover, the impact of female rule also meant that the ways in which queens were depicted in literature changed in the sixteenth and early seventeenth century. And these queens were so powerful in their representation that they continued to be depicted and discussed centuries after their deaths, even to this day.

The sixteenth century in England, and in Europe more generally, was a time of tremendous change, the fault line between medieval and modern. The universal Church in the West split into fragments: Catholic and a variety of sects of Protestants. The explorations into Africa and the Americas also made people think differently about the world in which they lived and the gender relations of people in that world. This time period likewise saw the further development of nation-states, with changing definitions of the nature of monarchy. Those definitions became even more complex when women moved into positions of political power. It may come as no surprise that the sixteenth century was not only a century of queens but also of witchcraft accusations, most of which were aimed at women.

There were queens particularly in England but also in Scotland and the Continent. Some of these were strong-minded wives of kings, others were their widows who acted as regents and procured powerful roles in the political structures as Queen Mothers, and some, such as Mary I, Elizabeth I, and Mary Stuart, were queen regnants. The impact of women who had power either through their marriages or, more remarkably by biological accident, held power in their own right, had a great influence on how strong women were perceived and presented. Being a queen regnant gave certain women more potential for power than being a queen consort or queen mother, and, indeed, the role of consort entailed different vulnerabilities than that of regnant.

Pamphlet literature, historical representation, and drama of the time all shared the debate on women's capabilities and nature. The impact of queens continued even beyond in the sixteenth century when women actually ruled in their own right. Questions about powerful women and the roles they might play were deeply debated well into the seventeenth century before the reigns of Mary II and Anne. The pamphlet debate on queenship in the sixteenth century had become by the next century a far more thoroughgoing debate over women's capabilities and roles in public as well as private life.

Ironically, the desire for a male heir led to a whole group of strong women as queen consorts and eventually as queen regnants in sixteenth-century England. Henry VIII's desperate wish for a son led to his decision to attempt to annul his marriage to his popular first wife, Catherine of Aragon, whose only child to survive infancy was their daughter Mary. Despite the fact that continuing the marriage with Catherine in the 1520s would have meant that the heir to the throne was female, many people in England were distraught over Henry's proposed divorce, especially when it also meant a break with the Church of Rome. Though Henry claimed that one reason he must have a son was that the role of king meant leading his people in war and "the battlefield was unmeet for women's imbecilities,"[2] Catherine's mother Isabella of Castile had been queen in her own right and had led troops into battle against the Moors. Catherine had been not only advisor to her husband in the early years of his reign, but was also a successful regent at home when he was fighting in France. Though Catherine stayed loyal to Henry despite her refusal to agree that she was not his lawful wife, both the king and those around him feared Catherine might take after her mother and lead the disaffected against the crown. Catherine of Aragon was not the only powerful wife that Henry eventually married.

Instead of replacing Catherine with a French Princess as Henry's Chancellor Cardinal Wolsey originally expected, Henry's second wife was Anne Boleyn, an English woman at the court whom Henry passionately loved. Anne refused to follow the path of her sister Mary and become Henry's mistress. Marriage to Anne and the break with Rome became intertwined as Henry pursued his goal of having a son. When Anne finally became pregnant in late 1532, Archbishop Cranmer early the next year declared Henry's marriage to Catherine null and void while Parliament declared "This realm of England is an empire" and no Pope nor Emperor can tell its king or its people what to do. Many people demonized the Protestant Anne for replacing Catherine and were arrested for slander. When Anne as well did not have a living son, and may well have given birth to a deformed male fetus, Henry's love turned to such hate that in 1536 he had her executed with five men, reputed to be her lovers. Their daughter Elizabeth, like her half-sister Mary, was declared illegitimate. On the day of her execution Henry announced his engagement to another lady at court, Jane Seymour, who was to give Henry the son he craved, though she died at childbirth. The fourth marriage to Anne of Cleves was annulled and the fifth marriage to Katherine Howard led to another execution for adultery. Henry's last wife Katherine Parr was also a strong woman who supported humanism and strived to bring together Henry's three children: Mary, Elizabeth, and Edward.

Though only one of Henry VIII's wives was actually the mother of a surviving son, all six wives resonated powerfully with the English people. In the decades after Henry's reign they were presented in both Catholic and Protestant polemical literature, in ballads, and in drama. More generally, the power and danger of Henry VIII's wives reflected the often contradictory role of the queen consort in seventeenth-century England as well, such as Anna of Denmark, wife of James I, or Henrietta Maria, consort to his son Charles. From 1553, after the death of Edward VI and the unsuccessful attempt to supplant the succession with Lady Jane Grey, England had women rulers, Mary I and Elizabeth, for the rest of the century. In Scotland, Mary Stuart was queen in her own right and in France the second half of the century was dominated by the Queen Mother, Catherine de Medici. Images of these queens also echoed for centuries to come.

These powerful women provided the possibility of expanded gender roles and were glorified and demonized on both sides of the religious divide—Catholic and Protestant. In 1558, the Scots Calvinist John Knox referred to this phenomenon as a "monstrous regiment of women."

Knox was the most famous of an entire group who debated whether or not a woman had the right to rule and to bear authority over men. Others who wrote in the 1550s against Catholic Mary I included Christopher Goodman and Thomas Becon. John Aylmer's *Harborowe for Faithful and Trewe Subjectes* (1559) was the first Protestant pamphlet of Elizabeth I's reign to support queenship, but Aylmer and other Protestants also showed reservations about women and power. The debate over legitimacy of female rule went to the heart of the question over the nature of womankind. The polemical debate used many historical, literary, and Biblical examples to argue for or against women's right to rule. Stories of earlier women often had as unmentioned shadows the parallels with the contemporary sixteenth-century queens. But while the debate over queenship reflected questions about the nature of womankind in general, for women who actually held power, there was another kind of issue at work: how to establish and maintain authority as a woman in power.

While there were celebrations of these strong women, they also caused great anxiety that was intertwined with the religious conflicts and the national rivalries that were going on at the same time. We can understand much more about the ambivalence felt about women in power from seeing how actual sixteenth-century queens, earlier historical queens, and legendary queens were represented in Renaissance drama and culture. By analyzing the different representations of Renaissance queenship we can gain a greater understanding of cultural anxieties about strong women, and of the difficulties and expanding possibilities of women in power.

***

This collection is divided into three parts. Part 1, "The Nature of Renaissance Queens," considers such queens as Catherine of Aragon, her daughter Mary I, and two queen consorts of the early seventeenth century, Anna and Henrietta Maria. Part 2, "Imaging Renaissance Queens and Power," examines a number of dramatic, poetic, and cultural texts about queens in the early modern period. While one essay considers the representation of Catherine of Aragon, other essays in this section consider mythical or fictional queens in drama and poetry. In Part 3, "Cultural Anxieties and Historical Echoes of Renaissance Queens," the essays examine later dramatic and poetic representations of Katherine Parr, Mary Stuart, Catherine of Aragon, and Anne Boleyn, as well as English and French representations of the French queen mother Catherine de Medici.

Timothy Elston's essay examines the impact of Spanish humanist Juan Luis Vives on the education of Princess Mary Tudor, later Queen Mary I. While some scholars argue that Vives was something of a proto-feminist, effecting transformative change in social and cultural attitudes toward the education of women, others argue that Vives simply reinforced the status quo. Elston sees Vives as adopting *a via media*, using his educational treatises for the Tudor queens as a means of changing women's educational experiences within the framework of existing patriarchal ideals.

Mary I is also the subject of Judith Richards's essay, a revisionist consideration of this often maligned queen. Challenging traditional notions of Mary as incompetent, stubborn, and ineffectual, Richards argues that Mary was, in fact, well-learned, politically accomplished, and astute. Richards maintains that Mary's religious policies were not simply conservative and narrowly conceived; in keeping with her humanist education, Mary brought new modes of instruction to conventional ceremonies and rituals of worship. It is time, Richards argues, to rescue Mary's legacy as a monarch from centuries of Protestant critique.

Louis Roper also argues for a reconsideration of a royal reputation: in this case, Anna of Denmark, queen-consort of James I. Roper expands upon the work of recent scholars who have demonstrated that, contrary to traditional views, Anna was no inept and powerless queen whose only interest was in frivolous entertainment and expensive court masques. This essay is particularly interested in how Anna and her associates contributed to English colonization efforts. In 1617, Pocahontas and John Rolfe visited the English court to muster support for the flagging Virginia Company; the queen's network responded positively by providing much-needed financial support. Roper argues that Anna deserves much greater credit for her role in this historical moment as well as for her influence on the choice of James's favorites and the adoption of political policies.

As several of the authors in this volume demonstrate, many of the early modern queens traditionally considered peripheral wielded far more influence than the historical record has claimed; Karen Nelson explores the different ways in which Charles I's sister Elizabeth and his wife Henrietta Maria promoted their own causes in their adopted countries and how they wielded influence on Charles. Henrietta Maria initially resisted assimilation to the English court, much to the dismay of her adopted people; as her reign progressed, she gradually came to acknowledge the expectations of her as an English queen. In contrast, Elizabeth, who well understood the necessity for popular support, made repeated and successful efforts to establish a cooperative relationship between herself and her adopted people of Bohemia. Nelson highlights the differences in the approaches of these two queens to their monarchies, but she argues that each queen was influential in her own way in negotiating the complexities of the Stuart court and in promoting her own particular political agendas.

Though a number of essays in the second part of the collection consider legendary or fictional queens, Matthew Hansen's essay, with its consideration of Catherine of Aragon and Patient Griselda, works as a bridge from historical queens to some mythical women. Hansen examines how the reputation of Queen Catherine of Aragon underwent a transformation in popular history and literature so that by the end of the sixteenth century she was portrayed as a paragon of wifely patience in the tradition of the legendary Patient Griselda. Hansen provides a careful analysis of a work that has received insufficient attention, William Forrest's 1558 verse history dedicated to Mary I, which specifically compares Catherine of Aragon to Griselda. Hansen, further, explores the literary development of the Griselda legend in sixteenth-century literature and the valorization of Catherine's historical persona in chronicle histories, and argues that these two traditions converge in Shakespeare and Fletcher's Henry VIII in which Catherine is presented as an exemplar of noble queenship.

Susan Dunn-Hensley's essay also focuses on Shakespeare's dramatic representations of queens. Dunn-Hensley considers Shakespeare's work in the context of attitudes current in the Renaissance: anxieties about the female body and sexuality were ubiquitous and such fears were exacerbated when the female body assumed the throne. Dunn-Hensley examines three plays in which Shakespeare portrays sexually active and transgressive queens: *Titus Andronicus*, *Hamlet*, and *Cymbeline*. Tamora, Gertrude, and Cymbeline's consort are all marked by a powerful, unruly sexuality that threatens to disrupt the orderly, patriarchal world.

Jo Eldridge Carney examines how early modern anxieties over female rule were manifest in the cultural preoccupation with Amazon queens. Sixteenth- and seventeenth-century literature and drama include numerous references to the Amazon woman, a figure that came to represent female monstrosity and violation of the natural order, particularly because she represented self-sufficiency and autonomy. In Shakespeare's *A Midsummer Night's Dream*, Shakespeare and Fletcher's *The Two Noble Kinsmen*, and Fletcher's *The Sea Voyage*, the threat of the Amazon queen is introduced but she is ultimately vanquished and orthodox patriarchy is reaffirmed.

Sid Ray's essay also considers the way in which the debate over female monarchy emerges in Shakespeare's plays. Ray explores the appropriation of the head/body metaphor in early modern political and marital theory and demonstrates how *Othello* and *The Tempest* challenge orthodox views of female authority in their references to "unnatural" bodies. In their evocations of differently formed bodies from newly explored worlds, both of these plays challenge traditional categories of "otherness," and in so doing, subtly but radically call into question traditional notions of female rulership in the political and domestic realms.

Kirilka Stavreva focuses on depictions of female power and authority in four of Shakespeare's later plays, *Macbeth*, *Cymbeline*, *The Winter's Tale*, and *The Tempest*. Stavreva explores the ways in which the language of witchcraft, "witch-speak," was appropriated and incorporated by dramatists and permeated the social world of their plays; as royal and noble characters exploit the possibilities of witch-speak, the potency of its expression complicates categories of female and male political authority and represents a powerful challenge to early modern notions of kingship.

The final set of essays examines how a number of sixteenth-century queens were reexamined and refashioned in literature, drama, and film in the centuries that followed. The various ways these Renaissance queens were depicted reflects the values and concerns of the people and times of these later periods. Carole Levin examines how Henry VIII's last wife Katherine Parr becomes the model queen of John Foxe's *Acts and Monuments* and then reads *The Taming of the Shrew* as an echo and counterpoint to Foxe's representation. Not only is Kate tamed as Henry tamed his wife, but Bianca, modest and scholarly, also reflects certain qualities of the queen. Joy Currie's analysis covers several centuries. Currie examines how Mary Stuart, particularly during her time of imprisonment in England, presented herself as a suffering woman, and compares Mary's own poems with those written about her by William Wordsworth (1770–1850). Wordsworth's evocation of the Scottish queen was part of the Romantic concern with the individual. Georgianna Ziegler also draws a thoughtful comparison while she examines nineteenth-century views of queenship given that a queen, this time Victoria, was again ruling. Ziegler focuses on Catherine of Aragon, examining not only Victoria's own view of this earlier queen but how nineteenth-century historians and actresses presented Henry VIII's brave but domesticated first wife.

Just as Catherine of Aragon was a positive image in the centuries after her death, across the Channel queen mother Catherine de Medici was used as a warning of the dangers of powerful women. That Catherine was Catholic, Italian by birth, and ruler in France made it all the easier for the English playwright Christopher Marlowe to characterize her as a villain. Elaine Kruse demonstrates how this portrayal of Catherine endured, and continued to be used for political measures, discussing how John Wyat in the late seventeenth century contrasted a cruel Catherine with a good Mary II. By examining both French and English depictions of Catherine, Kruse carefully delineates the connections between political representations of queens in the two countries.

The collection ends with Retha Warnicke's sweeping essay that examines how representations of Anne Boleyn have changed from the sixteenth century to the present day. Warnicke notes a startling change between earlier depictions of Anne and twentieth-century ones. Instead of showing a more sympathetic and multivalent use of Anne, modern dramatists present Henry VIII's second queen as ambitious and manipulative, demonstrating that even today the cultural anxiety over strong women remains.

Anne Bradstreet was not alone in the early modern period in her fascination with queens. As this collection demonstrates, the reality as well as the representation of queens played a significant role in the cultural context. Centuries later, sixteenth- and seventeenth-century queens still hold a strong fascination for many people, and the way they have been represented reflects not only ideas about the early modern period, but also the concerns of later times. The representations and historical analysis of these queens that continue to this day are part of the ongoing debate about women and their roles, which is the successor of the Renaissance debate. The rule of queens, as consorts, regents, or in their own right, caused great discussion about women's capabilities and their essential nature in the English Renaissance. The issues raised then still resonate as we begin a new millennium.

Notes

1. Anne Bradstreet, "In Honor of That High and Mighty Princess Queen Elizabeth of Happy Memory" in Sandra M. Gilbert and Susan Gubar, *The Norton Anthology of Literature by Women*, 2nd edn. (New York: W.W. Norton and Company, 1996), p. 87.
2. Carolly Erickson, *Bloody Mary* (New York: Doubleday, 1978).

Part I
The Nature of Renaissance Queens

Transformation or Continuity? Sixteenth-Century Education and the Legacy of Catherine of Aragon, Mary I, and Juan Luis Vives

Timothy G. Elston

If the education of a king was a daunting task in sixteenth-century England, how much more so was the deed if the future monarch was a woman. Yet, the very problem facing Henry VIII and his first wife, Catherine of Aragon, after the birth of their only surviving child, Mary, in 1516, was how to educate the Tudor heir. Although Erasmus's *The Education of a Christian Prince* (1516) existed to serve as a guide for a future king, and Henry even owned a copy, there was no such guide for a future queen.[1] Furthermore, the Tudor Dynasty was still young, and many, including Henry, feared that leaving England in the hands of a woman, educated or not, was an open invitation for foreign intervention or civil war. Therefore, the idea of educating Mary to rule almost certainly never entered Henry's mind. Catherine, however, most likely never harbored such concerns, though there was little she could do about them. She was, after all, the daughter of Isabel of Castile, and knew firsthand that a woman, properly motivated, could be a successful monarch. To create this triumphant queen would require at least two factors: a good education and history's good graces. While only the passage of time could achieve the latter, the education of Princess Mary was attainable, and, for this task, Catherine turned to the new learning of the day, humanism, and one of its prime proponents, her compatriot the Spanish humanist Juan Luis Vives. However, Catherine received more than she perhaps bargained for. Ostensibly, Vives's educational efforts were for Mary, but by extension benefited all women, including Catherine, because her failure to produce a male heir would cause her incredible hardship by the end of the second decade of the sixteenth century, when Vives's advice about her worthiness as a woman would be most needed. The long-term results of Vives's efforts would provide future generations of women a greater educational experience within the confines of a patriarchal society.

Educated at the *Estudio General* in Valencia, in 1508–09, Vives obtained a clear understanding of the debate between the old and new learning then expressed in Spain, and quickly allied himself with the less popular humanists led by Antonio de Nebrija. He then traveled to France where he attended the Montaigu School, a center of religious reform that infused his zeal for the ethical improvement of society and the individual, remaining there until 1512.[2]

After Paris, Vives moved to Bruges and then to Louvain in 1517, where he encountered the northern form of humanism as presented by Erasmus, quickly developing a propensity for Erasmian thought. Erasmus's impact upon Vives, as for so many others, was profound and Vives's time in Louvain was extremely productive. Erasmus was, as James McConica has stated, in command of "the allegiance of the best minds of his day for a reason. It was his genius to fuse into a single stream of thought the converging currents of the late fifteenth century: humanistic textual scholarship, Florentine neo-Platonism, Netherlands piety... and the manifold discontents of a middle class suddenly aware of its power and its needs. It was this blend which received the alluring label of *philosophia Christi*—a phrase rich with patristic overtones, signifying a life of wisdom entirely consecrated to God."[3] Certainly, if any of Erasmus's followers bought into this *philosophia Christi* it was Juan Luis Vives. For Vives, all human actions in this world should reflect the person and life of Christ, which is at the heart of the works that he produced for Catherine on women's education.

Through his contact with the Erasmian circle, Vives met Thomas More, who, in 1521, was Under-Treasurer of England. More made it possible for Queen Catherine to take Vives under her protection and provide him with a small pension. Vives, desiring a better income, quickly dedicated his commentary on *Civitas Dei* to Henry VIII in 1522, followed by *De Institutione Feminae Christianae* (*The Instruction [Education] of a Christian Woman*), which he dedicated to Catherine, in April 1523. By May of the same year, Vives was in England, employed, not by Catherine nor by Henry, but by Cardinal Thomas Wolsey, who offered him a job as reader of Latin, Greek, and rhetoric at Cardinal College, Oxford.[4] Thus began Vives's career in England, and he would continue in the favor of Catherine, Henry, and Wolsey until 1528.

Vives's presence in England and, eventually, at the English court, was not the first for a humanist. As David Loades has pointed out, by Henry VIII's accession, ideas concerning a properly educated monarch had changed with the spread of Italian humanism after the French invasions, and Henry recognized that he needed to have a library that reflected the new learning, lest other monarchs perceive him as incapable of "competing on the European stage."[5] Therefore, under Henry VIII, humanists found themselves among those who had established themselves at court. Thomas Linacre and William Blount, Lord Mountjoy, were two such men. Linacre was in attendance as Mary's tutor, while Mountjoy was a well-known and well-connected patron of the new learning, who studied under Erasmus, and served Queen Catherine as her Chamberlain beginning in 1509.[6] Eventually, the royal court was so favorable to humanist learning that Erasmus, in a letter to Richard Pace, the Latin secretary of the King, wrote, "How truly splendid is the court of your native Britain, the seat and citadel of humane studies and of every virtue! I wish you joy, my dear Pace, of such a prince, and I wish your prince joy, whose kingdom is rendered illustrious by so many brilliant minds."[7]

Catherine's backing of humanism and her support of a humanistic education for Mary demonstrates the depth of the new learning's affect upon the court and should not come as a surprise. Catherine was, after all, the product of the very same learning. Queen Isabel of Castile, herself a late bloomer when it came to education, saw the necessity of an educated monarch and encouraged several different humanist scholars to educate all of her children. Catherine, educated along with her brother Juan, the heir to the Spanish throne, came under the tutelage of two Italian humanist brothers, Antonio and Alessandro Geraldino, who educated Catherine and her sisters in the classics.[8] Alessandro, who later traveled to England with Catherine in 1501, wrote at the behest of Isabella a work on the education of girls, *De eruditione nobelium puellarum* (*On the Education of Well-Born Girls*). While this work has not survived,[9] the seeds of female educational success planted by both Isabel's example of an educated monarch and Catherine's tutors took root in Catherine, and, once queen in England, she indulged her passion for learning and patronage as had Tudor women before her.

Within the house of Tudor, there was a long tradition of supporting the new learning, though its establishment as the scholarship for the future monarch did not take place until Princess Mary's birth. Beginning with Lady Margaret Beaufort, Henry VII's mother, and extending to Mary, the Dowager Queen of France and Catherine of Aragon's sister-in-law, these women held in common their choices for receiving their patronage, which they limited to men who composed one of two types of literature: devotional works or educational treatises. Patronage also extended to certain religious houses, one of which Catherine visited often, the Bridgettine house of Syon. Therefore, Vives was only one of several people for whom Catherine chose to provide patronage. She supported in some form Linacre, Pace, John Leland, and several others. Furthermore, Catherine received several dedicatory works besides Vives's *De Institutione Feminae Christianae*, including works by Thomas Wyatt, Richard Pynson, and Alphonso de Villa Sancta.[10]

Catherine and Henry entered Oxford in October of 1523, and out of this visit, in what may be the first face-to-face encounter between these people, Vives received an invitation to spend the Christmas holidays at Windsor. From a letter he wrote to his friend, Francis Cranvelt, it is clear that the opportunity to spend time in the royal court was what Vives truly wanted. He believed it was his calling to educate the Christian Princes of his world, for only by educating them could he make any changes to society. At this time, Vives also wrote *De Ratione Studii Puerilis* (*A Plan of Study for Children*) for Princess Mary, which he personally gave to the Queen on her visit to Oxford.[11] It appears that this Spanish born Queen of England swept Vives off his feet and, in admiration of her, Vives wrote to Cranvelt in January of 1524, "At times I was able to have some philosophical talks with the Queen, one of the purest and most Christian souls I have ever seen."[12] No doubt, his meetings with Catherine confirmed for Vives his decision, as his dedication indicated, to model *De Institutione Feminae Christianae* largely upon the life of this remarkably educated queen, and offer to other aristocratic women the experience of humanistic education.

Modern readers of Vives's *De Institutione Feminae Christianae* and his second work for Princess Mary, *De Ratione Studii Puerilis*, both written in 1523, are often confronted with conflicting views of Vives's intentions regarding women's education when reviewing scholarly work from the last century. Two arguments have arisen concerning Vives's views on the education of women; the first interprets Vives's accomplishments as a "transformative" event in the lives of women, while the second reflects the political rhetoric of the mid to late twentieth century that perceived progress for women within the existing patriarchal system as less than acceptable.

In the autumn 1997 edition of the *Journal of Women's Studies*, Judith Bennett introduced a somewhat controversial theory concerning traditional scholarship on women's history, which provides an excellent way of examining this debate. In her article, entitled "Confronting

Continuity," Bennett concluded that historians of European women have too often interpreted a change in women's experience as "transformation" in their status within patriarchal Europe, whereas in reality research suggests that change in experience is simply that, a change in experience, and nothing more.

Specifically, Bennett applies this theory to her own work on the alewives of late medieval England. Her research demonstrates that these women did difficult work for low pay to supplement their family's meager income, and as brewing ale became more profitable, women gradually moved out of the industry, relegated to other equally difficult work of low status and low pay. Bennett therefore concludes that experiences changed for these women, but that there was not a transformation of their status within patriarchal society.[13]

Admittedly, the alewives of Bennett's research have little to do with this essay, but her theory is applicable to many situations, including the present discussion. Adherents to the "transformation argument," including Francis Utley, Foster Watson, Garrett Mattingly, and Pearl Hogrefe, have regarded Vives's ideas and Catherine's implementation of the same as the greatest progress for women and women's education up to the sixteenth century. As champions of this argument, they have either declared that the collaboration between Queen Catherine and Vives was vital to the efforts of educating women in England during the reign of Henry VIII, or since Vives recommended training women in humanistic methods, this same group came to argue that feminism began with the Renaissance.[14] Clearly, this approach views the mere acknowledgment of the need in the sixteenth century to educate women as a transformation in women's status, or, to put it more succinctly, a revolution in their value to patriarchal society. Yet, this analysis does not examine in depth what type of education Vives actually recommended for Princess Mary nor, as it turns out, for women whose parents were concerned with the upward mobility of their family.

On the other side of the debate, one finds those who argue that the words 'feminist' and 'Vives' do not belong in the same sentence. Not surprisingly, women scholars from the latter half of the twentieth century have tended to lead with this argument. Certainly, there is truth in this observation since some of Vives's comments are far from flattering to women. In fact, after the publication of *De Institutione Feminae Christianae*, which is often highly critical of marriage, Erasmus wrote to Vives offering his congratulations on the work, though stating that he believed Vives was too harsh on women and that he hoped Vives treated his wife better than he suggested in his writings.[15] Ultimately, modern scholars have tended to follow the lead of Gloria Kaufman, who concludes that Vives is simply ambivalent toward women's education, torn between religious and patristic orthodoxy and humanist learning.[16]

Modern scholars have responded to Vives's more romantic champions by asking, where are all the women who supposedly benefited from this revolutionary education? Since the resulting answer to this legitimate question is painfully obvious, many modern historians and literary critics have concluded that Vives's methods and proposals appeared no better than what already existed; it was the continued reinforcement of patriarchal ideals at the expense of women. Where one group has observed positive progress, the other has perceived continuity at its worst.

Yet, neither attitude appears realistic in its approach to Vives or to Catherine. As this essay will demonstrate, Vives was neither a Renaissance feminist nor some doctrinally confused and ambivalent scholar, but was instead someone attempting to provide a way of changing women's experience within the restricted roles allowed by the patriarchal society of his day, and limited by his own personal faith. Furthermore, Vives worked within the parameters of the life of Catherine, on whom he claimed to model *De Institutione Feminae Christianae*.

The focus of the study of *De Institutione Feminae Christianae* and *De Ratione Studii Puerilis* should be the differences between the education Vives presented in these treatises to Catherine and Mary, and the standard education for young women of early modern England. In a recent essay on the education of women in late medieval England, Sharon Michalove argues that Vives's views on a girl's education in *De Institutione Feminae Christianae* were typical of most aristocratic girls' education. Morality was the important goal, and immensely necessary for someone who was to run a large household.[17] For example, Michalove points to the Lisle family who considered their daughter's education as important as their son's. In the will of John Smyth, the Lisle family auditor, he made provision for all his children: the sons educated more formally but "honestly and diligently," with the daughters "to be brought up virtuously and honestly in learning until they marry."[18] However, in *De Institutione Feminae Christianae* Vives approached the traditional education from a different angle, changing women's experience but not transforming their status.

A couple of points concerning the *De Institutione Feminae Christianae* merit some discussion. First, it is worth noting that while *De Institutione Feminae Christianae* is one of the earliest treatises of its kind to appear in England, it was simply one among several written by Spanish men concerning the equality and worthiness of educated women. Beginning in 1443 with Juan Rodriquez de la Camara's *El triunfo de las donas* (*The Triumph of Women*), followed by Alvaro de Luna's *El libro de las virtuosas y claras mugeres* (*The Book of Virtuous and Famous Women*) in 1446, this phenomenon culminated in 1500 with Fray Martín Alonso de Cordoba's *Jardín de las nobles doncellas* (*The Garden of Noble Maidens*), which he wrote for the infanta Isabel, defending her right to the throne of Castile.[19]

Nor were Spaniards and Catholic humanists the only scholars considering education for women. In 1524, only one year after Vives's tutorial letter for Mary, Martin Luther wrote to the mayors and aldermen of the cities of Germany concerning educating the children of those same cities through Christian schools. Anticipating their complaints he wrote that he was not advocating the types of schools with which they were so familiar, schools where young men studied for "twenty or thirty years over Donatus or Alexander, and yet have not learned anything at all." Instead, he advocated a school which boys would attend two hours per day and girls one hour. This, Luther argued, would allow the children to be educated and still get their household duties done.[20]

Second, and perhaps more important, *De Institutione Feminae Christianae* is not a book on education as we have come to understand the term. Instead, it is a work on the proper deportment of women and its chief purpose is to provide guidelines for women to guarantee their chastity. For this reason, the volume is divided into three smaller books, one each for the maiden, the wife, and the widow, representing the three stages in a woman's life in which challenges to chastity were different. Valerie Wayne has rightly observed that Vives carried this idea of chastity to the point of obscuring all other possible virtues, and notes, "One good for women had become the only good."[21] Apparently, though, Vives was not alone in his thinking, for *De Institutione Feminae Christianae* was the most popular conduct book of its age going through at least nine English publications by the end of the century.[22]

Specifically, the first book of *De Institutione Feminae Christianae* concerns our present topic and is where one notices Vives advocating a more structured education for women than previously observed in English tradition. Believing an educated woman could not be impure, he praised specific role models from history, such as Cornelia, the mother of Gracchus, and Zenobia, the queen of Palmyra, to name just two. Vives then mentioned notable women of his own period, such as, Catherine of Aragon, Doña Mecia de Mendoza, and Thomas More's daughters, all of whom he held up as paragons of successfully educated women.[23] More importantly, he urged women to learn to read and write, though he does not actually say the language needed to be Latin, and then discussed authors and works that women should and should not read.

Authors and works approved by Vives will come as no surprise to modern readers. Reading like a who's who of exalted Christian fathers, Vives advocates the reading of both the Old and New Testaments, along with Saints Cyprian, Jerome, Augustine, and Ambrosius, followed by classics from Plato, Cicero, and Seneca. Vives's aim was for women to meditate upon these works, believing that they would strengthen their virtue.[24]

The works Vives opposed for women, and, a point that many have overlooked, opposed for men as well, were books on chivalry, erotic fiction, and most poetry. Vives provided examples of this forbidden literature based on language lines. Therefore, he listed *Amadís, Esplandián, Florisando,* and *Tristan* from Spain; from France he points out *Lancelot du Lac, Paris and Vienna, Ponthus and Sidonia*; and from Flanders *Floris and Blanchefleur, Leonella and Canamoro.*[25] As Carlos Noreña reminds us, morality and ethics were at the heart of Vives's philosophy of education, and he believed it was of utmost importance for teachers and parents to be responsible enough to protect children from any authors who might corrupt the minds of youth. Noreña provides a quote from *Vivis Opera Omnia,* which states, "First of all the boy must be kept away from any author who might encourage vice in general or who might aggravate the defects of the individual. For instance, a lascivious young man should be prevented from reading Ovid, a facetious and whimsical student should avoid Martial, Lucian is not for the cynic detractor, nor Lucretius for the irreligious pupil . . . . Cicero will be of little help to the conceited and vainglorious child."[26] From this reading, it should be obvious that Vives was not just concerned with a chastity of body for women, but also a chastity of mind and emotions for all.

In this sense, then, Vives was not advocating some transformation in a woman's educational status that would provide her some incredible opportunities to serve society. Yet, neither was he advocating education of women as traditionally performed. Where the norm in late medieval England had been for young girls to leave home and attach themselves to another household in order to train in the proper ways of running a large house, Vives changed the experience by encouraging parents, and especially mothers, to train their own daughters while they were young, and then to employ a male tutor, preferably an older married man. As Retha Warnicke points out, Vives's *De Institutione Feminae Christianae* indicates that he believed just as Thomas More did, that women were to be educated to "heighten their ability to please their husbands and to educate their children."[27] Who better to accomplish this task than the child's parents and a tutor under their watchful gaze?

While all of the above may be well and good for the average aristocratic daughter, determining what all of Vives's guidelines actually meant for Mary and her education as it pertains to *De Institutione Feminae Christianae* is another problem. It seems a bit presumptuous of Vives, though not completely out of character, to believe that his guidelines would somehow bind Catherine and Henry to a particular course of study for Mary. Certainly, Vives wanted Mary to resemble his ideal woman, and for him this could only come about by way of an education supervised by her already exemplary mother. It is also true that Catherine did take an interest in Mary's education, admonishing her on at least one occasion to keep working on her Latin,[28] yet, it appears, like most students Mary utilized some but not all of Vives's guidelines, which becomes increasingly clear when one considers his other work of 1523, *De ratione studii puerilis*.

This treatise is actually composed of two different letters, one to Mary, and the other to Charles Blount, son of William Blount, Lord Mountjoy, Catherine's Chamberlain. Vives makes it clear in his preface to the letter, which he refers to as a "rough sketch of studies,"[29] that Catherine of Aragon ordered him to produce a guide, or course of study, for Princess Mary's instructor, with the sole purpose of the plan for Mary to learn Latin.

To accomplish his objective, Vives included as many aspects as he saw fit: grammar, pronunciation, writing, memorization, and naturally, what he believed Mary should read. In this case, he suggested Cicero, Erasmus, More, Cato, Seneca, Plutarch, Jerome, Ambrosius, Augustine, and others along with daily readings in the New Testament.[30] He also wanted Mary to appreciate stories that "teach the art of life." These accounts included Papirius Praetextatus in Aulus Gellius, Joseph from the book of Genesis, Lucretia in Livy, and Griselda, all of which commend virtue and disdain vice.[31]

One wonders, however, how Princess Mary was to use this Latin in light of Vives's clear desire in *De Institutione Feminae Christianae* to hold to the traditional line of the Church that a woman was to keep silent. As Valerie Wayne has argued, this age-old stipulation became a major restriction on women's ability to express themselves through speaking and writing, and because *De Institutione Feminae Christianae* had many reprints, it reinforced the apostle Paul's prohibition among the general populace.[32] Yet, Vives made an exception for Mary through *De ratione studii puerilis*, where he encouraged her to be educated with other children, and insisted that she converse in Latin, being praised and praising others for their hard work. Furthermore, he suggested that Mary listen attentively so that she could imitate those more learned in written and spoken Latin than she was.[33] His encouragement of Mary to write down sentences and sayings that others had written indicates Vives's desire for Mary to utilize Latin in all of its aspects, including making what she learned part of her every day rhetoric. One must remember that Vives wrote this plan for a seven-year-old child, whom he believed would learn best through imitation and repetition.

Nevertheless, this in no way alters the fact that Vives did produce a different plan for Mary than for Charles Blount, who was only four months Mary's junior.[34] To some scholars this has suggested that Vives's decision to write out two different plans of education was made solely on the basis of gender, and for proof point to the differences in reading lists, where Mary's list is less detailed.[35]

Another possible explanation for this disparity may exist in Catherine's choice of Mary's teacher, as opposed to Lord Mountjoy's choice of tutor for his son. In the introduction to the letter for Mary, Vives went out of his way to praise the tutor whom Catherine had selected, and wrote, "I was content to point out details, as with a finger. He will explain the rest of the matters."[36] However, in the case of the plan for Charles Blount, though it is possible that Lord Blount was his son's tutor,[37] to the best of our knowledge, Vives does not have any information concerning a possible preceptor. Maria Dowling has noted that Mountjoy employed John Crucius as a tutor between 1522 and 1527,[38] but it is unclear how widespread this knowledge was, and there is no indication that Vives and Crucius ever met when the two were in England. Furthermore, we know of only two other instructors chosen for Charles Blount; one, at the urging of Erasmus, was Peter Vulcanius, about 1529–30, and the other, Andreas Hyperius, sometime later.[39] Therefore, Vives's attention to detail may simply be to inform the younger Blount about his responsibilities as a student, and about the type of tutor his father would employ.

Yet, the question remains: was Vives showing deference to gender or was his lack of direction a demonstration of his faith in Mary's teacher? The answer to this question lies in discovering whoever Mary's Latin teacher was. Determining her instructor's identity has often led to confusion, however, with some providing more credit for Vives than is his due. Foster Watson insisted that Linacre, a noted English humanist scholar and friend of Erasmus, was Mary's teacher along with Vives.[40]

Garrett Mattingly, writing forty years later, continued to lay stress upon Vives, claiming that upon his arrival in England in 1523, Catherine engaged him as Mary's tutor.[41] More recently, though, David Loades has argued for Thomas Linacre as sole instructor of Mary, at least until his death in 1525,[42] and therefore present when Vives wrote *De ratione studii puerilis*. Since Henry and Catherine employed Linacre at the court in some capacity, and since he was the author of a Latin grammar text, it stands to reason he would be Mary's instructor, making the need for Vives as anything more than an advisor unnecessary.

This all said, instructing Princess Mary to read and write Latin, and training her in the proper deportment of a Christian woman were not exactly preparing her to rule England. Furthermore, it is a mistake to believe Vives's intention was for any purpose other than to prepare her for the inevitable marriage negotiations as she fulfilled her role as political pawn, just as her mother had done in 1501 with her marriage to Prince Arthur. As Loades has stated, "Piety, chastity and humane letters were the objectives of those who guided her lessons from the very first, and the prospect of marriage dominated the schoolroom as much as it did her role in the political life of her father's court."[43] Vives understood that Mary needed training on how to be the proper young woman; a woman with an unsullied reputation was far more valuable politically. Once married, Vives, like Sir Thomas More, saw Mary's, and for that matter any woman's, education in the humane letters as providing for her the ability to give learned and wise counsel which her husband would use to rule in her name.

How did Catherine react to such a book and its obvious designs? Was there any advice that Vives directed at her? A careful reading of *De Institutione Feminae Christianae* recognizes that Vives wrote the book for both Mary and Catherine.[44] By 1523-24, it was evident to most of Europe that Catherine and Henry's marriage had fallen upon hard times, with the birth of Henry Fitzroy in 1519 and his subsequent elevation to Duke of Richmond in 1525 only making Catherine's inadequacies as a wife more prominent. Vives wrote *De Institutione Feminae Christianae* in three separate books corresponding to the life of Catherine when she was maiden, wife, and widow of Arthur, but book two on marriage and the wife's duty to her husband corresponded perfectly with her situation with Henry. By 1523, it is clear that Catherine will not have any more children and Vives, so Ruth Kelso surmises, intended to write to the needs of Catherine concerning the inability of some women to conceive, pointing out that infertility is not a sin, and that a woman was still a woman even if she could not have a baby.[45]

Advice on how to view herself with regard to infant production, however, no more endeared Vives to Catherine than his advice concerning her continued suffering in her marriage to Henry. Catherine knew her duty; as her mother, Isabel, had done with Ferdinand, Catherine would put up with Henry's philandering.[46] She was the model for Vives's ideal Christian woman, but she did not have to like it. Nor did she necessarily have to encourage her daughter to agree with Vives's rather harsh views of marriage and motherhood. For this reason, Catherine, through Mountjoy, engaged Erasmus to write a more positive piece on the preservation of marriage, *Christiani matrimonii instituti* in 1526,[47] a work that reflected more of Catherine's ideals and would, optimistically, influence Mary.

In the end, what did Mary learn from Vives and Catherine's influence, and did her tutors keep to Vives's principles? One finds that Vives's guidelines were only partially successful; Mary's Latin skills improved greatly, and later she translated Erasmus's *Paraphrase on St. John's Gospel*, edited and published by Nicholas Udall in 1547.[48] However, Vives's advice concerning Greek and that Mary be kept from frivolous activities such as bowls, card games, dances, and the like, was not heeded.[49] Yet, Mary learned to be a patron of this new learning from her mother. During her tenure as queen, Mary provided grants to Oxford and to Trinity College, Cambridge, and even bequeathed £500 to the "poor scholars" of those same schools in her will.[50]

In light of Mary's mixed response to Vives's work, and having determined that these two works on education from this period demonstrate Vives's belief of the necessity of maintaining virtue through education for both men and women, there exists a need to reexamine *De Institutione Feminae Christianae* and *De ratione studii puerilis* and question their influence in early modern England. In a discussion of Vives's influence on the conditions for women in Spain, Milagros Ortega Costa discusses the impact of two guides for the perfect woman written in sixteenth-century Spain. Noting that "the status of Spanish women deteriorated" during this time, Costa argues that neither Vives's nor Fray Luis de Leon's *La perfecta casada*, written sixty years after Vives's work, helped in halting the decline in women's status.[51] Neither, did these works halt the decline within England, despite the overwhelming popularity of *De Institutione Feminae Christianae*. If anything, Vives's work reinforced, intentionally or not, the existing patriarchal system.

Regardless, this reinforcement of patriarchy does not mean that Vives was a scholar who was ambiguous about women and their education; their education was something in which he believed strongly. His beliefs, however, do not mesh with the present-day scholarly desire for some sort of transformative event that denotes progress along positive lines, that is to say, throwing off the existing patriarchal system for a system of equality. The fact that Vives lacked the foresight to include in his works instructions that would transform women's status from the mundane domestic sphere allotted to them by patriarchal society to a higher plane of equality should not be viewed as ambiguousness but as being rather natural for the period.

In the end, we find that Vives was a man with his feet planted firmly in his conservative Spanish Catholic tradition while his head embraced liberal humanist ideals. We find that he, like most humanists, believed in the essential equality of men and women, with the stipulation that faithfulness in religion was paramount in life. For this reason, though Vives was willing to encourage the education of women on slightly different lines than normal, he was not prepared to recognize any other role for those same women than their domestic function. Still, as Ruth Kelso has noted, "But to do [Vives's view of education] justice, one must view it also against the whole background of the still recommended confinement of women to the home, and their training only for domestic duties. How much wider the door was that Vives opened for women."[52] While we may not like this progress amidst continuity, what else could we possibly have expected? Vives was after all, a man of his season, not a man for all seasons.

Notes

Portions of this essay were previously presented at the Sixteenth Century Studies Conference in Denver, October 2001. Thanks to Annette, Nikki, and Morgan for their support.

1. See Desiderius Erasmus, *The Education of a Christian Prince*, ed. Lisa Jardine, trans. Neil M. Cheshire and Michael J. Heath (Cambridge: Cambridge University Press, 1997) for the most recent English edition.
2. Carlos G. Noreña, *Juan Luis Vives* (The Hague: Martinus Nijhoff, 1970), pp. 39–57.
3. James Kelsey McConica, *English Humanists and Reformation Politics Under Henry VIII and Edward VI* (Oxford: Clarendon Press, 1965), pp. 14–15.
4. Noreña, pp. 61–81. See Garrett Mattingly, *Catherine of Aragon* (Boston: Little, Brown and Company, 1941), p. 187, for a different interpretation. Vives's letter to Erasmus is in P. S. Allen and H. M. Allen, eds., *Opus Epistolarum Des. Erasmi Roterodami* IV, p. 1222. For more views of Catherine of Aragon, see the essay by Hansen in this collection.
5. David Loades, *The Tudor Court* (London: B.T. Batsford Ltd., 1986), pp. 116–17.

6. Loades, *The Tudor Court*, p. 118; Stanford E. Lehmberg, "William Blount, fourth Baron Mountjoy, ca. 1478–8 November 1534," in *Contemporaries of Erasmus: A Biographical Register of the Renaissance and Reformation*, vol. 1, ed. Peter G. Bietenholz and Thomas B. Deutscher (Toronto and London: University of Toronto Press, 1985), pp. 154–56.
7. Translated in Maria Dowling, *Humanism in the Age of Henry VIII* (London: Croom Helm, 1986), p. 19.
8. John E. Paul, *Catherine of Aragon and Her Friends* (New York: Fordham University Press, 1966), pp. 62–63; Nancy Rubin, *Isabella of Castille* (New York: St. Martin's Press, 1991), p. 265; Mattingly, p. 9.
9. Charles Fantazzi, "Introduction," in *The Education of a Christian Woman: A Sixteenth-Century Manual*, by Juan Luis Vives, ed. and trans. Charles Fantazzi (Chicago and London: The University of Chicago Press, 2000), p. 24.
10. McConica, pp. 54–6.
11. Noreña, pp. 85–6.
12. Vocht, Henry de, ed., *Literae Virorum Eruditorum ad Franciscum Craneveldium (Letters of Learned [Educated] Men to Francis Cranvelt)*, 1522–28 (Louvain: Louvain Librairie Universitaire, Uystpruyst Publisher, 1928), pp. 232–33; Noreña, p. 87.
13. Judith Bennett, "Confronting Continuity," *Journal of Women's Studies* (Autumn 1997), pp. 73–94.
14. Francis L. Utley, *The Crooked Rib: An Analytical Index to the Argument about Women in English and Scots Literature to the End of the Year 1568* (Columbus: Ohio State University Press, 1944); Foster Watson, ed., *Vives and the Renaissance Education of Women* (New York: Longmans, Green and Co., 1912); Garrett Mattingly, *Catherine of Aragon* (Boston: Little, Brown and Company, 1941); Pearl Hogrefe, *The Sir Thomas More Circle* (Urbana: University of Illinois Press, 1959).
15. Fantazzi, "Introduction," p. 14.
16. Gloria Kaufman, "Juan Luis Vives on the Education of Women," *Signs*, 3 (1978), no. 4, p. 896. Also see: Constance Jordan, "Feminism and the Humanists: The Case of Sir Thomas Elyot's *Defence of Good Women*," in *Rewriting the Renaissance*, ed. Margaret W. Ferguson et al. (Chicago: University of Chicago Press, 1986); Janis Butler Holm, "The Myth of a Feminist Humanism: Thomas Salter's *The Mirrhor of Modestie*," in *Ambiguous Realities: Women in the Middle Ages and Renaissance*, ed. Carole Levin and Jeanie Watson (Detroit: Wayne State University Press, 1987), pp. 197–218.
17. Sharon D. Michalove, "Equal in Opportunity? The Education of Aristocratic Women, 1450–1540," in *Women's Education in Early Modern Europe: A History, 1500–1800*, ed. Barbara J. Whitehead (New York and London: Garland Publishing, Inc., 1999), p. 48. See Retha Warnicke, *Women of the English Renaissance and Reformation* (Westport, CN: Greenwood Press, 1983), p. 6, for a different definition of "well educated."
18. Michalove, p. 69.
19. Fantazzi, pp. 24–5.

20. Martin Luther, "Letter to the Mayors and Aldermen of all Cities of Germany in Behalf of Christian Schools," in *Readings in the History of Education*, ed. Ellwood P. Cubberley (Boston and New York: Houghton Mifflin Company, 1920), pp. 242–43.
21. Valerie Wayne, "Some Sad Sentence: Vives' Instruction of a Christian Woman," in *Silent but for the Word: Tudor Women as Patrons, Translators, and Writers of Religious Works*, ed. Margaret Patterson Hannay (Kent, OH: Kent State University Press, 1985), p. 24.
22. Betty S. Travitsky, "Reprinting Tudor History: The Case of Catherine of Aragon," *Renaissance Quarterly*, 50.1 (1997), p. 164.
23. Juan Luis Vives, "De La Mujer Cristiana," in *Obras Completas*, ed. Lorenzo Riber, vol. 1 (Madrid, 1947), pp. 997–1000; Noreña, p. 32.
24. Vives, "De La Mujer Cristiana," p. 1005.
25. Vives, "De La Mujer Cristiana," p. 1003. It is interesting to note that in the Hyrde edition of 1529, Hyrde adds works in English that he believed were of little or no benefit to readers. His list includes Parthenope, Genarides, Hippomadon, William and Melyour, Libius and Arthur, Guy, and Bevis. See Watson, ed. *Vives and the Renascence Education of Women*, p. 59.
26. Noreña, *Juan Luis Vives*, p. 178.
27. Warnicke, p. 35.
28. Henry Ellis, *Original Letters, Illustrative of English History*, vol. 2 (London: Harding, Triphook, and Lepard, 1825), letter cvii, pp. 19–20.
29. Juan Luis Vives, "De Ratione Studii Puerilis, Epistola I," in *Opera Omnia*, ed. Gregorio Mayans (1782, republished by Gregg Press Limited, 1964), p. 256; for a translation see Juan Luis Vives, "Plan of Studies for Girls," in *Vives and the Renascence Education of Women*, ed. with commentary by Foster Watson (New York: Longmans, Green and Co., 1912), p. 147.
30. Vives, "De Ratione Studii Puerilis, Epistola I," p. 269; Vives, "Plan of Study," p. 147.
31. Vives, "De Ratione Studii Puerilis, Epistola I," p. 265; Vives, "Plan of Study," p. 144.
32. Wayne, pp. 21–3.
33. Vives, "Plan of Study," p. 146.
34. Stanford E. Lehmberg, "Charles Blount, fifth Baron Mountjoy, 28 June 1516–10 October 1544," in *Contemporaries of Erasmus: A Biographical Register of the Renaissance and Reformation*, vol. 1, ed. Peter G. Bietenholz and Thomas B. Deutscher (Toronto and London: University of Toronto Press, 1985), p. 154.
35. Kaufman, p. 895.
36. Vives, "De Ratione Studii Puerilis, Epistola I," p. 256: "*res velut digito indicasse fui contentus, ille reliqua explicabit.*" I have chosen to use Foster Watson's translation from his Vives, "Plan of Study," p. 173.
37. Vives, "De Ratione Studii Puerilis, Epistola II: Carolo Montiojo Gulielmi filio," in *Opera Omnia*, ed. Gregorio Mayans (1782, republished by Gregg Press Limited, 1964), p. 270. "*Vale, et exemplum, quod domi haves sapientissimi patris, imitare.*" (Farewell, and imitate the example you have at home

of your very wise father.) This last sentence in Vives's preface may indicate that William Blount, Lord Mountjoy, was Charles's tutor based upon Vives's multiple references to the necessity of imitating one's preceptor.
38. Dowling, pp. 145, 191. Dowling takes her dates from the commentary to a letter from John Crucius to Erasmus in P. S. Allen and H. M. Allen, eds., *Opus Epistolarum Des. Erasmi Roterodami*, vol. 7, letter 1932.
39. *DNB* II, pp. 701–2; Gilbert Tournouy, "Petrus Vulcanius," in *Contemporaries of Erasmus: A Biographical Register of the Renaissance and Reformation*, vol. 3, ed. Peter G. Bietenholz and Thomas B. Deutscher (Toronto and London: University of Toronto Press, 1985), p. 420.
40. Watson, "Introduction," in *Vives: On Education, A Translation of the De Tradendis Disciplinis of Juan Luis Vives* (Totowa, NJ: Rowman and Littlefield, 1971), xxviii.
41. Mattingly, p. 188.
42. Loades, *The Tudor Court*, p. 118.
43. David Loades, *Mary Tudor* (Oxford, UK and Malden, MA: Blackwell Publishers, 1989, reprint, 1997), p. 33.
44. John A. Thomas, "A Moral Voice for the Restoration Lady: A Comparative View of Allestree and Vives," *Journal of the Rocky Mountain Medieval and Renaissance Association*, 7 (1986), p. 126.
45. Ruth Kelso, *Doctrine for the Lady of the Renaissance* (Urbana, Ill: The University of Illinois Press, 1956, 1978), pp. 116–17.
46. Recent biographies on Isabel of Castile are Nancy Rubin, *Isabella of Castile* (London and New York: St. Martin's Press, 1991), and Peggy K. Liss, *Isabel the Queen* (Oxford: Oxford University Press, 1992).
47. Fantazzi, p. 15.
48. Watson, p. 148.
49. Loades, *Mary Tudor*, pp. 43–44.
50. Loades, *Mary Tudor*, p. 372.
51. Milagros Ortega Costa, "Spanish Women in the Reformation," in *Women in Reformation and Counter-Reformation Europe: Public and Private Worlds*, ed. Sherrin Marshall (Bloomington, IN: Indiana University Press, 1989), pp. 89–90.
52. Kelso, p. 74.

Mary Tudor: Renaissance Queen of England

Judith M. Richards

Mary Tudor (1516–58) was the first queen regnant of England. As the only surviving child of the twenty-year marriage of Henry VIII and Catherine of Aragon, her ever becoming monarch was in itself an ironic comment on her father's long and destructive campaign to ensure a masculine succession to his throne. Mary was reared in the Catholic tradition. She remained faithful to that tradition all her life, and her commitment to the faith she was born into, has long been a potent weapon—and impetus—for critics of her reign. Even before her death, Protestant critiques of her reign highlighted her Spanish lineage and her Catholic allegiance. In 1563, John Foxe produced the first English version of his martyrology, *Actes and Monuments in these latter and perillous dayes*. There, Foxe introduced Mary's reign as "the horrible and bloudy time of Queene Mary."[1] He described, in varying degrees of detail, nearly three hundred martyrdoms suffered by Protestants. Foxe's widely available work was also soon drawn upon by historians[2] and, through several routes, the language of the "Fires of Smithfield" and "Bloody Mary"[3] has resonated through the years and well into the twentieth century.[4] Foxe's outrage has long been the more effective precisely because he was among a very small minority who deplored all heresy burnings at the time. More recently, another note was introduced, which impugned Mary's sexuality as well as her reign. A. F. Pollard wrote, "Sterility was the conclusive note of Mary's reign."[5] G. R. Elton agreed, "Positive achievements there were none."[6] Elsewhere he defined Mary as "arrogant, assertive, bigoted, stubborn, suspicious and (not to put too fine a point upon it) rather stupid.... She had ever been her mother's daughter rather than her father's; devoid of political skill, unable to compromise."[7] Recently, historians have moved to a more dispassionate stance, but still find little to respect in her reign. Her foremost biographer, David Loades has defined her limitations as those of "a profoundly conventional woman," her limitations as a ruler "largely those which were imposed by her sex." John Guy has described her, as she came to the throne, as "politically self-deceived. Her piety and unmarried state gave her the intensity of a nun." Susan Brigden notes that, like Henry VIII's other children, Mary "had received the best humanist education" but she doubts that Mary had the intelligence and astuteness to benefit from such education as ruler.[8] A feminist critique has recently added a further argument for her gendered conservatism, that "by marrying and by omitting any claim to the title of Supreme Head [Mary] thereby announced herself as subject in both her persons—as woman and as queen—to the authority of male superiors: her husband and king, Philip II of Spain; and the head of the universal church ... the Pope."[9]

* * *

For many reasons then, Mary has traditionally been viewed as a disappointing queen. This chapter offers an account of another Mary Tudor, one who was always pious, and who happened to be childless, but whose reign was also more worldly wise and more deeply influenced by her humanist education than is usually acknowledged. She has been most maligned for her decision to restore England to her own preferred religious allegiance, but it was, after all, less than two years after her accession, that the principle of *cuius regio, eius religio* across Germany was effectively formalized by the Peace of Augsburg (1555), and the Catholicism she reintroduced was informed by her humanist training. Also challenging for the first English queen regnant was establishing the rituals for representing female rule in England;[10] most remarkable was the path she followed in her marriage to a foreign prince while her preserving legal autonomy, a path inconceivable to almost all her English subjects.

There must necessarily be some revisionism in such an exercise; in this case it begins with Mary's mother. When Elton remarked of Mary that she "had ever been her mother's daughter rather than her father's", that much is uncontentious. The bad press Catherine of Aragon has received from English historians owes much to her resistance to Henry's wish to annul their marriage after some twenty years. The dominant image of Mary's mother comes from her final years, as Henry's rejected wife, the suffering Griselda of popular Catholic hagiography.[11]

But she was never simply a pathetic figure. She resolutely opposed Henry's wish to invalidate their marriage after more than twenty years, not least because she knew that the main effect would be to bastardize and disinherit their sole surviving child. In her resistance, Catherine demonstrated that she had considerable political skill. She repeatedly thwarted the king's intentions; it took Henry the better part of six years and the destruction of Papal authority in England to get the divorce he wanted. All the while, she consistently—and even plausibly—represented herself as the King's loving and obedient wife. She also consistently and vehemently denied the claim that did so much to validate Henry's case for the divorce, that her first marriage had been consummated.

The Catherine of Aragon of the earlier years of their marriage was no suffering Griselda. The youngest daughter of Isabel of Castile and Ferdinand of Aragon, she was educated beyond the level of any known English woman of her generation, indeed to a level almost unknown outside Spain for any female. Raised in the most splendid court in Europe, and betrothed to the heir to the English throne from the time she was three, Catherine was educated to be a king's wife. Throughout her time in England she was a consistent student of fresh humanist works; Maria Dowling reports that in her dying days she found consolation still in reading the most recent work of Erasmus on, appropriately, preparation for death.[12] Unlike her husband, who reportedly went no closer to that seat of learning than good hunting took him, she visited Oxford to discuss matters of learning with the scholars there. After the early death of Catherine's first husband, the ailing Arthur Tudor, her father Ferdinand of Aragon had nominated her as his ambassador to the English court, a responsibility she seems to have fulfilled to the satisfaction of both sides until well after her marriage to Henry VIII, Arthur's younger brother.

The reputation of the younger Catherine had been spectacular. The early diplomatic reports about the English royal couple were dazzling, well beyond familiar matters of court splendour. In late 1512, Henry VIII was planning war against France, and Catherine was closely involved. One Venetian diplomat reported: "The king will prepare a fleet and attack France in the spring. The Queen very warm about this and would like to get four great galleasses and two bastard from the Signory, asking the cost and saying that France was building two bastard galleasses.... The king is for war, the Council against and the Queen for it."[13] Such messages transmitted across Europe reflected a general appreciation of the remarkable wife of Henry VIII. In June 1513, a rumor that she would go with Henry to the battlefield of France was quickly followed by the news that actually she would remain as regent of England, with unprecedented powers. With Henry VIII in France, the Scots declared war against England. Catherine took an active role in the preparations, and there were further rumors that she would personally lead an English army to Scotland. In the event, as Peter Martyr wrote to Erasmus, "Queen Catherine, in imitation of her mother Isabella... made splendid oration to the English captains, told them to be ready to defend their territory... and they should remember that English courage excelled that of all other nations. Fired by these words, the nobles marched against the Scots... and defeated them".[14] The battle of Flodden proved to be one of the most comprehensive defeats England ever inflicted on Scotland. When Henry had sent a captive French duke to Catherine, she wrote to him that "a duke is a great gift, but she hopes to send him a king."[15] As it transpired, she had to send Henry a piece of the dead king's coat, along with evidence of the French encouragement for Scotland to renew attacks on England. There is any number of such reports extolling the leadership qualities of the first wife of Henry VIII, written by men who had no obvious vested interest in praising her.

The leading humanists, and particularly Erasmus, frequently praised her learning, and its depth. In November 1524, Vives wrote to Erasmus, describing the royal responses to his *De Libero Arbitrio*. The summarized letter reported that Henry read "a few pages, seemed pleased, and said he would read it through. He pointed out... a passage where Erasmus deters men from immoderate curiosity as to Divine mysteries, which, he said, pleased him much. The Queen is also much pleased. She desired Vives to salute him for her, and says that she thanks him for having treated the subject with so much moderation...."[16] Like her sisters, Catherine had received an unusually broad education under her mother's supervision. She was proficient with keyboard and harp; she was schooled in philosophy, literature, and religion, and as well as Latin she had studied Castilian, French, English, and German.[17] She was, in her turn, in an excellent position to ensure that Mary Tudor received an extensive humanist education, the *sine qua non* for any Renaissance figure. She commissioned the Spanish scholar Vives to outline Mary's proposed studies in his *Education of a Christian Woman*. It is a platitude worth repeating that humanists valued education precisely because it developed the rational and moral capacities of all its students. But Vives's recommendations for Mary's education included much more besides. In exemplary humanist mode he advised Catherine to refine the educational program as her daughter developed: "Time will admonish her to more exact details, and thy singular wisdom will discover for her what they should be." Vives worked with others on a collection of proverbs, from classical sources, and anecdotes from his own experience, designed for her study both as private person and future ruler. He advised that she be thoroughly grounded in scripture, the church fathers and other edifying works as essential preparation for a governor.[18] Giles Duwes, once French tutor to her uncle and her father, prepared a French-based study, which dealt not only with conventional philosophical and religious discussions, central to the education of any humanist pupil, but also introduced material dealing with court life and foreign affairs.[19] Under her mother's supervision, she was educated for future rule.

From the late 1520s onwards Mary's status as heir apparent was being reassessed by her father. A combination of old and new factors—the lack of a male heir was a far more significant one than the presence of Anne Boleyn at court—worked sufficiently on Henry's consciousness for him to develop considerable qualms about having married his deceased brother's wife.[20] After his first marriage was finally annulled by Henry's own nominees in England, he kept Catherine and Mary apart. When a royal physician warned him about the gravity of Mary's illness, and asked that her mother be able to take care of her, the king explained that for the safety of the realm they had to be kept separate; Catherine, he explained, "was so haughty in spirit, she might, by favor of the Princess, raise a number of men, and make war, as boldly as did [the] queen...her mother."[21] He at least remembered the reputation of the formidable queen whose daughter he had married.

The adolescent Mary, separated from her mother, still shared her mother's humiliations, in ways which seem to have reinforced her mother's enduring influence. In the aftermath of the English break from Papal authority, she was reduced from royal princess to royal bastard, as Catherine was degraded from queen consort to dowager princess. Mother and daughter were always forbidden by Henry to meet, even when Catherine was dying, but they had still corresponded, though only a few letters have survived. During the aggressively Protestant reign of Mary's much younger half brother, Edward VI (1547–53) it was the protection of the Emperor Charles V, Catherine's nephew and Mary's cousin, which probably saved Mary from the worst consequences of her resistance to the zeal of her brother's regime. On the throne, one of Mary's earliest statutes nullified her mother's divorce,[22] and she adopted Catherine's badge, the pomegranate of Aragon, as her personal symbol. In her will, she asked to have her mother's body moved close beside her own.[23] Given Catherine's close supervision of her upbringing, it is no surprise that Mary honored her mother in many ways throughout her reign.

When Edward VI died, his council, the mayor and aldermen of London, and the (Anglican) church leaders all acquiesced in the proclamation of Edward's distant cousin and preferred heir, Lady Jane Grey, as queen. The Janeite coup was backed by France; in the absence of any strong evidence that Mary would win, Charles V decided not to intervene. While Edward VI lay dying, his elder half sister, privately warned of her imminent danger from Northumberland, had fled to her estate of Kenninghall, in Norfolk. Separated for these reasons from her usual advisers, Mary was thrown back on her own resources. She wrote to members of Edward's Privy Council once she knew of her brother's death. She was, she disingenuously wrote, dismayed she had heard nothing from them. After all, she was next heir to the crown of England and title of France after Edward by act of parliament, by the last will and testament of Henry VIII, besides (rather obscurely) "other circumstances advancing our right." She warned them she knew the reasons for their delay in proclaiming her, and advised she had arranged for her proclamation to be made herself. She also warned them against taking up arms against "this our just and rightful cause," not least because of the allegiance "which you owe to God and us."[24] The language resonates with her confidence that she was indeed as fully a monarch as any of her predecessors.

Placing her faith in her lineage and her father's will, Mary duly proclaimed herself the true queen of England. She quickly rallied an effective resistance to the coup, and provided a sound focal point for it. One eyewitness account described a gathering of her forces at her stronghold in East Anglia:

> To encourage her people, two or three days before the armies were expected to engage, her Highness commanded that all her host should put itself in battle array, and came to the camp, where all, with shouts and acclamations, casting their helmets into the air, and with many other tokens, showed their joy and the great love they bore to her Highness, crying "Long live our good Queen Mary" and "Death to traitors." And by reason of the great outcry of the people, and the many discharges of artillery and arquebusses, the Queen was obliged to alight to review the troops, for the fright and much rearing of the palfrey she rode; and she inspected the whole camp, which was about a mile long, on foot.[25]

The attempt to put Lady Jane Grey in Mary's place collapsed without any bloodshed, essentially because of Mary's unexpected resistance. Her popular support even *before* the internal collapse of the Edwardian Privy Council was strong in crucial local communities.[26] The surviving rhetoric in favor of Mary was consistently cast in terms of her accession rights, confirmed by statute. Richard Troughton described how John Haryngton of Exton responded to the Northumberland plan to place Jane on the throne. In support of Queen Mary he "sodenly went into his parlor, and broughte forthe a Statute book, and layde it awpon uppon the borde, that every man myghte rede hit; and had noted the substaunce of the Statute for the declaracion of the Quenes Maiesties ryght to the Crowne of England, after the deathe of Kynge Edward."[27] Her legal right to the throne was what her supporters most consistently evoked. In one contemporary effusion praising Mary's accession ("which brought us comforte al, / Through God, whom wee of dewtye prayse / that gives her foes a fal"), one verse in particular illustrates how the preferred language of legal right sidestepped the issue of confessional preferences. "Our soueraygne & rightioyse Queene / Wyl vyce and syn depresse: / Will cheafly love the churche of God / And punyshe wickednesse."[28] In London, 'Poor Pratte' was in print within days of Gilbert Potter's punishment for speaking against Queen Jane and for Queen Mary. The author insisted that "thousands more then thy selfe" shared his view "yet durst they not (suche is ye fragility & weakenes of the flesh) once move their lippes to speake y^t whiche thou did speake." His great anxiety was that, before all could be put to right "God wil take frō us the vertuouse Lady Mary oure lawfull quene."[29] There is much less evidence available to consider the role of religious affiliation in shaping responses to the attempted coup by Northumberland. Nevertheless, even in London, the heart of the Protestant reformation, it was immediately obvious how well the old religion had survived when Mary came to the throne.[30] According to Cranmer's biographer, by the first week in September, the "unofficial revival of the mass throughout the country" was a matter of critical concern for the Archbishop.[31]

Once on the throne, Mary secretly entered into negotiations with her cousin, the Emperor Charles V, to marry his son, Philip of Spain. None of her political advisers knew of the negotiations until the marriage was agreed: her failure to consult them has been cited as another example of her wilful obstinacy. But almost all of those advisers who had not served under Edward VI had served Henry VIII after her mother's humiliations and the break with Papal authority. It must have been extraordinarily difficult for her to know whom she could trust. She anticipated—and faced—opposition to her marriage from within her council, from parliament, and from many of her subjects. The French response to the news of her impending marriage echoed the expectations of many of her subjects as well. In December 1553, Wotton reported from France to the English Council the Constable of France's view that "When the Prince hath married the Queen, he shall be King himself, and then what councillors will or dare counsel against his King's pleasure and will?" Wotton's reply, that the right to England's crown was grounded on the Queen, and that councillors would do their duty, and advising her "according to their minds, according to their duty and conscience" was not seen as powerful. Rather, he was reminded how things had been in the "late King's time. And when [Philip] is a King, who shall be councillors but such as will please him?"[32] The fundamental premise, after all, was that masculine will should prevail, which in the French view of things meant that England would soon be at war with France.

The belief that her marriage would endanger the independence of her realm worried many besides the French. In early 1554, there was an uprising (with French foreknowledge, and possibly with French backing) against the proposed Spanish match, culminating with rebel forces in the streets of London. As the situation grew more threatening Mary went to the Guildhall, where she made another public speech, a lengthy one, to the Londoners gathered there, successfully rallying them to her support. She was, manifestly, an effective public speaker well before the plaudits started for the same "unwomanly" skills of her half sister Elizabeth. Both had been well educated in humanist traditions and skills, but Mary also had the examples of her mother and grandmother to emulate. General hostility to her marriage was based upon the conventional, divinely ordained model of husband–wife relationships, which meant that Mary must be subordinate to her husband, and the control of her kingdom would pass to him, a foreigner, a Spaniard and a staunch Catholic. What those expectations ignored was an extraordinary set of precedents, which Mary had good reason to know better than did anyone else in England. With her support, and probably with her guidance, two unanticipated steps were taken as part of her marriage arrangements. One was a parliamentary act, which Mary therefore had to endorse before it had legal force; that act declared that after her marriage she would continue to be as much and as solely the queen as she had been before it.[33] The second was a marriage treaty which named Mary's husband as king, and allowed his title precedence over hers, but which confined his role to that of assisting his wife, especially in military matters. It explicitly prevented him from exercising any authority in England independently of his wife. Philip was to be, except in military matters, effectively political wife to the monarch of England, although some coinage, charters, seals, and other representations showed them as equals. It is not surprising that Philip had privately reserved his right not to be bound by the treaty.

It is argued here that the terms of the marriage by which Mary metaphorically emasculated her husband reflect too closely for sheer coincidence the marital arrangements finally achieved by/or for her maternal grandmother, Isabel of Castile. Isabel had been the only surviving child of the younger brother of Henry IV of Castile. As Henry's reign became increasingly erratic, she emerged as his preferred heir apparent.[34] To strengthen her power base, Isabel had married Ferdinand of Aragon in 1469. When Henry died, her right was disputed, and Ferdinand was away in Aragon. To minimize opposition, Isabel's advisers had believed she should claim the Castilian throne immediately. After Henry's death, in 1474, Isabel attended his funeral in the morning, and that afternoon, she was installed as the first queen regnant of Castile. After the ceremony she rode under the canopy of state in a lengthy procession through Segovia. At the head rode a man, "in his right hand a naked sword, held by the pummel, point up...so all could see even at a distance that the bearer of royal authority who could punish the guilty was approaching." She was proclaimed as Queen "and our Proprietress" and her absent husband proclaimed as "the King Don Ferdinand, her legitimate husband."[35] It was not until eight days later that her husband Ferdinand heard about the coronation. He was angry that the ceremony had taken place without him and amazed that the unsheathed sword, the "ancient symbol of the highest sovereign authority," had been raised for his wife. "I never heard of a Queen who usurped this male privilege" he reputedly observed.[36] He was dismayed to have been defined as king consort rather than king regnant; he had not expected that the marriage contract would be taken so literally. Marital and political breakdown loomed until a compromise was worked out by the royal couple's respective advisers. Ferdinand's legally subordinate position in Castile was qualified by public representations of a fully shared monarchy; "the two agreed to use one seal, joint coats-of-arms, and that both their portraits were to appear on the coinage. And so it was that their coins showed both monarchs, their shared coats-of-arms, and such mottoes as 'whom God has joined, let no man separate.'" To achieve this public equality, there was one compromise on the queen's side, that the king's name was to precede Isabel's on all documents and ceremonial addresses, and that Ferdinand was also to take "full responsibility for waging war."[37]

Both monarchs retained preeminence in their own kingdom (and Isabel willed hers to a daughter, away from her husband). But the public equality of Isabel and Ferdinand was always rigorously observed. When the English ambassadors negotiated with her parents for the marriage of

Catherine, they had been so struck by the displays of the equality of the two that they retained the Spanish usage in their reports, which referred to the two monarchs as "the kings."[38] There is a tradition that Henry VII, the father of Catherine's two husbands, never spoke of her parents, Isabel and Ferdinand, "without touching his hat as a sign of respect."[39] There was every reason for Catherine, who had lived in her parents' court until she was sixteen, to keep the memory of her parents' arrangements alive for her own daughter. By 1520, it was becoming clear that she would have no further children, and the strategies of Catherine's mother would have been set before her daughter, as she contemplated the probability of Mary inheriting the English throne.

Like her grandmother before her, after her marriage Mary was careful to maintain an appearance of shared power, in many forms of royal representations and in more material forms, as an undated instruction from Mary to an unnamed Privy Councilor, makes clear. He was "fyrste to tell the Kyng the whole state of this Realme in all thynges appartaynyng to the same as muche as ye knowe to be trewe, seconde to obey hys comandment in all thyngs, thyrdly in all thyngs he shalle ask your advyse to deliver your opinion as becometh a faythfull conceyllour."[40] More generally, the steps Mary took to define her regal authority in relation to her husband's followed closely those that her grandmother had also deployed. From this view, Mary's marriage was much less a wilful act, much more a carefully calculated (and, as it transpired) successful political act. She chose a husband distant from the English disputes and intrigues, whose powers were carefully circumscribed by legislation and treaty, which she had sanctioned, and, above all, whose interests in England could only be served by protecting her interests.[41]

The Mary being presented in this chapter was a women of excellent education, with unexpectedly good leadership skills and political competence, a truly Renaissance queen. She also well understood the role of magnificence in establishing her authority. Her own appearance on public occasions was always richly embellished, and her appreciation of sumptuous dress and spectacular jewelry, reflected in her portraits, is well known. She well understood the uses of princely magnificence which, as Sydney Anglo has written, "served as the external sign of intrinsic power."[42] One of the main markers of Renaissance political thought is now seen as being shifting understandings of what we now call the state. Whether Mary was responsive to such shifting political values is still unclear, but she had strong views on the scope of her own authority. She always wished to restore papal authority, but had no reason to see that as a political constraint. The European monarchies of the time all exercised political autonomy despite their formal recognition of papal authority. In her restoration of the Catholic Church, she several times used her royal authority to override existing parliamentary legislation. She was consistently represented wearing the closed crown, the crown imperial, which Henry VIII had used to such effect to signal his establishment of the imperial and fully autonomous realm of England.[43] How far Mary was influenced by shifting humanist understandings of the state is a subject in need of further investigation. John Foxe reported that as she lay dying she lamented above all else the loss of Calais. What that meant to her, it is harder to know; it was always shameful to diminish rather than expand a realm as it was an estate, and she had lost the last European toehold of a once great kingdom. Her understanding of foreign policy is also due for reconsideration. The traditional suggestion is that she joined in her husband's war against the French out of marital solidarity. If so, it had taken over two years for Philip to win her over. Moreover, from the beginning of her reign she had every reason to dislike and mistrust the French who had, however discreetly, backed the Northumberland plot for Lady Jane Grey, probably supported the Wyatt uprising, and given refuge to various opponents of the Marian regime, including Thomas Stafford. His attempted uprising at Scarborough in April 1557 provided the final excuse for England to declare war on France, thereby joining the longer-standing Franco-Spanish struggle. There are good grounds for thinking of Mary as a political realist, who like other contemporary monarchs, conflated her realm's interests with her own. It is not at all obvious that she was, as Elton put it "devoid of political skill, unable to compromise."

Until the end of 1554, Mary remained legally head of the English church, and although it was not a power she sought, she did on occasion use it to further her preferred religious interests. Thereafter, the program to reclaim England as a member of the Catholic Church was formally overseen by Reginald Pole, as Papal Legate, and Queen Mary. Together they shared final responsibility for the whole spectrum of religious policy.[44] For many years, as Mary grew to maturity in a household supervised by his mother, the exiled Pole was a leading member of the *spirituali*,[45] and as such was later treated by Paul IV as a suspect heretic. The gulf between the *spirituali* and Protestants was not always self-evident, and many of the former had aspired to restoring union within the church. Until she realized how obdurate the Protestant party was, Mary may genuinely have intended to maintain her initial offer of a *de facto* toleration as a way of maintaining dialogue with—and thereby reclamation of—"her" heretics, on similar assumptions.

Mary's religious policy, her project to recover England for the Catholic Church, bore many hallmarks of her Erasmian humanist education. A childhood marker of this has survived. In *An Introductorie for to learne to speke Frenche Trewely*, Giles Duwes recalled how the young princess, perhaps in 1527, had quizzed him about prevailing practice. He reported the dialogue which followed his explanation "that we ought nat to pray at masse, but rather onely to here and harken."

"In my God, I can nat se what we shall do at the masse, if we pray nat."
"Ye shall thynke to the mystery of the masse and shall harken to the wordes that the preest say."
"Yea, and what shall do they which understande it nat?"
"They shall behold, and shall here, and thynke, and by that they shall understande."[46]

In the 1520s, that was an informed orthodox view, taught, for example by John Fisher.[47] Mary's questioning attitude, however, may have endured well beyond 1527, for one of the most striking aspects of the Marian regime is the attention that was paid to ensuring that the people should have a much better understanding of the religious ceremonies they were to "behold." Some of her clergy were also active in instructing the laity in the Catholic meaning of those scriptures. Jennifer Loach, indeed, has demonstrated that there were similar patterns for printed instructional material under Mary as there had been under Edward. Catechisms were drawn up for basic instruction of all in the Catholic faith, as were homilies, for use by those clergy who were not equipped to preach. The printing press was never the only weapon, as indeed it had never been the only weapon for Protestants. But it was an important instrument, and it is much more difficult to distinguish between Edwardian and Marian uses of the printing press than the traditional dichotomy between Word-based Protestant and ritual-based Catholic would suggest.[48]

Before Reginald Pole was able to enter England, in late 1554, the reeducation campaign was substantially the work of Bonner and his leading clergy. It seems likely that they continued to lead the way after Pole took up his position. As Susan Brigden had summarized the output, "On July 1 1555 thirteen Homilies were published. Composed by [Bonner] and his chaplains, they were concerned with the central issues of faith: of man's fall and redemption, Christian love and charity, the nature and authority of the Church, the centrality of the sacrament of the altar, and an assertion of the doctrine of transubstantiation."[49]

Best known is probably the children's catechism, printed in red and black to help them read: *An honeste godly instruction*, apparently prepared by Bonner himself. He also "caused... to be set forth" *A profitable and necessary doctrine for every Christian man* in 1555. In that, amongst many other matters, he confronted the troublesome, and by the 1550s, strictly Protestant, doctrine of "faith alone," insisting instead that the Scriptural "we be justified by faith" meant "faith... containing the obedience to the whole doctrine and religion of Christ."[50] Although there were, inevitably, divisions within the Marian Catholic hierarchy about the desirability or dangers of having the Bible available in English, the Westminster synod presided over by Pole, did also agree to have the New Testament translated into English.[51] That decision was never translated into action, perhaps because of the very limited time remaining for the Catholic hierarchy to reclaim England.

Given that Pole was not active in the publication of religious manuals, the necessary general support may have come from Mary. This probability is made the more plausible by the royal proclamation of 1555, confirming the right of Wayland to print all "authorized" primers.[52] Moreover, by the time he arrived in England, Reginald Pole had moved away from his earlier attachment to preaching and became more deeply committed to the saving power of ceremony.[53] Mary remained more strongly committed to the active promotion of preaching, as a way of remedying "the evil preaching in time past,"[54] although there is no evidence she ever spared a thought for having it supersede, rather than inform, the importance of religious ceremonial.

So the Catholicism that was reintroduced under Mary, and with her strong support, was not simply conservative. It reflected in a number of ways the ambitions of the more humanist of the Catholic clergy; the combination of new modes of instruction and older ceremonies of worship, with all the visual splendor of the church rituals restored, seems to have been considered by her the most palatable religious route. Mary's policies are increasingly being seen as having shown many signs of succeeding before she died. If she had lived, or if, since she was childless, she had managed to establish a recognized Catholic heir, there seems little doubt that England would, within a few years have returned solidly to the Catholic camp. And the historical judgment on Mary would have been very different. Perhaps it would have taken more account of a humanist, Renaissance queen, well educated for rule, well schooled in politics, and well versed in the iconography and the practice of power. Mary has been buried for too long by the aftermath of John Foxe's powerful Protestant polemics.

Notes

1. John Foxe, *Actes and Monumentes of these latter and perillous dayes* (London, 1563), p. 889.
2. For details of how Holinshed's initially more sparing use of Foxe was expanded in later editions to render Mary "an object of comic disesteem," see Annabel Patterson, *Reading Holinshed's Chronicles* (Chicago: University of Chicago Press, 1994), esp. p. 57.
3. John Strype, *Ecclesiastical Memorials* (Oxford, 1822 edn.), III, ii, p. 153. Cited in Philip Hughes, *The Reformation in England*, 3 vols. (New York, Macmillan, 1963), 2: 255.
4. An extraordinarily popular collection of 'school-yard' history asserts that Mary's brother Edward had forced all his subjects to become Protestant 'so that Bloody Mary would be able to put them all to death afterwards for not being Roman Catholic.' W. C. Sellar and R. J. Yeatman, *1066 and All That* (London: Methuen, 1930).
5. A. F. Pollard, *The History of England from the Accession of Edward VI to the Death of Elizabeth (1547–1603)* (London: Longmans Green, 1910, reprinted New York, 1969), p. 172.
6. G. R. Elton, *England Under the Tudors* (London: Methuen, 1964), p. 214.
7. G. R. Elton, *Reform and Reformation: England, 1509–1558* (London: Edward Arnold, 1977), p. 376.
8. D. M. Loades, *Mary Tudor: A Life* (Oxford: Basil Blackwell, 1989), p. 8; John Guy, *Tudor England* (Oxford: Oxford University Press, 1990), p. 227; Susan Brigden, *New Worlds, Lost Worlds. The Rule of the Tudors 1485–1603* (Harmondsworth: Allen Lane, 2000), p. 199.
9. A. N. McLaren, *Political Culture in the Reign of Elizabeth 1 Queen and Commonwealth 1558–1585* (Cambridge: Cambridge University Press, 1999), p. 16. See also, pp. 90–103.
10. See my "Mary Tudor as 'Sole Quene'?: Gendering Tudor Monarchy," *The Historical Journal*, 40:4 (1997), pp. 895–924.
11. William Forrest, *The History of Grisild the Second*, ed. W. D. Macray (London: Chiswick Press, 1875). See Matthew Hansen's essay in this collection for more on this text.
12. Maria Dowling, "A Woman's Place? Learning and the Wives of Henry VIII," *History Today*, 41 (June 1991), p. 38.
13. *Letters and Papers, Foreign and Domestic, of the Reign of Henry VIII*, ed. J. S. Brewer, J. Gairdner and R. H. Brodie (23 vols. in 38 parts, 1862–1932) (Hereafter *L & P*) vol. I, i. 1475.
14. *L & P* I, ii. 2268, 2778,
15. *L & P* I, ii. 1970, 2261.
16. *L & P* IV, ii. 828.
17. Peggy K. Liss, *Isabel the Queen Life and Times* (New York: Oxford University Press, 1992), p. 253.
18. Maria Dowling, *Humanism in the Age of Henry VIII* (London: Croom Helm, 1986), pp. 224–25, 226. Significantly, Dowling adds that the collection *Satellitium vel Symbola* was subsequently used in the education of Prince Edward, who was always educated to rule.

19. Dowling, *Humanism*, pp. 227–28.
20. *Calendar of State Papers Spanish* IV, pt 2, ii Chapuys to the Emperor 11 July 1533, 739.
21. *L & P*, V, viii. No. 429; Chapuys to the Emperor 21 March, 1535, 167. Catherine apparently shared this view.
22. "An act declaring the Queen's Highness to have been born in a most just and lawful matrimony; and also repealing all Acts of Parliament and Sentence of Divorce had or made to the contrary." 1 Mary 2 cap 1.
23. John N. King, *Tudor Royal Iconography. Literature and Art in an Age of Religious Crisis* (Princeton: Princeton University Press, 1989), p. 185. Mary's will is reproduced in Loades, *Mary Tudor*, pp. 370–83.
24. "Letter from Mary to the members of Edward VI's Privy Council, dated 9 July 1553 from Kenninghall" transcribed (and modernized), Robert Tittler, *The Reign of Mary I* (London: Longman, 1991), pp. 81–82.
25. *The Accession of Queen Mary: Being the contemporary narrative of Antonio de Guares, A Spanish Merchant resident in London*, ed. and trans., Richard Garnett (London: Lawrence and Bullen, 1892), p. 92. The work was first published, in Spanish, in 1554.
26. For a significantly modified view of this assertion, see Robert Tittler and Susan L. Battley, "The Local Community and the Crown in 1553: The Accession of Mary Tudor Revisited," *Bulletin of the Institute of Historical Research*, LVII, 136 (November 1984), pp. 131–39.
27. "A Petition of Richard Troughton... relating to the share taken by him in the Duke of Northumberland's Plot," *Archaeologia, XIII* (1834), p. 31.
28. Richard Beeard, "A Godly Psalme, Of Mary Queene, which brought us comfort al" in *Fugitive Poetical Tracts*, ed. Henry Huth (London: n. p., 1875) Series 1, 1493–1600, No. 17. An editorial note indicates the author subsequently became an incumbent of St-Mary-at-Hill, London, and had previously commented on a controversy between Churchyard and Camel in the reign of Edward VI, which indicates a longstanding Protestant tendency.
29. [Poor Pratte] *The copie of a pistel or letter sent to Gilbert Potter* dated 1 August 1553, sig (Aiiv, B). That incident and Potter's punishment—prison and having his ears cut off—is mentioned in several contemporary sources, including, particularly briefly, *The Diary of Henry Machyn*, ed. J. G. Nichols (London: Camden Society, 1848), p. 37.
30. Susan Brigden, *London and the Reformation* (Oxford: Clarendon Press, 1989), pp. 530–31, 587–89.
31. Diarmaid MacCulloch, *Thomas Cranmer* (New Haven: Yale University Press, 1996), p. 351.
32. Quoted in P. F. Tytler, *England under the Reign of Edward VI and Mary I*, 2 vols. (London: R. Bentley, 1839), 2: 267–68.
33. The occasion for this statute, passed only in the third parliamentary session (April 1554), is still the subject of much speculation now, as it was then. See Jennifer Loach, *Parliament and the Crown in the Reign of Mary Tudor* (Oxford: Clarendon Press, 1986), pp. 96–97, and Richards, "Mary Tudor as 'Sole Quene'?" pp. 904–05.
34. For a brief introduction to the problems, see Felipe Fernández-Armesto, *Ferdinand and Isabella* (London: Weidenfeld & Nicolson, 1975), pp. 44–45.

35. Liss, *Isabel the Queen*, pp. 97–99; see also Nancy Rubin, *Isabella of Castile The First Renaissance Queen* (New York: St Martins Press, 1991), pp. 3–5.
36. Rubin, *Isabella of Castile*, pp. 128–29.
37. *Ibid.*, pp. 130–32; Liss, *Isabel the Queen*, pp. 104–07.
38. Liss, *Isabel the Queen*, p. 221. I am grateful to Glyn Redworth for pointing out to me the Spanish standard usage of 'los reyes' for king *and* queen, because the masculine form was conventionally used for husband and wife in many social forms. I suggest that the English observers retained the form because they had no term in their language for the reality of the shared regal power they saw before them.
39. J. S. Brewer, *The Reign of Henry VIII from his Accession to the Death of Wolsey*, 2 vols. (London: J. Murray, 1884), 1: 45.
40. BL Cotton Vesp F III no. 23
41. For an argument for much more power exercised by Philip, see Glyn Redworth, "'Matters impertinent to women': male and female monarchy under Philip and Mary" *English Historical Review*, vol. 112, 447 (1997), pp. 597–613; for another approach again, see David Loades, "Philip II and the government of England," *Law and Government under the Tudors*, ed. Claire Cross, David Loades and J. J. Scarisbrick (Cambridge: Cambridge University Press, 1988), pp. 177–94.
42. Sydney Anglo, *Images of Tudor Kingship* (London: Sealey, 1992), p. 6.
43. See Dale Hoak, "The iconography of the crown imperial," in *Tudor Political Culture*, ed. Dale Hoak (Cambridge: Cambridge University Press, 1995), pp. 54–103.
44. Dermot Fenlon, *Heresy and Obedience in Tridentine Italy: Cardinal Pole and the Counter Reformation* (Cambridge: Cambridge University Press, 1972), p. 223.
45. *Spirituali* have been consistently characterized as a group within the Catholic Church who were much attracted to the "protestant" doctrine of justification by faith, but could not accept the Lutheran extrapolation which attacked church tradition and the role of ceremonial in worship. They were, it has been suggested inheritors of "pre-Lutheran Paulinism." Thomas F. Mayer, *Reginald Pole Prince & Prophet* (Cambridge: Cambridge University Press, 2000), p. 3. Until the early sessions of the Council of Trent, a number of them had still had ambitions to achieve a reunion of the West European church. That had been the hope of Contarini, another prominent member of the *spirituali*, and formative influence on Pole, at Regensburg in 1541. See Peter Matheson, *Cardinal Contarini at Regensburg* (Oxford: Clarendon Press, 1972).
46. Cited in *The Lay Folks Mass Book or the Manner of Hearing Mass*, ed. T. F. Simmons (London: Early English Text Society, 1879), p. 158. Duwes's work was probably first published in 1533, perhaps for the infant Elizabeth.
47. Eamon Duffy, *The Stripping of the Altars: Traditional Religion in England c.1400–c.1580* (New Haven: Yale University Press, 1992), p. 531.
48. Jennifer Loach, "The Marian Establishment and the Printing Press," *English Historical Review*, CI (1986), pp. 135–48.
49. Susan Brigden, *London and the Reformation*, p. 578.

50. Cited Hughes, *The Reformation in England*, v. 2:244
51. Mayer, *Reginald Pole*, p. 242.
52. Duffy, *The Stripping of the Altars*, p. 538
53. His commitment in 1542 to "preaching as the means for pastoral regeneration: the 'simplex evangelium', without scholastic theology" had long since disappeared because of the aftermath. Fenlon, *Heresy and Obedience*, p. 255. For the ambiguities of Pole on the importance of preaching, see also Mayer, *Reginald Pole*, pp. 246–51.
54. Loades, *Mary Tudor*, p. 243.

Unmasquing the Connections between Jacobean Politics and Policy: the Circle of Anna of Denmark and the Beginning of the English Empire, 1614–18

Louis H. Roper

On January 6, 1617, the popular team of Inigo Jones and Ben Jonson presented their masque, *A Vision of Desire*, at court.[1] While of academic interest to students of Jacobean theater and the settlement of Virginia— since the audience included the Powhatan "princess," Pocahontas, and her planter-husband, John Rolfe—this occasion actually had the greatest ramifications for English history, especially the history of empire, and, correspondingly, sheds light on the nature of the political world of Jacobean England. In the first instance, the masque provided the backdrop for the elevation of George Villiers to earl of Buckingham, an important step in the development in the continuing emergence of this new court favorite. It also constituted part of the itinerary of the "Indian princess" and her consort on their successful tour to drum up support for the flagging Virginia Company. But, secondly, the timing of Buckingham's creation and the appearance of the Virginians may not have been coincidental since both the establishment of the new favorite and the resurgence of the Jamestown colony were policies favored by Anna of Denmark, queen of "Great Britain," and members of her political and literary circle, a group then ascending to power.

In the end, their triumphs—the preeminence of Villiers at the expense of Robert Carr, earl of Somerset, and his Howard friends, as well as the 1618 recapitalization of the Virginia Company—proved temporary: Villiers, once ensconced as the lover of James I (1603–25), disappointed his backers by pursuing an independent course of action

both as controller of royal patronage and as chief minister, while the
Company collapsed amidst factional bickering, mismanagement, and
corresponding finger pointing in the aftermath of the devastating Indian
attack on Jamestown in 1622.

But in the longer term, Villiers, as duke of Buckingham, created a
controversial administration that created thorny political problems for
James and his son, Charles I (1625–49) that, arguably, stretched the liga-
ments that connected English monarchs with their subjects. In addition,
although the Virginia Company was consigned to the historiographical
rubbish heap by the royal takeover of its operations in 1624, the momentum generated in terms of capital and migration by the visit of
Pocahontas and Rolfe in 1617 made it possible for Virginia to survive the
disaster and compelled a lukewarm monarchy to maintain the colony
rather than give it up. Instead of joining its counterpart, Saghedoc
(founded by the Virginia Company of Plymouth in present-day Maine
in the same year as Jamestown, 1607, but abandoned after the first
winter amidst accusations of cannibalism among the colonists), Roanoke
(1585), Guiana (1612), and Providence Island (1641) as wrecks along
the colonization motorway, Jamestown survived to become, famously,
the first permanent English settlement in North America. Thus, an
analysis of Anna's associates helps to restore the connection between
metropolitan politics and English colonization that succeeding generations of scholars of Anglo-American settlement have artificially severed.[2]

Revisionism, as battle-weary students of early Stuart England know
all too well, has sought to transform our understanding of English political history prior to the Civil Wars. At the least, the Whiggish–Marxist
high road to Civil War upon which parliamentary liberty supposedly tram-
pled over Stuart absolutist pretensions, as engineered by S. R. Gardiner,
Wallace Notestein, and their disciples, has been demolished. Yet, as "post-
revisionists" have taken pains to point out, conflict certainly did occur
within the early seventeenth-century English political nation and in its
shires and people did oppose—even hamstring—governmental policies
both in and out of parliaments.[3]

How to address the realities of political conflict and opposition in
early Stuart England without teleologically linking it to the outbreak of
hostilities in 1641? That question has plagued the field for over a generation. Actually the answer, as so often happens in historiography, may
have been staring us in the face. We have known for some time that
factions, traditionally downplayed as engineers of policy (as opposed to
political) change, and their competition for favor created many of the
disputes that broke out at this time, especially during the reign of

James.[4] We also know something of the character and personnel of these networks—clients, and even patrons, shifted allegiances, using the privileged forums provided by parliaments in which to express displeasure with policy and to attack ministers, such as Buckingham in the 1620s.[5]

Yet, perhaps because of the relative paucity of parliamentary meetings and perhaps because it falls between the two stools of the "Elizabethan Era" and the doomed reign of Charles I, rather less attention has been focused on the politics of the Jacobean period. Correspondingly, the behavior and effects of arguably the greatest of Jacobean factions—or, perhaps more accurately, networks—has only recently started receiving proper consideration, largely thanks to the work of Leeds Barroll and Barbara Lewalski. But these studies have not worked out the ramifications of their findings. An examination of this network, in turn, must of necessity reveal something about the purpose, beliefs, and behavior of these political associations and especially the one that revolved around James I's queen, Anna of Denmark.

Barroll has spent a considerable amount of time successfully rehabilitating Anna's reputation as a political operator. Until recently, Anna has been dismissed as a feather-brained backer of expensive and frivolous court entertainments with no aptitude or understanding of court politics. Barroll's research in Scotland (where Anna was the queen-consort of James VI for fourteen years before they moved south but a nation still customarily ignored in English history) and Denmark (where Princess Anna, sister of the Danish king, Christian IV, may have been exposed, at an early age, to the notion of pompous, overblown male monarchs) has revealed that Anna played a very active and substantial political role in the northern kingdom. She formed her own household and attempted, often successfully, to use those connections to advance her associates even against the wishes of her husband.[6]

When that husband succeeded to the English throne, Anna registered several significant and immediate successes in establishing herself as an autonomous political figure: she regained control over her eldest son, Prince Henry, from her enemy, the earl of Mar; she established her own English household whose makeup did not jibe with the plans of the king and his council; and she used that household as the nexus for political and literary patronage. Most significantly, a group of noblewomen, led by Lucy Russell, countess of Bedford, and including Penelope Rich (*nee* Devereux) and Mary, countess of Pembroke (*nee* Sidney), took it upon themselves (apparently) to travel north to meet the new queen at Newcastle and it was this group who formed the core of Anna's household and of her network of associates, which included their husbands, brothers, and sons as well as the leading lights of Jacobean literature and theater.[7]

Perhaps inevitably (and, therefore, tiresomely), the gender of this "feminine commonwealth" has led to its historiographical devaluation.[8] The evidence uncovered so far would seem to suggest, though, that, not only did these women—notably within the context of a monarchy that took great pains to codify patriarchy as its ideology—engage in political activity of the sort customarily assigned to the "public" (viz. male) sphere of early modern European societies, they also shared a full-fledged political platform (albeit a negative one) of opposition to Spain and to the Scottish retainers whom James brought south with him. This opposition manifested itself, especially early in the reign, in the plays and masques created by the literary talents who attached themselves to patrons within the queen's circle.[9]

Barroll and Lewalski, scholars of early modern English culture, have demonstrated Anna's political nous and her success at establishing a third center of political power (along with the king and Prince Henry), but have characterized her English career as one dedicated to maintaining queenly independence (and resistance to patriarchy) as well as a sense of regal majesty as queen consort largely through the masques and other entertainments she underwrote.[10] Yet, although they have sketched out the extent of her connections—and noted a trail back from them to the "Protestant" faction of Robert Devereux, second earl of Essex (the leader of the abortive 1601 rebellion against Elizabeth)—they have not suggested that the queen-consort involved herself in politics for policy reasons. Unfortunately, we have no "smoking gun," but the circumstantial evidence indicates that Anna had an interest in government, in policy and in effecting that policy, as well as in attacking her opponents (which, naturally, went hand in hand). After all, she had been a major political player in Scotland, why should the leopard have changed her spots in England? Moreover, she seems to have created an even larger network (in an admittedly larger realm) in her new role.[11]

Of course, as a newcomer to the English scene and as consort to the reigning monarch, Anna, even with the ready retinue who joined her at Newcastle, would have had to undertake a preliminary investigation of the political landscape. From 1603 until his death in 1612, Robert Cecil, the successful architect of the peaceful accession of the Scottish king to the English throne, handled much of the day-to-day administration of government and, correspondingly, dominated the political scene by keeping various claimants for power at arm's length. Anna seems to have largely acquiesced in this state of affairs: Cecil served as the high steward of her estates and he took charge of the mourning when her infant daughters died, they exchanged gifts and correspondence, and she attended him "diligently" during his final illness.[12]

Nevertheless, the record reveals that individuals with close connections to the queen consort scored significant hits against the king and Cecil even early in the reign. Sir Edwin Sandys, Sir Thomas Ridgeway, and Sir Maurice Berkeley (members of Anna's new Council) together with the earl of Southampton, the earl of Pembroke, Pembroke's client-associate, Sir Benjamin Rudyerd, and Sir William Strode, a relation of Sandys, led the successful parliamentary fight against the effort to unite the realms of England and Scotland against the deepest wishes of the monarch. Of course, who was directing whom (and indeed whether "direction" is an accurate assessment of this "opposition") remains unknown since early seventeenth-century English people engaging in politics outside the recognized organs of government did not take minutes of their meetings although we do know that unofficial political gatherings took place both privately and at court.[13] We also know that the Scots who accompanied James VI on his sojourn to becoming James I—and so had the most to benefit from Union—had already, with the exception of the duke of Lennox, earned the enmity of Anna (the earls of Dunbar and Mar especially so). They had also irritated prideful English nobles, such as Southampton and the earls of Pembroke and Arundel, by crowding them toward the margins of the patronage picture. And the Scots were foreigners who might not have the best interests of England at heart—or at least so Sandys and his associates relentlessly and successfully argued in the parliament of 1604.[14]

Cecil's death removed his steadying hand from the tiller of the ship of state and a bitter fight to control the government between the queen's group and the Howard family ensued. Somewhat curiously, we have known for some time, notwithstanding the old view of Anna as a political lightweight, that the queen consort played a role in the opposition to the Howards that culminated in the emergence of Villiers.[15] It seems clear, though, especially in light of her rehabilitation by Barroll, that she was one of the leaders—if not *the* leader—of the anti-Howard group. The evidence we have suggests that Anna's attitude stemmed, in part, from personal reasons. She loathed, for instance, Sir Thomas Overbury, chief associate of Somerset, apparently for laughing about her and for failing to tip his hat to her, and she quarreled with Henry Howard, earl of Northampton, for instance, over control of Greenwich Park in 1613.[16]

Also, it is quite clear that Northampton (a pensioner of Spain from the 1580s), led (until his death in 1614) the pro-Madrid wing of

James I's government and, correspondingly, earned the enmity of the leaders of Anna's circle—the countess of Bedford, Penelope Rich, the earls of Pembroke and Southampton, Sandys, Rudyerd, George Abbot, the archbishop of Canterbury—who generally styled themselves standard-bearers for international Protestantism in the manner of their relative and friend, Sir Philip Sidney.[17] But to what degree, if any, did Anna share these views and to what degree, if any, was she willing to act on them?[18]

Relatively considerable debate, both contemporary and historiographical, has concerned itself with the issue of whether Anna herself may have been a Roman Catholic. A satisfactory conclusion has not been reached—and may be unreachable given the various religious perspectives of observers and the tendency among Jacobean Protestants to identify Lutherans (the creed in which the queen was instructed as a child) as Roman Catholics. In any event, whether "papist" ("crypto-" or otherwise) or not, the evidence we have suggests that Anna had no particular feelings for Spain. On the one hand, like her brother, Christian IV, she refused to meet commissioners from the United Provinces on the grounds that they were rebels against their natural sovereign, Philip III, and she allegedly entertained matches between her sons and Spanish princesses. On the other, she seems not to have taken any noticeable steps to protect Catholics and Catholicism in England, she did not especially favor a Spanish match for her children (as opposed, say, to a French one), confirmed Protestants (and members of the queen's circle) had constant charge of the education of those children (and formed close ties with them), and she unsuccessfully sought a pardon for the Protestant "martyr" Sir Walter Ralegh (who, of course, had numerous connections in her circle) before his execution in 1618 following his misadventures in Guiana.[19]

Then, there is the circumstantial evidence that the most prominent opponents of Spain in England actively, consistently, and immediately sought associations with her. Either the queen had no particular interest in politics and attracted these people to her court through their common literary and theatrical interests into which faction came to be incorporated (the revisionist twist on the traditional argument) or the countess of Bedford, Mary Wroth, Pembroke, and Southampton recognized (even before she came to England) that they had a political affinity with Anna. Such an affinity would have had to have included a frosty attitude toward Spain.

We already know that she went further than that—at least in the short-term, factional sense—since she famously orchestrated—in alliance with Canterbury, Pembroke, Southampton, and others—the launch of Villiers (in conjunction with Jonson's masque *The Golden Age Restored*) into the affections of James with the avowed purpose of replacing the Howard-backed favorite, Somerset. Helped to no end by the folly of the latter and his wife, Frances Howard (culminating in their implication in the alleged murder of Overbury in the Tower and their banishment from court), Villiers rose through the king's bedchamber to become, in quick order, viscount, earl, marquis, and duke (the first in England since the execution of the duke of Norfolk in 1572). The death of Northampton, the aging of the Howard earls of Suffolk and Nottingham, and the collapse of Somerset cleared the decks for Anna's group by 1615: in addition to the continuing preeminence of Villiers, Pembroke became Lord Chamberlain in that year ("an appointment strongly influenced by Queen Anne," according to his biographer).[20]

We also know that Anna commissioned the publication of William Welwood's contribution to the debate over freedom of the seas, *De Dominio Maris* (1616). The discoverer of this patronage relationship put it down to the queen's desire to preserve her monopoly to license foreign fishing expeditions in British waters, obtained in 1614—a 21-year patent she purportedly obtained so that she could "maintain her elegant life style without the necessity of a further increase in her allowances from the state." This is possible, but why did Anna pursue this particular monopoly and how did she know to encourage Welwood? Since we have no evidence either way, it seems equally possible that the queen did have an interest in navigation, international law, and British interests (which, of course, she would have regarded as indistinct from her own).[21]

Perhaps more crucially, though, but generally overlooked, Anna had effective charge of the English government for much of 1617 whilst her husband made his return to Scotland. In the king's absence, the queen ruled in conjunction with Prince Charles (just 17 years old at the time), her allies, Canterbury, Worcester, and Lord Chancellor Ellsmere (stepfather of Elizabeth de Vere, countess of Derby and Susan de Vere, countess of Montgomery and, therefore, Pembroke's sister-in-law, both active members of Anna's household) who easily outnumbered the sole Howard (but not pro-Spanish) member, Thomas, earl of Suffolk and Lord Treasurer. The Venetian ambassador, for one, had little doubt that the political center of England shifted to Anna's palace at Greenwich.[22]

The eclipse of the generally pro-Spanish Howards enabled the plans of Pembroke (whose reputation has also received a new glow), Southampton, Sandys, and others to kick-start the moribund colonization of Virginia. Again, although we have no direct evidence that Anna had an interest in American colonization (a phenomenon which, since it was a constant irritation to the Spanish, would also have provided convenient direct evidence of an anti-Spanish demeanor on her part), we do have circumstantial evidence—in the form of the attendance of Pocahontas and Rolfe at the masque previously cited, in an address made by Captain John Smith in 1618 on the progress of Jamestown, and in her subscription to the Virginia Company's recapitalization campaign of the same year—that she, at least, had knowledge of the colony and was expected to have an interest in its success. The resuscitation of Virginia also demonstrates the character and limits of state involvement in English colonization: the monarchy seems to have given no encouragement to the colony, leaving it to those involved—and their connections—to sort their venture out satisfactorily.[23]

The trials and tribulations of the Virginia Company constitute another seemingly well-known story in the annals of James I's England. To recapitulate briefly, the Crown originally chartered two companies, one in Plymouth and one in London in 1606. The Plymouth Company received title to essentially the northern half of North America (demarcated at the site of modern Philadelphia), planted the failed colony at Saghedoc, and gave up. The Virginia Company of London, granted the powers to govern and recruit settlers in southern North America (so long as, significantly, they did not interfere with or "molest" the Spaniards), sent colonists to Chesapeake Bay where they settled at Jamestown, then an island in the estuary of the James River.

There, most of them suffered and died—at the hands of hostile indigenous neighbors, led by the noted sachem, Powhatan (father of Pocahontas), from lack of food, and from the "bloody flux" (dysentery)—whilst their government argued amongst themselves and failed to provide necessary leadership. Famously, at least according to his own account, Smith, to the annoyance of many of the leaders in the party, stepped in, implemented a "work or starve" policy to force "gentlemen" (apparently unwilling to get their hands dirty) to toil in the fields, ordered the settlers to follow the practice of the Indians by dispersing in the summer, and stopped the rot. Captain John, though, suffered an "accident" in 1609 and had to return to England although he maintained his interest in Jamestown and in colonization generally.[24]

More misery followed, although the company tried constantly to promote its effort as a Hakluytian answer to the nation's perceived problems (Richard Hakluyt, the Elizabethan colonial promoter, had been an investor and early advisor) of overpopulation and dangerous dependence on foreign trade in hopes of securing more capital and more settlers. Unfortunately, reports filed by early settlers placed the credibility of the company literature into doubt and it had difficulty attracting continued support. Moreover, the relief fleet sent in 1609 wrecked itself on Bermuda (as noted in Shakespeare's *Tempest*), the colony's leaders returned to bickering and the settlers to starving (whilst the Powhatans amused themselves by picking off stragglers). Indeed, the colonists had decided to abandon the effort when a new governor, Lord de la Warr, finally arrived and convinced them to stay. Still, Virginia remained so unsettled that de la Warr's successor, Sir Thomas Dale, had to implement a version of martial law to ensure a proper defensive system and distribute food equitably. Then, the deaths of Cecil and his merchant friend, Sir Walter Cope, deprived the company and the colony of much of its support in England. In 1616, by all accounts the situation in Virginia was, almost literally, grave.[25]

By this time, though, matters had begun to improve in the Jamestown saga. First, Powhatan made peace with the English, punctuated, in accordance with indigenous diplomatic custom, with the marriage between Pocahontas and Rolfe, a leading Virginia planter. Secondly, Rolfe successfully and famously introduced the cultivation of tobacco brought to the colony by his connections in Venezuela. This commodity, as produced in that part of the Spanish Empire, had already attracted a substantial market in England to the extent that the king had felt the need, in his inimitable fashion, to issue *A Counter-blaste to Tobacco*, which outlined what he regarded as the demerits of the weed for the realm and his subjects (1604). We do not know whether Rolfe himself or someone else (probably in London) provided the impetus for introducing tobacco cultivation into the Chesapeake. We do know, though, that by 1616, the Virginian had completed his preparations to introduce what he undoubtedly knew would be a successful commodity into the English market; Rolfe and, significantly, his wife, went to England to spread the word. Clearly, those in charge of the company's operations brought about the reinvigoration of their enterprise with a degree of consciousness. They laid the groundwork in 1615 with the publication of Ralph Hamor's *A True Discourse of the Present Estate of Virginia* that announced the peace between the English and Powhatan and the corresponding marriage of Pocahontas and Rolfe as well as the now-assuredly excellent prospects for the colony.[26]

Here, we must restore the colonization of Virginia to its proper context of Jacobean political history (in accordance with the reconfiguration of that history in line with our new appreciation of Anna of Denmark and the earl of Pembroke) in order to properly understand how and why the venture did finally succeed. The story of Jamestown has focused primarily on the settlement itself (perhaps inevitably since most interested scholars have been anachronistically seeking the "origins" of American society, with some attention paid to the Virginia Company, or of the "British Empire") with scant regard to the reality that the effecting of an English imperial moment in the early seventeenth century required an encouraging atmosphere at court.[27]

Can it really have been a coincidence that Pocahontas and Rolfe made their sensational visit to court and spread the "good news" of tobacco at the very time when Anna controlled the government of England? In the event, Virginia, long regarded with disdain, became a watchword for the first time since the disasters of 1609: the company succeeded in attracting a wave of new money, with Pembroke at the top of the table of investors, and, along with private undertakers, a wave of new settlers; the population rose, notwithstanding continued demographic difficulties with "seasoning." It seems fair to say that without this dual influx, achieved a decade after the founding of Jamestown, this once-precarious toehold of English empire in America would have remained tenuous at best. Would it have been able to survive a determined Indian attack such as the one led by Powhatan's brother and bitter enemy of the English, Opechecanough, which wiped out one-quarter of the colony's population in 1622?[28] Even though the attack exposed the Company's shortcomings, and it dissolved amidst wrangling and finger-pointing, the 1622 reality remained that the colony had become too valuable and too numerous to be abandoned and the crown took direct control.

With the king on his way to Scotland and the Howards in disgrace, we find some evidence that the friends of Virginia certainly believed that they had friends in high places in 1617. Rolfe, upon his arrival in London, published *A True Relation of the State of Virginia* dedicated to Pembroke and referencing Hamor's pamphlet, whilst, around the same time, Captain Smith took it upon himself "to make [Pocahontas'] qualities known" to Anna herself in his history of Virginia. Rolfe acknowledged the painful birthpangs that the colony had suffered—"envie, dissentions and iarrs" brought on by an "Aristocratycallie" chosen government deterred husbandry while the "vulgar sort looked for Supplies out of England," along with "Enmytie with the Indians." But now that Sir Thomas Dale had concluded peace with Powhatan and established order (in a "more absolute gouerment") and, most importantly, now that tobacco ("knowen to them to be verie vendible in England") had been planted, he did not doubt but that the colony's potential would finally be realized. To finally perfect this ambition, Rolfe implored Pembroke and "many right Honorable and worthy personages both here and [in] Virginia" to uphold "this Christian Cause" against the "evill reports" of "murmerors, slanderors, and backsliders."[29] In the meantime, based at the earl of Northumberland's house in Richmond (Northumberland was a friend of Ralegh), the tobacco planter and the Indian princess made the rounds from the summer of 1616 until April 1617 (when Pocahontas died of smallpox and the now-widowed Rolfe returned to America).[30]

The promotional campaign, no matter how coordinated it was, had a palpable effect. Pembroke and his friends put their money where their mouths were and encouraged others to do the same; a remarkable number of Anna's associates held remarkable prominence on the lengthy list of 1618 investors in the Virginia Company: the earl of Bedford subscribed £120, Sir Maurice Berkeley £80, the archbishop of Canterbury £75, Sir Oliver Cromwell (another member of the queen's council) £65, Sir John Harington £187 10s, Viscount L'Isle £90, Southampton £350, Sandys £287 10s, Suffolk and his son (constituting the Howard presence on the list and Suffolk had also been involved in the government of the company previously) £133 6s 8d and £87 10s respectively, and Pembroke himself £400 (the third highest subscription after Lord de la Warr and the Company of Grocers).[31]

The thousands of pounds raised and the rekindled interest in the colony translated into a new charter and reorganization for the company (now led by Sir Edwin Sandys), and a reformation of land distribution and local government (the celebrated House of Burgesses created in 1619). The company also began to permit private proprietors to bring settlers independently to work their own lands. Although claims arose that too many people were brought too quickly (resulting in straggling settlements, starvation, and the Opechecanough disaster), it is most significant that, according to our best figures, some 3,500 to 4,000 people came to Virginia from England between 1619 and 1623 bringing the total population of the colony to between 4,500 and 5,000, although only some 2,500 inhabitants remained in 1623 after the Indian attack. Even so, the English were in the Chesapeake to stay.[32]

While Pembroke, Southampton, Sandys, Lord Robert Rich, and others of her associates figured prominently in the company's affairs, Anna of Denmark did not. Ironically, having engineered the greatest political *coup* of her career and now poised to become an even greater political figure as the mother to the heir to the throne and "maker" of the new favorite, the queen's health fatally intervened. Even as Villiers progressed in late 1616, she had developed pleurisy or congestive heart failure. By the time James returned to England in November 1617 she seems to have been seriously ill and remained so for most of 1618 before her death on March 2, 1619.

Gardiner claimed that Anna's "death was of no political importance" based on his belief that she exercised little influence over her husband and that "she seldom attempted to employ it with any settled and deliberate purpose. Her real sphere was the banquet and the masque." Thus, although her acquaintances regarded her with fondness, for "the mass of the nation she was as completely forgotten as though she had never lived."[33] Undoubtedly, we cannot have expected too much from a queen consort but it seems that this traditional view presumed more than it analyzed. In the first place, "banquets and masques" can serve as avenues for political expression.[34] But more importantly, the evidence indicates quite clearly that, *pace* the Gardinerian view of reality, Anna did generate substantial political gravity (certainly as much, if not more so, than her celebrated son, Prince Henry, did before his death at eighteen) that attracted substantial political actors. Within their firmament, the most significant sort of political activity took place.

Notes

1. A shorter version of this paper was read at the 2001 Sixteenth-Century Studies Conference, Denver, CO.
2. Wesley Frank Craven, *The Dissolution of the Virginia Company: The Failure of a Colonial Experiment* (Gloucester, MA.: Peter Smith, 1964 [1932]); Kenneth M. Andrews, *Trade, Plunder and Settlement: Maritime Enterprise and the Genesis of the British Empire, 1480–1630* (Cambridge: Cambridge University Press, 1984).
3. Richard Cust and Ann Hughes, eds., *Conflict in Early Stuart England* (London: Longman, 1989).
4. Kevin Sharpe, ed., *Faction and Parliament: Essays on Early Stuart History* (London and New York: Methuen, 1978); Linda Levy Peck, *Court Patronage and Corruption in Early Stuart England* (Boston: Unwin Hyman, 1990).
5. Conrad Russell, *Parliaments and English Politics, 1621–1629* (Oxford: Oxford University Press, 1979).
6. Leeds Barroll, *Anna of Denmark, Queen of England: A Cultural Biography* (Philadelphia: University of Pennsylvania Press, 2000), pp. 14–35.
7. Barroll, *Anna of Denmark*, pp. 36–73; Barroll, "The Court of the First Stuart Queen," in Linda Levy Peck, ed., *The Mental World of the Jacobean Court* (Cambridge: Cambridge University Press, 1992), pp. 191–208; Barbara K. Lewalski, "Lucy, Countess of Bedford: Images of a Jacobean Courtier and Patroness," in Kevin Sharpe and Steven N. Zwicker, eds., *Politics of Discourse: The Literature and History of Seventeenth-Century England* (Berkeley and

Los Angeles: University of California Press, 1987), pp. 52–77; Barbara K. Lewalski, "Enacting Opposition: Queen Anne and the Subversions of Masquing" and "Exercising Power: The Countess of Bedford as Courtier, Patron, and Coterie Poet" in idem, *Writing Women in Jacobean England* (Cambridge, MA: Harvard University Press, 1993), pp. 15–43, 95–123.
8. The observation of Edward Somerset, earl of Worcester, quoted in Michael Brennan, *Literary Patronage in the English Renaissance: The Pembroke Family* (London and New York: Routledge, Chapman & Hall, Inc., 1988), p. 104.
9. Lewalski, "Enacting Opposition," p. 24 and "Exercising Power," p. 107.
10. Barroll, *Anna of Denmark*, p. 73; Lewalski, "Enacting Opposition," *passim*.
11. Peck, *Court Patronage and Corruption in Early Stuart England*, pp. 68–74.
12. Pauline Croft, "Robert Cecil and the Early Jacobean Court," in *The Mental World of the Jacobean Court*, ed. Peck, pp. 134–47 at 142–43.
13. Barroll, *Anna of Denmark*, pp. 56–62, Brennan, *Literary Patronage in the English Renaissance*, pp. 104–5.
14. Barroll, *Anna of Denmark*, p. 34. Peck, *Court Patronage and Corruption in Early Stuart England*, lists Anna's Council, p. 223n.
15. Roger Lockyer, *Buckingham: The Life and Political Career of George Villiers, First Duke of Buckingham, 1592–1628* (London and New York: Longman, 1981), pp. 19–20.
16. Barroll, *Anna of Denmark*, pp. 136–37; Linda Levy Peck, *Northampton: Patronage and Policy at the Court of James I* (London: Unwin Hyman, 1982), pp. 40, 74.
17. Brennan, *Literary Patronage in the English Renaissance*, pp. 123–24; Peck, *Northampton*, pp. 70–71; Barroll, *Anna of Denmark*, pp. 36–73.
18. It was the view of the redoubtable Victorian, Samuel Rawson Gardiner (who regarded her as a staunch papist) that Anna, under the alleged influence of her Scottish lady-in-waiting, the Catholic Jean Drummond, countess of Roxborough, accepted a Spanish pension and worked hand-in-glove with the Spanish ambassador, Sarmiento, to wield her weak influence on her husband. S. R. Gardiner, *History of England from the Accession of James I to the Outbreak of the Civil War, 1603–1642*, 10 vols. (London: Longman, Green and Co., 1883–84), 2: 224. In light of Barroll's research, this verdict cannot be sustained: indeed, the queen dismissed this "influential" lady, curiously, at the beginning of 1617. Thus, he determined that Anna geared her political activity against the Howards, *Anna of Denmark*, pp. 155–59.
19. Barroll, *Anna of Denmark*, pp. 117–21, 162–72.
20. Brennan, *Literary Patronage in the English Renaissance*, pp. 129–46; Barroll, *Anna of Denmark*, pp. 130–51.
21. Cf. J. D. Alsop, "William Welwood, Anne of Denmark and the Sovereignty of the Sea," *Scottish Historical Review*, 59 (1980), 171–74 (quotation at 172).
22. The council to rule the realm in the king's absence had been created by January 19 and James finally crossed into Scotland from May 13 until November, Gardiner, *History of England*, 1: 215; 3: 224, 228; Barroll, *Anna of Denmark*, pp. 51–54 for Derby and Montgomery and p. 153 for the creation and make-up of the council.

23. Cf. Michael Braddick, "The English Government, War, Trade, and Settlement, 1625–1688," in Nicholas P. Canny, ed., *The Origins of Empire*, vol. 1 in Wm. Roger Louis, ed., *The Oxford History of the British Empire*, 5 vols. (Oxford: Oxford University Press, 1998), pp. 286–308.
24. John C. Appleby, "War, Politics, and Colonization, 1558–1625," in Canny, ed., *The Origins of Empire*, pp. 55–78 at 71–74.
25. In 1616, the English population of Virginia numbered 351, Craven, *The Dissolution of the Virginia Company*, p. 34.
26. Previous promotion campaigns had come in response to "scandalous reports" made in print and on the stage, e.g., William Barret, *A True Declaration of the Estate of the Colonie in Virginia* [London, 1610] in Peter Force, ed., *Tracts and Other Papers Related to the Settlement of the United States*, 4 vols. (Washington, DC, 1838–1846), 3: 3–27, quotation at 8. Naturally, these attempts to refute such "reports" styled Virginia as fertile, the Indians as friendly, the colonial government as benevolent, and the Virginia Company as civic-minded (as opposed to nakedly pursuing profit). Whether the "ideology" publicly articulated by the company bore any connection with reality is another matter, cf. Andrew Fitzmaurice, "The Civic Solution to the Crisis of English Colonization, 1609–1625" in *Historical Journal*, 42 (1999), 25–51. Jacobeans interested in America knew about (and some illegally engaged in) the tobacco trade with Venezuela, Guiana, and Trinidad, Joyce Lorimer, "The English contraband tobacco trade in Trinidad and Guiana, 1590–1617," in K. R. Andrews, N. P. Canny, and P. E. H. Hair, *The Westward Enterprise: English Activities in Ireland, the Atlantic, and America, 1480–1650* (Liverpool: Liverpool University Press, 1978), pp. 124–50.
27. James Horn, "Tobacco Colonies: The Shaping of English Society in the Seventeenth-Century Chesapeake" in Canny, ed., *The Origins of Empire*, pp. 170–92. Pembroke receives just one mention in Canny's volume; Anna of Denmark, inevitably, does not appear in its index.
28. Of course, the expansion of the English settlement and the high-handed attitude of the newcomers in demanding and taking food from the Indians, as well as the threat now posed to hunting grounds sparked this attack. But it is not beyond the realm of possibility to suggest that Opechecanough, who replaced Powhatan as the leading Chesapeake sachem after his brother's death in 1618, would have attacked the English anyway, Peter C. Mancall, "Native Americans and Europeans in English America, 1500–1700," in Canny, ed., *The Origins of Empire*, pp. 328–50 at 337–38.
29. John Rolfe, *A True Relation of the State of Virginia lefte by Sir Thomas Dale Knight in May last 1616* (London, 1617).
30. Captain John Smith, *The Generall Historie of Virginia, New-England, and the Summer Isles with the Names of the Adventurers, Planters, and Governours from Their First Beginning An. 1584 to this Present 1624* [London, 1623], in Philip L. Barbour, ed., *The Complete Works of Captain John Smith (1580–1631)*, 3 vols. (Chapel Hill, NC: University of North Carolina Press, 1986), vol. 2. Smith's letter to Anna, which recounts the famous tale in which Pocahontas purportedly saved him from the "barbarous power" of her father, appears at pp. 258–62.

31. "A Complete List in Alphabetical Order of the 'Adventurers to Virginia,' with the Several Amounts of their Holdings," 1618[?], Susan Myra Kingsbury, ed., *The Records of the Virginia Company of London*, 4 vols. (Washington, DC: Government Printing Office, 1933), 3: 79–90.
32. Craven, *Dissolution of the Virginia Company*, p. 301. Samuel Purchas reported that "twelve hundred persons and upward" went to Virginia in 1619 "and there are neere one thousand more remaining of those that were gone before," *Hakluytus Posthumus or Purchas His Pilgrimes: Contayning a History of the World in Sea Voyages and Lande Travells by Englishmen and Others*, 20 vols. (New York: AMS Press, 1965), 19: 122.
33. Gardiner, *History of England*, 3: 294.
34. Although calling them "subversive" may be a step too far, cf. Barbara Kiefer Lewalski, "Anne of Denmark and the subversion of masquing," *Criticism*, 35 (1993), pp. 341–56.

Negotiating Exile: Henrietta Maria, Elizabeth of Bohemia, and the Court of Charles I

Karen L. Nelson

On December 24, 1632, soon after the death of her husband Frederick, Elizabeth of Bohemia apologized to her brother, King Charles I of England, for not visiting him as he commanded, "Nevertheless, I entreat you to pardon me, if I cannot at present obey your command and my own wishes; the custom in Germany being not to stir out of the house for some time, after such a misfortune. And since I was married into this country, I should wish to observe its customs carefully, so as to give no occasion for scandal. And moreover, I doubt whether, even after the expiration of the aforesaid term, I shall be able so soon to enjoy this happiness, until my poor children can be re-established in the empire, or at least in a fair way of being so."[1] In this passage, Elizabeth carefully acknowledged her obedience to the brother who had at this point invested eight years of England's resources and soldiers upon her behalf and whose very marriage hinged upon efforts to regain the Palatinate for Elizabeth, her husband, and their offspring. At the same time, Elizabeth recognized her status as a foreign bride in exile and her obligations to the ways of her adopted homeland as she reminded her brother of his obligations to the rights of her children. Even, perhaps especially, in this time of mourning her husband, Elizabeth astutely used all of the weapons in her arsenal to keep her brother allied with her cause. She operated in sharp relief to her brother's wife, Henrietta Maria de Bourbon, who also hoped to influence Charles's policies, both foreign and domestic, but whose methods differed drastically. Whereas Elizabeth tailored her methods to her audience and tried to make the way for herself and her family as smooth as possible throughout her career as queen, Henrietta Maria expected her hearers to conform to her desires and enjoyed the hubbub of contention, particularly at the beginning of her reign as consort to Charles I.

The contrast in the approaches these two women used as they attempted to direct Charles's policies, and the scope of their successes, is especially evident in controversies at court in which each became involved. These periods of crises—for Henrietta Maria, the first years of marriage, 1625 to 1630, and for Elizabeth, the years immediately following the death of Frederick, 1632 to 1634—reveal the strategies inherent to their success as queens living in foreign lands.[2] Henrietta Maria sought a number of goals: loosening of English restrictions for English Catholics; control over the affairs of her own household; power over Charles. Elizabeth was more focused upon gaining the return of the Palatinate for her husband, which would result in their return from exile in the Hague and ultimately lead to management of her own affairs. Neither queen was content to remain a conduit of foreign policy or a marker for dynastic union; instead, each influenced Charles and those around him in efforts to advance their own agendas for their adopted countries.

The level of their success with Charles hinged in large part on three areas: their recognition of local practices; their ability to use alliances and networks to further their own projects; and their knowledge of Charles, in particular their awareness of his weaknesses and insecurities. Henrietta Maria, after initially ignoring most of these aspects of queenly politics, incorporated them to some degree into her own behavior, and saw a resultant rise in her success with Charles. However, many aspects of domestic policy remained beyond either Charles's or Henrietta Maria's power. The puritan faction at court was strong enough to scrutinize and redirect the "popish" practices of John Cosins, Bishop of Durham, and of Richard Montague. Charles could not have returned England to the pope or completely removed restrictions against Catholics even if he had wanted to, and he did not. In the same vein, while Elizabeth of Bohemia used all of these tools adroitly and managed to keep her brother involved in negotiations for the Palatinate, she could not recast him as a king powerful enough to marshal England's financial, military, and diplomatic resources for her cause or as a charismatic leader of a united force against the Hapsburg empire.[3] Clearly, while both women's influence played a role in Charles's reign, neither were able to rule through him, nor were they able to overcome the larger context within which Charles worked.

Especially during the first years of her marriage to Charles, Henrietta Maria repeatedly ignored local custom, particularly concerning religion.

In part, she responded to the family obligations placed upon her by her mother Queen Marie d'Medici, her brother King Louis XIII of France, and her godfather Pope Urban VIII. They charged her with serving as missionary to England and hoped she would restore England to Roman Catholicism. Henrietta Maria acknowledged these obligations and assumed the missionary mantle with zeal in her letters thanking the pope for dispensation to marry outside of the faith.[4] She offered similar assurances to her brother, "and as I desire religiously to heep [sic] and observe your majesty's sincere intentions, as well in what concerns me and mine, as in what may be useful and advantageous to the religion and the Catholics of Great Britain, I give your majesty my faith and word of conscience, that if it so be that it please God to bless this marriage, so as to give me the favour of progeny, I will make no selection of persons to bring up and serve the children who may be born, except from Catholics; I will only give the charge of choosing these officers to Catholics, obliging them to take none but those of the same religion."[5] Despite these promises, Marie d'Medici, with ghostwriting assistance from her spiritual advisors Cardinal Richelieu and Father Bérule, wrote instructions for the fifteen-year-old princess, "of which [Henrietta] should keep a copy in the most precious of her caskets, in order that the maternal advice should be constantly before her eyes."[6] Many in England were equally anxious that she would be swayed by her surroundings and imagined her possible conversion to the English church and to English culture more generally. Dr. Meddus wrote to the Reverend Joseph Mead from London on June 17, 1625, to inform him that the queen "hath already given some good signs of hope that she may ere long, by God's blessing, become ours of religion."[7] Another correspondent relates one of these signs. He describes Henrietta Maria's first meeting with Charles and tells that, "At dinner, being carved pheasant and venison, by his majesty (who had dined before), she eat heartily of both, notwithstanding her confessor (who all the while stood by her) had forewarned her that it was the eve of John the Baptist, and was to be fasted, and that she should take heed how she gave ill examples or scandal at her first arrival."[8] In these early days of the match, French and English, Catholic and Protestant envisioned conversion as a possible solution to the mixed marriage.

Henrietta Maria almost immediately destroyed these hopes with her provocative response to the English settlements regarding religion. Not content to profess outward conformity, or even to practice Roman Catholicism with the discretion Charles preferred in his subjects, she insisted upon emphasizing her own Roman Catholicism publicly and repeatedly at a moment when Roman Catholics were viewed as potential terrorists against the state and Charles was suspected of double-dealing with the pope as part of the marriage settlement. She refused to attend her husband's coronation service, claiming that a Catholic could not participate in a protestant service, although she viewed his procession to Westminster Cathedral from the gatehouse of Whitehall, the home of Abraham Williams, the agent in England for Elizabeth of Bohemia.[9] In this way, she assumed her place within the family even as she stood separated from her husband in religious practice. The country, though, noticed her absence from the ceremony more than her presence as a witness, and her refusal to participate in the coronation caused rumblings that she was no Queen of England since she had refused to be crowned.[10]

In her first year in England, Henrietta Maria made every effort to keep faith with her mother's behests and created an exile community, a "Little France," for herself in England. She and her household denigrated all things English, ranging from the furnishings provided them upon their arrival, the temporary Catholic chapel, and the treatment they received from courtiers they met. Henrietta Maria made nominal, if any, effort to understand her new country's language or practices, and her insistence upon continuing to act as a French queen in the English court provoked an immediate critical response. Letters and histories list infraction after infraction on the part of the teenaged queen and her circle: her lutenist was charged with spying; she and her maids disrupted protestant sermons; she acted in masques and pastorals, and some of her women even wore men's clothing and beards upon the stage.[11] Moreover, as Laura Hunt Yungblut has observed, England at this time was characterized by "twin traditions of asylum and xenophobia"; elsewhere, she suggests that the English crown "publicly supported but privately suspected" immigrants.[12] The critical reaction to Henrietta as a French Catholic princess was in part due to larger suspicions on the part of English people for foreigners.

Henrietta Maria exacerbated this response with her reliance on her French court. Charles I's letters to Buckingham throughout 1625 and into 1626 repeatedly reveal his exasperation with Henrietta Maria's reliance upon her advisors at his own expense and also reflect his private concerns. He repeatedly presented himself as a scorned lover, one who had made multiple efforts at reconciliation only to be rebuffed by his bride at the instigation of her advisors. In a letter to Buckingham dated November 25, 1625, he offered his standard complaint, "You know what patience I have had with the unkind usages of my wife, grounded upon a belief that it was not in her nature, but made by ill instruments, and overcome by your persuasions to me, that my kind usages would be able to rectify those misunderstandings. I hope my ground may be true, but I am sure you have erred in your opinion; for I find daily worse and worse effects of ill offices done between us, my kind usages having no power to mend anything."[13] He repeatedly described the slights from Henrietta Maria to Buckingham, and he continually placed the blame for her behavior upon her councilors in an effort to construct a working relationship with her.

He, like many others in England, was suspicious not only of their interventions in his personal life but also in public policy and in religion. In letters of this period, he complained of the influence of "the monsieurs" and worried about their "making plots with my own subjects" (40). His response, and his country's, was fairly typical for a king and a court encountering a new consort. Henrietta Maria's mother, Marie d'Medici, and her contemporary Anne of Austria met with similar sorts of criticism as they brought the traditions of their homelands to their adopted countries and as they created exile communities of their own. Charles referred to other clashes between cultures that served as precedents when he asked Buckingham, his ambassador to the French court, to apprize Henrietta Maria's mother of the situation. In the letter to Buckingham from November 25, 1625, which detailed Henrietta Maria's foibles and her advisors' interference, he continued with this plea:

> Now, necessity urges me to vent my self to you in this particular, for grief is eased being told to a friend; and because I have many obligations to my mother-in-law (knowing that these courses of my wife are so much against her knowledge, that they are contrary to her advice) I would do nothing concerning her daughter that may taste of any harshness, without advertising her of the reasons and necessity of the thing.... You must, therefore, advertise to my mother-in-law, that I must remove all those instruments that are causes of unkindness between her daughter and me, few or none of the servants being free of this fault in one kind or other; therefore I would be glad that she might find a means to make themselves suitors to be gone; if this be not, I hope there can be no exceptions taken at me, to follow the example of Spain and Savoy in this particular.[14]

In addition, he recognized his obligations as a son-in-law and hoped to have councilors she valued intervene on his behalf. He also asked Buckingham to offer similar justifications to his brother-in-law, Louis XIII of France.[15] He wanted to remind both of Henrietta Maria's advocates that kings before him had needed to disband these exile communities in order to assimilate their brides into their courts.

Neither Louis XIII nor Marie d'Medici interceded for Charles, but the priests in Henrietta Maria's household enabled him to take the action he had desired for months when they required Henrietta Maria to make a penitential trip to Tyburn, in part to atone for her sins but also to expiate the sins of her adopted country's treatment of Catholic martyrs. In a letter dated July 12, 1626, describing Henrietta Maria's trespasses, Charles concluded, "Thus, having had so long patience with the disturbance of that which should be one of my greatest contentments, I can no longer suffer those, that I know to be the cause and fomenters of these humours, to be about my wife any longer, which I must do, if it were but for one action which they made my wife do, which is, to make her go to Tyburn in devotion to pray: which action can have no greater invective against it than the relation."[16] This public, inflammatory, confrontational display of Catholic piety gave Charles the excuse he needed to expel the priests and the bulk of Henrietta Maria's household, in contradiction to the private terms of the marriage treaties but to the approbation of the English public.

Henrietta Maria's family connections often made the English people, particularly the more Calvinist members of Parliament, suspicious of French intervention and Catholic meddling. The French and papal efforts to use the marriage settlement as a wedge for rights for English Catholics served almost to their detriment; prior to the treaties, anti-Catholic laws were only sporadically enforced, but following Henrietta Maria's arrival, Parliamentary members agitated successfully for reforms of the anti-Catholic policies. By March 18, 1630, one English observer noted: "From court the newes is that the king by his councell hath made a strict order that the foraigne ambassadors house be attended by pursuivants to attach all that goe thither to mass, and that the queen's chappell is not priveleged now for any but her household. From Ireland the newes is of like nature: the 2 justices have so suppressed the priests, jesuites and fryars that neither public mass is sayd nor any of the rabble presumes to walke abroad with theire former confidence, so that there is great hope of much better times in that kingdom, thankes be to God."[17] The knowledge that secret treaties existed caused speculation on the part of Parliament and, for a period from 1629 to 1630 at least, more enforcement than might otherwise have occurred.

Once Henrietta Maria was denied the French home-away-from-home she had constructed for herself, she began to make use of the English networks available to her. To replace the French maids, Charles provided her with an English Catholic circle of maids of honor and priests,[18] a circle he had proffered as early as her arrival in England but that she had refused until the removal of the French.[19] She expressed her own suspicions that these new advisors would exert too much control over her, but she eventually developed productive relations with the Countess of Buckingham and Lady Hay.[20]

By 1632, Henrietta Maria was more astute at working within the confines of her adopted culture than she had been upon her arrival in England in 1626, although her impulsive actions and her maintenance of French customs continued to cause controversy. Judith Barrington related this story to her mother in a letter from Whitsunweek 1632, "A neighbour of mine... sufred a great... disgrace some fortnight agone in Hide Park, whear the queen, as she thought, espyed one of her gounes [gowns] that she had lately lost on Mrs Kimpton's back and so sent to her to kno whear she had itt. She being out of countenance at such a speach would not answear, which made it the more suspitious, so that at last she was sent to a justice of peace whear she answered also crossly. But at last the truth was knowen. The kinge cryed her pardon, would have her brought to kiss the queen's hands, but she would not. He offred to knight her husband but she refused that also, but parted fairly, a poor recompence for so publicke a disgrace; yet the kinge did nobly in itt."[21] The king did his best to recover the situation, but Henrietta Maria continued to make public display of her ire, a tendency that had caused difficulties between her and Charles and that continued to give trouble. Her concessions to her new nation, too, were not always well received. The seven-hour pastoral she enacted with her ladies was in English, "aswell for her recreation as for the exercise of her Englishe," as one correspondent noted in September 1632.[22] However, that action was equally controversial, as a letter from January 31, 1632–33, reveals. George Gresley informed Sir Thomas Puckering that

> Mr. Prinne an Utter Barrister of Lincons Inne is brought into the High Commission Court and Star Chamber for publishing a Booke (a little before the Queene's acting of her Play) of the Unlawfullness of Plaies, wherein the Table of his Booke and his briefe Additions thereunto he that these words, "Women actors notorious whores;" and that S. Paul prohibits women to speake publicly in the Churche; "and dares then" sayth he "any Christian woman be so more than whoreshly impudent as to act, to speake, publiquelie on a Stage (perchaunce in man's apparell and cut haire) in the presence of sundrie men and women?" which wordes it is thought by some will cost him his eares, or heavily punnisht and deeply fined.[23]

While Henrietta Maria's choreography of and performance in ballets had earned her the approbation of the French court and French society more generally, the English response to this sort of public display remained mixed at best and aroused suspicions especially in her Calvinist critics. Henrietta Maria, throughout her tenure, charted a course based on her own standards, desires, and expectations rather than upon the norms of her new nation.

In contrast to Henrietta Maria's tempestuous entrance and term in England, Elizabeth of Bohemia entered the Hague as a mature, grateful refugee of twenty-three in 1621. By the late 1620s, she was in her thirties. She had seen first her father and then her brother promise aid and then fail to deliver upon those promises, either because they relied too heavily upon treaties or because England could not provide the troops it owed its allies. She was a queen thrice exiled, first in 1613 by her marriage to Frederick V, Elector of Heidelberg. In late 1619, Calvinists in Bohemia rebelled against Habsburg control and asked Frederick to rule their independent state; when Frederick acceded to this request, Elizabeth went with him to Prague. In 1621, the Catholic League joined with the Hapsburgs to overthrow the rebels, and Frederick's forces were defeated during the Battle of White Mountain. Bohemia was handed to the Roman Catholic Maximilian of Bavaria, and Elizabeth and Frederick fled first to Germany and then to the Netherlands. The Calvinist rebel forces who had invited Frederick to assume the Bohemian throne had also hoped that James would come to their aid, much as Elizabeth I had intervened when the Dutch Provinces declared their independence from the Spanish Hapsburgs. James, however, refused this role, in large part because of his "royal insolvency," as Jonathan Scott describes it, and also because of his desire to be seen as a peacekeeper.[24] By 1622, the Catholic League had defeated the Upper Palatinate and the Rhineland as well. At this point, James refused Elizabeth and her children refuge, fearing it might interfere with his efforts to treat with Spain for Charles's then-proposed marriage to the Infanta. For the remainder of his reign, James preferred treaties to military action, and his refusal to intervene militarily continued to frustrate Elizabeth and lose ground for her husband.[25]

Even before Frederick's fall from fortune, though, Elizabeth had recognized the importance of popular support for her reign in ways that Henrietta Maria never did. As a new bride and young Electress, in 1613, she walked through the crowds of Dutch people who had come to meet her at her arrival from England and began to develop friendly feeling on the part of the Dutch. Once in Heidelberg, she dismissed the bulk of the English hangers-on and made attempts to assimilate, although she refused to become the German housewife her mother-in-law hoped she would be.[26] She communicated alongside her husband in the Lutheran church when pressed by her husband's new constituents in Prague, although she expressed concern and asked for guidance from her father as far as the protocol of continued communion.[27] Even when young and assured of her position as Electress or as Queen, Elizabeth made efforts to create bridges to her adopted community in ways that Henrietta Maria refused to do, and these allegiances served her in good stead in later years.

Elizabeth was continually cognizant of the fact that her husband was battling to regain his lands and that she owed her residences in the Hague and Rhenen to the kindness and hospitality of her friends, especially the Prince of Orange. She could not join with Frederick's forces, but she could facilitate the return of her husband's lands by building relationships and by bringing military and monetary support to the Protestant alliance. She corresponded with many of the members of James's and Charles's courts and kept her suit at the forefront by reminding those around both kings of her plight. Letters that have survived include those to Sir Julius Caesar, Sir Dudley Carleton, and George Villiers, Duke of Buckingham; the Earl of Dorchester evidently burned those he received.[28] She relied heavily upon Sir Thomas Roe and Sir James Hay, Earl of Carlisle, to keep her apprized of the news in England and to intercede on her behalf. She maintained regular contact with the Duchess of Tremoille, her husband's aunt, and included letters to her uncle the King of Denmark, to her Danish cousins, and to the Swedish King whenever a reliable courier afforded her the opportunity. She agitated, politely, at the Dutch and German courts and encouraged her brother to send the most effective ambassadors to the Protestant Union and to the Dutch and German states. Her agents, particularly Thomas Roe, pursued her suit at the courts of France, Denmark, and Sweden, as well as in England. While observers in England believed her excuses to her brother for not answering his call for her return upon her husband's death,[29] they also were aware of her unvoiced motives and of her need to keep her suit in front of the Germans and Dutch, especially since it was now the suit of a widow and her orphaned children.[30] Roe advised her, in a letter from February 6, 1633–34, that "she must try all things and some will take."[31] Elizabeth had already been employing such a strategy for many years.

Throughout her exile, Elizabeth strove especially to persuade first James and then Charles to intervene militarily to save the Palatinate. During James's reign, Elizabeth attempted to use Charles as her agent with James:

> My only dear brother, I am sure you have heard before this, that Spinola hath taken some towns in the lower Palatinate, which makes me to trouble

you with these lines, to beseech you earnestly to move his majesty that
now he would assist us; for he may easily see how little his embassages are
regarded. Dear brother, be most earnest with him; for, to speak freely
with you, his slackness to assist us doth make the Princes of the Union
slack too, who do nothing with their army; the king hath ever said that
he would not suffer the Palatinate to be taken; it was never in hazard but
now, and I beseech you again, dear brother, to solicit as much as you can,
for her that loves you more than all the world. I doubt not but you will
do it, since you have hitherto solicited his majesty for us, where you do
shew your affection to me, which I beseech you to continue."[32]

Elizabeth astutely sent her criticisms of James's policies not to James but
to her trusted intermediary, one whose counsel carried weight with the
king. She played upon Charles's sympathies by treating him as trusted
confidant, and she sandwiched her presentation of her dire situation and
her concerns between appeals to his family feeling. Elizabeth successfully
enlisted Charles's support; one contemporary remarked that he "believed
there was never prince better affected to a sister, or to a cause, than his
Majesty, but by what necessity, which we ourselves create and worship,
they are bound up, is a mystery inscrutable."[33] However, Charles was
unable either to persuade his father to commit to the outlays required for
military action or, later, to convince Parliament to provide similar
support for her cause. While Elizabeth was able to capitalize upon
English pro-protestant, anti-Hapsburg sentiment to further her cause,
she was nevertheless unable to erase what Parliament perceived as
Buckingham's mismanagement of a series of efforts on her behalf. First,
Mansfeld's forces fighting for the Protestant Union did not receive the
promised English backing in 1625, then the naval forces led by
Buckingham at Cadiz and at Rhe sustained mighty losses, in part because
Parliament had never provided the funds, supplies, or trained men they
promised. Rather than admit their own culpability, Parliament used
those failures as an excuse not to grant additional funds, and Charles was
unwilling to lay the groundwork for success with Parliament.[34]
Elizabeth's rhetoric had a reach limited by internal politics in England.

Nonetheless, Elizabeth saw these particular methods—charming an
intercessor with praise and confidential critique of the king's policies—
as productive, and she continued to employ them once Charles's reign
began, although she turned to George Villiers, Thomas Roe, and to her
official representative in England, Francis Nethersole, as the beneficiaries of her pleas. Elizabeth's willingness to exploit her connections
almost severed Charles I's sympathy for her cause in the winter of
1633–34, and at that moment, her methods for persuading her brother

to side with her cause become particularly clear. A thread running through her letters from 1630 onwards was a sister's lifelong knowledge of and frustration with her younger brother; she claimed Charles was slow to act, relied too much on the words of foreign emissaries and domestic counselors, and was too easily led to believe that treaties themselves would solve the crisis of the Thirty Years War.[35] She complained in one letter to Roe, "I am sure you know how my business goeth in England, like a crabbe, for as yet I see no great hopes of anie thing to be done, The French King hath all sortes of Ambassadours and agents in Germaine and my deare brother hath none."[36] Elizabeth offered similar comments on numerous occasions, but she knew her brother well enough to defer to him as king, and to keep her criticisms private, rather than to create the public scenes Henrietta Maria seemed to favor.

However, Elizabeth's agents were not always as tactful as she was. Sir Francis Nethersole created enormous difficulties for her when he wrote a private letter, at her behest, to Secretary Cooke in which he asked for support for anti-Hapsburg forces so "that the King be not the second time accused for the loss of the Palatinate."[37] His words were misconstrued by the Secretary, in part because of his history of inflammatory and impulsive speech; Nethersole was arrested so that the Council could inquire into his correspondence with Elizabeth and investigate concerns that Nethersole was fomenting rebellion. The Council demanded to see Elizabeth's letters, and Nethersole attempted to escape his imprisonment and have the letters sent to the Dutch Embassy in a misguided effort to protect her honor. Elizabeth was incensed that "the lords of the councell have seased upon Nethersoles papers and my letters have been read at the council table; though I doe not care who seeth my letters and commands I have given him having never so much thought and much less written aniething to him, that can be against the love and respect I beare to my deare Brother, yett I have verie good reason to take it ill that those papers should be seased on and seene, as if I had anie evill plott against my Brother."[38]

Elizabeth objected in large part to the disrespect paid to her agent and to the public display of inquiry, much as her brother despised similar show. She recognized, at least for argument's sake, her brother's right to know her communications and her affairs: "as for my Brother if [he] should have desired to have [seen] what I writt to Nethersole or what privat commands I did give him I was ever verie willing he shoulde see all, as I have ever given Nethersole that charge that whatsoever my brother shoulde command him of my private or publick command he should doe it for I doe not desire to hide the least thought of my heart from my deare brother."[39] However, the Council did not have the same rights. She complained, "I confess that this that the Councill hath done doth trouble me," and elsewhere commented crossly to Roe, "I hope that you doe not wonder that I have not written to you.... There are alreadie too manie of my letters scene by the Councell: they need no increase of them" (91). Nethersole lost his position at court, and Elizabeth eventually repaired her relationship with Charles, but Charles never led English forces to rally on her behalf, in part because the Germans and the Dutch had restored her son to the Lower Palatinate in early 1634.

While their efforts with their general adopted communities were very different, Henrietta Maria shared with Elizabeth of Bohemia a reliance on family alliances. Here, both women operated within a very traditional trajectory for royal women. Magdalena S. Sanchez, in her study of Margaret of Austria, Margaret of the Cross, and the Empress Maria, identifies three methods of influence that these women employed as they negotiated Hapsburg court life: "familial connections, their reputations for piety, and even frequent illnesses."[40] Henrietta Maria especially looked to the intervention of her mother, Marie d'Medici, her brother, Louis XIII, and their ambassadors. She was also aware of the concerns of the pope. These people carried varying credibility in England; while Charles was concerned about maintaining favorable relations with his mother- and brother-in-law, the English people were suspicious of all dealings with France, especially as the diplomatic situation with France shifted throughout the early years of Henrietta Maria's tenure. France served at times as an ally, at times as an enemy in negotiations with the Hapsburgs, and was always an historical rival, so Henrietta Maria's reliance upon her family caused its own set of problems. To a large extent, the same could be said for Elizabeth; her husband was called upon to rule Bohemia because of his connections to England, a nation viewed by many in Europe as the hope for Protestantism, and a power whose reputation for military intervention was still feared in the 1620s and early 1630s. Indeed, Kevin Sharpe suggests, "for all their sense of England's impoverishment, the ambassadors of Europe, of Spain, France, Sweden and the Netherlands have never dismissed England as lightly as have historians.... For all England's incapacity to mount a major campaign, she had, as they recognized, a navy which could... facilitate or obstruct communications in the Channel and North Sea which were crucial."[41] However, for each queen, the family network provided a crucial line of defense of honor and interests, and both women exploited these connections and bore the responsibilities of them.

For Elizabeth of Bohemia and for Henrietta Maria, piety and religious feeling caused difficulties rather than providing the means of support they offered the Hapsburg women. Frederick, Elector Palatine, was chosen to rule Bohemia precisely because he would lead the nation as a Protestant king against the surrounding Catholic forces. The Bohemia rebellion was quashed by anti-Protestant forces, and neither Elizabeth nor Frederick nor their supporters throughout Europe could build a Protestant alliance that was able to defeat the combined Catholic forces bent upon keeping the electoral seat from a Calvinist. Henrietta Maria, on the other hand, viewed herself as someone who could return England to the Roman Catholic fold, and that mission was viewed with intense suspicion by her subjects. Her efforts to model Catholic piety for England caused more controversy than conversion, although she eventually constructed a private circle of protected space for high-ranking Catholics and was seen throughout her rule as a patron saint for Catholic writers and priests. Elizabeth of Bohemia and Henrietta Maria were both successful politicians, though, as they navigated the complexities of the English court.

Notes

1. Unless otherwise stated, quotations from the letters of Elizabeth, Queen of Bohemia, are from *The Letters of Elizabeth, Queen of Bohemia*, ed. L. M. Baker (London: Bodley Head, 1953), pp. 86–87.
2. For studies of key figures in this period, see Alison Plowden, *Henrietta Maria: Charles I's Indomitable Queen* (England: Sutton Publishing, 2001); Josephine Ross, *The Winter Queen: The Story of Elizabeth Stuart* (1979. New York: Dorset, 1986); Roger Lockyer, *The Early Stuarts: A Political History of England, 1603–1642* (1989. London: Longman, 1999); and *Buckingham: The Life and Political Career of George Villiers, First Duke of Buckingham, 1592–1628* (London: Longman, 1981); Roy E. Schreiber, *The First Carlisle: Sir James Hay, First Earl of Carlisle as Courtier, Diplomat and Entrepreneur, 1580–1636* (Philadelphia: American Philosophical Society, 1984); and Kevin Sharpe, *The Personal Rule of Charles I* (New Haven: Yale University Press, 1992).
3. For an overview of events, see Jonathan Scott, *England's Troubles: Seventeenth-Century English Political Instability in European Context* (Cambridge: Cambridge University Press, 2000), especially pp. 1–134.
4. *Letters of Queen Henrietta Maria, Including Her Private Correspondence with Charles the First*, ed. Mary Anne Everett Green, History of Women microfilm series (1857. New Haven, Connecticut: Research Publications, 1975), pp. 9–10.
5. Mary Anne Everett Green, p. 8.
6. Alexis Francois Artaud de Montor, *The Lives and Times of the Popes* (New York: The Catholic Publication Society, 1911).

7. Thomas Birch, ed., *The Court and Times of Charles I* (London: Henry Colburn, 1848), 1: 30.
8. Birch, 1: 31.
9. Great Britain, Historical Manuscripts Commission, *The Manuscripts of his Grace the Duke of Rutland, G.C.B., Preserved at Belvoir Castle*, twelfth report, appendix, part 4 (London: Eyre and Spottiswoode, 1888), 1: 476.
10. *Diary of John Rous, Incumbent of Santon Downham, Suffolk, from 1625 to 1642*, ed. Mary Anne Everett Green, Camden Society, no. 66 (London: J.B. Nichols and Sons, 1856), pp. 11–12.
11. Birch, 1: 30, 31, 32, 39, 50, 52. For letters concerning the queen's masque and her lutenist, see *The Manuscripts of the Duke of Rutland*, 1: 478, 481. See also *The Court and Times of Charles I*.
12. Laura Hunt Yungblut, *Strangers Settled Here Amongst Us: Policies, Perceptions and the Presence of Aliens in Elizabethan England* (London: Routledge, 1996), pp. 3, 6–7, 47–51, 85–94.
13. *The Letters, Speeches and Proclamations of King Charles I*, ed. Charles Petrie (1935. London: Cassell, 1968), p. 40.
14. *The Letters, Speeches and Proclamations of King Charles I*, pp. 40–41.
15. *The Letters, Speeches and Proclamations of King Charles I*, pp. 42–45.
16. *The Letters, Speeches and Proclamations of King Charles I*, pp. 44–45.
17. *Barrington Family Letters, 1628–1632*, ed. Arthur Seale, Camden Fourth Series, no. 28 (London: Royal Historical Society, 1983), pp. 137–38.
18. Richard Montague writes, "The Queen hath three preists, Father Phillipps, I thinck, her Confessor, a Scottishman, Father Godfrey, and Mr. Potter, all honest moderate men as they say.... The French ladies are all gon, I thincke. There be of her Majesty's bedchamber the Duchesse of Buckinghame and the Lady Savage; Roman Catholicks. The rest Protestants." In *The Correspondence of John Cosin, D.D., Lord Bishop of Durham*, ed. George Ornsby, Surtees Society, vol. 55 (Durham: Whittaker, 1872), 1: 102.
19. Plowden lists the people waiting to greet Henrietta Maria at Dover as "his mother, his sister, the Countess of Denbigh, and his niece, the Marchioness of Hamilton. Also present was Sir Toby Mathew, son of an Anglican bishop but a recent convert to Catholicism, who had come along to act as interpreter," p. 24. Buckingham's mother was a known Catholic.
20. Schreiber describes the mercurial relations Henrietta Maria had with Lucy Hay, Countess of Carlisle from 1627 through 1630, *The First Carlisle*, pp. 125–27.
21. *Barrington Family Letters*, pp. 245–46.
22. Letter from Mr. Pory to Sir Thomas Puckering, Sept. 20, 1632, in Henry Ellis, ed., *Original Letters Illustrative of English History, Including Numerous Royal Letters*, second series (London: Harding and Lepard, 1827), 3: 270.
23. Ellis, *Original Letters*, second series, 3: 280–81.
24. Scott, *England's Troubles*, p. 98.
25. See Scott, *England's Troubles*, pp. 98–103; *Letters of Elizabeth* and Baker's commentary, 48–67, especially p. 57.
26. Ross, *Winter Queen*, p. 48.

27. See *Letters of Elizabeth*, 51, dated April 23, 1620.
28. Great Britain, Public Record Office, *Calendar of State Papers, Domestic Series, of the Reign of Charles I, 1625–1649* (1858. Nendeln, Liechtenstein: Kraus Reprint, 1967), 5: 469.
29. See her letter from December 1632, quoted in the opening page.
30. See letter from George Gresley to Sir Thomas Pickering, January 31, 1632–33, in Ellis, *Original Letters*, second series, 3: 280.
31. *Calendar of State Papers, Domestic Series*, 6: 453.
32. *Letters of Elizabeth*, p. 54.
33. Sir Thomas Roe to John Dinley, *Calendar of State Papers, Domestic Series*, 6: 105.
34. Kevin Sharpe, in *Personal Rule of Charles I*, outlines the pressures facing Charles and England, both internally and externally. See especially pp. 9–70.
35. *Letters of Elizabeth*, p. 83.
36. *Letters of Elizabeth*, p. 86.
37. *Letters of Elizabeth*, p. 91.
38. *Letters of Elizabeth*, p. 90.
39. *Letters of Elizabeth*, p. 91.
40. Magdalena S. Sanchez, *The Empress, the Queen, and the Nun: Women and Power at the Court of Philip III of Spain* (Baltimore: Johns Hopkins University Press, 1998), p. 5.
41. *Personal Rule of Charles I*, p. 70.

Part II
Imaging Renaissance Queens and Power

"And a Queen of England, Too": The 'Englishing' of Catherine of Aragon in Sixteenth-Century English Literary and Chronicle History

Matthew C. Hansen

In her 1997 article "Reprinting Tudor History: The Case of Catherine of Aragon" Betty Travitsky focuses her attention on an early modern

Vxoriæ virtutes.
To my Sister, M. D. COLLEY.

THIS reprefentes the vertues of a wife,
Her finger, ftaies her tonge to runne at large.
The modeft lookes, doe fhewe her honeft life.
The keys, declare fhee hathe a care, and chardge,
    Of hufbandes goodes: let him goe where he pleafe,
    The Tortoyfe warnes, at home to fpend her daies.
            M 3

Plautus in Amph.
Non ego illam mihi
dotem duco effe, qua
dos dicitur,
Sed pudicitiam & pu-
dorem, & fedatum
Cupidinem,
Deûm metum, paren-
tum amorem, & co-
gnatium concordiam,

Inuidiæ

Uxoria Virtutes from Geffrey Whitney, *A Choice of Emblems*.
By permission of the Newberry Library.

queen about whom much remains to be said. After tracing the editorial manipulations of commentary on Catherine of Aragon in the prefatory materials to eight editions of Juan Luis Vives's *Instruction of a Christen Woman* appearing between 1529 and 1592, Travitsky observes that the editions of 1585 and 1592 represented a return to the most favorable and flattering portrayal of Catherine, that of the 1529 edition, despite being published by the "strongly Protestant printers Robert Waldegrave and John Danter." Travitsky goes on to note that the "Catherine of Aragon celebrated thirty years later in Shakespeare's *Henry VIII* had become depoliticized by the latter part of the sixteenth century, that she was seen by that time in decidedly non-threatening and non-sectarian terms, and perhaps that the type of pious, learned, domesticated woman she had come to represent had become more widely celebrated in that age."[1] I use Travitsky's work as the starting point for a discussion of several texts in which this transformation occurs. My particular focus here traces the strategies employed in sixteenth-century chronicle histories to present Catherine of Aragon as a figure who demands to be compared to—and praised for the same attributes as—the literary archetype of wifely devotion found in the legend of Patient Griselda.

One seriously neglected literary artifact that contributed to the valorization of Catherine of Aragon as a paragon of patience is a manuscript history in verse written by William Forrest and dedicated to Mary Tudor in 1558 entitled *The History of Grisild the Second*. In this work, Forrest narrates the history of Catherine of Aragon, replacing her name throughout with "Grysilde" and King Henry VIII with "Walter."

The History of Grisild the Second exists in only one known edition, that of the Rev. W. D. Macray, who edited it in 1875 from the author's manuscript now in the Bodleian Library.[2] Macray asserts that his text copy is "evidently the copy presented by the author to Queen Mary, being beautifully written on vellum, and having been originally 'bound in laced satin'" (xx–xxi). Macray does not catalog the existence of any other copies of this manuscript although he does include, as appendices, a number of other short works by Forrest. David M. Loades in his work on Mary Tudor references Forrest's panegyric verses on the accession of Queen Mary, the *New Ballad of the Marigolde* (1553) as well as his 1551 *Metrical Versions of Some Psalms*.[3] However, Loades does not reference Forrest's curious "history" of Griselda nor the equally interesting "An Oration consolatorye to Queen Mary" attached as an appendix to Forrest's unique history of Catherine of Aragon. Garret Mattingly provides a note on Forrest's history at the end of his biography of Catherine of Aragon, but is largely uninterested in the work.[4]

There is nothing remotely veiled in Forrest's history; in the "Prologue to the Queenis Majestee," Forrest praises Catherine's virtue and extols her as a model to be emulated by her daughter. The primary strength in his comparison of Griselda and Catherine is in their equivalent abundance of patience:

> Her I heere lyken to *Grysilde* the goode,
> As well I so maye, for her great patience;
> Consyderinge althingis with her howe it stoode,
> Her geavynge that name theare is none offense;
> Your noble Father working like pretence
> As *Walter* to *Grysilde*, by muche unkyndenes,
> By name of *Walter* I dooe him expresse.[5]

This is, at its most basic level, an unapologetic bid for Queen Mary's patronage. As such, Forrest must tread a thin line, for a sympathetic portrayal of Catherine in an account of the divorce proceedings can easily result in a narrative that portrays Henry VIII as a villain. Whatever her personal feelings toward her father may have been, Queen Mary—like her sister after her—needed to maintain a living relationship with her dead father as the surest security for the succession of the Tudor line. That Forrest is sensitive to this tension can be seen in the prologue. In a discussion of the extent to which good parents are models for good behavior to their children and bad parents models consciously to reject, Forrest relies on platitudes and non-specifics to avoid casting aspersion on Henry. His choice in these lines of the masculine pronoun further distances the generalized concept of good and bad parental models from the specific instance of Mary and her famous parents:

> What more renowne to childe redounde maye,
> Then as to reade or heeare, by recomptinge,
> Howe his parentys in their lyvynge daye
> Had heere God in high reverencinge,
> His honour, service, and lawes mayntayninge,
> That hee, not degeneratinge thearfro,
> May (in his lyvynge) practice the like so.
>
> Or, whoe dothe reade or heeare the contrayre,
> His parentys to be nocyous and yll,
> But that it mae geve motyon ynwardelye
> As to beeware the like to fulfyll.[6]

Forrest only becomes explicit when he comes to highlight the positive example that Catherine abundantly provides:

> Howe much (O novle and excellent Queene!)
> Maye then delyte youre domynation
> Youre Mothers meeke life of youe to bee seene,
> Or reduced to commemoration,
> That was of moste worthye commendation,
> Perfectely knowne to hundreadys that yeat bee,
> As most especyall to youre majestee.[7]

Forrest deliberately avoids an indictment of Henry VIII for the ordeals a patient Catherine must endure. The "Schsmys and Sectys" into which the realm has fallen are "of Sathans owne raysinge" and in praising Catherine's virtuous patience, Forrest makes her enemy out to be "The sathanyke Serpent, who had her in hate, but never cowlde her (to his purpose) culpate."[8]

The author goes still further, making certain to praise Queen Mary's noble Father by claiming that he "Was leadde in some parte by means of the light," a claim illuminated in a presumedly authorial marginal gloss as meaning that "Oure Kynge [was] somewhat ledde by the counsell of undiscreet persons."[9] Satan is a prevalent force throughout Forrest's account and his agents—notably bad, unnamed counselors—ply on the fleshly appetites and desires of an all too human king. This is not to suggest that Forrest himself did not see the course of human history as an eternal struggle between the forces of good and evil, but as a politically savvy churchman writing during the religiously and politically tumultuous years in which he did, it is also an effective strategy for avoiding potentially overly dangerous polemic.

While such strategies are sensible—given Forrest's likely hopes for this manuscript to serve as a means of self-promotion—they also aim to please an audience in the Tudor period, one interested in celebrating England's history and the nobility of English monarchs; the realization of such strategies frequently links and elides history and myth. While the only known extant copy of Forrest's history is the supposed royal presentation copy, it seems highly unlikely that this would indeed have been the only copy ever made. While dedicated to and aimed explicitly at Queen Mary, Forrest's prologue nonetheless hints at a larger audience for his work. His purpose in part, he asserts, is to assure that the memory of the virtuous Queen Catherine remain alive once the "hundreds that yeat bee" to whom her "worthye commendation" is "Perfectely knowne" have shuffled off this mortal coil; he aims

> Her hereby unto remembrance to call
> And els (withoute this) not so to bee fall
> But, as yee and the godlye dothe the same,
> So, oure posterytee to heare of her fame.[10]

The extent to which Forrest was successful in this aspect of his project will be taken up below.

Following the prologue, Forrest provides a detailed outline of the twenty chapters that follow. The first four are devoted to a discussion of Catherine's parentage and simultaneously present testaments to the extent of her learning, her piety, and her charity. Her ill-fated match with Henry's brother, Arthur, is briefly discussed and Henry VII—referred to as a second Solomon—is treated with a respect that subsequent historians would certainly challenge.[11] Forrest's summaries are nearly as instructive as the chapters themselves as they often reveal not only the material contents therein presented, but the author's take on those matters as well. His fifth chapter begins the saga of the divorce proceedings and Forrest again takes pains to avoid sullying Henry VIII's image by casting significant blame for the King's actions on unnamed counselors who either give him bad advice or fail to give him good advice.

> Caput 5
> How at the Dyvyllis (and certaine of his) instigation, *Walter* sought meanys to bee dyvorsed from *Grisilde*, for that hee had no prynce by her tenheryte after hym, and for also that she was his brother's wief [sic]. *Walter*'s Counsell perceavynge his entent, durste not contrarye the same, hee was a man so headye furyous.[12]

Forrest places the blame for the discourse between the heretofore seemingly happily married Walter and Griselda on "The cursed Enemye, sower of discord." The King in Forrest's presentation is the unfortunately malleable patsy caught in the middle of corrupt counselors; the progress of such a narrative should be familiar to anyone with even a cursory understanding of the psychomachia—the battle between good and evil—at work in the morality plays.[13] The enemy remains faceless and non-specific:

> Some wycked theare weare, at his exitation,
> (To picke a thanke of hym their soveraygne)
> That prompted *Walter* after this fashyon.[14]

To blame external agents makes perfect sense given the narrative framework Forrest has imposed upon the history. In the generic Griselda myth, Walter's actions are motivated as a test of her requisite womanly patience, aiming to insure that despite her lowly birth she does indeed possess an innate nobility. However, no such test is necessary for Catherine—although she endures it nonetheless, thus reaffirming her noble lineage, which Forrest recounts in chapter 1. Forrest grounds the second Walter's motivation in part on Walter's desire for a male heir; interestingly, earlier versions of the Griselda legend, including Chaucer's Clerk's telling of it, have counselors who implore their Marquis to marry expressly to insure that he will produce an heir to whom the kingdom can pass peacefully.[15] A further tension exists in that those familiar with the Griselda legend—as Forrest clearly intends his audience to be—would know also that the ending is a happy one in which Griselda and Walter are reconciled, her children restored to her, and the future prosperity of the royal family on both domestic and dynastic levels a seemingly sure thing.

To avoid any potential confusion, Forrest offers, in his eighteenth chapter, a brief comparison and contrast of the first Griselda and Walter with the second (reminding his readers, just in case, that he means Catherine of Aragon and Henry VIII). He does not fully disclose all the details he massaged or omitted in order to make Catherine better conform with the legendary patience of Griselda. In particular, Forrest explicitly stresses Catherine's relative silence throughout by, for example, omitting details of the court at Blackfriars and Catherine's reported speech at this and other semi-public events. The rich details of these events do appear in the near-contemporary chronicle histories, which I will discuss further below. Forrest's presentation of Catherine stresses her natural inclination to charity and Christian devotion; the one moment of recriminatory speech which he invents for her in chapter 10 is offered with the caveat that she spoke such words "syttinge all solytarye." Like Griselda, she would never openly voice discontent or dissatisfaction before her lord. The people—who support Catherine/Griselda and, like Forrest, believe the injustice she suffers to be the direct result of "Noughtys els but Mannys fragylytee / Noughtis els but Mannys sensuall mynde"—do not rise up in public revolt.[16] They too contain their complaints within a strictly private discourse: "Suche, of the rude and pooare Comynaltee, / Was (secreatlye) their tawlke and wisperinge."[17]

It is easy to understand Catherine's life as an imitation of Griselda. Catherine's poignant final letter to her estranged spouse is remarkably

Griselda-like in its expression of devotion and wifely duty:

> *My most dear lord, king and husband*: The hour of my death now drawing on, the tender love I owe you forceth me, my case being such, to commend myself to you, and to put you in remembrance with a few words of the health and safeguard of your soul which you ought to prefer before all worldly matters, and before the care and pampering of your body for the which you have cast me into many calamities and yourself into many troubles. For my part, I pardon you everything, and I wish to devoutly pray to God that He will pardon you also. For the rest, I commend unto you our daughter Mary, beseeching you to be a good father unto her as I have heretofore desired. I entreat also, on behalf of my maids, to give them marriage portions, which is not much, they being but three. For all my other servants I solicit the wages due them, and a year more, lest they be unprovided for. Lastly, I make this vow, that mine eyes desire you above all things.[18]

It is important to note that Catherine wrote this letter in her own hand, in English. Forrest adapts, in chapter 12 (99–105), the sentiments in this letter and fits them to his metric form although he directs Griselda's devotion more toward God than to Walter. Forrest also references this letter or "Bill" itself, written and dispatched to Walter, "Whoe ofte theron thought, though lytlle he spake."[19] Forrest likely knew of Vives's *Instruction of a Christen Woman*, a text outlining for Catherine an educational scheme for Mary; if he was also familar with Vives's subsequent epistle to Catherine outlining further particulars of *de ratione studii puerilis*—a plan of study for girls—he would have found there Vives's endorsement of the Griselda legend as one of a precious few stories sanctioned for the Princess Mary's perusal.[20] The echo of Catherine's final letter to her husband and Forrest's use of Griselda as the framing legend suggest that he had a close connection, and perhaps quite privileged access, to Catherine.

In Forrest's conclusion, Catherine ascends into heaven and takes her place among the saints. Once there, she joins the chorus pleading for England's protection and salvation. In a larger sense, Forrest also ushers Catherine into the realm of literary legend by presenting her as a real-life Griselda.

Forrest clearly intended both to chronicle and reinspire popular sympathy for Catherine of Aragon. While clearly pro-Catherine, pro-Mary, and pro-Catholic, Forrest is not a Papist and does not endorse a return to allegiance with Rome.[21] Indeed, by appropriating a popular folk legend as the framework for his history, Forrest successfully de-emphasizes much of the religious controversy and sectarianism that resulted from the divorce.[22] As noted above, Forrest couches this in broader terms as a battle between good and evil but doesn't go so far as to paint Protestants as evil or agents of the Devil; rather he points out the constant temptations of sin and wickedness that can lead even the noblest and best-intentioned astray.

Just as Forrest's work has largely been ignored by historians, so too have literary historians analyzing the various versions of the Griselda legend failed to take Forrest's *Grisild the Seconde* into account. The remainder of this essay therefore offers an examination of the interrelated development of popular history representations of Catherine of Aragon and the developmental literary history of the Griselda legend, two histories which coalesce in William Shakespeare and John Fletcher's *Henry VIII*.[23]

Several scholars have recently provided excellent accounts of the development of the Griselda legend in the sixteenth century, linking it to larger social and political issues. That history, briefly, includes the original legend as attributed to Petrarch and later adapted by Chaucer in the *Canterbury Tales*. Several versions then appear during the sixteenth and seventeenth centuries: John Phillip's moralistic interlude *The Comodye of Pacient and Meeke Grissill* (ca. 1565); a ballad version in Thomas Deloney's *The Garland of Good Will*, which was first registered for publication in 1593 although the earliest extant edition is dated 1631; a prose narrative purportedly translated from French, dated 1619; and Thomas Dekker, Henry Chettle, and William Haughton's 1599 play *The Pleasant Comodie of Patient Grissill* which was first performed in 1600 and published in 1603. Viviana Comensoli traces the developmental literary history of the Griselda legend from the fourteenth to the seventeenth century with a particular focus on how the representative rehearsals of the Griselda legend and their treatment of marriage are intertwined with historical developments and changes in attitude toward marriage.[24] As England moves away from Catholicism and slowly becomes a more Protestant-leaning nation-state, the monastic life is concomitantly devalued; hence in the legends, Gaulter (Walter) is increasingly less resistant to marriage. As the title of her article implies, Comensoli's focus is principally on the 1599 Dekker et al. play. In this dramatic version, marriage is given a fuller explication and multiple models of wifely behavior beyond the traditional Griselda figure (chaste, silent, and obedient) are explored. Comensoli sees these changes as indicative of larger patterns of domestic and social conflict which in turn "register a high degree of skepticism, corroborating Early Modern England's increasing disenchantment with the institutions it upheld."[25]

Lee Bliss investigates the "remarkably widespread appeal" of the Griselda legend throughout the sixteenth century, exploring the range of implications from Phillip's staunchly Protestant appropriation of the story to the proto-feminism present in the tensions and contradictions of Dekker, Chettle, and Haughton's comedy.[26] What is unfortunately missing is the inclusion of Forrest's *Grisild the Seconde*, itself polemic in its appeal for sympathy toward Catherine of Aragon if not also for English Catholicism. That only seven years later John Phillip could use the same fiction to promote Protestant values is a testament to both the richness of the core legend and the inventiveness of sixteenth-century English authors. There is an underlying project of social programming at work in these texts and their insistent promotion of patience and obedience as principle feminine virtues. Read alongside characters like Mary in the anonymous *Arden of Faversham* and Moll Firth in *The Roaring Girl*—both fictionalized representations of real women—one could perhaps identify a driving need on the part of the patriarchal hegemony to preach patience as an act of containment.

While the fictional Griselda was being reworked in the popular imagination, so too was Catherine of Aragon's popular historical persona being written and personified. Both John Foxe and Raphael Holinshed—staunchly Protestant historians—valorize Catherine of Aragon. Like Forrest, they seem to do so without taking the overt risk of portraying Henry VIII as the villain in the suffering that provides Catherine the opportunity to be an exemplar of patient endurance. Among the various chronicle histories of England produced—and frequently reproduced—throughout the sixteenth century one can identify ready patterns of influence. This is certainly true when reading the materials the chroniclers present concerning Catherine of Aragon. Foxe, whose *Acts and Monuments* first appeared in 1563 and by 1583 had been reissued in four editions (1563, 1570, 1576, 1583), follows Edward Hall (1548) essentially verbatim in his details of Catherine; while John Stowe in his *Annales* (1580, 1592, 1605) draws on materials from both Hall and Holinshed (1577, 1587), his presentation of Catherine follows Holinshed in most regards.[27] Although these various chronicles agree in—and share—most details, there are subtle differences. Reading those differences proves quite revealing, particularly in the materials added and deleted in Stowe's far more character-driven approach to chronicle history. In essence, there are two, somewhat competing chronicle traditions to compare and contrast: Hall/Foxe and Holinshed/Stowe.

Hall's chronicle first appeared in 1548 and is thus the closest contemporary account of Henry and Catherine's divorce. That is not to say it is the most accurate nor am I interested here with historical accuracy; rather, I am interested in reading how the presentation of Catherine is shaped by the various chroniclers. Hall is not necessarily anti-Catherine but is essentially pro-Henry. Forces greater than either of them affected the fate which befell them—that is, the divorce. Hall notes marginally that "The Kynges mariage [was] doubtefull at the beginnyng" and excuses are made: "The kyng beyng young, and not understandyng the lawe of God...."[28]

In his details of the divorce proceedings, Hall publishes an "Oracion" of the King followed by the Queen's response. The King's speech details that his conscience was pricked when the French ambassador, working on the arrangement of a marriage between Henry and Catherine's daughter Mary and the Duke of Orleans, questioned "whither she be the kyng of England his lawfull doughter or not, for well known it is that he begat her on his brothers wife which is directly against Gods law & his precept."[29] The King's speech concludes with praise of Catherine:

> For I assure you all, that beside her noble parentage of the which she is discended (as all you know) she is a woman of moste gentlenes, of moste humilitie and buxumnes, yea and of al good qualities appertainyng to nobilitie, she is without comparison, as I this xx. yeres almost have had the true experiment, so that if I were to mary againe if the mariage might be good I would surely chose her above all other women: But if it be determined by judgement that our mariage was against Goddes law and clerely voyde, then I shall not onely sorowe the departing from so good a Lady and lovyng a companion, but muche more lament and bewaile my infortunate chaunce that I haue so long lived in adultry to Goddes great displeasure, and have no true heyre of my body to inherite this realme.[30] (755)

The Queen responds with a strong counterargument, opening with a pair of rhetorical questions: "Alas my lordes is it now a question whether I be the kynges lawful wife or no? When I have been maried to him almost xx. yeres & in the meane season never question was made before?"[31] Catherine outlines a strong argument, betraying perhaps some indignation (not wholly unjustified) at the doubts about her marriage and her character being raised in this "trial." Catherine blames Cardinal Wolsey for this trouble, believing his actions to be in retaliation for her open abhorrence of his "volupteous life, and abhominable Lechery."[32] In her response, she reveals a wounded, angry woman willing to expose the villainy she perceives against her. Hall claims that Catherine spoke these words in French and that they were recorded by Cardinal Campeius and later translated by Hall himself, subtly reminding his readers of Catherine's status as a foreigner, an outsider. A court is then assembled at Blackfriars to rule on the divorce and Henry addresses the legates; according to Hall the queen departs from this meeting in silence and from here Hall moves on to other matters.

In Holinshed's chronicle account of the divorce proceedings (second edition, 1587), the King's address to his subjects prior to the calling of the court at Blackfriars is published along with a response from the Queen not included in Hall. The queen does not depart in silence from the court at Blackfriars, as Hall reported, but instead delivers the following speech later adapted by Shakespeare and Fletcher: "Sir (quoth shee) I desire you to doo mee justice and right and take some pitie upon mee, for I am a poore woman, and a straunger, borne out of your dominion...."[33] Once she concludes, "she arose up, making a low curtesie to the king, and departed from thence...."[34] Her exit is described with some pathos, for as she leaves, she is aided in doing so by her general receiver, Master Griffith. (One might suspect that the visually telling entrance of Henry, leaning on Wolsey per the stage directions of Act 1, scene 2 of Shakespeare and Fletcher's *Henry VIII* is a subtle inversion of this.) Here the complementary details that concluded Henry's oration in Hall are magnified: "The king perceiving she was departed thus, and considering her words which she pronounced before him, said to the audience these words in effect: For as much (quoth he) as the Queene is gone, I will in her absence declare unto you all: She hath been to me as true, as obedient, and as comfortable a wife, as I would wish or desire: she hath all the vertuous qualities that ought to be in a woman of her dignity, or in any baser estate: she is also surely a noble woman borne, her conditions will well declare the same."[35]

From here Wolsey interjects, asking the King to proclaim that he was not the prime mover in prompting the King to divorce, "for [he was] greatlie suspected herein."[36] In fact, Holinshed claims that Catherine directly accused Wolsey of being her enemy in open court—an act that Holinshed paints as highly indecorous for the queen. Henry responds to Wolsey's request by attesting that the Cardinal was not responsible for calling the King's marriage into question and then goes on to explain that what prompted his conscience were the questions of the French ambassador.

What follows in Holinshed is another scene familiar to readers of Shakespeare and Fletcher's *Henry VIII*: Wolsey comes to Catherine with the charges of the court; he speaks to the Queen in Latin but she stops him, asking that he speak to her in English: "Naie good my lord (quoth she) speake to me in English."[37] After he delivers the charges, Catherine voices her concern over finding any just council in England where all fear stirring the King's displeasure and because her true friends remain in her native Spain.

Of the later chroniclers, Foxe follows Hall, omitting the additional materials Holinshed provides. Stowe combines elements from both Hall and Holinshed and ultimately produces the most fully rounded character portrait of the queen (and later of Cardinal Wolsey) in the various chronicles. While it is a long rehearsed fact that Shakespeare drew on Holinshed for the chronicle history plays in his early career, it strikes me that the republication of Stowe's *Annales* in 1605 may well have significantly contributed to Shakespeare's return to the writing of history plays with *Henry VIII* near the conclusion of his career.

Stowe introduces some significant lines not in Holinshed when, for example, Wolsey addresses Catherine concerning the court's refusal of her appeal to Rome: "Then began the cardinall to speak to her in Latin: Nay good my Lord (quoth she) speak to me in English for I can (I thank God) bothe speake and understand English, although I understand some Latin." Arguably Shakespeare read Stowe's slightly expanded account and was here inspired to expand this added detail into a moment in which Catherine adamantly embraces her adopted realm.

Judith H. Anderson has argued that Shakespeare was indebted to Stowe's 1592 *Annales* and its use of George Cavendishe's *Life of Wolsey* for the portrait of the Cardinal in the play.[38] Annabel Patterson is lukewarm in her endorsement of Anderson's argument. An equally compelling scenario is one in which Shakespeare read and reacted to the 1605 Stowe—either instead of, or in addition to, the 1592 edition. He had clearly read and been influenced by the second edition of Holinshed (1587) earlier in his career. I would suggest that *Henry VIII* may be Shakespeare's reaction to the 1605 edition of Stowe—rather than his re-reading (or recollection) of the 1587 Holinshed. In discussing the aforementioned scene Patterson does not quote the additional lines "for I can (I thank God) bothe speake and understand English, although I understand some Latin." Patterson inexplicably omits the latter portion of this line, introduced by Stowe; this material adds additional strength to Anderson's argument that Shakespeare's greater debt here is to Stowe rather than Holinshed.

Stowe's narrative frequently provides longer, fuller speeches than those quoted by Holinshed—although Holinshed is clearly a source for Stowe. Stowe also omits material, further shaping his characters. For example, while Stowe reports the King's oration to his subjects he omits the Queen's argumentative reply. He silences her—just as Forrest silenced his Griselda by omitting all mention of the trials—and elevates her success in satisfying the silent ideal his culture sought in women. In the courtroom at Blackfriars, however, Stowe does provide the Queen's oration there which, significantly, is a plea for justice and pity for the Queen, "a poore woman and a straunger, borne out of your dominion."[39] As Annabel Patterson has noted, the autograph manuscript of Cavendish notes that these lines were "sayd in effect in broken Englyshe, as followythe. . . ."[40] Hall and Foxe claim the speech was delivered in French and later translated. There is thus a gradual process that moves Catherine, at least in language, toward being English. Stowe especially de-emphasizes Catherine's foreignness, referencing it when he does, not to alienate Catherine from a sixteenth- and seventeenth-century English readership, but to stress her isolation and the suspiciously stacked-deck nature of the divorce proceedings from her perspective.

Stowe, more so than previous chroniclers, contributes to a process whereby Catherine is increasingly "Englished"—to appropriate the uniquely English coinage that frequently replaced the Latinate "translated" on the title pages of numerous translations of materials throughout the sixteenth and seventeenth centuries. Catherine's foreignness and specifically her Spanish origins are de-emphasized in order to present her as a portrait of womanly virtue and perhaps, specifically, of those virtues most desired of Englishwomen by Englishmen. It is difficult, if not impossible, to register the effect Stowe's portrait of Catherine—as distinct from Foxe's—had on English readers writ large. Foxe is the more re-issued and widely-circulated author, but the extent to which his readers fixated on Catherine—as opposed to the infamous Protestant martyrs who eventually become the namesake for the shorthand version of Foxe—cannot be adequately gauged. As I will show below, it is clear that Shakespeare and Fletcher adapted—directly or indirectly—a presentation of Catherine more in line with Stowe's rendering than Foxe's; and, ultimately, the influence of the popular theater on the popular imagination, while likewise an unknown quantity, is undeniable. Still more striking is the extent to which Shakespeare and Fletcher present Catherine as a Griselda-like figure and paragon of English feminine virtue. It seems all but impossible that they could have been familiar with Forrest's manuscript history although the resulting presentation of Catherine in the two works is strikingly similar.

As surveyed above, the literary figure of patient Griselda appeared and reappeared in various manifestations throughout the sixteenth century. There is a tantalizing sense of coincidence in the 1603 publication of Dekker et al.'s *Pleasant Comodie* (composed around 1599) and the 1605 publication of Stowe's *Annales* followed a few years later by

Shakespeare and Fletcher's *Henry VIII* in which a patiently suffering and Griselda-like Queen Catherine is presented in a play whose alternate title, *All Is True*, provides a telling insight into how we perhaps ought to read chronicle histories produced in the sixteenth century. This is at best coincidence, but it is tantalizing coincidence.

Shakespeare and Fletcher's portrayal of Katherine of Aragon in *Henry VIII* fully Englishes Catherine by presenting her as the apotheosis of wifely duty and a character of Griselda-like patience. Shakespeare and Fletcher's Katherine is, to be sure, not entirely chaste, silent, and obedient as the ideal Griselda would be, but two out of three isn't bad and Katherine is decidedly chaste and obedient.

Katherine only appears in four scenes in the play and yet, as Jay Halio notes, one of the most recent professional productions of the play effectively made Katherine the star.[41] Katherine is clearly lionized in the play, her four appearances showcasing her charity, obedience, intelligence, and regal bearing even in the face of extreme adversity.

In her first appearance—Act I, scene ii—a scene wholly invented it would seem by the dramatist(s) (there is no correspondent scene in any of the chronicles), Katherine lobbies for the oppressed clothworkers overburdened by Wolsey's excessive taxes. She is concerned for her people, a figure who defends the impoverished and weak against those tyrants who would do them harm. Later she herself becomes the poor and oppressed, a fact that she stresses frequently.

In Shakespeare and Fletcher's handling of the Blackfriar's scene, Katherine speaks, positioning herself as a "poor woman" and an outsider:

> Sir, I do desire you do me right and justice,
> And to bestow your pity on me, for
> I am a most poor woman, and a stranger,
> Born out of your dominions.... (2.4.13–16)[42]

Later in this same scene she characterizes herself as "a simple woman, much too weak / T'oppose [Wolsey's] cunning" (2.4.106–07). Katherine is not unaware of the politics of gender and in fact, manipulates these politics to her rhetorical advantage.

When Katherine's servants apprise her that Wolsey and Campeius have come, in Act 3, scene 1, Katherine's questioning response underscores her gender: "What can be their business / With me, a poor weak woman, fall'n from favor?" (3.1.19–20). Receiving the news Campeius and Wolsey offer, Katherine makes a request: "Let me have time and counsel for my cause. / Alas, I am a woman friendless, hopeless" (3.1.79–80). She again stresses her feminity. While she characterizes herself as "a poor weak woman" and "a woman friendless," she goes on to recognize her exemplarity as a woman and a wife:

> Have I lived thus long—let me speak myself,
> Since virtue finds no friends—a wife, a true one?
> A woman—I dare say without vainglory—
> Never yet branded with suspicion?
> Have I with all my full affections
> Still met the King, loved him next heav'n, obeyed him,
> Been—out of fondness—superstitious to him,
> Almost forgot my prayers to content him?
> And am I thus rewarded? 'Tis not well, lords.
> Bring me a constant woman to her husband,
> One that ne'er dreamed a joy beyond his pleasure,
> And to that woman when she had done most
> Yet will I add an honour—a great patience. (3.1.125–37)

Shakespeare and Fletcher return to Katherine's opening theme, employing the gender politics that envelop her to soften her tone at the scene's conclusion:

> You know I am a woman, lacking wit
> To make a seemly answer to such persons. (3.1.177–78)

Katherine—as she must—speaks up for herself rather than suffering all in silence; but even as she does so, she craftily acknowledges and uses to her best advantage the hegemonic power structure that views her as a weak, frail woman. Her most passionate, angry defense in 3.1. when Cardinals Campeius and Wolsey come to her is delivered in "rage" according to Campeius (3.1.101), and yet it is cooly logical and well developed in its rhetorical argument. What has yet to be noted about this speech is that it is to a large extent an adaptation of Catherine's reply following Henry's oration to his subjects in Holinshed. The change in context is important here. Catherine does not, as in Holinshed, deliver this speech in open court, but in private, when confronted at home by two men, one an emissary for the King and one an emissary for the Pope. There is a subtle decorum in this shift of context, a shift in keeping with the sort of editorial move on Stowe's part to excise the claim that Catherine accused Wolsey of conspiring against her in open court, and of Forrest who allows his Griselda to complain only privately. Katherine's anger is given vent in a private, domestic space and is not for the public viewing of the realm.

In addition to her rhetorical prowess, other aspects of Katherine's language arts contribute to the increased Englishness of Shakespeare and Fletcher's portrayal.

Unlike other contemporary texts that frequently rely on phonetic spellings and deliberate word alterations in an effort to capture a particular accent (as with the "-ish's" of the Irish Captain MacMorris in *Henry V* (3.2.89 ff.) or the Welsh accents of Sir Owen ap Griffith and his wife Gwenthian in Dekker, Chettle, and Haughton's *Patient Griselda*), Katherine speaks plain English and makes that point herself:

> O, good my Lord, no Latin;
> I am not such a truant since my coming,
> As not to know the language I have lived in.
> A strange tongue makes my cause more strange, suspicious;
> Pray speak in English. (3.1.42–46)

Katherine is a Queen, and a Queen of England, too. Moreover, her insistence on plain-spoken English allies her with the audience—especially at the Globe—assembled to hear the play: "Pray speak in English. Here are some will thank you, / If you speak truth for their poor mistress' sake" (46–47). While Katherine refers immediately to her assembled waiting women, one can quite easily identify the thankful, longing to hear the truth regarding their poor mistress, to include the playhouse audience, many of whom (at best) would have had small Latin.

The domestic privacy of this scene, noted above, affects not only the substance of Katherine's speech but its mode of delivery as well. Wolsey and Campeius maintain a formal register, addressing Katherine with either honorifics or "you" (as opposed to the less formal "thou"). Katherine is initially formal as well, but as she is increasingly moved in passion, her register downshifts to a more colloquial English and her speech is frequently punctuated with "ye's." Compare this with Katherine's first appearance—at court—where her language is notably and consistently formal. In the earlier scene (1.2) she primarily addresses characters according to their titles: "your majesty" (14); "My good lord Cardinal" (23); "my lord" (to Wolsey, 43). When she does use a pronoun here it is "you" (lines 44 ff.).

When Jane Lapotaire took the part of Katherine in the 1996–97 Royal Shakespeare Company production, she and the director, Greg Doran, chose to present Katherine's English as Spanish-accented and almost rigidly formal. Their decision to do so grew from a desire to underscore Katherine's vulnerability, her place in the play as a truly isolated figure. They drew their inspiration for such an interpretation to a significant degree from the exclamation of the Old Lady in 2.3: "Alas poor lady! / She's a stranger now again" (16–17).[43] While their decision decidedly focused the emotional attention of the play on Katherine and her patient suffering, to do so by highlighting her alien status reads against the grain of the play and the larger tide of history's popular presentation of Catherine that I am arguing for here. Indeed, even in the lines on which they based this interpretation, they seemingly overlook the final two words of that line: Katherine is said to be "a stranger *now again*" (emphasis added). The underlying suggestion is that she had ceased to be a stranger and, indeed, through her well-documented charity toward her English subjects—represented by her advocacy for the clothworkers in Act 1, scene 2—Katherine has clearly come to see the English as her people. Katherine's language throughout the play is more suggestive of her having become fully Englished rather than remaining a permanent alien. Notably, she is comforted and entertained at the opening of Act 3, scene 1 not by a Spanish folk song, but by an English madrigal.

Doran and Lapotaire were certainly correct, however, in their efforts to read the play as, in large part, a hagiography. Shakespeare and Fletcher's Katherine is undeniably saintlike in her patient endurance, a fact that is in part expressed in the heavenly access she is granted in her dream-vision in 4.2 and made more fully explicit in Henry's description of her in Act 2, scene 4:

> Thou art, alone—
> If thy rare qualities, sweet gentleness,
> Thy meekness saint-like, wife-like government,
> Obeying in commanding, and thy parts
> Sovereign and pious else, could speak thee out—
> The queen of earthly queens. (2.4.137–42)

Moreover, in his single line praising simultaneously Katherine's "meekness saint-like" and "wife-like government," Henry provides the formulaic feminine ideal that so thoroughly links Katherine to Griselda. Katherine, as noted above, self-consciously practices the patience these descriptions subsume (3.1.137).

Scholarly discussions of Shakespeare's histories have firmly established that Shakespeare goes beyond merely dramatizing his source materials and actively interrogates the construction and reproduction of history. Whether fully consciously or not, Shakespeare and Fletcher in *Henry VIII* contribute to a larger effort that employs history as a tool for shaping culture and influencing thought in whatever present in which that history is read (or heard). Their play is yet another chapter in the almost overwhelming conduct book for early modern Englishwomen; it is social programming. What is in part remarkable about this is the exemplar offered here is a conflation of two foreign women who over time have been Englished, Catherine of Aragon and Patient Griselda. The fulsome title page of a 1619 prose retelling of the legend of Griselda is enormously revealing in that as it reminds the readers of Griselda's status as a foreigner, it is simultaneously unapologetic in advertising itself as precisely the same sort of self-conscious social programming offered by Shakespeare and Fletcher:

> The
> Ancient True and Admirable
> History of Patient Grisel,
> a Poore Man's Daughter in France:
> Shewing
> How Maides, By Her Example, In Their Good Behaviour
> May Marrie Rich Husbands;
> And Likewise Wives By Their Patience And Obedience
> May Gaine Much Glory
> ---
> WRITTEN FIRST IN FRENCH, AND
> Therefore to French I speake and give direction,
> For English Dames will live in no subjection.
> BUT NOW TRANSLATED INTO ENGLISH, AND
> Therefore say not so, for English maids and wives
> Surpass the French in goodnesse of their lives.[44]

There is almost a suggestion of reverse psychology in the details here. The text itself, like all other English versions of Griselda privileges Griselda's chaste, silent, and patient obedience as the consummation devoutly to be wished in all Englishwomen. Perhaps there is also a subtle, ironic shaming at work: the most ideally English of Englishwomen are foreigners.

It is a well-rehearsed fact of Queen Mary I's will that she desired a monument be erected to her mother.[45] No such action ever took place. In his history of Catherine of Aragon, Forrest clearly aimed to provide a sort of monument that would celebrate Catherine's virtues for posterity. His efforts were seemingly as ineffective as those of the Queen to whom he dedicated his works. The curious elision of popular and literary history—perhaps entirely by coincidence—would realize a resurgence throughout the later sixteenth and into the early seventeenth century with several reappraisals of the Griselda legend and of the person of Queen Catherine. These two traditions, seemingly divergent, converge again in the late works of Shakespeare, his valedictory play proving a striking comment on history, fame, and popular perception. As Katherine's gentleman usher Griffith says to her late in the play, "Noble Madam, / Men's evil manners live in brass, their virtues / We write in water" (4.2.44–46), he reveals a kind of keynote to the project Shakespeare and Fletcher undertake. They aim to set down Catherine's virtues in somewhat stronger stuff, to celebrate her patience and her virtue and to provide a monument not simply to a noble woman, but to an exemplary English queen.

Notes

I am deeply grateful to Professor Travitsky for her invaluable advice and suggestions after reading through an earlier version of this essay. I also owe a debt of gratitude to the Women's Studies Program at the University of Nebraska-Lincoln for awarding this essay a 2002 Karen Dunning Graduate Scholarly Paper prize.

1. Betty Travitsky, "Reprinting Tudor History: The Case of Catherine of Aragon," *Renaissance Quarterly*, 50:1 (Spring 1997), 164.
2. W. D. Macray, ed., *The History of Grisild the Second: A Narrative, in verse, of the divorce of Queen Katharine of Aragon. Written by William Forrest, sometime Chaplain to Queen Mary I, and now edited, for the first time, from the author's MS in the Bodleian Library* (London: Whittingham and Wilkins, 1875). Hereafter Forrest. I have regularized the use of i/j and v/u in all quotations but otherwise maintained Forrest's spellings as rendered by Macray.
3. David M. Loades, *Mary Tudor: A Life* (Oxford: Oxford University Press, 1989).
4. Garrett Mattingly, *Catherine of Aragon* (London: Jonathan Cape, 1942), p. 314.
5. Forrest, p. 5.
6. Forrest, p. 2.
7. Forrest, p. 3.
8. Forrest, pp. 4, 3.
9. Forrest, p. 5.
10. Forrest, pp. 3, 5.
11. See, for example, John E. Paul, *Catherine of Aragon and Her Friends* (London: Burns & Oates, 1966). Paul is especially critical of Henry VII's miserly pursuit of the dowry and the subsequent hardship it caused Catherine (pp. 16–27).
12. Forrest, p. 10; the same material reappears on p. 49.
13. See David Bevington, *From Mankind to Marlowe: Growth of Structure in the Popular Drama of Tudor England* (Cambridge, MA.: Harvard University Press, 1962).
14. Forrest, p. 49.
15. "Delivere us out of al this bisy drede,

    And taak a wyf, for hye Goddes sake!
    For if it so bifelle, as God forbede,
    That thurgh youre deethe youre lyne sholde slake,
    And that a straunge successour sholde take

Youre heritage, O wo were us alyve!
Wherefore we pray you hastily to wyve!" (134–40)

Geoffrey Chaucer, "The Clerk's Tale" in *The Riverside Chaucer*, ed. Larry D. Benson (Boston: Houghton Mifflin, 3rd edn., 1987).

16. Forrest, p. 71. There was, of course, open, popular dissent at times in reaction to the marriage. See Geoffrey de C. Parmiter, *The King's Great Matter: A Study of Anglo-Papal Relations 1527–1534* (New York: Barnes & Noble, 1967), pp. 71, 197–98.
17. Forrest, p. 72.
18. Mattingly, *Catherine of Araagon*, p. 308.
19. Forrest, p. 106.
20. Juan Luis Vives, *Opera Omnia* (Reprint London: Gregg Press, 1964), p. 275; an English translation of this Latin epistle is available in Foster Watson, ed. *Vives and the Renascence Education of Women* (New York: Longmans, Green & Co., 1912), p. 144. See also Timothy Elston's essay in this collection.
21. Macray offers details from the corpus of Forrest's writings which convincingly support the same conclusion: "Although Roman, he was not Papal; he shared that old English dislike to the usurped domination of the Bishop of Rome, which so largely helped to the general acceptance of the high-handed measures of Henry VIII" (xvi).
22. Gordon McMullan, in his Arden Third Series edition of *Henry VIII*, provides a brief but insightful commentary on some of these issues, further relating them to their complex transmission in the late plays. He alludes glancingly to the Griselda legend having a part in this as well, with Katherina in *Taming of the Shrew*, Katherine in *Henry VIII* and Hermione in *The Winter's Tale* all being manifestations of the Griselda figure. Certainly more remains to be said on the complex inter-relationships at work amongst these historical and literary materials than space will allow here. See Gordon McMullan, ed., *Henry VIII* (London: Thomson, 2000), pp. 120–36.
23. McMullan is the first editor of Shakespeare and Fletcher's *Henry VIII* to even cite the text. He refers to it in a footnote to 3.1.137 (326), noting as he does so the recollection of Patient Griselda. See also Ann Rosalind Jones and Peter Stallybrass, "(In)alienable possessions: Griselda, clothing and the exchange of women" in *Renaissance Clothing and the Materials of Memory*, ed. Jones and Stallybrass (Cambridge: Cambridge University Press, 2000).
24. Vivian Comensoli, "Refashioning the Marriage Code: The *Patient Grissil* of Dekker, Chettle and Haughton," *Renaissance and Reformation, Renaissance et Reforme*, 13:2 (Summer 1989), pp. 199–214.
25. Commensoli, p. 212.
26. Lee Bliss, "The Renaissance Griselda: A Woman for All Seasons," *Viator: Medieval and Renaissance Studies* 23, (1992), pp. 301–43.
27. I have deliberately simplified the relationships here and it should be noted, as Annabel Patterson has argued, that a label like "Holinshed" suggesting an autonomous author is misleading given the fact that these chronicles were

highly collaborative and regenerative in their use and re-use of materials from earlier chronicle compilations. See Annabel Patterson, " 'All is True': Negotiating the Past in *Henry VIII*" in *Elizabethan Theatre: Essays in Honor of S. Schoenbaum*, ed. R. B. Parker and S. P. Zitner (Newark: University of Delaware Press, 1996), pp. 147–68.
28. Edward Hall, *Hall's Chronicle* (London J. Johnson, 1809), p. 507. I have regularized the use of i/j and v/u in all quotations.
29. Hall, p. 754.
30. Hall, p. 755.
31. Hall, p. 755.
32. Hall, p. 755.
33. Raphael Holinshed, *Chronicles*, 3 vols. (London, 1587), 3: 907. All matter discussed here is from the third volume.
34. Holinshed, 3: 907.
35. Holinshed, 3: 913–14.
36. Holinshed, 3: 914.
37. Holinshed, 3: 908.
38. Judith H. Anderson, *Biographical Truth: The Representation of Historical Persons in Tudor-Stuart Writing* (New Haven: Yale University Press, 1984), pp. 136–42.
39. John Stowe, *The Annales of England* (London: 1605), pp. 912–13.
40. Patterson, p. 165.
41. This was the 1996–97 Royal Shakespeare Company production in the Swan Theatre, Stratford. Halio notes "Refusing to compromise her principles right to the end, and suffering for them, this Katherine emerged as the real star of the production, winning from the audience the highest acclaim" (60). Jay L. Halio, ed., *King Henry VIII, or All Is True* (Oxford: Oxford University Press, 1999).
42. All references here are to *The Riverside Shakespeare* text, ed. G. Blakemore Evans and J. J. M. Tobin (2nd edn. Boston: Houghton Mifflin, 1997).
43. See "Queen Katherine in *Henry VIII* in Robert Smallwooed, ed., *Players of Shakespeare 4* (U Cambridge P, 1998), pp. 132–151.
44. *Ancient, True, and Admirable History of Patient Grisel* (London: 1619).
45. Loades, in *Mary Tudor: A Life*, includes Mary's will as an appendix.

Whore Queens: The Sexualized Female Body and the State

Susan Dunn-Hensley

In the summer of 1567, a rebellion forced Mary Stuart off the throne of Scotland. Mary's political failure resulted, in part, from her unwise personal choices: her preference for her court favorites, particularly David Rizzio; her inability to extricate herself from the suspicion surrounding the murder of her husband, Lord Darnley; and her hasty marriage to James Hepburn, Earl of Bothwell, who was also suspected of taking part in Darnley's murder. By 1567, the queen, whose "grace and good humour [had] made her appeal to the general populace" earlier in her reign, could no longer command the loyalty and respect of the nobility or the people.[1] As Mary was taken to Edinburgh as a prisoner, the crowds revealed their contempt for their queen, crying out "burn the whore!... burn her, burn her, she is not worthy to live, kill her, drown her."[2] Their response to the fallen monarch, presented in unambiguously gendered terms, reveals a preoccupation with Mary's physical body and her alleged sexual transgressions. In the eyes of her people, Mary was not only a murderess, she was a whore, and her sexual "taintedness" proved as deplorable as her other "crime." Because of her position as queen, Mary's physical body possessed political significance, and the crowd's condemnation of Mary suggests anger at a woman who had sullied not only herself but also, by extension, Scotland.

In reacting to Mary, the crowd addresses the specific actions of one monarch; however, the language the crowd uses and the sentiments that they express connect this incident with a broader historical and social framework surrounding issues of female rule. During a time when women were legally and socially subordinate to men, the idea that a woman could rule an entire nation was almost inconceivable; yet, in the middle to late sixteenth century, England, Scotland, and France were all ruled by women. Mary Tudor ruled England from 1553 until her death in 1558. Elizabeth Tudor succeeded her sister and reigned until 1603. From 1542 to 1567, Mary Stuart ruled Scotland, a throne which her mother, Mary of Guise, had held as regent until her daughter returned from France in 1561. Across the channel, Catherine de Medici played a major role in French politics for thirty years as queen mother.[3]

Despite major differences in the individual women and in their methods of rule, each queen's reign was complicated by the position that women held in Renaissance society and by prevailing attitudes about women and their bodies. Fear of the female body and anxiety about female sexuality pervaded Renaissance literature and culture. In a time when women were being tried for witchcraft and when the penalty for transgressing social norms was severe, the sexualized female body represented all that was frightening and dangerous in the Renaissance world. Not surprisingly, this fear increased when the female body occupied the throne. To many, the presence of a woman on the throne seemed at odds with natural and divine law. Her position as the head of state was seen as threatening the very assumptions on which patriarchal society rests.

The controversy surrounding the fitness of a woman ruler inspired numerous tracts and treatises, but it also found more subtle expression in the art and literature of the day. Like many of his contemporaries, Shakespeare addresses the issue of queenship in a number of his works, including his depiction of sexually active and transgressive queens in *Titus Andronicus*, *Hamlet*, and *Cymbeline*.[4] In each of these plays, Shakespeare links the rampant, uncontrollable sexuality of the queen with the world of nature, and, in each case, the chaotic world of nature and sexuality threatens to disrupt the ordered world of politics. In *Hamlet*, Gertrude holds no political power; however, her sexualized body has the power to contaminate the state even though she exerts no influence on the politics of her kingdom. In *Titus Andronicus* and *Cymbeline*, Tamora and Cymbeline's queen are queen consorts, not queen regnants; however, through their positions as wives and mothers, they wield a great deal of power, and their evil schemes, wedded to their sexual bodies, threaten to bring contamination and destruction to their kingdoms.[5]

The Debate over Female Rule

In the year 1553, eleven years before Shakespeare's birth, England crowned her first queen regnant in over 400 years. Not surprisingly, Mary I's accession caused a great deal of anxiety as the female body moved from the margins to the very center of political power. Not since Matilda (1127–35), the daughter of Henry I, had England been ruled by a woman, and in an era rife with misogyny, the crowning of a woman forced a rethinking of the role and position of women in English society. Having a woman on the throne posed a number of potential problems for England. According to the church, the woman was subordinate to the man, and under the law, the English wife was subordinate to her husband. Mary's accession forced English society to address two important questions: could a woman be head of England's church in spite of ecclesiastical law, and could a woman rule over men in spite of civil law? These theological and legal questions were eclipsed by a more practical question: would England's sovereignty be compromised if the queen married a foreign prince, who, as husband, would serve as the head of the queen's household?[6]

Mary's accession to the throne incited a heated debate about the legitimacy of a female monarch. Even those writers who opposed Mary because of her Catholicism tended to focus their attacks on her gender. Anti-Catholic writers repeatedly "invoked scripture against gynecocracy and identified Mary with such figures as Jezebel."[7] In *How Superior Powers ought to be obeyd*, Christopher Goodman argues that Mary, by taking on the role of queen, has disobeyed God because "she has disregarded the authority of scripture [Deuteronomy XVII] which declares that Israel shall choose a king from 'one of their brethren.'"[8] Even a writer like Thomas Becon, who primarily objects to Mary's Catholicism, supports his points with scriptures that limit the public activities of women. In *An humble suplicacioun unto God for the restoring of his holye woorde unto the churche of England* (1554), Becon goes so far as to argue that the lack of a male heir in England is God's punishment against the nation.[9] One of the harshest criticisms of Mary's reign comes from John Knox, who calls women's rule "repugnant to Nature," "a contumlie to God," and a "subversion of good order." In *The First Blast of the Trumpet against the Monstrous Regiment of Women*, Knox echoes the sentiments of many as he addresses female "deficiency" and the monstrosity of female rule.

Many of these writers, some of whom were in exile during the reign of the Catholic Mary, were embarrassed when the Protestant Elizabeth came to the throne. In response to Elizabeth's accession, John Aylmer wrote in defense of a woman's right to rule. In his 1559 *An Harborowe for Faithful and Trewe Subjectes*, Aylmer argues against Knox's ideas about divine and natural law, suggesting that "while neither nature nor scripture are decisive in denying the legitimacy of woman's rule, providence can be seen to support it." He argues that the absence of a male heir fits into God's divine purpose, and "if He put to his hande she cannot be feable, if he be with her who can stand against her."[10] Using the theory of the king's two bodies, Aylmer argues that gender is part of the natural body and that it is overcome in the body politic.

Aware of the debate about a woman's right to reign, Elizabeth consciously constructed herself in ways that addressed objections to her gender. Leah Marcus argues that Elizabeth "constructed a vocabulary of rule that was predominantly male."[11] One of her strategies was to invoke the political theory of the king's two bodies to construct herself in a manner that separated her female physical body from her "male" political body. She styled herself as a "female Prince"; and, in the "Address to the Troops at Tilbury," which Elizabeth supposedly delivered on August 9, 1588, she presented herself as a warrior. However, although Elizabeth's careful self-construction helped address theological and legal concerns, she could not completely counteract the deep anxieties that early modern men must have felt at the prospect of female authority. Employing the legal theory of the king's two bodies to justify female rule could not fully erase anxieties produced by the fact that one of the bodies was gendered female. After all, as Alan Smith points out, "most men of the day would have agreed with Knox's sentiments" about female rule, "if not necessarily with the violence with which Knox expresses them."[12] Despite her best efforts to control her own image, Elizabeth's private life and desires did not escape public censure and debate.

Many people felt that England would only be safe if its sovereign were to wed and produce heirs, thus securing a clear and unchallengeable line of succession. Remaining unmarried placed Elizabeth outside of Protestant society's expectations for a woman, leaving her open to attacks that presented her as transgressive and lascivious. Even careful construction of herself as a virgin could not quell rumors that Elizabeth was a "whore" queen. As Carole Levin makes clear, Elizabeth's status as unmarried female ruler produced much speculation about her sexual behavior and her physical body. Throughout her reign, rumors circulated about her sexual exploits and the illegitimate children that they had produced. According to Levin, rather than subsiding as the queen aged, these rumors intensified during the last two decades of Elizabeth's reign. Indeed, the rumors were so widespread and insistent that they persisted even after Elizabeth's death.[13]

The accession of James I did not stop the debate about and interest in queenship. We can attribute this interest, in part, to the nostalgia for Elizabeth that followed her death. According to Levin, "within two or three years of Elizabeth's death there began to be a nostalgia for 'good

Queen Bess' and the glories of her reign."[14] In addition to nostalgia for their former queen, writers were no doubt interested in their new queen, James's wife, Anna. Indeed, Carol Chillington Rutter argues that Shakespeare bases Cleopatra on Anne, not Elizabeth. As evidence, she cites Anne's "breathtaking extravagance, her astuteness in politicizing spectacle, her subversive wit, her rages and political relentlessness, her volatile relationship with the king, her stunts...her female 'government,'...her vulnerability to erotic betrayal..." and her "fertility."[15] Regardless of what specific sources inspired Shakespeare's creation of Cleopatra, we can certainly argue that the coming of a capricious, political, fertile queen consort could not help but feed interest in the concept of queenship and in the connection between female power and the female body.

Tamora

During the early modern period, the female body was associated with contamination and sin. Contemporary medical attitudes about menstruation held that the female body was a site of contagion and uncleanness,[16] and many contemporary theologians argued that women, like their foremother Eve, were more susceptible to temptation and more likely to repeat the fall. Some men feared the possibility of the sexualized female body running rampant and subjecting patriarchal civilization to the chaotic forces of nature. Although this fear of the disorderly woman may have been the result of displaced anxieties about the social upheavals of the period, to many people in the early modern period, unruly women suggested a very real threat. As Underdown points out, "anxiety about patriarchal order was more than a literary phenomenon."[17] Indeed, Mendelson and Crawford argue that "the period from around the mid-sixteenth century to the Civil War was one which was particularly dangerous to women." During that time, society was "obsessed with disorder, and women who challenged the accepted order were perceived as a more serious threat."[18] Evidence of this concern can be found within court records of the period; according to Underdown, "between 1560 and 1640 local court records show an intense concern about unruly women."[19] In many of his plays, Shakespeare addresses society's concern with unruly women.

Perhaps more than any of Shakespeare's other queens, Tamora illustrates male fear of the transgressive, contaminating female. In the opening act of *Titus Andronicus*, Shakespeare makes clear that Tamora has no legitimate claim to power in Rome. A queen of her own people, Tamora has been defeated in battle and has come to Rome as a prisoner. Her status as Queen of the Goths, rather than legitimizing her right to rule, calls into question her very nature, for throughout the first act of the play, we are repeatedly reminded that the Goths are barbarous. Any power she could have in Rome would be illegitimate; however, only moments after Titus has given Tamora as a gift to Saturninus, she begins to exert control over the emperor. As if bewitched, he asks her to be his empress and agrees to her bargain that, "If Saturnine advance the Queen of the Goths, / She will a handmaid be to his desires, / A loving nurse to his youth" (1.1.330–32). Her words suggest the power dynamic that she envisions for them: she will play the handmaid, fulfilling his sexual desires, if she can also play the nurse, guiding him as a mother would a child.

Tamora begins to exert her power almost immediately; bent on revenge, she convinces Saturninus to publicly make peace with the Andronici while she privately plots their ruin. Her language in the passage reveals her transgressive nature: "My lord, be rul'd by me, be won at last, /.../... let me alone, / I'll find a day to massacre them all, / And rase their faction and their family..." (1.1.442–51). In exhorting Saturninus to be ruled by her, Tamora attempts to transgress the prescribed limits of her power and, in doing so, challenges the social order. She is Saturninus's subject, his prisoner, and soon to be his wife. In each of these roles, she is subordinate to him; however, from this point forward, she controls him and, by extension, Rome. That he allows her to control him reveals his weakness of character and suggests the threat that Rome will face under "the rule" of a sexually transgressive queen consort.

Although Act I provides us with the opportunity to feel sympathy for Tamora, whom we have seen plead fruitlessly for the life of her son, Act II quickly undercuts these feelings and establishes Tamora as a dangerous foe to civilized Rome. In the soliloquy that opens Act I, Aaron calls his lover "Semiramis." He then labels her a "siren" who "will charm Rome's Saturnine, / And see his shipwrack and his commonweal's" (2.1.23–24). In each comparison, he links Tamora with the forces of disorder that threaten the lives of men and the stability of civilization. Aaron's reference to the Assyrian queen, who was known for her "promiscuity and cruelty," immediately alerts the audience to the dangerous nature of Tamora's sexuality.[20] In Aaron's description, Tamora will bring ruin not only to Saturninus, but to Rome as well.

Aaron's assertion about Tamora's destructive sexual power proves to be accurate, for Tamora's desires threaten the state even before her murderous schemes begin to unfold. Tamora's sexual appetite is intimately linked to one of the central concerns of *Titus Andronicus*, the conflict between civilization and barbarism. While the Andronici represent the stabilizing forces of city, family, and order, Tamora represents unruly nature, passion, and disorder. Both symbolically and literally, Tamora poses the chief threat to Roman civilization. Symbolically, Tamora is linked to barbarism because of her position as queen of the Goths and because of her intimate connection with the play's two central images of barbarism, the blackamoor child and the gaping hole in the forest. Just as Tamora's promiscuity links her to the archetypal image of dangerous femininity, her choice of a lover provides a visual emblem of her contaminating threat. To early modern society, Tamora's preference for Aaron, a Moor, whom the other characters refer to as "a devil," reveals the danger that she poses for Rome. Aaron's racial identity allows Shakespeare to make visible Tamora's personal deviance and the contamination that she brings to the empire. Tamora's influence over Rome is more than symbolic, however. Both Tamora and Aaron represent, in Alan Sommers's words, "the barbarism of primitive, original nature."[21] Because she is empress, Tamora has the power to infect Rome with barbarism, through her influence over the emperor and her role as bearer of the royal offspring.

The literature of early modern society reveals a great deal of concern with the issue of female sexual desire, particularly as it relates to marital infidelity and questions of paternity. Because of primogeniture, much depended on the purity of the mother. In the case of a queen, the entire state depended on the purity of her body, for as the bearer of the royal offspring, she served as the continuer and preserver of the integrity of the royal line. When Tamora joins with Aaron and produces a child, her lust contaminates the royal progeny and, by extension, the kingdom. Through the language used to describe the child, Shakespeare reveals the threat that Aaron's offspring poses for Rome. When the nurse brings the child to Aaron, she calls it a "devil" and "a joyless, dismal, black and sorrowful issue" (4.2.63–66). In her words, he is "loathsome as a toad amongst the fair-fac'd breeders of our clime" (4.2.67–68). When Aaron is captured and brought to Lucius, Lucius calls the child the "base fruit of their burning lust" (5.1.43) and refers to it as the "growing image of thy fiend like face" (5.1.45). Tamora's tainted body has produced a "fiend," a child so loathsome to his mother that she sends him to its father to be christened at the point of a dagger. To an early modern audience, who associated the Moors with barbarism and disorder, Tamora's giving birth to a blackamoor babe would have suggested that her womb quite literally bred disorder for Rome.

Although Aaron's child proves a powerful emblem of Tamora's contaminating power and the dangers of female sexual desire, it is ultimately overshadowed by the play's central image, the dark, gaping hole in the forest. Through the image of this bloody pit, Shakespeare links female sexual transgression and the disorder of the natural world. The pit's centrality to the text is difficult to miss; for, throughout the scene in which Martius and Quintus find the hole, they repeatedly describe its dark, bloody character. Upon seeing that Martius has fallen in the hole, Quintus describes it as a "subtile" hole "whose mouth is covered with rude-growing briers, / upon whose leaves are drops of new shed blood (2.3.224, 210, and 199–200). From within the pit, Martius describes his surroundings as an "unhallowed and blood-stained hole" (210). Both men are filled with an undeniable anxiety at their encounter with this mysterious hole, and throughout the next fifty or so lines, they offer repeated descriptions of the hole, calling it variously a den that contains "a fearful site of blood and death" (215–16); a "detested, dark, blood-drinking pit" (225); a pit with "ragged entrails" (230); a "fell devouring receptacle / As Hateful as [Cocytus'] misty mouth" (236); and finally a "swallowing womb" (239).

Through these descriptions, Shakespeare makes the connection between this vile pit and the female body overt. The pit is the womb of the feminized earth, and it represents the full spectrum of female threat: the "nothingness" of the sexual organs, the devouring womb, the uncontrollable forces of nature and female desire. The images of blood associated with the pit suggest menstruation, breaking of the hymen, and childbirth, as well as death, for the Earth's womb is also a tomb. Martius and Quintus's anxiety when faced with the pit mirrors early modern anxiety about the female body. Throughout Act II, the devouring womb in the forest is connected to Tamora's contaminating womb. It is Tamora who introduces the pit to the audience through her story of Bassianus and Lavinia's attempt to kill her. Her imagination links the pit with terror, madness, and death. Later in the play, the connection between Tamora and the devouring womb becomes even stronger as she literalizes her position as devouring mother by consuming her own children, albeit without her knowledge.

All of Tamora's actions have serious consequences for Rome; however, it is her participation in the rape and mutilation of Lavinia that most clearly reveals Tamora's depravity and the danger she presents for the empire. Throughout the play, Shakespeare draws strong parallels between Lavinia and Rome. David Willbern makes this point quite effectively, suggesting that Lavinia, who is "[f]ought over by imperial claimants, attacked by barbarian Goths, and finally avenged by the Andronici... repeats by her personal fate the larger fate of Rome herself."[22] In attacking Lavinia, Tamora metaphorically attacks Rome. Shakespeare underscores the threat Tamora's actions pose to the empire through references to Tarquin's rape of Lucrece. Shakespeare makes the connection between Tarquin and Tamora in two different parts of the text. As Aaron encourages Tamora's sons to rape Lavinia, he reminds them, "Lucrece was not more chaste than this Lavinia" (2.1.109). Later, the connection becomes more explicit as Lucius promises his father that he will avenge his father by making Tamora beg at the gates "like Tarquin and his queen" (3.1.297). These references suggest that just as Sextus Tarquinius's violent lust brought an end to his family's rule in Rome, so too will Tamora's lust destroy Saturninus and perhaps Rome itself. Although some critics argue that Aaron is the principle instigator of the attack on Lavinia, and his role in the play makes Tamora superfluous, these lines, as well as several other key parts of the text, suggest that Tamora bears the responsibility for the attack on Lavinia.

Although plotted by Aaron and executed by Chiron and Demetrius, the rape of Lavinia plays a crucial role in Tamora's plan for revenge on the Andronici. Because Tamora cannot rape Lavinia, her sons must act as her surrogates, perpetrating the act for the love of their mother. Tamora cleverly spurs her sons in their purpose by accusing Bassianus and Lavinia of trying to kill her. After recounting her harrowing tale, Tamora exhorts her sons "Revenge it, as you love your mother's life, / Or be not henceforth call'd my children" (2.3.114–15). Tamora repeats this sentiment as her sons are preparing to drag Lavinia away: "Use her as you will, / The worse to her, the better lov'd of me" (2.3.166–67). In the first statement, she calls for revenge on both Bassianus and Lavinia, a request that is answered by the death of Bassianus. In the second statement, she speaks specifically of the rape. In encouraging this act, Tamora, who has already maneuvered her way into a position of influence in Rome, extends her power even further into patriarchal territory. By linking her love for her sons to their ability to enact her revenge, Tamora co-opts their bodies to her use. Just as Hamlet serves as surrogate for his father, who cannot take action himself because he no longer holds corporeal form, the sons must become the body for Tamora, who cannot rape Lavinia because she lacks the male part.

Tamora's role in the rape of Lavinia goes far beyond her words that incite her sons, however. Tamora bears responsibility for the actions of Demetrius and Chiron because she is their mother. Both the language of the text and contemporary medical views support the assertion that

Demetrius and Chiron's behavior results from and is an extension of their mother's evil nature. Because her polluted body formed them and because she nursed them at her breast, their character is inextricably bound to hers. Lavinia's assertion that the milk Chiron and Demetrius "suck'st from her did turn to marble / Even at thy teat thou hadst thy tyranny" (2.3.144–45) is not merely figurative. According to Mendelson and Crawford, early modern society believed that the mother's milk could literally taint the child: "the nurse's character, and whatever food she ate or activity she engaged in had the potential to affect the child she fed." The belief that "the nurse's qualities were transmitted to her child by her milk" was widespread in early modern society.[23] Because Tamora's sons "sucked" their wickedness from her body, the crimes they commit are more a result of her evil than of Aaron's coaxing.

Shakespeare's text reinforces Tamora's connection to her sons's physical bodies by connecting Tamora to Chiron's sword. During an argument with Chiron, Demetrius refers to his brother's sword saying "our mother, unadvis'd, [g]ave you a dancing-rapier by your side..." (2.1.37–38). These lines, although easily missed, are fascinatingly evocative. Tamora, as mother, gave her son a sword. A phallic symbol, the sword represents the gift of masculinity bestowed by the mother. Not only did she form their bodies in her tainted womb, not only did they suck forth tainted milk, but she also gave Chiron the representation of his manhood. If we assume that the sword given by Tamora could have been used in the dismembering of Lavinia, then this piece of evidence would support the idea that the rape is an assault by proxy.

Tamora's actions have serious ramifications for the state. Tamora's sexual transgressions threaten to contaminate the royal line, and her plot to destroy the Andronici becomes so brutal that it almost leads to the downfall of Rome. Ultimately, even the barbaric Goths find her behavior unacceptable and join with Lucius to purge Rome of her stain. Though Rome is restored at the end of the play, Tamora's sexual desires and lust for revenge cost Saturninus his reign and his life.

Gertrude and Cymbeline's Queen

Although Shakespeare's queen Gertrude does not actually rule Denmark, her transgressions have a tremendous impact on the ruling family and, by extension, on the state. She makes no attempt to exert power over state affairs, yet her body has the power to bring contamination to the state. References to Gertrude's transgressive sexuality fill the text and, at times, even overshadow Claudius's crime. Janet Adelman argues that Hamlet's revulsion at his mother's sexuality is as "intense as anything directed toward the murderer Claudius."[24] In addition, according to Steven Mullaney, "Mourning for a dead king, even revenge, is displaced or at least overlaid and complicated by misogyny toward a queen who is too vital, whose sexuality transgresses both her age and her brief tenure as widow."[25] Gertrude transgresses expectations by allowing herself to take another husband so soon after the death of the first; in doing so, she produces deep anxieties in her son and in the court.

A rapid remarriage is not the only indication of Gertrude's sexual uncontrollability. Indeed, Gertrude's very status as widow serves to implicate her as lascivious and insatiable. According to Dorothea Kehler, "although some twenty-five to thirty-five percent of sixteenth- and seventeenth-century English marriages were remarriages, censuring remarriage was tantamount to a convention for early modern writers. Pernicious clichés about widows (but not widowers) are found in polemics, household manuals, and plays of the period."[26] One particularly widespread myth about widows presented them as excessively lustful and socially disruptive. Having already experienced sexual pleasure, they were thought to be insatiable in their desires. Even if early modern society could at times envision chaste widowhood, a widow's unique legal position threatened patriarchal society. Wealthy widows "were often the executors of their husband's estates and trustees of their children's inheritance." Within these roles, the widow had "a legal identity" and "legal rights."[27] Not surprisingly, such freedom proved threatening to the existing social structure. Remarriage did not necessarily set the early modern mind at ease, however. As we see in *Hamlet*, the remarriage of a widow reminds patriarchy of its own mortality and replaceability.[28] Thus, the role of widow was destabilizing in and of itself, a fact that might explain why many of Shakespeare's transgressive queens are widows.

Throughout the play, Hamlet is concerned with his mother's transgressive behavior. In his first soliloquy, Hamlet discusses the problems of the state and his mother's sexuality in terms of a contaminated garden: "Fie on't, ah fie, 'tis an unweeded garden / That grows to seed; things rank and gross in nature / Possess it merely..." (1.2.135–37). The fact that Hamlet's garden reference comes directly after his statement "How weary, stale, flat, and unprofitable / Seem to me all the uses of the world" (1.2.133–34) suggests that the garden to which Hamlet refers is Denmark. However, the garden could also be Gertrude's contaminated body. The fact that the garden can represent either Gertrude or the state suggests the interchangeability of the queen and the land. If we link the play's references to decay and corruption, we find further evidence of the connection between queen and state, as well as evidence that Gertrude's sexual behavior has tainted Denmark. Marcellus's assertion that "Something is rotten in the state of Denmark" can be read as a reference not only to Claudius's crime but also to Gertrude's sexual transgressions (1.4.90). Further, Hamlet's comment that "Denmark's a prison" can be taken as an allusion to Gertrude's contaminated body (2.2.239). Notably, the prison image suggests the enclosed spaces of the female body. Hamlet's use of garden imagery also suggests an Edenic allusion. Gertrude, like Eve, has turned the garden to weeds, and just as Eve's sin is visited on all of her offspring, Gertrude's sins are visited on her children—Hamlet and the people of Denmark.[29]

From a practical perspective, Gertrude's actions carry serious consequences for the royal family and for the kingdom. Adelman argues that "Gertrude's failure to differentiate [between Old Hamlet and Claudius] has put an intolerable strain on Hamlet by making him the only repository of his father's image, the only agent of differentiation in a court that seems all too willing to accept the new king in place of the old."[30] If we view this assertion in terms of its significance to the state, we find that Gertrude's inability to differentiate between the two men may help explain the court's willingness to accept Claudius. By embracing Claudius, Gertrude makes it easier for the court and the kingdom to accept him as a legitimate substitute for the former king. Thus Gertrude's desires lead to a marriage that in many ways legitimates the rule of a regicide.

The Queen in Cymbeline also proves to have a contaminating influence on her land. Although Shakespeare does not explicitly deal with the Queen's sexual transgressions, he does suggest her sexual disruptiveness by making her a remarried widow and linking her schemes to witchcraft. Although the Queen is the wife of a king and not a ruler in her own right, her behavior can be viewed as an example of the dangers of female rule. She is dangerous because, although she has no legitimate political power, she uses her body to control the king and, through him, the kingdom. In order to secure her position, she attempts to marry her son to the king's daughter. When her plan fails, she attempts to poison Imogen to make her son heir to the throne. She even exerts her influence in the realm of politics: it is she who urges her husband not to pay tribute to Rome, thus instigating war.

The prototype for the Queen comes right out of a children's fairy story. The fact that Shakespeare has not given her a name might suggest the universality of the character: she is the archetypal contaminated woman who has haunted society's fantasies for centuries. Shakespeare, himself, makes reference to the tradition from which her character comes when he has the Queen inform Imogen that she does not intend to play the part of the stereotypical stepmother: "be assur'd you shall not find me, / daughter / After the slander of most stepmothers, / Evil-ey'd unto you" (1.1.69–72). By presenting herself as "not the typical stepmother," the Queen's words evoke all of the folklore surrounding the stepmother character. In fairy tales, stepdames are frequently presented as evil witches, and although Shakespeare does not explicitly call the Queen a witch, he provides numerous clues that link her with witchcraft. The Queen is fascinated by herbs, flowers, and poisons. She studies with the doctor to learn the secrets of nature; however, she seeks not to heal but to destroy. Shakespeare makes direct reference to witchcraft only twice in the text: Iachimo calls Posthumus a "holy witch" (1.6.166), and Arviragus prays that no witchcraft will charm Imogen's presumably dead body (4.2.277). Yet, the imagery of the witch pervades the scenes involving the Queen. The Second Lord refers to the Queen as "a crafty devil" who "bears all down with her brain" (1.6.52–54). According to him, the king is "by the step-dame govern'd," and she is "hourly coining plots" (1.5.58–59). In a time when people were being prosecuted and killed for witchcraft, the use of the witch image is telling. In early modern literature, the witch represents all of the forces of disorder that threaten the stability of society. She is dangerous, sexually promiscuous, and potentially disruptive.

In addition to connecting her to witchcraft, the Queen's fascination with flowers and the natural world also links her to Eve. Several times in the first act, Shakespeare connects the queen and the garden, a reference, perhaps, to Eve and the contamination that she brought to humanity. When Posthumus and Imogen want to be alone, the Queen says she will "fetch a turn about the garden..." (1.1.81). Later, we see her in the garden again, this time collecting flowers. Like Gertrude, the Queen is intimately linked to nature, and like Gertrude, the Queen and her transgressions threaten the stability of the kingdom.

That the Queen threatens to disrupt order is evident throughout the play. *Cymbeline* takes place during the time of Christ's birth, and although we find no specific reference to Christ, Christian allusions fill the text. The structure of the play emphasizes the coming of peace in the last scene, and the Queen is an obstacle to that peace. Even at the moment of her death, the Queen refuses to repent of anything except for the fact that "the evils she hatched were not effected" (5.5.60). According to the doctor, she "grew shameless desperate" and "died despairing" (5.5.58–61). Her refusal to ask for forgiveness excludes her from participating in the community that forms in the last scene of the play. Because she and her son do not repent, they die. Once she has been removed, the characters enter into a realm of peace and harmony that foreshadows the Nativity of Christ. The king is reunited with his daughter and his presumed dead sons, and in this atmosphere of forgiveness and restored fellowship, the king, now free of the Queen's evil counsel, decides to continue paying tribute to Rome. The fact that the Queen and her son are the only characters absent from this peaceful end makes clear the disruptive power of the sexual female (and her offspring) and establishes the necessity of her removal.

Conclusion

At the end of each of these plays, the queen dies and patriarchal order is restored. At the end of *Hamlet*, the entire royal family lies dead on the floor. At this point, Fortinbras, a masculine warrior figure, enters and restores order to the land. At the end of *Cymbeline*, the king, no longer under his wife's control, agrees to pay tribute to Rome and inaugurates an era of peace concurrent with the birth of Christ. In *Titus Andronicus*, Tamora makes literal her role as devouring mother before dying by Titus's blade, and Lucius takes the throne and restores order to Rome, burying his dead and tossing Tamora over the wall to be eaten by the beasts and the birds. Ultimately, no matter how powerful these dramatic queens are, no matter how transgressive and dangerous, they all must die, and the patriarchal order must be restored. Interestingly, the move from allegedly transgressive queens back to patriarchal order parallels the scene played out in the streets of London as James entered the city. Unlike in the plays, however, the death of the female ruler and the return of patriarchal rule in England did not end the debate/discussion about queenship. Concern about women's bodies, nature, and the body politic continued to haunt and intrigue the nation throughout James's rule and beyond.

Notes

1. Mike Ashley, *British Kings and Queens* (New York: Carroll and Graf Publishers, 1998).
2. Carole Levin, *The Heart and Stomach of a King: Elizabeth I and the Politics of Sex and Power* (Philadelphia: University of Pennsylvania Press, 1994), p. 77.
3. For more on Catherine de Medici, see the essay by Kruse in this collection.
4. All quotations from these texts come from *The Riverside Shakespeare*, ed. G. Blakemore Evans et al. (Boston: Houghton Mifflin, 1974).

5. It is worth noting that, in each of the aforementioned plays, Shakespeare's presentation of queenship merely reinforces the negative representations of women popular in the Renaissance. Shakespeare does not always present female rule in this manner, however. In *Antony and Cleopatra*, for example, Shakespeare challenges conventional representations and complicates contemporary notions about female sovereignty and female sexuality.
6. That this was a major concern is evident from the terms of the 1554 marriage treaty between Mary I and Philip. The provisions of the treaty, which limited Philip's political power in England, were ratified in 1554 in an Act of Parliament, which "declared that Mary's rule was to be as authoritative as that of a male monarch" (428). Unfortunately, neither the treaty nor the act could prevent Philip from influencing Mary. In fact, Philip's attempts to gain control were "hindered chiefly by Parliament" because "the queen herself wished he were more powerful" (Constance Jordan, "Women's Rule in Sixteenth-Century Political Thought," *Renaissance Quarterly*, 40.3 [1987]: 428.)
7. Jordan, "Women's Rule," p. 425.
8. Jordan, "Women's Rule," p. 432.
9. Jordan, "Women's Rule," p. 430.
10. Jordan, "Women's Rule," p. 439.
11. Theodora Jankowski, "'As I am Egypt's Queen': Cleopatra, Elizabeth I, and the Female Body Politic," *Assays: Critical Approaches to Medieval and Renaissance Texts*, 5 (1989): 93.
12. Alan Smith, *The Emergence of the Nation State: The Commonwealth of England 1529–1660* (Harlow: Longman, 1984), p. 78.
13. Levin, p. 82.
14. Levin, pp. 168–69.
15. Carol Chillingsworth Rutter, *Enter the Body: Women and Representation on Shakespeare's Stage* (London: Routledge, 2001), p. 98.
16. According to Sara Mendelson and Patricia Crawford, "Medical theories gave substance to the Old Testament view that a menstruating woman was polluted and polluting" (21). One medical theory speculated that "because women could not purify their blood, as men could, by exercise and heat, they accumulated the impure blood which they shed monthly" (21).
17. David Underdown, *Revel, Riot and Rebellion: Popular Politics and Culture in England 1603–1660* (Oxford: Oxford University Press, 1985), p. 39.
18. Mendelson and Crawford, p. 69.
19. Underdown, p. 39.
20. At least one account credits Semiramis with ordering the death of her husband, and, after his death, taking numerous lovers from her army, "killing them to make way for their replacements." (Dorothea Kehler, "'That Ravenous Tiger Tamora': *Titus Andronicus*'s Lusty Widow, Wife, and M/other," in *Titus Andronicus: Critical Essays*, ed. Philip C. Kolin [New York and London: Garland Publishing, 1995], p. 321.)
21. Alan Sommers, "'Wilderness of Tigers': Structure and Symbolism in *Titus Andronicus*," in *Titus Andronicus: Critical Essays*, ed. Philip C. Kolin (New York and London: Garland Publishing, 1995), p. 116.

22. David Willbern, "Rape and Revenge in Titus Andronicus," in *Titus Andronicus: Critical Essays*, ed. Philip C. Kolin (New York and London: Garland Publishing, 1995), p. 174.
23. Mendelson and Crawford, p. 29.
24. Janet Adelman, "'Man and Wife Is One Flesh': *Hamlet* and the Confrontation with the Maternal Body," in *Hamlet*, ed. Susanne L. Wofford (Boston: Bedford Books, 1994), p. 258. Originally published in Janet Adelman, *Suffocating Mothers: Fantasies of Maternal Origin in Shakespeare's Plays, "Hamlet" to "The Tempest"* (New York: Routledge, 1992).
25. Steven Mullaney, "Mourning and Misogyny: *Hamlet, The Revenger's Tragedy*, and the Final Progress of Elizabeth I, 1600–1607," *Shakespeare Quarterly*, 45 (1994): 149.
26. Dorothea Kehler, "The First Quarto of *Hamlet*: Reforming Widow Gertred," *Shakespeare Quarterly*, 46 (1995): 399–400.
27. Theodora Jankowski, *Women in Power in Early Modern Drama* (Urbana and Chicago: University of Illinois Press, 1992), p. 36.
28. Although much critical discussion has been devoted to the male fear of replacement and subsequent anxiety about remarried widows, it is worth noting that this fear of being forgotten was not strictly the concern of the male. In a world where diseases killed many and childbirth was a major cause of death, many women must have shared the concern that Margaret Cavendish recorded in her autobiography: "I hope my readers will not think me vain for writing my life...I write it for my own sake.... Lest after-ages should mistake, in not knowing I was daughter to one Master Lucas of St John's...second wife to the Lord Marquis of Newcastle; for, my lord having had two wives, I might easily have been mistaken, especially if I should die and my lord marry again." (Elspeth Graham et al., *Her Own Life: Autobiographical Writings By Seventeenth-Century Englishwomen* [London and New York: Routledge, 1989], p. 99.)
29. Interestingly, both Claudius and Gertrude contaminate their world; he brings death through Cain's sin, and she brings sexual impurity through Eve's sin. As Janet Adelman points out, according to this analogy, Gertrude's sin would be the more serious of the two. After all, according to Renaissance theology, Eve's fall brought sin into the world and, therefore, caused Cain's iniquity.
30. Adelman, p. 257.

"Honoured Hippolyta, Most Dreaded Amazonian": The Amazon Queen in the Works of Shakespeare and Fletcher

Jo Eldridge Carney

English and continental literature from the late Middle Ages well into the seventeenth century includes numerous references to Amazon queens, from Christine de Pizan's *The Book of the City of Ladies* in 1405 to Thomas Heywood's *Exemplary Lives...of the Nine Most Worthy Women* in 1640 and Thomas D'Urfey's *A Commonwealth of Women* in 1685.[1] Amazon legends acquired particular topicality in the sixteenth century when explorers of the Americas and Africa recounted stories of alleged Amazonian tribes in the New World; Elizabethan playwrights were quick to incorporate the figure of the exotic Amazon into several of their dramatic productions.[2] Though the particulars of the legends varied, the Amazons were reputed to be warrior women who burned off one breast to allow for more skillful archery;[3] mated with men enthusiastically albeit for reproductive purposes only; raised their daughters but surrendered their sons, or killed them, or, even worse—forced them to perform domestic duties; and finally, lived in all-female communities. Any one of these behaviors would have challenged contemporary notions about the nature of the ideal woman; in toto, the description of the Amazon woman provided Elizabethans with a paradigm of female monstrosity. In a few cases, the Amazon myth was called up in a more positive fashion: for example, poets exploited Amazon references to emphasize Elizabeth as martial queen in connection with the Armada threat,[4] but in general, even Elizabethan iconography eschewed Amazonian association. Far more frequently, the figure of the Amazon was appropriated to represent violation of the natural order.

For some early modern authors, it was the notion of the military prowess of the Amazon woman that signaled transgression; for others, it was the Amazon's exotic otherness that was compelling; yet others were drawn to her unnatural rejection of domesticity. For Shakespeare and his sometime collaborator, John Fletcher, what seemed most intriguing and threatening about the Amazon legend was the notion of a female community ruled by a queen, a government that bore semblance to paradigms of monarchy with which they were familiar. Amazonian society was not without its own hierarchy: these self-sufficient women were led by a queen, a queen who ruled successfully without a king. That women could thrive in a separate world without men was clearly a threat to conventional cultural and political ideologies. Thus, Shakespeare and Fletcher introduce the Amazon queen into their works only to erase her, or, more specifically, to subsume her into the larger world of orthodox patriarchy. In their works, the power of the Amazonian ruler gives way to a less subversive model of queenship: the queen is vanquished, and she and the female community she represents are forced to accept a supporting role in a world ruled by men. This strategy can be traced through Shakespeare's *A Midsummer Night's Dream* (ca. 1595) to Shakespeare and Fletcher's *The Two Noble Kinsmen* (ca. 1613) and then to Fletcher's *The Sea Voyage* (ca. 1622): a sequence of plays that begins in comedy and ends in caricature.

In *A Midsummer Night's Dream*, the subjugation of Hippolyta and her Amazonian past provides a subtle but insistent backdrop for the ultimate erasure of female community and power in the play. Heterosexual relationships and the promise of fruitful marriage strike the note of generic comic triumph in the end, and while the friendships of men are not threatened, homosocial relationships of women have been silenced. The power of the queen figure has also been erased, except for the power associated with procreation. In *The Two Noble Kinsmen* anxiety about female relationships and appropriate queenship figures even more prominently: thus, as this play also ends in a triumph of heterosexual marriage and male homosocial resolution, the concomitant defeat of female community and female rule is even more dramatic. In *The Sea Voyage*, the concept of female community and rule is presented as both implausible and undesirable: the women no longer need to be coerced or persuaded to abandon their same-sex and self-governed community; rather, they are practically begging to be conquered and subdued. In short, the status quo is so compelling that the queen ultimately abdicates and the pseudo-Amazons turn themselves in.

Chaucer's *The Knight's Tale* provided Shakespeare with the mythological framing of *A Midsummer Night's Dream*: the play, like Chaucer's tale, begins with the imminent wedding celebration of Theseus, ruler of Athens, and Hippolyta, Amazon queen. With his now (in)famous pronouncement, "Hippolyta, I wooed thee with my sword / And won thy love doing thee injuries, / But I will wed thee in another key" (1.1.16–17),[5] Theseus simultaneously acknowledges and suppresses his bride's martial past.[6] Moreover, his reference to their upcoming nuptials— "*I* will wed *thee*"—is not a claim of mutuality; rather, the subjective and objective pronouns signal domination. Theseus's authority is immediately reasserted in the same scene in his arbitration of the dispute between Egeus and his daughter, Hermia. Theseus, not surprisingly, rules in favor of Egeus's right to enforce Hermia's marriage to Demetrius, though he offers Hermia death or a religious vocation as alternatives to enforced marriage: "Either to die the death or to abjure / Forever the society of men" (1.1.65–66). Theseus then disparages female community in his description of the cloistered life as "barren" and "fruitless." He seems as unable to imagine that a society of celibate women could provide an appealing option as he is unable to imagine Hermia's unnatural resistance to her father's demands. Throughout this interchange, Hippolyta has been present, but silent, for Theseus turns back to her and asks, "Come, my Hippolyta. What cheer, my love?" (1.1.122). His question implies that Hippolyta disapproves of his decision to rule against Hermia. Theseus does not ask for her opinion; he only asks her acquiescence. Hippolyta's relative silence, however, speaks volumes. Her seeming lack of "cheer" suggests that she sympathizes with Hermia's plight; indeed, the society of women that Theseus denigrates recalls the very same-sex community from which Hippolyta was severed by Theseus's sword. Yet, even though Hippolyta refrains from supporting Theseus, she does not speak up to defend Hermia. Notions of female solidarity have seemingly bowed to the sword as well.[7]

Hippolyta does not appear again until Act IV, as she and Theseus ride out to the hunt. The Amazons were noted for their accomplished hunting skills, so it is not surprising that Hippolyta would indulge in a nostalgic recollection of a hunting episode with Hercules, Cadmus, and their famous "hounds of Sparta." This is the only time in the play that Hippolyta invokes her past life. Theseus, rather than inviting her to speak of her experience further, immediately points out that his hunting dogs are also Spartan bred and are superior to any other dogs. A small moment, perhaps, but it is another instance of Theseus's silencing of his queen, his erasure of her past Amazonian life, and his own self-promotion.

By the end of the play, Hippolyta appears to be generally resigned to her place in Theseus's kingdom, yielding to the decisions of her husband

and ruler. While Demetrius, Lysander, and Theseus banter amiably, there is no verbal exchange among the women and in fact, Helena and Hermia speak no lines at all in the final act. And while Hippolyta briefly disagrees with Theseus about the young lovers' "story of the night" and then jokes about the rude mechanicals' play, her resistance is brief. Ultimately, Hippolyta is only the queen to Theseus's king: Athens must be peopled and her purpose, we are reminded at the end of the play, is to go the "bridebed...and issue there create" (5.1.379–81).

But the felicitous tone at the end is surely undercut by the fact that legends of Theseus would have predetermined what that issue was: the son of Theseus and Hippolyta was the handsome Hippolytus. After Hippolyta's death, Theseus marries Phaedra, who falls in love with her stepson; Hippolytus's rejection of her results in both his own violent death at the instigation of Theseus and in Phaedra's suicide. We cannot know to what extent Shakespeare's audience would have recalled the Hippolytus legend as the fairies offer their fertility blessing at the end of *A Midsummer Night's Dream*, but clearly Shakespeare had Hippolytus in mind in the naming of his Amazon queen. Many sources refer to the Hippolyta figure as Antiopa; in conflating the two figures and naming his Amazon as he does, Shakespeare seems to be hinting at the more ominous results of the Amazon conquest.[8]

Indeed, many critics have pointed out that Shakespeare's audience would have recognized the minatory undertones throughout *A Midsummer Night's Dream*, suggested in large part by the familiar legends of Theseus. Shakespeare's debt to Chaucer is clear, but he also relied on Plutarch's *Lives* and Ovid's *Metamorphoses*; from all three sources, Theseus emerges as a victorious and illustrious hero, but one still plagued by a history of faulty judgment and betrayals of women.[9] Theseus's exploits include the seduction, rape, kidnapping, and abandonment of a series of women; the fact that Oberon refers to many of them—Perigenia, Aegles, Ariadne, and Antiopa—in his argument with Titania suggests that Theseus's less than admirable track record with women had not been overlooked by Shakespeare.

In *A Midsummer Night's Dream*, it is the subjection of Hippolyta that seems to matter—for otherwise, she plays a small role. Theseus's conquest of Hippolyta provides Shakespeare with an apt parallel to both Egeus's control of Hermia and Oberon's domination over his queen, Titania. Hippolyta's former community of women also parallels the girlhood friendship of Helena and Hermia as well as Titania's friendship with the changeling boy's mother. But by the play's end, Hippolyta and Titania have left behind their female communities as well as their power;

they have been subsumed into their roles as consorts: in the final scene, Titania joins Oberon and Puck in blessing Hippolyta's ill-fated marriage bed. And while Hermia achieves her desire to marry Lysander, her satisfaction is not without considerable cost to her friendship with Helena and her own loss of voice. The female community, evoked by Amazonian mythology, is successfully erased and subsumed under a secure heterosexual patriarchy that can allow for homosocial bonding among men but not among women. Just as every Jack needs his Jill, every king needs a queen, but a queen who will acquiesce and reinforce—and perpetuate through her procreative role—his own monarchy.

When Shakespeare returns to *The Knight's Tale* almost twenty years later in his collaboration with John Fletcher, the Amazon figure yields an even greater opportunity to examine the issue of the place of female power and community within a male world. When Shakespeare and Fletcher wrote this play, James had been on the throne for almost a decade, but the specter of female rule still loomed large in the collective memory of early modern society. In *The Two Noble Kinsmen*, the Amazon queen Hippolyta is given a somewhat larger voice and role as well as the female companionship of another Amazon via her relationship with her sister, Emilia. *The Two Noble Kinsmen* does not, however, ultimately endorse or celebrate the female community of these women. Even more emphatically than in *A Midsummer Night's Dream*, this play clearly brings the issue of same-sex friendship and community to the forefront of the play, only to eliminate the possibility of sustaining female friendship in a world of romantic relationships and marriage. Likewise, the play introduces the example of queenship only to diminish the power of female monarchy and emphasize the procreative role of queens.

As in *A Midsummer Night's Dream, The Two Noble Kinsmen* opens with the imminent nuptials of Theseus and Hippolyta, but here the wedding ceremony is abruptly interrupted by the arrival of three widowed queens who seek Theseus's help in defending their husbands' honor.[10] Though quite an assembly of queens, this is no monstrous regiment; they are not asserting their power as monarchs or consorts, they are only acting as good wives, seeking proper burial rites for their lords who were slain in war. Immediately, they turn to both Hippolyta and Emilia for help in convincing Theseus to adopt their cause. In an appeal to Hippolyta, the second queen first asks the Amazon queen to help, "For your mother's sake / And as you wish your womb may thrive with fair ones" (1.1.26–27).[11] This request provides a pointed reference to Hippolyta's female heritage but it also reminds Hippolyta of her present function as queenly vessel. The second queen then evokes Hippolyta's warrior past, but, perhaps not surprisingly, she does not ask Hippolyta for help on the battlefield:

> Honoured Hippolyta,
> Most dreaded Amazonian, that hast slain
> The scythe-tusked boar; that with thy arm, as strong
> As it is white, wast near to make the male
> To thy sex captive, but that this thy lord,
> Born to uphold creation in that honour
> First nature styled it in, shrunk thee into
> The bound thou wast o'erflowing, at once subduing
> Thy force and thy affection. (1.1.77–85)

This grieving queen does not merely ask Hippolyta for assistance: she specifically calls upon the Amazon queen's martial past but then immediately evokes her conquered status. Hippolyta may once have been as powerful as she is beautiful, but her days of active queenship are over. The second queen explains that the subjection of Hippolyta was necessary, for the Amazon queen was "o'erflowing" the bounds of nature; indeed, it was Theseus's task to conquer Hippolyta and "uphold creation" by restoring the proper hierarchy; clearly, the Amazon community is seen as a violation of natural order.

The widowed queen is thus evoking conventional ideology in which the hierarchical structure of the family was ideally modeled after public order. In *A Bride-bush: Or, A Direction for Married Persons* (1617) the Puritan preacher William Whately set forth the popular view on the need for "a man's keeping his authority" in familial structure: "... be it known that every man is bound to maintain himself in that place in which his Maker hath set him... he must not suffer this nature of order to be inverted... it is not humility but baseness to be ruled by her whom he should rule."[12] Whately's was only one of many voices in early modern England who spoke against the unnatural rule of queens.[13] In conquering Hippolyta and establishing himself as ruler, Theseus was fulfilling his duty in reestablishing the appropriate world order "that first nature styled it in." It is significant that it is another queen who is advising Hippolyta how to act appropriately; as much as we might want to view this scene—with five female characters on the stage—as a depiction of female community, it instead serves as an example of queenship being relegated to its proper place: we are wives and mothers, not rulers in our own right, the grieving queen seems to warn Hippolyta, and our duty is to our husbands.

The widowed queen further advises Hippolyta to plead on their behalf, reminding her to be soft-spoken and tearful—in other words, appropriately feminine: "Speak't in a woman's key; like such a woman / As any of us three; weep ere you fail" (1.1.93–94). Hippolyta agrees to plead on their behalf, but adds that she "had as lief trace this good action with you / As that whereunto I am going..." (1.1.102–03). Hippolyta acknowledges that she would happily be soldier rather than bride. Immediately, however, she adds that she is, nonetheless, going to her nuptials willingly: Hippolyta seems to be caught uncomfortably between her past and her present status, between her willingness to help the queens by taking on the task herself and her awareness that she must resign herself to her imminent position as consort to Theseus. While it might be argued that this appeal from the queens to Hippolyta and Emilia suggests a certain female solidarity, and while both women ultimately plead on the queens' behalf, Hippolyta is also distancing herself from the community of women and from her former abilities by transferring the task to Theseus, a task that she could have performed herself in her previous life as an Amazon. Again, the community of women is assimilated—reluctantly—into the larger world of male rule. The widows serve as the appropriate paradigm for queenship, not Hippolyta.

When Theseus departs to fight on behalf of the widowed queens, Hippolyta invokes her own warrior past in the service of recognizing that battle is important for Theseus: "We have been soldiers and we cannot weep / When our friends don their helms..." (1.3.18–19). Likewise, her same-sex friendships help her to understand Theseus's friendship with Pirithous. It is as though her past experiences as Amazon are only worthy insofar as they enable her to accept her husband's need for homosocial bonding and marital experience.[14] Her ties to the Amazon life are now relegated to the past and her task is now to maintain her place in Theseus's heart. The younger Emilia, however, still speaks wistfully of female community and of her childhood friend, Flavinia:

> You talk of Pirithous' and Theseus' love.
> Theirs has more ground, is more maturely seasoned,
> More buckled with strong judgement, and their needs
> The one of th'other may be said to water
> Their entangled roots of love—but I
> And she I sigh and spoke of were things innocent,
> Loved for what we did... (1.3.55–61)

Emilia's eloquent evocation of female friendship, reminiscent of Helena's appeal to Hermia in *A Midsummer Night's Dream*, concludes with her insistence "that the true love 'tween maid and maid may be / More than in sex dividual" (1.3.81–82). Emilia later appeals to the altar of Diana to rescue her from imminent marriage: "I am bride habited, but maiden hearted" (5.1.150–51). Diana does not answer her pleas, and Hippolyta chides Emilia that her desire to remain chaste and unmarried is "sickly appetite." At this point, Hippolyta is herself fully subdued; she has surrendered her own role as Amazon queen and is prepared for her role as Theseus's queen consort. As Emilia is sent off to be claimed as a wife to one of the kinsmen, Hippolyta comforts her with the reminder to "weep not" for "wench, it must be"—Hippolyta's tone is clearly one of resignation rather than enthusiasm. Even more so than in *A Midsummer Night's Dream*, this Hippolyta seems to be trying to resign herself to her fate and attempting to persuade Emilia to accept hers, but there is small joy in the process. Ironically, Emilia's presence in the play contributes little to an atmosphere of female companionship, since the community of women is so clearly compelled to yield to male desire and the demands of marriage. The friendship of the eponymous kinsmen is also tested against the demands of heterosexual romance, but their differences are resolved in the end; likewise, the friendship of Theseus and Pirithous suffers no damage. What the Amazon women must sacrifice from their previous lives, the men are able to maintain. Female community and authority, represented by the Amazonian lifestyle, has been conquered and eliminated. Not only has Hippolyta been conquered, but Emilia also has been won in battle, "the prize," according to Theseus. Emilia's exclamation, "Is this winning?" (5.3.138) is only superseded by her more haunting comment, "I am extinct" (5.3.20).

By 1622, Fletcher was still intrigued by the Amazons, for he returns to the subject in his comedy, *The Sea Voyage*.[15] This less familiar work calls for a brief summary. The play begins with echoes of *The Tempest*: a ship wrecks near a small, barren island; the passengers, a group of French pirates, survive, though they have lost all of their provisions and their treasure. With this group of men, there is a woman, Aminta, who has been captured by one of the Frenchmen, Albert; just as Theseus conquered Hippolyta and then married her, Albert abducted Aminta and then became her lover. His rapacious behavior seems to be forgiven when he vows to remedy his crime against Aminta by finding her long lost brother, Raymond. On this very island, the shipwrecked men encounter two Portuguese men who were forced from their homes by these French pirates' fathers; after distracting the French men with treasure, the Portuguese manage to escape with the French ship.

To help the stranded and starving group, Albert swims to a nearby island in search of food; this island happens to be inhabited by a group of self-proclaimed Amazons, and it is, perhaps not surprisingly, a more fertile landscape. These women are actually the relatives of the Portuguese exiles from the previous island; they were separated from their husbands at sea and their ship foundered on this island that had at one time been occupied by Amazons. Not realizing that their husbands are stranded on the nearby island, the women decide to adopt the lifestyle of the Amazons and they agree "never to look on man but as a monster" (2.2.208). Like Aristophanes's Lysistrata, the self-proclaimed queen Rossella preaches to the younger women about the evils of men:

> Have I not taught thee
> The falsehood and the perjuries of men?
> On whom, but for a woman to shew pity,
> Is to be cruel to her selfe; the soveraignty
> Proud and imperious men usurp upon us,
> We conferre on our selves, and love those fetters
> We fasten to our freedomes." (2.2.192–98)

Rossella reminds her band of women that fortune brought them to this very island, once inhabited by Amazons, for a reason; surely they are meant to emulate the lifestyle of the female government and community and rethink their places in the hierarchy of power.

However, the younger women are beginning to rebel and long for male companionship. When Albert arrives on the Amazons' island, the women are thrilled; they are even happier when they discover that there are more men who survived the shipwreck. Rossella finally agrees to allow the women to "choose a husband and enjoy his company a month" but, in imitation of the Amazons, this mating is to be for procreative purposes only.[16] Eventually Rossella's own long-lost husband finds his way back to the island and Rossella—who had so fiercely defended the Amazonian life—now quickly abandons the error of her ways. Ostensibly, all ends well as the couples go off to couple.

Whereas in *A Midsummer Night's Dream* and *The Two Noble Kinsmen*, the Amazonian culture is gradually erased and subsumed into the larger heterosexual culture, here the Amazon community seems doomed from the beginning, for the women seem less threatening than ludicrous. The queen here is not a real queen, but a ruler who claims seniority and appoints herself monarch and the Amazons are only would-be Amazons. Our first encounter with the alleged Amazons is when we first see three women—Hippolyta, Juletta, and Crocale—who are half-heartedly attempting to hunt a stag that easily manages to escape them. Hippolyta bears little resemblance to her counterparts in the previous plays; unlike Hippolyta in *A Midsummer Night's Dream*, this Hippolyta and her companions admit that they are incompetent hunters. Fletcher's Amazon women appear to be caricatures of their predecessors, particularly as they begin to rail against their celibate lives. Crocale complains:

> The strictness of our Governess that forbids us
> On pain of death the sight and use of men,
> Is more than tyranny: for her self, shee's past
> Those youthfull hearts, and feeles not the want
> Of that which young maids long for. (2.2.22–26)

Rossella, presumably being older and therefore less desirous of sexual encounters, apparently cannot understand the libido of youth. Hippolyta agrees with Crocale and adds that she herself was not "made for this single life" and that rather than spend her time in the typical Amazonian pastime of hunting, she would like to *be* the hunted: "... nor do I love hunting so, / But that I had rather be the Chace than the hunted" (2.2.35–36). This desperate longing is a dramatic contrast to Hippolyta's pride in her hounds of Sparta and in her own hunting ability in *A Midsummer Night's Dream*.

Crocale then recounts her previous night's dream of a "sweet young man" who "stole slylie to my cabin, all unbrac'd / Took me in his arms and kiss'd me twenty times" (2.2.59–60). Crocale continues:

> Lord, what a man is this thought I
> To doe this to a mayd!
> Yet then for my life I could not wake.
> The youth, a little danted, with a trembling hand
> Heav'd up the clothes. (2.2.62–66)

This dream, entirely transparent in its erotic longing, reminds us that we have come a long way from *The Two Noble Kinsmen* and Emilia's reluctance to "love any that's called man" and her desperate appeal at the altar of Diana. Juletta and Hippolyta take obvious vicarious pleasure in Crocale's dream; this scene marks an occasion of female companionship, but the focus of their discussion is their intense longing for male lovers, not their friendship with each other or their present female community.[17]

That longing is soon satisfied when Albert swims ashore; Crocale's response is that he "is a handsome beast / Would we had more o' the breed" (2.2.73–74). Queen Rossella's young daughter Clarinda arrives soon after; having grown up on the island among women, Clarinda has no recollection of men. Her response, "what a brave shape it has," (2.2.113) clearly echoes the pronouncement of Shakespeare's Miranda: "Oh brave new world, that has such people in it." Clarinda is immediately smitten with Albert and revives him from his exhausted, swooning state. When Rossella arrives and finds her daughter in raptures over a man, she quickly reminds Clarinda that men are the monstrous species, an interesting inversion of the popular assumption that the Amazons were monstrous aberrations of nature. Clarinda, however, rebels against her mother's claims and repudiates the Amazon life of celibacy, reminding her mother that without men, the world would only be peopled with beasts. Clarinda's abdication of the Amazonian lifestyle is echoed by Hippolyta's passionate and determined claim, "We must and will have men" (2.2.216).

When Albert affirms that there are more survivors on the nearby island, Rossella agrees that her company of women can meet with the men, but only for the requisite one-month mating period. The need to populate the earth was a convenient argument to persuade Rossella to allow the women male company, but in fact the young ladies seem far more interested in sexual activity as an end in itself. In the subsequent scenes, the plot turns to the appropriate pairing up of the men and women, replete with numerous references to sexual satisfaction. A good deal of bawdy humor occurs at the expense of Rossella, who repeatedly urges the younger women to forego the company of men. But when one of the sailors claims attraction to Rossella, insisting, "I must and will enjoy you" (3.1.333) she responds flirtatiously, "I like your wooing and your discourse" (3.1.362). Even Rossella's devotion to the celibate life is short-lived in the face of such irresistible courting. Interestingly, this particular sailor, Tibalt, claims that Rossella's age appeals to him; he wants to choose an older, "barren" mate, "For though I like the sport, I do not love / To Father children" (3.1.329–30). It could not be stated more emphatically that the sexual pairing is not for procreative reasons.

In addition to the ubiquitous references to sexual appetite, the play abounds in references to food and hunger. The shipwrecked men are dying for want of meat and drink and the women are starving for the company of men; indeed, references to the desire for food and the desire for sexual satisfaction are often conflated. At one point, some of the shipwrecked men contemplate the sleeping figure of Aminta and consider cannibalism. One of the shipmen, Lamure, claims that there is precedent for cannibalistic practice:

> Of such restoring meates, we have examples,
> Thousand examples and allow'd for excellent;

Women that have eate their Children,
Men their slaves, nay their brothers: but these are nothing;
Husbands devoured their wives (they are their chattels). (3.1.100–04)

Lamure's examples, interestingly enough, all refer to examples of cannibalism in familial relationships; what might have been considered savage and uncivilized has now become domesticated and common. The men then proceed to argue over what delicate piece of meat they will each devour: one sailor claims that "shee's young and tydie, / In my conscience she'll eat delicately; / Just like young Pork a little lean" (3.1.106–08) to which another replies that she may need to be salted and powdered first. Their ravenous designs on Aminta are only prevented with the arrival of some of the other sailors who charge them with villainy and devilry. Grotesque in its own right, this scene constitutes a curious inversion of Amazonian savagery, since the Amazons themselves were sometimes charged with cannibalistic practice.[18] Throughout the play, Fletcher appears to be diluting the Amazonian threat: just as the women on the island are only pretending to be Amazons, some of the practices associated with them are now displaced onto the men. The women are described as essentially dainty and weak creatures, while hunger, predation, and hunting are appropriated as expected male behavior. When Rossella commands the women to imprison and guard the men, their female power resides in the ability to provide or withhold food. The men are portrayed at the point of starvation while the women are described as equally hungry—but hungry for male companionship.

Not only does heterosexual desire take over the community of women, but competition over the men introduces an element of discord among the women. Clarinda had promised friendship and protection to Aminta, but the sisterly vows are forgotten in the face of their rivalry over Albert. Ultimately, we see no evidence that the women have taken pleasure or solace in their commonwealth of women, and in fact, they are eager to leave their paradise island. They only become Amazons in the first place out of revenge for loss of their husbands, not out of a desire for autonomy or female community. Even Rossella, the self-appointed queen, is willing to "give up her selfe / Her power and joyes, and all, to you, / To be discharged of 'em as burthensome / Wellcome in any shape..." (5.4.97–100) and return to her proper place in the world as Sebastian's wife when he reappears at the end of the play. Sebastian suggests that the voyage has been a nightmare, but now all is well and "wee'l returne' To our severall homes" (5.4.113–14). Order has been restored and everyone can resume his and her rightful places in society.

The Amazon community of women, according to Fletcher, has been caricatured, diluted, and ultimately eliminated as an embodiment of threatening female power, for *The Sea Voyage* portrays a world in which it is inconceivable that women could survive without the society and governing power of men.

Notes

1. For an encyclopedic survey of Amazon references in sixteenth-century literature, see Celeste Turner Wright, "The Amazons in Elizabethan Literature," *Studies in Philology*, 37 (July 1940): pp. 433–56. See also Simon Shepherd, *Amazons and Warrior Women: Varieties of Feminism in Seventeenth-Century Drama* (New York: St Martin's Press, 1981). Shepherd's book includes some discussion of the Amazon figure in early modern literature, though not as much as his title would suggest. See also Kathryn Schwarz, *Tough Love: Amazon Encounters in the English Renaissance* (Durham: Duke University Press, 2000). Schwarz's excellent study examines representations of Amazons in the Jacobean masque, in *The Fairie Queene*, and in *The Arcadia*, as well as in Shakespeare's plays.
2. See Jean E. Gagen, *The New Woman: Her Emergence in English Drama, 1600–1730* (New York: Twayne Publishers, 1954), for a brief overview of the Amazon figure in seventeenth-century drama. Gabriele Bernhard Jackson discusses Shakespeare's use of the Amazon tradition in his representation of Joan of Arc in *Henry IV, Part I*: "Topical Ideology: Witches, Amazons, and Shakespeare's Joan of Arc," *English Literary Renaissance*, 18 (Winter 1988): pp. 40–65. See also Louis Montrose, *The Purpose of Playing: Shakespeare and the Cultural Politics of the Elizabethan Theatre* (Chicago: University of Chicago Press, 1996), pp. 124–34. Montrose discusses the Amazon tradition in connection to *A Midsummer Night's Dream*: "Amazonian mythology seems symbolically to embody and to control a collective (masculine) anxiety about women's power not only to dominate or to repudiate men but also to create and destroy them."
3. See Gail Kern Paster, *The Body Embarrassed: Drama and Disciplines of Shame in Early Modern England* (Ithaca: Cornell University Press, 1993), for a fascinating discussion of the cultural implications of the Amazonian mastectomy. According to Paster, "The Amazons' significance as ambivalently powerful figures of aggressive, self-determining desire is epitomized by their self-mutilation."
4. Winfried Schleiner discusses Amazonian references to Queen Elizabeth and claims, "Significantly, all the direct Amazon references I have seen relate to the Armada conflict, the most serious challenge to her reign." Schleiner also suggests, "If the references to Elizabeth as an Amazon are few, the main reason may be that she preferred the reputation of a peaceful ruler." "*Divina Virago*: Queen Elizabeth as an Amazon," *Studies in Philology*, 75 (1978): pp. 163–80.
5. All references to *A Midsummer Night's Dream* are from the Bedford/St. Martin's edition, 1999, ed. Gail Kern Paster and Skiles Howard.

This excellent edition also includes a helpful discussion of Amazons in connection to the play, pp. 194–216.

6. It is interesting to note that Theseus's well-known opening line was cut from Michael Hoffman's recent film version of *A Midsummer Night's Dream*. Though regrettable, this omission is in keeping with the film's portrayal of a relatively mild-mannered Theseus.
7. There has been a good deal of discussion of the importance of female friendship and community—or lack thereof—in reference to *A Midsummer Night's Dream*. For example, see Shirley Nelson Garner, "*A Midsummer Night's Dream*: 'Jack Shall Have Jill/Nought Shall Go Ill," *Women's Studies*, 9 (1981): pp. 47–63.
8. On the irony of Oberon's final blessing of the marriage of Theseus and Hippolyta, see Peter Holland, "Theseus' Shadows in *A Midsummer Night's Dream*," *Shakespeare Survey*, 47 (1995), pp. 139–51.
9. For example, see D'Orsay W. Pearson, "'Unkinde Theseus': A Study in Renaissance Mythology," *English Literary Renaissance*, 4 (1974): pp. 276–98.
10. Though Carol Thomas Neeley does not discuss *The Two Noble Kinsmen*, her arguments about interrupted weddings apply to this play. See Neeley, *Broken Nuptials in Shakespeare's Plays* (New Haven: Yale University Press, 1985).
11. All references to *The Two Noble Kinsmen* are from the Arden edition, ed. Lois Potter, 1997.
12. William Whately, *A Bride-Bush; Or, A Direction for Married Persons*, quoted in Lloyd Davis, ed., *Sexuality and Gender in the English Renaissance: An Annotated Edition of Contemporary Documents* (New York: Garland Publishing, 1998), p. 247.
13. For more commentary on early modern pronouncements against female monarchy, see the essays in this collection by Susan Dunn-Hensley and Sid Ray.
14. See Geraldo de Sousa, *Shakespeare's Cross-Cultural Encounters* (New York: St. Martin's Press, 1999). De Sousa makes a similar point, arguing that Hippolyta and Emilia "momentarily project their now-repressed same-sex comradeship on the relationship between Pirithous and Theseus," p. 33. See also Jeanne Addison Roberts, *The Shakespearean Wild: Geography, Genus, and Gender*. (Lincoln: University of Nebraska Press, 1991). Roberts focuses on Theseus's struggle "to come to grips with a central male dilemma, namely, the conflict between his need for the female Wild represented by Venus and his preference for the male Wild of Mars," p. 129.
15. All references to *The Sea Voyage* are from *The Dramatic Works in the Beaumont and Fletcher Canon*, ed. Fredson Bowers, vol. IX (Cambridge: Cambridge University Press, 1994). Massinger also had a hand in *The Sea Voyage*, but the exact nature of the collaboration has been difficult to determine. See Bowers, pp. 7–8.
16. In his description of the Amazon culture in *The Discovery of the Large, Rich, and Beautiful Empire of Guiana*, Sir Walter Raleigh refers to the monthly procreative sessions: they "do accompany with men but once in a year, and for the time of one month. At that time all the kings of the borders assemble, and the queens of the Amazons, and after the queens have chosen the rest cast lots for their valentines. This one month, they feast, dance, and

drink of their wines in abundance, and, the moon being down, they all depart to their own provinces. If they conceive and be delivered of a son, they return him to the father; if of a daughter, they nourish it and retain it...."

17. See Peter Holland, "'Travelling hopefully': the Dramatic Form of Journeys in English in English Renaissance Drama," in *Travel and Drama in Shakespeare's Time*, ed. Jean-Pierre Maquerlot and Michele Willems (Cambridge: Cambridge University Press, 1996). Holland comments briefly on *The Sea Voyage*: "The hungry confrontation with a hostile environment and the impossibility of suppressing heterosexual desire are the play's main concerns...," p. 160.

18. See Michael Hattaway, "'Seeing Things': Amazons and Cannibals," in *Travel and Drama in Shakespeare's Time*, ed. Jeanne-Pierre Maquerlot and Michele Willems (Cambridge: Cambridge University Press, 1996), pp. 179–92.

"No head eminent above the rest": Female Authority in *Othello* and *The Tempest*

Sid Ray

As for the head of the naturall body, the head hath the power of directing all the members of the body to that use which the judgement in the head thinkes most convenient. It may apply sharpe cures, or cut off corrupt members, let blood in what proportion it thinkes fit, and as the body may spare, but yet is all this power ordained by God.
(King James, A Speech to the Lords and Commons of the Parliament at Whitehall, 1609)

Paul, Ephesians 5 sayeth this: ye wyves, submit yourselves unto your husbands, as unto the lorde, For the husband is the wyves heads, like as Christ also is the head of the congregation, ... so let the wives also be in subjection to theyr husbands in all thynges.
(Heinrich Bullinger, *The Christen state of matrimonye*, 1543)

It was my hint to speak—such was my process—
And of the Cannibals that each [other] eat,
The Anthropophagi, and men whose heads
Do grow beneath their shoulders.
(*Othello*, 1.3.142–44)

Othello and *The Tempest* seem unlikely plays to illustrate queenship. They revolve around strong males tyrannizing over females—a wife and a daughter—who display few of the authoritative qualities of Shakespeare's model woman ruler, Elizabeth I. However, the plays do present ways of thinking about female authority that were new, even revolutionary, for an early modern English audience. References in each play to sightings of differently formed humans—men whose heads stand below their shoulders—allow for rethinking the human body as

Sir John Mandeville, Travels (1574)
By permission of the Houghton Library, Harvard University.

a model for political and marital hierarchies. When these references are analyzed in conjunction with the plays' politics, *Othello* and *The Tempest* suggest that, despite early modern beliefs about the unnaturalness of woman rulers, queenship could arise organically in the known world. This suggestion is surprising in light of the plays' bold exhibitions of male power. More significant is the radical political perspective that the differently formed body implies, given that constructions of early modern authority rest on the idea that a human head is and will always be above and thus superior to the human body.[1] This essay will examine early modern marital and political theorists' manipulation of the body metaphor as a way of legitimizing exclusive male rulership and proceed with an analysis of the plays, ultimately demonstrating Shakespeare's subtle undermining of early modern political and social orthodoxy.

Female monarchy, or gynecocracy, was vigorously debated in the early modern period. In *The First Blast of the Trumpet Against the Monstrous Regiment of Women*, published in 1558, John Knox claimed "it is a thing moste repugnant to nature, that women rule and governe over men."[2] His argument rested on St. Paul's dictum that a wife must obey her husband; according to Knox, a woman should never be a magistrate of the people, always being subject first to her spouse. Knox, who wrote his treatise to support the Calvinist reform movement, was not primarily concerned with repudiating the right of a female to inherit the throne but instead with challenging absolutism—the belief that the monarch has been chosen by God and is thus protected from popular will. By focusing on the inferiority of females, however, the Protestant Knox could challenge the "divinely" planned successions of the Catholic queens Mary Tudor and Mary Queen of Scots and motivate Protestant rebels. Though his treatise was directed at the Marys, its argument also applied to the Protestant Elizabeth. Not surprisingly, Elizabeth detested Knox, but during her reign she did little to counter his contention.[3] She remained unmarried, never testing his theories about the incompatibility of marriage and queenship. She resisted being named "head" of state at all, choosing instead the title of "Supreme Governor," while her father, Henry VIII, and her brother, Edward VI, had each been "Supreme Head over the Church of England."[4] Carole Levin theorizes that Elizabeth's decision to forgo being "head" derived, "not only from the idea of the monarch as head but from the perception of blasphemy that a woman could take this role."[5] Elizabeth claimed that her female body natural yielded to her male body politic, reinforcing female subordination to male authority. She often referred to herself as a "prince" or a "king" and famously claimed to rule with the stomach of her father. Elizabeth's deliberate blurring of gendered titles, her self-fashioning as virgin, and her refusal to marry made her an anomalous queen.[6] She avoided the difficult gynococratic questions—how a female monarch would depart from the male monarchical model and whether a married queen was superior or inferior to her husband. Inevitably, Elizabeth's compromise left room for people to imagine, no doubt fearfully, a very different kind of queen: a married one whose ruling authority over both her people and her husband could upset early modern marital and political hierarchies.

In part to curry favor with Elizabeth, John Aylmer, in *An Harborowe for Faithful and Trewe Subjectes* (1559), rebutted Knox's argument against gynocracy: "But because we see by many examples, that by the wholle consent of nacyons, by the ordinaunce of god, and order of lawe, women have reigned and those not a fewe, and as it was thoughte not againste nature: Therefore it canne not bee saide, that by a generall disposition of nature, it hathe bene, and is denyed them to rule."[7] Though queens who ruled in their own right were rare, they did exist: a passel of unhealthy sixteenth-century princes made ruling women more common by this time. In 1500, Queen Isabella had ruled Castile alone for twenty-six years and many other women had ruled by default—as mothers of children unable to rule because of age or imprisonment or as wives of dead kings. Later in the century, Mary of Guise would rule Scotland as regent for her baby daughter who would grow up to be queen of Scotland, if only for a short time. Mary and Elizabeth Tudor, of course, ruled in England for a combined fifty years, though not without opposition.

The reality of queenship in the sixteenth century allowed Aylmer to present a simple and compelling argument: queens exist; therefore they must be natural. But he had to contend with Knox's manipulation of the body metaphor that had by then become ingrained in beliefs about power in both political and domestic spheres. Knox concretized his misogynist abstractions by evoking the analogy of the human body, appropriated from medieval political philosophy and sixteenth-century jurisprudence. In the body paradigm, there can be only one head, and that head has to be male; otherwise the relationship between subject and ruler, wife and husband, is a monstrous one. Knox describes the monstrosity as such: "if her husband will commaund her in the publike weale, she being the magistrate, and not he: she may say to him.... Law make my husband to obey, for heare he is not my hed, but my subject."[8] In this situation, the husband is paradoxically a head and no head to his queenly wife. Knox continues: "For who wolde not judge that bodie to be a [m]onstre, where there was no head eminent above the rest, but that the eyes were in the handes, the tongue and mouth beneth in the belie, and the ears in the feet.... And no lesse monstrous is the bodie of that commonwelth, where a woman beareth empire. For ether doth it lack a lawfull heade... or els there is an idol exalted in the place of the true head."[9]

Because to his knowledge humans have only one head, Aylmer could only counter Knox by referring to divine precedent: "[God] sendeth a woman by birth, we may not refuse hir by violence. He stablisheth hir by lawe, we may not remove hir by wronge. He maketh hir a head, we may not make hir a hande or foote."[10] Accepting the body metaphor, Aylmer ignored the husband's paradoxical position as both inferior and superior to his ruling wife, and asserted that a female monarch is simply the head of the body politic whether she is married or not.

For Aylmer and Knox, the link between political and marital rule and the human body was incontrovertible. By extension, the model of a monarchical head governing a body of people was presumed to be as organic and universal as the structure of the human body itself. But the belief that the relationship between a ruler and his people replicates the relationship between the head and the body in every human being had emerged over centuries of writings by political theorists and jurists, which shows that whatever connection exists between the body and politics, it is constructed, or synthetic, rather than organic. Ernst Kantorowicz describes the evolution of the theory, citing Lucas de Penna as an influential jurist who "transferred to the Prince and the state the most important social, organic, and corporational elements normally serving to explain the relations between Christ and the Church—that is, Christ as the groom of the Church, as the head of the mystical body, and as the mystical body itself."[11] After Lucas de Penna came the political theorists John Fortescue and William of Lyndwood who "expounded the organic oneness of the realm, and compared it to that of the human body and its limbs and, with regard to the unanimity of the will and of mutual love, to a corpus *mysticum*."[12] Kantorowicz notes that in "mediaeval England, the marriage metaphor seems to have been all but nonexistent,"[13] but by 1603, King James, fresh to the throne when Shakespeare wrote *Othello*, could famously state without fear of redress, "'What God hath conjoined then, let no man separate.' I am the husband, and all the whole island is my lawful wife; I am the head, and it is my body; I am the shepherd, and it is my flock."[14] He thus indelibly intertwined marital and political power for the people of early modern England.

This head/body basis for authority was, even by 1559, so ingrained that Aylmer missed an obvious opportunity to undermine Knox's stance. If monarchy were considered natural because the relationship between a king and his people replicated the relationship between a husband and his wife, which in turn replicated the relationship between Christ and the Church, which then replicated the anatomical relationship between the head and the body, as dubious and convoluted as that theory was, one way to subvert it would be to posit the existence of natural bodies whose parts related to each other in different ways. Othello, of course, does just that in his "round unvarnished" traveller's tale, and, by his own admission, it is precisely his story of monstrous other bodies that seduces Desdemona (1.3.165–67).[15] Gonzalo does so as well in *The Tempest* when he claims the existence of "such men / Whose heads stood in their breasts" (3.3.46–47), a statement ironically meant to soothe King Alonzo's fears of his vulnerability on the strange isle but which does just the opposite.

In his story, Othello describes exotic places—"anters vast and deserts idle"—and disfigured humans—"And of the Anthropophagi, and men whose head / Grew beneath their shoulders." To that last, Othello says, "these things to hear / Would Desdemona seriously incline" (1.3.140–47). Othello claims to have seen humans whose heads are in a very different relationship to their bodies than was considered the norm. His provocative observations suggest that what is natural and normal in early modern European thought is unnatural and abnormal in other parts of the world. Intriguingly, men whose heads grow beneath their shoulders make possible an inversion of order in which the man as "head" can exist beneath or within the woman as "body" and in which the "head" of state can exist beneath or within the people as the "body." In addition to making female authority a more viable proposition, the differently formed body allows for a more constitutional interpretation of monarchy, something Knox would, ironically, have appreciated. As indicated by the Duke's response to Othello's narrative, "I think this tale would win my daughter too" (1.3.171), such a creature would have had much allegorical resonance for both Desdemona and Shakespeare's audience.

Accounts of men without heads, or whose heads were below their shoulders instead of above them, were not new. Reports had existed in narratives for generations before Shakespeare, from Pliny's *Historia Naturalis* (AD 77) to *The Travels of Sir John Mandeville* (ca. 1355), and they had a history of being regarded allegorically.[16] That Desdemona "inclines" to Othello directly after his promising description of different bodies shows that, unlike those who regarded reports of such monstrous creatures as evidence of God's wrath, she interprets them as evidence of a brave new world. These tales excite Desdemona, increasing her attraction to Othello who, as a Moor, also deviates physically from the European norm. Brabantio recalls that, before meeting Othello, Desdemona was, "So opposite to marriage, that she shunn'd / The wealthy curled darlings of our nation" (1.2.67–68). According to her father, she abhorred the very idea of a conventional marriage. Perhaps Desdemona married Othello because with him she saw the possibility of a marriage without hierarchy, a no-headed marriage whose precedent is evoked by Othello's stories of differently formed humans and which is reinforced by his own obvious difference. Desdemona may then be attracted to Othello *because* of his blackness, not despite it. In fact, the heterodoxy of Desdemona's marriage to Othello, figured so visually in their contrasting skin colors, makes it fertile ground for exploring the connections between marital and political authority in early modern thinking.[17]

Indeed, Desdemona is an ambitious, iconoclastic female character. Her position as the sole daughter of a highly influential Senator of

Venice grants her some degree of inherent power and authority before her marriage. Her union with Othello, who claims to "fetch [his] life and being / From men of royal siege" (1.2.21–22) and acts as de facto ruler of Cyprus for most of the play, gives her additional status as the wife of a king-like figure. She displays independence of thought and action, refusing to be ruled by her father, and her lengthy, persuasive speeches before the Senate suggest that she is a burgeoning politician. That Desdemona is heir to her father's wealth and status and has an adventurous, forthright personality would make an unconventional, more equitable marriage appealing to her. In a conventional marriage she would have to transfer her wealth to her husband simply because he is considered the head and she the body beneath him. Desdemona further unsettles prenuptial orthodoxy by eloping with Othello, a "gross revolt" against her father (1.1.132). Desdemona's opposition to customary marriage indicates both a refusal to be confined by it as defined and regulated by her culture and a willingness to cultivate a different kind of marriage, one that she is led to believe exists in the non-European world Othello has inhabited where heads can exist below the shoulders. Her actions before the elopement are certainly unorthodox; she makes the first move in the courtship and is "half the wooer" (1.3.176), according to her father. In fact, like men with heads beneath their shoulders, she goes "Against all rules of nature" (1.3.102) in loving Othello.

Once married, Desdemona behaves as if she can throw the concept of female inferiority to the wind. Othello admits that before the marriage "she wished / That heaven had made her such a man" (1.3.163–64), and when married, she behaves as if she were entitled to male privileges. She tells the Senate of the pleasure she finds with her new husband: "That I did love the Moor to live with him, / My downright violence, and scorn of fortunes, / May trumpet to the world" (1.3.243–45), defying injunctions against women's outspokenness and hinting that she is eager to sleep with him. Early on, Othello reveals that he values Desdemona as a counselor as well as a bedmate, when, knowing they have only an hour before he is dispatched to battle the Turks, he thinks not only of spending the precious time on matters of love, but also on "worldly matter and direction" (1.3.299). Desdemona's request to meet Othello in Cyprus is in and of itself a daring maneuver. Once ensconced in that military outpost, she refers to herself as a soldier, "warrior as I am" (3.4.152), and even braves investigating Cassio's drunken skirmish with Roderigo and Montano in the middle of the night as if it were her business. When Desdemona later reminds Othello that Cassio "Hath ta'en your part" (3.3.73) in what are presumably lovers' quarrels, we discover that Desdemona and Othello have clashed in the past.[18] Desdemona acts the part of a high-ranking officer in the army, or, as Cassio implies when he calls her "our great captain's captain" (2.1.75), even higher than her husband, the general himself.

Greeting her as "my fair warrior" (2.1.182) in Cyprus, Othello appears to play along with Desdemona's claim to authority, and Shakespeare's audience would recall the warrior woman themes attached to Queen Elizabeth as defeater of the Spanish Armada and supposed descendant of Brutus and Arthur. But when Desdemona begins to talk like a Petruchio, planning to dominate Othello in her effort to redeem Cassio—"My lord shall never rest, / I'll watch him tame, and talk him out of patience; / His bed shall seem a school, his board a shrift, / I'll intermingle every thing he does with Cassio's suit" (3.2.22–26)—Othello does not respond in kind as an equal partner, much less a dutiful wife. Desdemona's authority threatens Othello who recognizes its ability to subvert the established hierarchy. He observes, "she might lie by an emperor's side and command him tasks" (4.1.182), imagining a side-by-side spatial relationship with her, rather than the "head over body" one. Where Desdemona believes her dominating behavior to be acceptable, possibly because of Othello's "otherness" and his experiences in distant worlds, the reports of men with heads beneath their shoulders resonate differently for Othello. As the tragedy unfolds and Iago uses all evidence of Desdemona's independence and authority against her—"Our general's wife is now the general" (2.3.310), it is clear that Othello wants Desdemona to keep within the boundaries delineated by conventional European marital ideology—that she as the body be subservient to him as the head.

A steadfast Christian, Othello believes in St. Paul's pronouncement about marital hierarchies. When Desdemona proves to be less of a subject than a ruler, Othello sees the world turning upside-down. Her hot and moist hand needs "A sequester from liberty, fasting and prayer, / Much castigation, exercise devout" (3.4.40–41) to be brought back in line with his Christian ideals. Desdemona misreads Othello's discontent as relating to political matters rather than personal ones and, as a result, her over-reaching plays beautifully into Iago's damning innuendo. The more Desdemona asserts power, the more she appears to be the adulteress Iago claims her to be. Quick to exploit an opportunity, Iago crudely insinuates a connection between a strong-willed woman and her sexual licentiousness: "Foh! one may smell in such a will most rank, / Foul disproportion, thoughts unnatural" (3.3.236–37). By mingling references to the powerful, sexual female body with the idea of bodily disproportion, Iago reminds Othello of proper spousal behavior: it is monstrous for the wife to be dominant.

Here Iago does nothing more than echo what many early modern marriage theorists were preaching. William Whately, in his tract, *A Bride-Bush* (1616), uses language of monstrocity and unnaturalness to describe the dominating wife, evoking a literally deformed human body to make his point:

> Nature hath framed the lineaments of his body to superioritie, and set the print of government in his very face, which is more sterne, and lesse delicate than the womans; he must not suffer this order of nature to be inverted. The Lord in his Word hath intitled him by the name of head: wherefore *hee must not stand lower than the shoulders*; if he doe, doubtlesse it makes a great deformitie in the family. That house is a misshapen house, and (if we may use that terme) a *crump-shouldered, or hutch-backt house*, where the husband hath made himselfe an underling to his wife, and given away his power and *regiment* to his inferiour: without question it is a sinne for a man to come lower, than God hath set him. It is not humilitie, but basenesse, to be ruled by her, whom he should rule. No *Generall* would thanke a *Captaine*, for surrendring his place to some common souldier; nor will God an husband, for suffering his wife to beare the swey (emphasis mine).[19]

Though written a decade after *Othello*, the language of Whately's tract reminds us of Desdemona's pressuring of marital, military, and political hierarchies. More, the "crump-shouldered" marital body eerily resembles Othello's description of men in Africa whose heads grow beneath their shoulders. But unlike Desdemona, Whately sees the deviant marriage as a deformed body, "misshapen," instead of as normal or naturally occurring. His value judgment on "othered" bodies reminds us how blackness necessitates Othello's strict adherence to European principles even as Desdemona challenges them. Whately's language also recalls Knox's invective from his tract against gynecocracy—"For who wolde not judge that bodie to be a monstre, where there was no head eminent above the rest.... And no lesse monstrous is the bodie of that commonwelth, where a woman beareth empire."[20] It appears that the ethnocentric European belief system is stacked against Desdemona's defiance of the perceived natural order.

The other characters in *Othello* ignore the possibility of there being alternative paradigms of rulership, although Iago's dissatisfaction with the system should be noted. When we meet him, Iago chafes at "knee-crooking" and "obsequious bondage" and complains that "Preferment goes by letter and affection / And not by old gradation, where each second / Stood heir to the first" (1.1.35–37). Soldiers would otherwise not be inclined to challenge hierarchy, and the contrast between Desdemona's attempt to be on at least equal terms with her husband and the behavior of the soldiers so bent on following military protocol is striking. Othello challenges the status quo least of all—that is, until he strikes and then kills his wife. As Anthony Gerard Barthelemy writes, "Shakespeare's black Moor never possesses the power or desire to subvert civic and natural order."[21] Even if he wanted to, he could not rule any other way in this culture. Othello knows not to make Antony's mistake of giving his "potent regiment to a trull" (*Antony and Cleopatra*, 3.6.95). To do so would, perhaps, be even more monstrous in the culture than for a black man to marry a white woman against her father's wishes. Indeed, Othello's blackness forces him to tow the line on white European conventions of manliness as well as those of civic and natural order, manliness and authority being intertwined. After Othello's seizure, Iago plays on that connection by asking, "How is it, general? Have you not hurt your head?" (4.1.59), capturing Othello's fall to the ground, his effeminacy as a cuckold, and his wife's dominance in a single, devastating play on words.

Spurred by Iago, Othello over-reacts to Desdemona's insurgency and to her supposed infidelity with Cassio. Initially, he wants to poison her, perhaps literally addressing what he believes to be the crimes of her body. But he opts instead to smother the talkative, "head-strong" Desdemona, attacking her literal head as if her crime were a capital one. His smothering of Desdemona performs the secondary function of silencing her radical words and stopping her seditious political voice. Ultimately, however, this murder is merely a brief and empty victory over the upstart woman.

Although Desdemona dies for her heterodox behavior, her death enables Emilia to exert her own power and transcend the woman's place. Indeed, Shakespeare frames Emilia's defiance of Iago as the legitimate revolt of a wife against her husband. Desperate to prevent his wife from revealing his villainy, Iago orders her away as a superior would an inferior: "Be wise, and get you home" (5.2.223), but she disobeys. In the end, Emilia, who, as Irene Dash has written, resembles the modern-day battered wife, having "no speech" in Act II and stealing for her husband in Act III, renounces all duty to her husband, a duty that Desdemona herself extols in Act I (1.3.180–89), and becomes the authoritative witness against him.[22] She is the body heroically rebelling against the head, dying for truth and justice, values that are, the play tells us, loftier than those of wifely obedience. Emilia's heroism at the end of *Othello* leaves female power and the right to wield power as a female unsmothered and thus uncontained.

Emilia has the final say and, through her, Shakespeare leaves open the natural possibility for women to wield authority, and not simply by default as sixteenth-century queens did. Even so, the tantalizing reference to men with heads below their shoulders seems not to have been included for the sake of women, but to promote a more republican form of government than the model of an absolute head governing over an inferior body. The side-effect is a conferring of more power to women— to defy their husbands, to have equality rather than equity in the marital relationship, to rule with their husbands (if not over them) in political contexts. In *The Tempest*, written about seven years after *Othello*, Shakespeare revisits reports of men with heads beneath their shoulders, showing a continued interest in exploring what are and are not "natural" paradigms of government—marital and political.[23] As in *Othello*, *The Tempest* shows how reports of different forms of government could impact European beliefs about order. But the meaning of the reference in the later play, which was written during a period when King James was marshalling his own absolute power in head/body terms,[24] is more subtle and enigmatic than in *Othello*. The remainder of this essay analyzes *The Tempest*'s reference to men with heads below their shoulders in light of Miranda's status, focusing on dynastic issues and their interplay with the colonial *topos*, both of which involve female power and queens in particular.

Though critics have long noted Miranda's isolation, obedience, and passivity, we often forget that she is born to be a ruling woman. The play's proliferation of puns on "heir," "air," and "hair," do not, after all, relate to Ferdinand alone. Miranda is the sole heir to Prospero's duchy and to his ruling power on the island. When she marries Ferdinand and he inherits his father's kingdom, Miranda will become queen consort, *lessening* her potential to wield power as a woman. Given Milan's vassalage to Naples and the wife's prescribed subordination to her husband, we can hardly expect that Miranda and Ferdinand will rule jointly. English playgoers would no doubt think of Mary's problematic marriage to Philip of Spain and the Knox–Aylmer debate, which would make them believe an equal, joint rulership unlikely or doomed. Miranda, "who [is] ignorant of what [she is]" (1.2.18), seems content with being a pawn, never realizing that her potential power is about to be reduced. Prospero carefully circumscribes her political knowledge; when Miranda hears of other European women in the play, she learns only about their part in a marriage—Claribel's to the King of Tunis,

Miranda's own mother's to Prospero. When Prospero finally informs Miranda that she is his heir and a princess, he does so in a circuitous, detached manner, using third-person narration and conditionality to distance himself from his disclosure:

> Thy mother was a piece of virtue, and
> She said thou wast my daughter; and thy father
> Was Duke of Milan, and his only heir
> And princess no worse issued. (1.2.56–59)

Instead of hailing her power and grooming her for authority, Prospero reinforces her destiny to be a body with her husband as head, most notably when he has the Roman goddesses Juno and Ceres appear at her wedding masque. Together, these goddesses associated with marriage and fertility emphasize Prospero's wish for Miranda to be a *producer* of heirs rather than *his* heir. Meanwhile, the Italian men's many references to "the widow Dido" mock Miranda's (and other women's) birthright and underscore the female ruler's vulnerability to the ambitions of husbands and lovers.[25] That the play was performed at the celebrations prior to the politically expedient marriage of King James's daughter, Lady Elizabeth, to Frederick, the Elector Palatine, further underscores the European response to ruling women—marry them off to dilute their power. Critics have drawn parallels between Princess Elizabeth's marriage to Frederick and Miranda's to Ferdinand. A key difference, however, is that Elizabeth, having younger brothers, was not her father's direct heir. Miranda is, in fact, an only child.[26] Dispossession being a central theme of the play, it is important to remember that Miranda, like Prospero and Caliban, is dispossessed of her authoritative position.

The references to disempowered queens and politically expedient marriages betray the Europeans' fear of female autonomy and rulership. Unlike her European counterparts, the Algerian Sycorax does appear to have been a ruling woman: as Caliban says, "This island's mine, by Sycorax my mother, / Which thou tak'st from me" (1.2.334–35). Her power, which, like a true queen, she only relinquished at death, gives additional credence to the suggestion in *Othello* that, despite European experience, rulership in the new world is not always absolute or male. Prospero describes Sycorax as "grown into a hoop" (1.2.259), a line editors have glossed as meaning she was bent with age.[27] In fact, she may have been hunch-backed, a condition similar to having a head beneath the shoulders, as Whately observes in his marriage tract quoted above. Prospero's harping on Sycorax's physical form, though he never saw her, shows how fearful it is to him. Literally, with a head beneath her shoulders, Sycorax challenges the European "head over body" paradigm in form and function.

Just so, as Gonzalo tells us, the explorers of the new world were reporting back to Europe that indigenous people were governing themselves in divergent ways—some of which not only challenge the head/body "norm" of government but which also, as in descriptions of the Amazons in *The Travels of John Mandeville*, challenge the belief that men are always more suitable rulers.[28] Significantly, when Gonzalo recalls the men with heads beneath their shoulders, he does so to soothe Alonso's fears of the "strange shapes" that Prospero has conjured for the antimasque. He says, "though they are of monstrous shape, yet note, / Their manners are more gentle, kind, than of / Our human generation" (3.3.31–33), suggesting, as Montaigne did, the greater civility of these "others." Gonzalo continues,

> Faith, sir, you need not fear. When we were boys,
> Who would believe that there were mountaineers,
> Dew-lapp'd, like bulls, whose throats had hanging at 'em
> Wallets of flesh? Or that there were such men
> Whose heads stood in their breasts? Which now we find
> Each putter-out of five for one will bring us
> Good warrant of. (3.3.43–49)

His speech does little to allay the king's anxiety (or that of Shakespeare's audience) as it further underscores the vulnerability and even the meaninglessness of European notions of authority in this non-European land. Alonso's power is not given in this setting where heads can grow beneath shoulders.

Immediately after Gonzalo's mentioning the men with heads in their breasts, Ariel chastises the royals in the form of a harpy, a predatory bird with a woman's face, increasing the Europeans' anxiety. This female monster temporarily dispossesses the ship-wrecked men of their power: "Your swords are now too massy for your strengths / And will not be uplifted" (67–68), continuing the assault on European principles of authority. Alonso's response is, "O, it is monstrous! monstrous!" (95), but it is unclear whether he refers to the harpy, her power over him, or to his own unnatural complicity in the usurpation of power from Prospero. The harpy's disempowering of Alonzo parallels Antonio's usurping of Prospero's duchy, poetic justice indeed. However, for Miranda and Caliban, also dispossessed islanders, there is no justice. Prospero studiously contains them both with an array of power apparatus—the panopticon, withholding knowledge, labeling, controlling sexuality, alienation. Certainly, there are many parallels between Caliban and Miranda, and a useful way of further examining Miranda's position is to compare it with Caliban's.

Shakespeare defines Caliban ("thou earth," 1.2.317) in physical terms. Caliban represents the body—he is prone to the physical weaknesses of the body, hunger and lust, and his labor is distinctly of a physical nature, as opposed to Ariel's arty magic. Whether Caliban is an Amerindian, the fabled European "wildman," an Irish colonial subject, a "mestizo," an African slave or prince, or all of the above, it is nevertheless clear that Caliban is a would-be "head" who has been relegated to the subservient position of the body: He makes his reversal of fortune plain to Prospero: "For I am all the subjects that you have, / which first was mine own king" (1.2.344–45). We also learn that the "head over body" hierarchy was alien to Caliban until Prospero arrived, suggesting that it had not been adopted by his ruling mother, Sycorax. As Constance Jordon points out, "At first, he 'lov'd' the man who later would become his master: unaware of meum and tuum [mine and yours], Caliban did not understand that the island (and presumably even Miranda) could not be shared between them."[29] Caliban's understanding of rulership before Prospero imposes his hierarchy follows the paradigm Desdemona derives from Othello's stories of the men with heads beneath their shoulders—that women can be rulers, that property can be shared, and that a "head over body" form of rulership is parochial, not universal.

Meanwhile, having learned hierarchies from Prospero—"how / To name the bigger light, and how the less" (1.2.338)—Caliban cannot *unlearn* them, instantly prostrating himself at the sight of Stephano (2.2.145) whom he assumes to be a god. Likewise does Prospero teach Miranda body-based subservience ("my foot my tutor?" 1.2.474), causing her to assume Ferdinand to be a spirit (1.2.413) or "a thing divine." In fact, to Caliban and Miranda, the Italians seem "nothing natural" (422) just as men with heads below their shoulders seemed unnatural to the European explorers. The play, then, suggests chiastic outcomes: the imposition of European beliefs ineluctably changes the nature of the people they colonized, and the people they colonize ineluctably change the nature of European beliefs. Caliban cannot go back to the way things were. Neither can Miranda, who must be safely married before she gains too much more knowledge. Similarly, despite Prospero's meticulous reordering of his world and the return of the non-natives to Europe and its conventions, the isle and its radical possibilities will not leave their imaginations or, more importantly, our imaginations. As in

Othello, Shakespeare makes us see the naturalness and thus the possibility of alternative paradigms of rulership. Though Miranda is safely contained in her marriage to Ferdinand, the Sycoraxes of the new world do not appear to need marriage at all.

Like John Knox, Prospero is at pains to prevent and demonize female authority, to the point of erasing his own daughter's chance to be an autonomous ruler. Not even Henry VIII was foolish enough to do that. But the poignancy, if not tragedy, of dispossession that the play grants to Prospero and Caliban must also extend to Miranda. Dispossession and usurpation are the worst of evils in the play—as Deborah Willis has observed, Antonio the usurper is the true "other" in the play, the one who is indeed "unnatural."[30] Thus, though Miranda does not prevail, the injustice of dispossession does. As in *Othello*, the thwarting of female authority in *The Tempest* is only provisional. The Emilias and Sycoraxes of the world still lurk both in and away from Europe. In *Othello* and *The Tempest*, Shakespeare uses the references to differently formed bodies pointedly to draw attention to the promises of newly explored non-European worlds, and in doing so, he leaves open the possibility of female autonomy in both the domestic and political spheres. In both plays, a collateral effect is a questioning of categories of "otherness" in general. By repeating, even if erroneously, reports of the existence of humans whose heads do not tyrannize over their bodies, Shakespeare flirts with political and social heterodoxy and might even betray constitutionalist leanings.

Notes

1. The body's use as a metaphor for the state and marriage has had a varied and complex history. At least three strands of thought appear to have blended by the early modern period: The first originates with Aristotle's concept of a body politic described in *The Politics*; the second comes from the first letter to the Ephesians where St. Paul dictates the marital hierarchy—"Wives, be subject to your husbands, as to the Lord." *The New Oxford Annotated Bible with the Apocrypha*, ed. Herbert G. May and Bruce M. Metzger (New York: Oxford University Press, 1973), 5: pp. 22–24. The third, developed by Aquinas and dogmatized by Pope Boniface VIII, is the idea of the church as a body, a *corpus mysticum*. The three strands became intertwined over the course of centuries of writing by European jurists, philosophers, and marriage theorists. For a comprehensive explanation, see Ernst H. Kantorowicz, *The King's Two Bodies: A Study in Medieval Political Thinking* (Princeton: Princeton University Press, 1957), pp. 193–232. Henry VIII adopted this "organological" understanding of authority when, in 1542, he spoke to his council about the relationship between the king and Parliament: "we as head and you

as members are conjoined and knit together in one body politic," quoted in Kantorowicz, 228. The understanding of state, church, and marital power as a head governing over a body becomes commonplace in the early modern period. Even though marriage tract writers and political theorists adopted the head/body metaphor, most interpreted or manipulated it to fit their understanding of how power should be exercised. *The Law's Resolutions of Women's Rights* (London, 1632) provides a particularly graphic interpretation of women's subordination to men: "when [the wife] hath lost her husband, her head is cut off, her intellectual part is gone, the very faculties of her soul are (I will not say) clean taken away, but they are all benumbed, dimmed, and dazzled," quoted in *Daughters, Wives and Widows: Writings by Men about Women and Marriage in England, 1500–1640*, ed. Joan Larsen Klein (Urbana and Chicago: University of Illinois Press), p. 50. Bishop John Thornborough used the head/body metaphor to make an argument supporting King James's call for the union of England, Scotland, and Wales: "The King is the countries Parent...one head to one body...What God hath so joyned together, let no man put asunder," *A Discourse Plainely Proving the evident utilitie and urgent necessitie of the desired happie union of the two famous Kingdomes of England and Scotland* (London, 1604), p. 15. It also allowed constitutionalists such as John Ponet to argue for a constitutional government: "Kings, Princes and other governours, albeit they are the headdes of a politike body, yet they are not the hole body." *A Short Treatise of politike power* (London, 1556), sig. G7v. Marriage tract writer William Gouge used it to declare that the husband is superior to the wife even when she is born above him: "by vertue of the matrimoniall bond the husband is made the head of his wife, though the husband were before marriage a very beggar, and of meane parentage, and the wife very wealthy and of a noble stocke," *Of Domesticall Duties* (London, 1622), p. 272. Ironically, it enabled marriage theorists to argue against wife-beating and for husbands to provide for their wives generously, "Is it not a signe of an improvident head, when the body goes naked, and is halfe hunger-starved?" William Whately, *A Bride-bush; or a Direction for Married Persons* (London, 1616), p. 177. In short, the head/body metaphor for government was a pliant and useful construct for defining power.
2. John Knox, *The First Blast of the Trumpet against the Monstrous Regiment of Women* (London, 1558), sig. B4v.
3. See Anne Somerset, *Elizabeth I* (New York: Knopf, 1991), p. 122.
4. See Carole Levin, *The Heart and Stomach of a King: Elizabeth I and the Politics of Sex and Power* (Philadelphia: University of Pennsylvania Press, 1994), p. 14.
5. Levin, p. 14.
6. See Leah Marcus, "Erasing the Stigma of Daughterhood: Mary I, Elizabeth I, and Henry VIII," *Daughters and Fathers*, ed. Lynda E. Boose and Betty S. Flowers (Baltimore and London: Johns Hopkins University Press, 1989), p. 408.
7. John Aylmer, *An Harborowe for faithfull and trewe subjects* (London, 1559), sig. C4v.

8. Knox, sig. G3.
9. Knox, sig. D3–D3v.
10. Aylmer, sig. C.
11. Kantorowicz, p. 218.
12. Kantorowicz, p. 224.
13. Kantorowicz, p. 223.
14. James I, *Political Works of James I*, ed. Charles H. McIlwain (London: Russell and Russell, 1965), p. 272. James drew on the analogy in much of his writing. In *The Trew Law of Free Monarchies*, he writes, "The King towards his people is rightly compared to a father of children, and to a head of a body composed of divers members.... And the proper office of a King towards his Subjects, agrees very wel with the office of the head towards the body and all members thereof: For from the head, being the seate of Judgement, proceedeth the care and foresight of guiding, and preventing all evill that may come to the body or any part thereof," p. 64.
15. Quotations from *Othello* follow the Arden edn., ed. E. A. J. Honigmann (Surrey, England: Thomas Nelson, 1997). Quotations from all other Shakespeare plays follow *The Riverside Shakespeare*, ed. G. Blakemore Evans (Boston: Houghton Mifflin, 1974).
16. According to Rudolf Wittkower in the *Gesta Romanorum*, men without heads represented humility, while in a fourteenth-century translation of Thomas of Cantimpre's *Liber de monstruosis hominibus*, men without heads were "lawyers who take excessive fees in order to fill their bellies." St. Augustine believed such creatures were part of God's great design: "God may have created fabulous races so that we might not think that the monstrous births which appear among ourselves are the failures of his wisdom." Quoted in Rudolf Wittkower, "Marvels of the East: A Study in the History of Monsters," *JWCI* 5 (1942), pp. 168 and 178.
17. For a thorough examination of the relationship between marital governance and political governance, see Constance Jordan, "The Household and the State: Transformations in the Representation of an Analogy from Aristotle to James I," *Modern Language Quarterly*, 54 (1993), pp. 307–26.
18. For an insightful discussion of Desdemona and Othello's relationship and this moment in particular, see Irene G. Dash, *Wooing, Wedding, and Power: Women in Shakespeare's Plays* (New York: Columbia University Press, 1981), p. 101.
19. Whately, pp. 97–98. William Gouge makes a similar suggestion in his marriage tract, *Of Domesticall Duties*: "Should the head be put under any parts of the body, the body and all the parts therof could not but receive much dammage thereby," p. 354.
20. Knox, sigs. D3–D3v.
21. Anthony Gerard Barthelemy, *Black Face, Maligned Race* (Baton Rouge: Louisiana State University Press, 1987), p. 181.
22. Dash, p. 123. For more on the prevailing of female authority at the end of *Othello*, see Emily C. Bartels, "Strategies of Submission: Desdemona, the Duchess, and the Assertion of Desire," *Studies in English Literature 1500–1900*, 36:2 (1996), pp. 429–31.

23. The editors of *The Riverside Shakespeare* note that *Othello* was probably not written before 1603 when one of its sources was available and not after November 1, 1604 when it was performed at Court. In the 1997 Arden *Othello*, Honigmann argues for an earlier date, 1602. *The Tempest* could not have been written before September 1610 or after November 1, 1611. See pp. 85 and 87.
24. Though it is in James's 1603 speech to Parliament that he uttered the famous lines, "I am the Husband, and all the Whole Isle is my lawfull Wife; I am the Head, and it is my Body" (McIlwain, 272), the speech he made in England in 1609 also employs those body metaphors in forceful ways. In the 1609 speech, though he concedes to Parliament a certain degree of authority (in the interests of getting money from it), he still claims that the King as head may "cut off corrupt members" (McIlwain, 308), particularly those who rise up against him.
25. There are two versions of the Dido story, both of which feature a powerful woman undone by men who see themselves as superior to her. In the "near historical" version, Dido stands by as her younger brother inherits her father's kingdom of Tyre. Later, when Dido builds Carthage, her rival, the King of Libya, proposes marriage to blend the two kingdoms; Dido kills herself rather than comply. In the more famous version, Dido falls in love with Aeneas and is abandoned by him for glory in finding Rome. See Robert E. Bell's *Women of Classical Mythology: A Biographical Dictionary* (New York: Oxford University Press, 1991), pp. 164–65.
26. See Lorie Jerrell Leininger, "The Miranda Trap: Sexism and Racism in Shakespeare's *Tempest*," *The Woman's Part: Feminist Criticism of Shakespeare*, ed. Carolyn Ruth Swift Lenz, Gayle Greene, and Carol Thomas Neely (Urbana and Chicago: University of Illinois Press, 1983), especially pp. 285–87. As David Scott Kastan points out, Princess Elizabeth's marriage more logically parallels that of Claribel to the Prince of Tunis. See *Shakespeare After Theory* (New York: Routledge, 1999), p. 190.
27. *The Norton Shakespeare*, based on the Oxford edn., ed. Stephen Greenblatt et al. (New York and London: W.W. Norton and Company, 1997) and the Bedford *Tempest*, ed. Gerald Graff and James Phelan (Boston and New York: Bedford/St. Martins, 2000), both gloss the line as meaning bent with age. *The Riverside* does not gloss it at all.
28. Mandeville describes the island of the Amazons where, "There is always a queen to rule that land, and they all obey her. This queen is always chosen by election, for they choose the woman who is the best fighter. These women are noble and wise warriors; and therefore kings of neighbouring realms hire them to help them in their wars." See *The Travels of John Mandeville*, translated by C. W. R. D. Moseley (London: Penguin Books, 1983), p. 117.
29. Constance Jordan, *Shakespeare's Monarchies: Ruler and Subject in the Romances* (Ithaca and London: Cornell University Press, 1997), p. 168.
30. Deborah Willis, "Shakespeare's *Tempest* and the Discourse of Colonialism," *Studies in English Literature 1500–1900*, 29:2 (1989), p. 281.

"There's Magic in Thy Majesty": Queenship and Witch-Speak in Jacobean Shakespeare

Kirilka Stavreva

Witches and royalty were a sure thrill for the theater-going crowds of Jacobean London, though it was not always easy to distinguish between these character types. In Thomas Middleton's tragicomedy *The Witch* (ca. 1616), for example, the Duchess of Ravenna traffics with Hecate, the Witch Queen, who repeatedly calls her "daughter." In the comedy *The Humorous Lieutenant* (1619) by John Fletcher and Philip Massinger, Antigonus, king of Syria, uses a love-potion to win Celia, his son's beloved. The Satanic Machiavellian villains driving the complex plots of murder and psychological torture in John Webster's dark tragedies *The White Devil* (1612) and *The Duchess of Malfi* (1614) are dukes or members of the royal family. William Shakespeare's tragedy *Macbeth* (ca. 1606) and his romance *Cymbeline* (ca. 1609) both feature evil queens who resort to devilish practices and rhetoric for political ends; in *The Winter's Tale* (1611) Queen Hermione and her lady-in-waiting Paulina prove masters of image magic and vituperative witch-speak; *The Tempest* (ca. 1611) features a magician whose supernatural powers blend Neo-Platonic magic with low-style witchcraft.

The chief practitioners of witchcraft and malediction in these plays are not village hags, but rather, court ladies, princesses, and royalty whose theatrical witchcraft was only a distant relative to countryside witch-speak. In the spaces where the King's Men performed, whether the newly opened Blackfriars Theatre or the Great Hall of Whitehall Palace, dazzling supernatural spectacles with swiftly flowing action were punctuated by fire and lightning, earthquakes and sea storms, while enchanting music and kaleidoscopic dance cast a spell over the senses of diverse spectators. Jacobean playwrights blended effortlessly illusionistic spectacle with Hermetic and fairy magic, intermingled the ancient rites of Hecate and Circe with figure-casting and love-magic, mixed Latin formulae of Satanic worship with the rantings of the village hags.

Yet, for all these trappings, regal theatrical witch-speak resonates clearly with the discursive violence of its low-born predecessor. Both are characterized by a quality described by Stephen Greenblatt as Aristotelian *enargeia*, "the liveliness that comes when metaphors are set in action, when things are put vividly before the mind's eye, when language achieves visibility."[1] Uttered in early modern households or on the Jacobean stage, witch-speak is the kind of theatricalized discourse that draws attention to the female body of its frequently eroticized speaker even as this body hardens its nurturing fluids into a masculine "undaunted mettle."[2] Whether theater professionals and audiences had had any real-life exposure to "the dark art" or not, the striking discursive performatives of real-life witches would have been familiar to them from numerous documentary pamphlets, which came out on the heels of witchcraft trials in the last decades of Queen Elizabeth's reign. "She candled her eyes upon her like a cat as big as two saucers," testified one Ann Wright about the alleged bewitchment of her daughter by her longstanding foe Mary Briscoe. Margaret Landish, another accused witch, produced "a strange howling in the court to the great disturbance of the entire bench." Joanna Powell cursed a churchwarden from her village "in Welsh language, kneeling down upon her bare knees and holding up her hands, but otherwise the words he could not understand."[3] Through such mysterious incantations, moans, giggles, equivocations, and suggestive body language, real-life witch-speak presented an enticing opportunity to mount on stage a superbly dramatic kind of violent speech.

The fulminations of real and theatrical witches alike taunted, shamed, emasculated, and hurled their victims' bodies on the ground. At the same time, whether grumbled on the commons of a poor Yorkshire village or in a resplendent royal court on the Blackfriars's stage witch-speak had the uncanny power to *connect* witches and bewitched in a bond described by Kenneth Gross as almost erotic.[4] Violent words begot a violent response in these exchanges, but also a liberating energy to body forth the violence of history. The witch-speak of the theatrical Jacobean queens, princesses, and their ladies-in-waiting, I will argue, provided the kind of discursive bond within the social world of the plays that could hold a kingdom together. This was a lesson, which theatrical kings were quick to learn and practice, potentially tainting the very concept of marvelous kingcraft.

Prior to the Jacobean era, demonic female nobility, royalty, and military leaders had appeared on stage in the 1590s, in Shakespeare's first four tremendously popular historical plays. These Elizabethan masters of malediction—most of them foreign queens—lacerate social bonds and threaten the English polity, unlike their Jacobean successors who use witch-speak to hold a polity together and to govern it. In *The First Part of the Contention* (*2 Henry VI*), the Duchess of Gloucester, a "woman of an invincible spirit" (1.4.7), not only resorts to the services of a witch and a conjurer to learn the future of the main figures in England's political life, but also prophesies the demise of her husband, the Lord Protector, even as she shames him for failing to support her.[5] The sharp tongue of Joan la Pucelle, the French military leader in *1 Henry VI* who is portrayed as conjuring spirits on stage in the play's final act, propels the hesitant French nobles into battle. It also batters "like roaring cannon-shot" the conscience of the Duke of Burgundy (3.7.79), eventually converting him to the French cause, and later on mercilessly tears down the military reputation of the English hero Lord Talbot. Queen Margaret, who appears in all four plays of Shakespeare's first tetralogy, wields a political and military power, which earns her the titles of a "she-wolf of France" and "an Amazonian trull" by her vanquished enemies (*Richard Duke of York* 1.4.112, 115). Her power is clearly related to a capacity to turn words into deadly weapons, conquering humans, nature, and history. It is her tongue, as much as her theatricalized mockery, that "more poisons than the adder's tooth" the Duke of York, when she puts a paper crown on his head and offers him a handkerchief dipped in the blood of his slaughtered son Rutland. On finding herself driven back to France "by awkward winds," Margaret confesses to having "cursed the gentle gusts / And he that loosed them forth their brazen caves," the ruler of the winds Aeolus (*The First Part of the Contention* 3.2.88–89). Helpless, Aeolus himself yields to her witch-speak and sends her a fair wind. Her curses upon the House of York in *Richard Duke of York* 5.5 and especially in *Richard III* 1.3 would eventually twist the course of English history into the plot of Margaret's revenge tragedy.

Yet, unlike the ubiquitous Jacobean theatrical witch-speak, in Shakespeare's Elizabethan plays queenly witch-speak typically dies with its practitioner. Its rare and pitiful mimics are helpless with injurious words: a Lady Anne who does not know any better than to curse herself along with the murderer of her first husband and father-in-law (*Richard III* 1.2), or a desperate Queen Elizabeth, who appeals to the violent-spoken prophetess Margaret in *Richard III*, "My words are dull.

O quicken them with thine!" (4.4.124). In Shakespeare's Jacobean drama, however, the politically advantageous witch-speak of queens and noble ladies clearly informs the discursive violence of kings and their subjects.

"O most delicate fiend": Yielding to the Evil Queen in *Macbeth* and *Cymbeline*

It is not the titular monarchs who are the makers of politics and history in Shakespeare's *Cymbeline, King of Britain* and *The Tragedy of Macbeth*. In these plays, two nameless queens, both fantastically educated for their times, use fighting words to whip their husbands into violent action. They dictate the fates of dynasties and nations, only to die like common witches, "shameless-desperate." They wield power through *enargeic* malevolent speech that channels the attention of spectators and interlocutors to their women's bodies, hardened like men's. This rhetoric brings the monarchs in the two plays, direct addressees of queenly witch-speak, into a state of erotic rapture. Furthermore, theatrical witch-speak reaps political victories for the two queens and their realms. Lady Macbeth sets her husband on the Scottish throne, and buys Scotland a much needed reprieve from the plotting of the factional thanes and their foreign allies. Cymbeline's "wicked queen," in turn, earns Britain its sovereignty from the Roman Empire, however briefly.

Witch-speak seems to haunt the words of characters both low- and high-born from the very opening of *Macbeth*. Indeed, Macbeth's first words in the play, "So foul and fair a day I have not seen" (1.3.36), echo closely the alliterating chant of the weird sisters in scene one, "Fair is foul, and foul is fair, / Hover through the fog and filthy air" (1.1.10–11). But at this point of the dramatic action the valiant thane can hardly be called a master of witch-speak: while his words diagnose Scotland's political climate precisely, they cannot effect deeds. Not so with the rhetorical performance of Lady Macbeth. At a pivotal point in the play when her husband's Christian pity and sense of social decorum convince him to put a stop to the plans of the assassination of King Duncan, Scotland's future queen lashes out a diatribe, which, in Macbeth's own words, does "bend up / Each corporal agent to this terrible feat" (1.7.79–80). To make her husband's will her own, his body an extension of hers, Lady Macbeth resorts to the rhetorical strategy of shaming, so popular with the demonic regal women from Shakespeare's first tetralogy:

> Was the hope drunk
> Wherein you dressed yourself? Hath it slept since?

> And wakes it now to look so green and pale
> At what it did so freely? From this time
> Such I account thy love. Art thou affeard
> To be the same in thine own act and valour
> As thou art in desire? (1.7.35–41)

Her charge is clear: going back on the assassination plans would prove Macbeth to be not only a coward, but also an impotent drunken braggart whose "act and valour" fail to match his desire. This suggestion stings the Scottish warrior to the heart, and he promptly asserts his manhood, "I dare do all that may become a man; / Who dares do more is none" (1.7.46–47).

At this point Lady Macbeth resorts to a rhetorical tactic favored by real-life witches: overspeaking, getting the upper hand in a verbal strife with her superior in the gender and social hierarchy. She asserts her own concept of manhood, one which transcends social conventions and historical constraints: "When you durst do it, then you were a man... / ... Nor time nor place / Did then adhere, and yet you would make both" (1.7.49–52). A man, the future queen asserts, is a maker of space and history. Neither social nor physical bonds can withstand manly determination, continues Lady Macbeth, rendering her point through an *enargeic* metaphor of uniquely female experience:

> I have given suck, and know
> How tender 'tis to love the babe that milks me.
> I would, while it was smiling in my face,
> Have plucked my nipple from his boneless gums
> And dashed the brains out, had I sworn
> As you have done to this. (1.7.54–59)

This image of manhood as a disrobed and violent female body stuns Macbeth and shatters his peace-making plans. It is an image viciously erotic, unnatural, and—as it appears—supernatural. Through it Lady Macbeth's female body acquires something of the destructive power of divine wrath, as described by the Biblical poet: "O daughter of Babylon, who art to be destroyed; happy shall he be, that rewardeth thee as thou hast served us. / Happy shall he be, that taketh and dasheth thy little ones against the stones."[6]

In the outcome of this speech, queenly witch-speak achieves its goal: Macbeth's will is completely subjugated to Lady Macbeth's. If there is any remnant of the royal "we" in his hesitant agreement: "If we should fail?", Lady Macbeth is quick to reword "we" as plural: "We fail! / But screw your courage to the sticking place / And we'll not fail"

(1.7.59–61). Queen-witch and bewitched have become one as a result of this masterful display of *enargeic* overspeaking. And Macbeth is quick to bring out the erotic dimension of this conjoining of violent wills. "Bring forth men-children only," he gasps before laying out the specifics of Duncan's assassination (1.7.72).

Witch-speak is also audible in the strong cadences, vivid metaphors, and beguiling insinuations of Cymbeline's beloved Queen. At a crucial moment in Britain's history, when the Roman ambassador Caius Lucius has come to court to demand the tribute owed to Britain's Roman conquerors, it is the Queen, and not Cymbeline, who announces her country's absolute sovereignty. Her speech, targeting both the Romans and her royal husband, is a masterpiece of shaming. She opens up by reminding Cymbeline that he has yet to live up to the valiance of his ancestors or indeed to "the natural bravery of [the] isle" over which he reigns (3.1.18). She then goes on to taunt Lucius with an image of Julius Caesar's double defeat on the British seas. Her sarcasm culminates in a vision of the Roman ships crushed not by human but by supernatural powers:

> his shipping,
> Poor ignorant baubles, on our terrible seas
> Like eggshells moved upon their surges, cracked
> As easily 'gainst our rocks... (3.1.26–29)

The Queen does not quite claim that it was weather magic that sunk Caesar's fleet, but the suggestion is apparent. At least one of her on-stage spectators, her son Cloten, seems to believe that Caesar's ships were indeed sunk by witchcraft. Accordingly, the slow-witted Cloten decides that Caesar's only hope to collect a tribute from Britain is to demonstrate an ability to command the sun and the moon. Any lesser witchcraft would apparently be ineffective against the powers evoked by Cloten's mother.

Like Lady Macbeth, the Queen in *Cymbeline* suggests that she partakes of a power unconfined to time or place. If Caesar's ships "cracked" "like eggshells" during the reign of "the famed Cassibelan," they can certainly be "cracked" again during Cymbeline's reign. Time stands still in the tableau she draws for her on-stage spectators of the Roman shipwreck, where the violence of nature is rendered strangely domestic through similes belonging to a goodwife's kitchen. The mishmash of apocalyptic and domestic imagery, coupled with the majestic rhythm of the Queen's speech, blends together a potent potion of nationalism and ridicule. Cymbeline (though perhaps not the Roman envoy) is struck with awe. When Cloten interrupts his mother to provide a prosaic summary of her words, the king impatiently protests: "Son, let your mother end" (3.1.38). Cloten fails to heed to the royal command, so the king eventually finds his own voice and declares Britain's independence from Rome. He motivates this huge political risk by recalling his ancestor's law-making and ridiculing "Caesar's ambition, / Which swelled so much that it did almost stretch / The sides o'th'world" (3.1.46–48)—thus echoing the Queen's discursive stabs, though with a less pointed delivery.

Cymbeline is not the only one at court to yield his will to the Queen's demonic discourse. The British lords agree that she is a "a crafty devil," since she "bears all down with her brain" (2.1.49, 50). Unlike the king, however, the nobles see clearly through the Queen's stratagems, perhaps because they pay scant attention to her erotic posturing. For Cymbeline, on the other hand, the impact of the Queen's witch-speak is apparently rendered irresistible by her histrionic eroticism. When told that on her deathbed she confessed to plotting his murder and using him in order to install her son to the British throne, the king exclaims:

> Mine eyes
> Were not at fault, for she was beautiful;
> Mine ears that heard her flattery, nor my heart
> That thought her like her seeming. It had been vicious
> To have mistrusted her. (5.6.62–66)

Both *Cymbeline* and *Macbeth* foreground the diabolical origins of queenly witch-speak, though the two queens in these plays belong to different witchcraft traditions. For Cymbeline's Queen, witch-speak is one in an array of injurious tools. She is also a herbalist and she aspires to master the male science of alchemy. Early in the play the Queen is shown issuing urgent orders to her ladies-in-waiting to gather certain flowers "whiles yet the dew's on ground" (1.5.1) and to deliver them promptly to her closet. She then discusses her progress in distilling perfumes and compounding medicines with Doctor Cornelius, and announces her intentions to test on animals the "most poisonous compounds" delivered by the doctor (1.5.8). Suspicious of the Queen's devilish nature, Cornelius summons the courage to suggest to her face that alchemic experimentation is bound to contaminate her nature and turn her into a hard-hearted, manly woman.

Lady Macbeth acquires witch-speak after a passionate plea to the "spirits that tend on mortal thoughts," those "murd'ring ministers . . . who wait on nature's mischief" (1.5.39–40, 46–48). She seems to be well aware of the capacity of witch-speak to harden the body and, conversely, of the body's power to enhance a witch's fighting words. Accordingly, she prays for the ability to liquefy her spirits and pour them like poison into Macbeth's ear, for a tongue of manly valor that would "chastise" her husband into murdering King Duncan, and for a body whose leaky womanly elements (blood and milk) would congeal into a strong alloy with her fighting words, so that "no compunctious visitings of nature" would misdirect her performance (1.5.23–28, 38–48).

It does not take long before we witness Lady Macbeth abandon the blank verse of nobility to resort (albeit in private) to the sing-song of the weird sisters. Shortly before Macbeth's coronation banquet, we find Lady Macbeth chanting to herself:

> Naught's had, all's spent,
> Where our desire is got without content.
> 'Tis safer to be that which we destroy
> Than by destruction dwell in doubtful joy. (3.2.6–9)

There is too much pattern, too many rhymes and alliterations in this incantation for a simple expression of rancor that no son of hers has been prophesied to inherit the Scottish throne. As soon as Macbeth enters, the queen interrupts her deadly alliteration of the very same sounds that the weird sisters mull around in their infamous "double, double, toil and trouble" (4.1.10). But it seems that the queen's spirits, along with her words, have already entered Macbeth's ear. By the end of their exchange in this scene, the king pledges that "a deed of dreadful note" will be done to Banquo and his son. He does not specify how, but bats, beetles, and crows—all of which have been traditionally associated with the "familiar spirits" of early modern English witches—figure prominently in his description of the dark "deed" (3.2.41, 43, 51).

If Lady Macbeth's magical incantation in this scene resonates with the musical patterns of the witches' sing-song, witch-speak informs Macbeth's choice of musical imagery to portray his "dreadful" plans for Banquo and Fleance: "ere to black Hecate's summons / The shard-borne beetle with his drowsy hums / Hath rung night's yawning peal, there shall be done / A deed of dreadful note" (3.2.41–44). The "drowsy hums" of the "familiar" beetle, which Macbeth seems to have borrowed from the night-queen Hecate, turn out to be indistinguishable from the "night's yawning peal" of church bells. Through these demonized "yawning peals," Macbeth literally sounds Banquo's death knell. The ominous pun on "note" at the end of this passage brings together musical notation, allusions to the night calls of the creatures summoned to carry out the dark deed, and the political advantage of Banquo's murder for Macbeth's dynasty.[7]

Macbeth then proceeds to evoke the circumstances of the projected murder:

> Light thickens, and the crow
> Makes wing to th'rooky wood.
> Good things of day begin to droop and drowse,
> Whiles night's black agents to their preys do rouse.
> Thou marvell'st at my words; but hold thee still.
> Things bad begun make strong themselves by ill.
> So prithee go with me. (3.2.51–57)

Whose brain, whose body conceived of this invocation? Light in Macbeth's *enargeic* image thickens like his demonic queen's blood in the outcome of her prayer to the "murdering ministers." The deadly *d*'s from Lady Macbeth's witch-song reverberate in Macbeth's pledge, made even more ominous by the rumbling of those strong Scottish *r*'s. The noble blank verse from the opening of Macbeth's murderous pledge eventually yields to ill-foreboding rhyme: "drowse"—"rouse," "still"—"ill," "prithee"—"me." In these lines queen and king, witch and bewitched are one being, living, breathing, and wielding a single supernatural discourse of political violence.

Mankind Witches: Binding the Polity in *The Winter's Tale*

If Macbeth's downfall is largely the effect of his receptivity to queenly and low-born witch-speak, the opening of *The Winter's Tale* portrays Leontes's resistance to the "potent" speech of his queen as the cause of a crisis in the polity and the royal family. In an uncontrolled eruption of jealousy, the Sicilian king accuses his queen of high treason and contemplates burning her at the stake, calls for the murder of the king of Bohemia, thus annihilating the age-long alliance between the two kingdoms, orders his newborn daughter abandoned in the wilderness, and causes the deaths of the heir to the throne and a devoted counselor. Sicily is left in international isolation and on the brink of a succession crisis. The king's counselors are alienated or exiled, while the king himself, awakening to the enormity of his actions, succumbs to a sixteen-year-long depression. The reason for this rampant desolation by royal discursive violence is Leontes's horrified realization that his status in the international arena as well as the continuity of the royal bloodline hang on the "potent" words of his queen—words of erotic charge and performative power, two important components of witch-speak.

There is no mistaking the erotic charge of Hermione's speech. Uttered by a woman whose advanced pregnancy is an overdetermined signifier of maternal fecundity and erotic activity,[8] her words alternate sexual taunts and playful sexual teases. Hermione parodies Polyxenes's professed desire to be reunited with his family as "limber vows," that is "limp, flaccid, flabby" (1.2.48). Shortly after shaming the Bohemian king into a predetermined choice ("My prisoner? or my guest?"), the queen urges a reward from her husband in no bashful terms, "Cram's with praise, and make's / As fat as tame things" (1.2.56, 93–94). A Cleopatra in her sexual openness, as Katherine Eggert reminds us, Hermione then hastens to suggest to her husband: "You may ride's / With one soft kiss a thousand furlongs ere / With spur we heat an acre" (1.2.96–98).[9]

As several critics have argued, Hermione's "potent" words are sorely needed for the legitimization and perpetuation of Leontes's political power, for what else can guarantee the legitimacy of the royal offspring?[10] It turns out that the queen's powerful rhetoric and the "boundless tongue" of her lady-in-waiting and chief defender Paulina are also indispensable for Sicilia's political redemption and the restoration of its political future. The two women are tough "physicians" of the state and the crown. They start out by shaming Leontes and delivering bitter public diagnoses of his attempt to eradicate the feminine from the political theater. Accused of witchcraft and heresy, Paulina storms back:

> I'll not call you tyrant;
> But this most cruel usage of your queen—
> Not able to produce more accusation
> Than your own weak-hinged fancy—something savours
> Of tyranny, and will ignoble make you,
> Yea, scandalous to the world. (2.3.116–21)

After Paulina labels Leontes's disastrous fear of female potency as "scandalous" and in dire need of radical reform, she proceeds to instruct the king's attendants that diplomacy would be of no avail in restoring Sicily's reputation.

In her self-defense, Hermione reiterates Paulina's charge against Leontes's tyranny and prophesies that "powers divine...shall make / False accusation blush, and tyranny / Tremble at patience" (3.2.26–30). Her prophesy (or is it a formal curse?) comes true as soon as the Apollo's oracle has been read: "Hermione is chaste, Polixenes blameless, Camillo a true subject, Leontes a jealous tyrant, his innocent babe truly begotten, and the King shall live without an heir if that which is lost be not found" (3.2.131–33). It is also obvious from the spontaneous reaction of the assembled nobles, "Now blessed be the great Apollo!" (3.2.134), that the witch-speak of the queen and her lady-in-waiting has already united them against Leontes's tyranny.

What remains to be done is to reconcile the king to the excessive signification of the female body and teach him receptivity to the excessive materiality of Hermione's and Paulina's witch-speak. Both goals are accomplished in the last scene of *The Winter's Tale*, in which Paulina repeatedly challenges the royal party to brand her "resurrection" of Hermione's "statue" as the "unlawful business" of witchcraft. Significantly, these challenges come up only after Paulina has already enticed Leontes into engaging in a series of discursive performatives typical of witch-speak. When the visitors to her chapel are dumbfounded at the sight of the "statue," Paulina urges Leontes to voice his "wonder." Leontes's prompted response, "Chide me, dear stone, that I may say indeed / Thou art Hermione" (5.3.24–25), begins to permeate the "statue" with a life of its own. Skillfully guided along by Paulina's suggestion, "No longer shall you gaze on't, lest your fancy / May think anon it moves," the king proceeds to word the "statue" into movement through the classic Austinian performative, "Let be, let be!" (5.3.60–61).

This is not Leontes's first experience in wringing reality out of words. As Carol Thomas Neely suggests, it was the king's language in the play's first act that reduced Hermione from a unique "she" to a grotesque "it," composed of the basest elements—"mingling bloods," "paddling palms," "pinching fingers."[11] But whereas Leontes's earlier performatives belong to a rigid script authored solely by the king, the performatives he utters in Paulina's chapel are communal and open-ended. In the opening of the play the king, in his capacity as supreme legal authority in the realm, wields autonomous injurious speech: "Away with her to prison!" "thou art here accused and arraigned of high treason" (2.1.105, 3.2.13). Under Paulina's direction, and with the incentive of the rest of Hermione's enchanted spectators, Leontes engages in a new kind of performative, authored by a collective speaking subject. Like historical witch-speak, his power to imbue the "statue" with life now rests not with himself as an individual office holder, but rather with an unfolding history of prior and future invocations that can grant or take away life.[12] When, having evoked this history, Paulina announces to her on-stage audience the imminent miracle of Hermione's resurrection, Leontes not only acquiesces to Paulina's supernatural art but virtually acts as her apprentice.

As is the wont of witch-speak, Hermione's and Paulina's rhetorical strategies are underscored by the power of theatrically displayed female bodies. If Hermione's "statue" was indeed done in Julio Romano's mannerist style, as the gentlemen at Leontes's court suggest (5.1.104–5), then her posture must have been dramatically exaggerated and perhaps somewhat contorted. The king comments on the emotional impact of Hermione's posture: "O, thus she stood, / Even with such life of majesty—warm life, / As now it coldly stands—when first I wooed her" (5.3.34–36). Perdita yearns to kiss Hermione's hand, Polyxenes lovingly muses on the apparent warmth of her lip, while Leontes, after gazing at the blood-pulsing veins of his queen, is stirred by the "air [that] comes from her" and moves to kiss her. In an extraordinary communal celebration of the female body, in which the king is cast in the lead role, Hermione is praised as lover, ruler, mother, Holy Mother, and a woman brimful of life.

In the statue scene, the bodily and the discursive components of witch-speak are split into Hermione's enchanting postures and Paulina's verbal performatives. Yet, this division does not signal a weakening or silencing of queenly witch-speak as soon as it has fulfilled its function of healing the polity.[13] Hermione's silence in this scene is no less powerful than the speech with which she fought the deathly legalese of her royal husband. For, as Janet S. Wolf has argued, in their fury and in their benevolence Paulina and Hermione overlap as much as Demeter and Hecate do in the Persephone myth.[14] They both nurse Perdita, publicly denounce tyranny, haunt the conscience of the guilty, and bring light to the truth. Arguably, the performative witchery of the statue scene is also the product of their *collective* authorship, directing, and acting. At the end of the play Leontes, for one, is left thirsting for more of these women's "potent" words. As the royal party exits the stage, he charges Paulina with the task of orchestrating the healing myth-making of his estranged and dispersed polity and family:

> Good Paulina,
> Lead us from hence, where we may leisurely
> Each one demand and answer to his part
> Performed in this wide gap of time since first
> We were dissevered. Hastily lead away. (5.3.152–56)

"This Damned Witch": The Island's Queen and Royal Witch-Speak in *The Tempest*

The Winter's Tale is unique among Shakespeare's Jacobean plays for its endorsement of women's "potent" words as a domestically and politically revitalizing art as "lawful as eating" (5.3.11). In other plays Shakespeare foregrounds the ubiquity of queenly witchcraft, including its echoes in the deeds and the majestic meter of theater kings, but is more ambivalent about its lawfulness. In *The Tempest*, for example, the magical incantations and theatrics of Duke Prospero—the chief means through which he wields power over the island's inhabitants—are clearly indebted to witch-speak, both low-born and queenly.

As various critics have noted, *The Tempest* is undecided about the nature of Prospero's supernatural powers. His learned Neo-Platonic magic is haunted by disturbing parallels to the "mischiefs manifold, and sorceries terrible" of the witch Sycorax, the island's previous ruler.[15] She is, of course, dead before the play begins, and we only know her history from Prospero's self-interested narrative. He does note, however, that Sycorax was active in Argiers's politics, and that even her powerful enemies were sufficiently indebted to her to suspend her death sentence for practicing sorcery.[16] Like other demonic queens from Jacobean drama, Sycorax's malevolent powers combine rhetorical *enargeia* and physical impact, although the tortures executed by her familiar spirits evoke much more clearly the style of real-life early modern witches. In his predilection for physical and mental suffering Prospero also bears a close resemblance to the low-born witches featured in the popular docu-fiction of the Elizabethan era. His spirits pinch, goad, and cramp Caliban, Stephano, and Trinculo, madden the Neapolitan party, paralyze Ferdinand and the "three men of sin," confine, imprison, and confuse the senses. He torments Caliban with apes, hedgehogs, and adders, and later releases his spirits in the shape of dogs upon the clownish conspirators. These tools of the magic trade are not all that different from Sycorax's toads, beetles, and bats, nor from the familiar spirits of countryside hags.

Exiled to the island, Sycorax must have ruled with an iron hand, judging from her punishment for Ariel's insubordination—imprisonment in "a cloven pine" (1.2.279). So does the usurper of her title. For all his professed aversion to "the foul witch," Prospero threatens to use his "art" to enact the same form of punishment on Ariel for resisting his commands: "I will rend an oak / And peg thee in his knotty entrails" (1.2.296–97). This is not simply an attempt to outdo Sycorax by choosing a tighter, more claustrophobic site of imprisonment for the insubordinate subject. As Mary Ellen Lamb has perceptively argued, if Sycorax's imprisonment of Ariel in a tree-trunk "cloven" like a vagina suggests a forced return to the womb, Prospero's description of the oak's entrails as "his" implies that Prospero's trunk has a womb-like interior.[17]

Entrapment in this securely knotted male womb would have lasted an eternity. It appears then that the duke's control over his subjects on the island is indebted not only to Sycorax's intimidating rhetoric, but also to his appropriation of female gestational powers.

It is Prospero's language, this powerful instrument of witchcraft, that is most heavily indebted to queenly witch-speak. Just when he renounces his "rough magic," the duke delivers a speech that, paradoxically, both performs and commemorates his "so potent art." Summoning the very elves and demi-puppets with whose help he "bedimmed / The noontide sun, called forth the mutinous winds," shaken "the strong-based promontory," "plucked up / The pine and cedar," and awakened the dead (5.1.33–50), Prospero intensifies verbal effect by a strange ritual performed under the accompaniment of "solemn music." He draws a circle in the ground, waves his staff and perhaps breaks it, thus adding bodily force to his *enargeic* supernatural discourse.

Several critics have noted that the duke's speech echoes the words of the witch Medea as rendered in Ovid's *Metamorphoses*.[18] It has not yet been observed, however, that Medea bears a number of similarities to two other royal women in *The Tempest*: Sycorax, the island's original ruler, and Miranda, the future Queen of Naples and Milan. Medea was the only surviving child of the rightful King of Corinth, Aeëtes. Like Miranda, she emigrated with her father to Colchis after the usurpation of the Corinthian throne by Corinthus. Like Miranda again, she managed to claim back her father's throne, and the Corinthians accepted her husband Jason as their king. Like Sycorax, Medea could not secure the throne for her children once Jason proposed to divorce her and marry Glauce the Theban. Medea's sons were subsequently stoned to death by the Corinthians, enraged at Medea's revenge on Glauce and her father—a fate that arguably was spared to Caliban only because his knowledge of the island was indispensable to Prospero.[19]

The play does not clarify how the Duke of Milan learned the cadences of Medea-Sycorax–Miranda,[20] but it does reveal the full measure of Prospero's debt to witch-speak in the language of the enslaved Caliban. When Caliban first bursts onto the stage, he spurts out an elaborate curse, which seems to be inspired by memories of his mother's "potent art":

> As wicked dew as e'er my mother brushed
> With raven's feather from unwholesome fen
> Drop on you both! A southwest blow on ye,
> And blister you all o'er! (1.2.323–26)

Caliban, however, cannot possibly remember Sycorax's witch-speak. As Miranda testifies, at the time of her arrival on the island, he was no bigger than a "freckled whelp" and had no words with which to make known his "purposes." He learned language from Prospero and Miranda or he would not have been such a master of pastoral blank verse.[21] But if the duke and the princess are Caliban's language teachers, then they are also the witch-speak masters whom the slave attempts to strike with his own witch-speak. Prospero, in fact, proves quite adept at cursing, when he overspeaks Caliban:

> For this be sure tonight thou shalt have cramps,
> Side-stitches that shall pen thy breath up. Urchins
> Shall forth at vast of night, that they may work
> All exercise on thee. Thou shall be pinched
> As thick as honeycomb, each pinch more stinging
> Than bees that made 'em. (1.2.328–33)

The duke's "bad tongue" makes physical pain come to life through phonetic pattern and live metaphor. His curses, fairly localized physical threats at first, gather momentum to a point when they threaten to turn Caliban's body into a shapeless mass "as thick as honeycomb." This is the kind of improvisatory discourse whose devastating effect depends on the ability of each clause to surpass the visceral threat of the previous one, unleashing a phonemic avalanche that would paralyze the response of its recipient.

Sycorax, the old witching queen, may be dead, but her potent word—taught to her son by Miranda, the youngest incarnation of the classical witch Medea—proves indispensable to Prospero in ruling over his island kingdom. However, even as ventriloquized witch-speak defines Prospero's marvelous monarchy, it undermines his moral right-to-rule. With this realization perhaps, he rejects his magic at the end of the play, which leaves him no choice but to retire to Milan, relinquish the political entity of his dukedom to the future King of Naples, and cast "every third thought" on his grave (5.1.314).

Of course, when Prospero's kingcraft, contaminated by queenly witch-speak, was viewed in the context of the Platonic–Pythagorean harmony of the Whitehall Banqueting House, it could be framed as an intricate compliment to the play's most privileged spectator, King James. We should remember that the courtiers flanking the hall were actually observing two concurrent spectacles: the on-stage action in Prospero's court and, directly against it, the symmetrical tableau in James's royal seat. Prospero's implicit feminization and demonization as a ruler could have underscored the infallibility of the other focus of the courtly spectacle. Uttered in the same hall where flamboyant Epiphany masques were wont to celebrate the presence of divinity in the person of the king, the Epilogue in which Prospero acknowledges that his "charms are all o'erthrown" (1) would have testified not so much to the vulnerability of James's mystical kingcraft as to the singularly masculine omnipotence of the royal spectator.[22]

In the commercial theaters of early modern London, however, Prospero's performance would have resonated quite differently. Without the physical presence of the harmony-restoring royal spectator, the assorted echoes of mythical and contemporary, countryside and queenly witch-speak in the duke's "art" would have marked his kingcraft as corruptible and untrustworthy. Addressed to the mixed audiences at the Blackfriars, which included fellows dismissed by Ben Jonson as "sinfull sixe-penny Mechanicks," Prospero's acknowledgment, "I must be here confined by you, / Or sent to Naples" (Epilogue 4–5) acquires considerable seditious power.[23]

Resounding in these commercial theater halls, the reverberations of witch-speak, from the incantations of mythical queens to the discourse of their male conquerors and consorts, and then further on, to the injurious speech of assorted disgruntled political subjects, bridged the moral gap between the supernatural manipulations at the court and in the countryside. Were the King's Men politically subversive in these representations? Hardly. Yet, neither were these socially engaged opportunists overly deferential to political authority. As they inscribed witch-speak onto female and male kingcraft, the mystical allure of the king was beginning to be tainted. The theaters were thus preparing a change in political mentality that some thirty years later would make it conceivable for the Puritan revolutionaries to put on trial and execute—like a low-born witch—God's lieutenant upon earth, King Charles I.

Notes

Many thanks to Cindy Benton, Tina Fetner, Michelle Mouton, and Jama Stilwell for their cheerful criticism of earlier drafts of this essay.

1. Stephen Greenblatt, "Shakespeare Bewitched," in *New Historical Literary Study: Essays on Reproducing Texts, Representing History*, ed. Jeffrey Cox and Larry J. Reynolds (Princeton: Princeton University Press, 1993), p. 121.
2. Macbeth describes his wife's composition as the kind of "undaunted mettle" that "should compose / Nothing but males" (1.7.73–74).
3. The three displays of witch-speak mentioned here are recorded, respectively, in John Addy, *Sin and Society in the Seventeenth Century* (London: Routledge,

1989), pp. 124–25; Gamini Salgado, *The Elizabethan Underworld* (London: J. M. Dent, 1977), p. 91; Keith Thomas, *Religion and the Decline of Magic* (New York: Charles Scribner's Sons, 1971), p. 508. On the structure and effect of early modern English witch-speak, see my "Fighting Words: Witch-Speak in Late Elizabethan Docu-Fiction," *Journal of Medieval and Early Modern Studies*, 30:2 (2000), pp. 309–38.

4. Kenneth Gross discusses cursing, a sub-type of witch-speak, as exemplary of the bond of "mutual need" that transforms both speaker and addressee in all forms of ill-speaking. See *Shakespeare's Noise* (Chicago: University of Chicago Press, 2001), p. 3.
5. All quotations from Shakespeare are from *The Norton Shakespeare*, ed. Stephen Greenblatt, Walter Cohen, Jean E. Howard, and Katherine Eisaman Maus (New York: W. W. Norton, 1997).
6. Ps. 137 AV. I am grateful to Alan Nagel for suggesting this intertextual connection.
7. My discussion of the musical imagery used by Macbeth in 3.2 is indebted to Allison Doherty's sensitive analysis of his language in an unpublished paper, "Macbeth: Confused Victim of Women or Despicable Proponent of Evil?" written for my Shakespeare class in 2001.
8. Valerie Traub, *Desire and Anxiety: Circulations of Sexuality in Shakespearean Drama* (New York: Routledge, 1992), p. 44.
9. Katherine Eggert, *Showing Like a Queen: Female Authority and Literary Experiment in Spenser, Shakespeare, and Milton* (Philadelphia: University of Pennsylvania Press, 2000), p. 162.
10. David Schalkyk, "'A Lady's 'Verily' Is as Potent as a Lord's': Women, Word and Witchcraft in *The Winter's Tale*," *English Literary Renaissance*, 22 (1992), p. 247; Eggert, *Showing Like a Queen*, p. 162.
11. Carol Thomas Neely, "*The Winter's Tale*: The Triumph of Speech," in *The Winter's Tale: Critical Essays*, ed. Maurice Hunt (New York: Garland Publishing, 1995), pp. 252–53.
12. On the collective subject of witch-speak (as different from its speaking subject), see my "Fighting Words," pp. 317–18.
13. For the opposite view, of women's words and worth as repressed and appropriated by patriarchal power, see, for instance, Traub, *Desire and Anxiety*, pp. 46–49, and Schalkwyk, "Women, Word, and Witchcraft," pp. 264–72.
14. Janet S. Wolf, "'Like an Old Tale Still': Paulina, 'Triple Hecate', and the Persephone Myth in *The Winter's Tale*," in *Images of Persephone: Feminist Readings in Western Literature*, ed. Elizabeth T. Hayes (Gainsville: University Press of Florida, 1994), pp. 32–44.
15. The extended debate on the blackness or whiteness of Prospero's magic has been summarized in Cosmo Corfield, "Why Does Prospero Abjure his 'Rough Magic'?" *Shakespeare Quarterly*, 36 (1985), pp. 32–33.
16. Anthony Harris, in *Night's Black Agents: Witchcraft and Magic in Seventeenth-Century English Drama* (Manchester: Manchester University Press, 1980), p. 143, observes that Charles Lamb interpreted Prospero's statement, "for one thing she did / They would not take her life" (1.2.268–69) as "a reference to the story of the witch who saved Algiers when it was besieged by Charles V in 1541."

17. Mary Ellen Lamb, "Engendering the Narrative Act: Old Wives' Tales in *The Winter's Tale, Macbeth, and The Tempest*," *Criticism*, 40:4 (1998), pp. 542, 545.
18. The relationship between Shakespeare's and Golding's translation of Medea's Ovidian speech was first detailed in T. W. Baldwin, *William Shakspere's Small Latine & Lesse Greeke* (Urbana: University of Illinois Press, 1944), 2:443–53. Lamb, "Engendering the Narrative Act," pp. 546–47, presses the analogy between Prospero's speech and Medea's incantation to show how early modern demonological discourse would have interpreted both as authored by the Devil.
19. Robert Graves, *The Greek Myths* (London: The Folio Society, 1996), pp. 557–58. As Graves clarifies, Medea's murder of her two sons is the creation of the dramatist Euripides, bribed with fifteen talents of silver by the Corinthians to absolve them from guilt.
20. A good candidate for a transmitter of Sycorax's witch-speak to Prospero would be Ariel. In "Engendering the Narrative Act," pp. 544–45, Lamb points to the overlaps between this supposed daemon of pure intelligence and the English fairies, as well as to Ariel's propensity for the lulling singsong and animal sounds of nursery rhymes, so similar to the incantations of the witches in *Macbeth*.
21. On Caliban's pastoral poetic, see Diane Purkiss, *The Witch in History: Early Modern and Twentieth-Century Representations* (New York: Routledge, 1996), p. 269, and David Norbrook, "'What Cares These Roarers for the Name of King?': Language and Utopia in *The Tempest*," in *The Poetics of Tragicomedy: Shakespeare and After*, ed. Gordon McMullen and Jonathan Hope (New York: Routledge, 1992), pp. 21–54.
22. The "frozen magic" embodied by the architecture of the Banqueting House is described in Vaughan Hart, *Art and Magic in the Court of the Stuarts* (New York: Routledge, 1994), pp. 136–54. On the double spectacle at Jacobean court performances, see John Orrell, "The Theaters," p. 96, and Ann Jennalie Cook, "Audiences: Investigation, Interpretation, Invention," p. 309, both in *A New History of Early English Drama*, ed. John D. Cox and David Scott Kastan (New York: Columbia University Press, 1997). Graham Parry, "Entertainments at Court," pp. 200–05, comments on the symbolic and political functions of the annual tradition of Twelfth Night royal masques.
23. *Ben Jonson*, 11 vols., ed. C. H. Herford, Percy Simpson, and Evelyn Simpson (Oxford: Clarendon Press, 1925–52), 6: p. 509.

Part III
Cultural Anxieties and Historical Echoes of Renaissance Queens

The Taming of the Queen: Foxe's Katherine and Shakespeare's Kate

Carole Levin

In considering the transmission of religious and gender ideologies in sixteenth-century England, we must consider John Foxe's *Acts and Monuments*, one of the most influential and widely read books of the English Renaissance, and a source for much Renaissance drama. Many early modern plays depict queens in perilous situations and some of these works drew on Foxe as a source. Henry VIII's sixth and last wife Katherine Parr is one such queen in peril whose story is chronicled in Foxe and then retold in part in Samuel Rowley's *When You See Me, You Know Me* (1605). While Rowley's version holds some interest historically, I would suggest the most intriguing parallel between Foxe's narrative and an early modern play is with Katherine Parr's namesake in one of Shakespeare's comedies, the one where Kate is known as a "curst shrew." I would argue that in *The Taming of the Shrew* we can see some deliberate echoes of the confrontation between Katherine and Henry, the threats to Katherine, and the cultural anxieties about an educated or strong-willed wife. Though Rowley's play follows Foxe more closely, it is *The Taming of the Shrew* that deals more thoroughly with the issue raised by Foxe. Furthermore, these concerns are found not only in the representation of Kate, but even, ironically, in Bianca as well. Though the traditional view of Bianca is that she is a brainless beauty who fools her father by her quiet and ladylike demeanor and then turns out to be actually spoiled and disobedient once married, I would argue that Bianca is really a model of an unruly woman who disrupts societal norms—but unlike both Katherine Parr and Kate—does not revert to the role of the pliant woman at the end of the play.

Henry VIII and Katherine Parr (1868) engraving from the painting by R. Smirke

Foxe presents a highly dramatic confrontation between Henry VIII and Katherine Parr, which leads to Henry planning to have Katherine arrested and examined for heresy because she has been too willing to speak back to him about what she has learned from her scriptural readings.

The lessons Queen Katherine learns from the event echo in the play Shakespeare wrote in the last years of Elizabeth's reign. For clarity's sake I refer in this essay to Katherine Parr as Katherine and Shakespeare's character as Kate. There are certainly differences between Katherine and Kate. And there are also real differences, and far more complexity, between what we know of the historic Katherine Parr and Foxe's representation of her. While Shakespeare shows a Kate who stoutly resists being married and doing anything that would please her husband, Foxe describes Katherine as trying very hard to be a good wife to Henry. Says Foxe: "For never handmaid sought with more careful diligence to please her mistress, than she did, with all painful endeavour, to apply herself, by all virtuous means, in all things to please his humour."[1]

But while Katherine Parr did indeed attempt to be a good wife to Henry, she had not gone willingly into the marriage. After surviving two arranged marriages that were both fraught with difficulties, the thirty-year old Katherine fell in love with the man courting her, Thomas Seymour, and looked forward to what she hoped would be a very different marriage. But Seymour diplomatically drifted from view once Henry began to demonstrate interest in Katherine. Given Henry's track record by this time, it is hardly surprising that she expressed the opinion she would rather be Henry's mistress than his wife, and saw her marriage as being more valuable to her family relations than agreeable to herself. She wrote to her brother William about her upcoming wedding that "[You are] the person who has most cause to rejoice."[2] She was not the happiest bride when Bishop Stephen Gardiner married her to the king at Hampton Court on July 12, 1543. But Katherine had as little choice about marrying Henry as Kate did about her nuptials with Petruchio; however, Katherine, "an impressive and agreeable woman,"[3] in the words of J. J. Scarisbrick, did, as Foxe suggested, all she could to please her difficult husband with her patience and good humor.

Despite these qualities, Katherine Parr had problems with her lord and husband, and the problems seem to come from her studies in theology. Scarisbrick and Susan James accept the presentation of Henry's threat to Katherine's well-being in Foxe as being historically accurate, though scholars would agree that the actual dialogue between Henry and Katherine is put in their mouths by Foxe.[4] Foxe describes how Henry, upon returning from France in 1546, learned that Katherine spent at least one hour a day in her studies of the holy Scriptures. Since Henry did not seem to mind, "this made her more bold" so that she would "frankly . . . debate with the king touching religion, and therein flatly to discover herself" (Foxe, 5.554). In the sixteenth century discover could mean "To disclose or expose to view (anything covered up, hidden, or previously unseen), to reveal, show," and with her study and her convictions Katherine began to show Henry more of who she really was, to her great peril; for Henry VIII, according to Foxe, "misliked to be contended withal in any kind of argument" (Foxe, 5.554).

Petruchio also desires Kate to agree with him unconditionally, threatening not to return to her father's house until she accept his word as truth:

> Now by my mother's son, and that's myself,
> It shall be moon, or star, or what I list,
> Or ere I journey to your father's house.[5]

By this time in the play Kate has learned her lesson by her husband's treatment:

> Be it moon, or sun, or what you please,
> And if you please to call it a rush candle
> Henceforth I vow it shall be so for me. (4.5.13–15)

For Katherine, the disagreement is even more disturbing. While Kate faces more abuse from her husband, and his refusal to bring her back to her father's house, Katherine could potentially lose her life. Because of her intense faith, Katherine "with reverent terms and humble talk" (Foxe, 5.555) would discuss the Scriptures with the king. But Katherine's reverence and humility were not enough when Henry was in an ill humor. At first their discussions were amicable enough; then "by reason of his sore leg (the anguish whereof began more and more to increase), he waxed sickly, and therewithal forward, and difficult to be pleased" (Foxe, 5.555).

Katherine left the room after one such discourse with Henry; the king then turned to Stephen Gardiner, bishop of Winchester—one of Foxe's principle villains—and muttered: "A good hearing . . . it is, when women become such clerks; and a thing much to my comfort, to come in mine old days to be taught by my wife" (Foxe, 5.555). Though Gardiner had performed the marriage ceremony he was delighted with Henry's disenchantment with Katherine, hoping that she could be replaced with a new queen of more conservative religious beliefs. Henry allowed Gardiner to write up articles against the queen, and the bishop began to secretly gather information against Katherine's religious practices. What happened next according to Foxe is an extravagant coincident that makes great drama despite its improbability. The bill of articles signed by Henry was mislaid and found by "some godly person"

(Foxe, 5. 558) who immediately warned Katherine. Not surprisingly, given the track records of her predecessors, she "fell incontinent into a great melancholy and agony" (Foxe, 5.558).

Katherine's weeping and wailing disturbed Henry so he sent his physician Dr. Wendy to see what was the matter, first confiding in him that he was about to have the queen arrested but swearing the doctor to secrecy. Despite his oath, Wendy, who thought highly of Katherine, "in secret manner" exhorted her "to frame and conform herself into the king's mind." Quite possibly this was Henry's plan—that the doctor would break his word and tell Katherine how she ought to behave to save herself. Should she show Henry "her humble submission unto him," Dr. Wendy assured her, "she should find him gracious and favourable unto her" (Foxe, 5.558). Here was a clear recipe of what was acceptable behavior for a woman. It is the same lesson Petruchio's friend advises Kate: "Say as he says, or we shall never go" (4.5.10).

Katherine had the presence of mind to tell her ladies to dispose of all their illegal religious books. Then she went to Henry, who immediately began to argue with her over religion. Katherine with "mildly, and reverent countenance" responded to Henry with a long speech that Foxe provides:

> Your majesty ... doth right-well know ... what great imperfection and weakness by our first creation is allotted unto us women, to be ordained and appointed as inferior and subject unto man as our head; from which head all our direction ought to proceed; and that as God made man to his own shape and likeness, whereby he, being endued with more special gifts of perfection, ... even so, also made he woman of man, of whom and by whom she is to be governed, commanded, and directed; who womanly weaknesses and natural imperfection ought to be tolerated, aided, and borne withal, so that by wisdom, such things as be lacking in her ought to be supplied.
>
> Since, therefore God hath appointed such a natural difference between man and woman, and your majesty being so excellent in gifts and ornaments of wisdom, and I a silly poor woman, so much inferior in all respects of nature unto you, how then cometh it now to pass that your majesty, in such diffuse causes of religion, will seem to require my judgement? ... I refer my judgment in this, and in all other cases, to your majesty's wisdom, as my only anchor, ... next under God, to lean unto. (Foxe, 5.559)

One would certainly expect such a submission to be enough, but Henry was still not placated. He accused Katherine of trying to teach him, rather than be taught by him: "You are become a doctor, Kate, to instruct us (as we take it) and not to be instructed or directed by us"

(Foxe, 5.559). Katherine protested that she was simply trying to learn, and that her other motive was to take Henry's mind off his leg. Finally, Katherine's words have delighted Henry. "And is it even so sweet heart! .... Then perfect friends we are now again" (Foxe, 5, 559, 560). Henry kissed and embraced Katherine, and told her words, out of her own mouth, had done him more good than a present of £100,000. This money, as well as Henry's pleasure, is perhaps a foreshadowing of Petruchio's behavior, who is equally pleased, and in fact wins a bet, because of Kate's submissive speech at the end of *Shrew*, which uncannily echoes Katherine's.

The taming of Katherine—and Stephen Gardiner, Bishop of Winchester—is not over, however. Henry does not cancel the arrest order. Gardiner and his colleagues, especially Wriothesley, unaware of the reconciliation, continued with their plans, with Henry doing nothing to stop them. Instead, the next day, Henry sat with Katherine in the garden and allowed the guards led by Wriothesley—Gardiner was to his good fortune not there—to come forward to start to arrest her. Only then did he berate them, as "arrant knave! Beast! and fool!" (Foxe, 5.560).

Though Henry had agreed to the drawing up the articles against Katherine, Foxe suggests that he never intended to use them. This is of course debatable. But even if that is true it was also a most effective way for Henry to teach Katherine not to behave in a manner he deemed inappropriate in a woman—to tame her. As Scarisbrick suggests, though we cannot know Henry's motives, and whether or not he had ever intended to go through with Katherine's arrest, this whole elaborate charade might well have been a way "to frighten Catherine, or to break her evident independence of mind."[6] Foxe, in his discussion of Katherine, clearly approves of her as one who while obviously highly intelligent, survives by posing as a "silly poor woman." Before we argue that Foxe himself is demeaning Katherine, however, I would add that "silly" can mean in the sixteenth century, "deserving of pity, compassion, or sympathy" or "helpless or defenceless." Certainly Katherine in this situation is deserving of compassion because of how defenseless—how in danger—she is.

The method of using force and threats to tame a wife uneasily echoes with that other Kate, tamed by her "lord and husband" Petruchio. Kate at her wedding has no intention of being tamed:

> Gentlemen, forward to the bridal dinner.
> I see a woman may be made a fool
> If she had not spirit to resist. (3.2.219–21)

But Petruchio will not allow his wife to show her spirit, certainly not after he has married her and thus has full legal control over her:

> She is my goods, my chattels, she is my house
> My household stuff, my field, my barn
> My horse, my ox, my ass, my anything. (3.2.230–32)

Petruchio's comments would hardly have shocked an Elizabethan audience. As Sara Mendelson and Patricia Crawford point out, "Very often women were legally constructed as property and possessions."[7] Moreover, Common law taught that husband and wife were one, and that one was the husband. In terms of property, "That which the husband hath is his own," and "that which the wife hath is the husband's."[8]

Petruchio takes Kate away with him where she has no relatives and no one who knows her. While an audience may well find their relationship amusing—Ruth Nevo calls the play "unencumbered enjoyment"[9]—Petruchio is also deliberately starving Kate of food and sleep as a means to "curb her mad and headstrong humor:"

> She ate no meat today, nor none shall eat.
> Last night she slept not, nor tonight she shall not.
> . . . .
> This is a way to kill a wife with kindness;
> And thus I'll curb her mad and headstrong humor.
> He that knows better how to tame a shrew,
> Now let him speak. (4.1.185–86; 196–99)

Petruchio's plan works well. As Kate tells his servant, Grumio,

> But I, who never knew how to entreat
> Nor never needed that I should entreat
> Am starved for meat, giddy for lack of sleep,
> With oaths kept waking, and with brawling fed.
> And that which spites me more than all these wants,
> He does it under name of perfect love. (4.3.6–11)

Again, an audience may find all this amusing, and indeed, Lynda Boose suggests that Shakespeare's wit "make[s] Kate's humiliation seem wildly comic,"[10] but it may be less so when one considers all the cases of husbands who abuse their wives "out of love." A fifteenth-century Sienese book on marriage advised husbands that "When you see your wife commit an offense, don't rush at her with insults and violent blows: rather first correct the wrong lovingly and pleasantly, and sweetly teach her not to do it again . . . . But if your wife is of a servile disposition and has a crude and shifty spirit, so that pleasant words have no effect, scold her sharply, bully, and terrify her. And if this still doesn't work . . . take up a stick and beat her soundly . . . not in rage, but out of charity and concern for her soul."[11]

This sentiment is echoed in William Whately's early seventeenth-century marriage manual, *A Bride-bush*. While he agrees that it is better for a husband not to beat his wife, if "she give just cause, after much bearing and forebearing, and trying all other ways, in case of utmost necessity," he can indeed beat her, but should "exceed not measure."[12] This perspective was certainly not universal, and some authors of manuals, such as Thomas Gouge writing in the early seventeenth century, were clearly opposed to wife beating; Gouge argues that husbands should treat wives "mildly," adding "if he reprove her, it must be with all mildness and meakness imaginable," particularly since "it doth not appear, that he hath any power or liberty thereupon to beat her."[13] English law, however, was on the side of those who did provide "reasonable correction."[14] Scholars have found from examining evidence of the early modern period that "wife beating was rife among all social groups."[15]

Linda Bamber suggests that the play demonstrates triumph "over the feminine," a point made even more strongly by the director Michael Bogdanov, who argues that *The Taming of the Shrew* is "a play about a male wish-fulfillment dream of revenge upon women. The humiliation to which Kate is subjected is what happens in a world ruled and dominated by men, where any woman who challenges male supremacy has to be smashed down by any means possible, until she is submissive, pliant . . . and comes when called"[16]—which is of course exactly what we see Kate do at the end of the play.

And while Petruchio's servants are certainly not being literal when one [Peter] tells another [Nathaniel] "He kills her in her own humour," Petruchio's treatment of Kate could certainly be harmful to her health. As Lena Orlin points out, "Kate's physical torture is intensified" during the time she is at his residence.[17]

An Elizabethan audience would have been aware of how common abuse of wives actually was. Mendelson and Crawford tell us that, "Married women experience a whole spectrum of mistreatment, ranging from verbal and psychological harassment and threats of violence, physical assault and attempted murder, to actual homicide. In some matrimonial cases which have been preserved in church and secular court records, we can document an escalating spiral of mental and physical cruelty."[18] As Keith Thomas points out, while theoretically in early modern England accused witches were not tortured to gain confessions, there were a number of cases where the accused, most of whom were women, were kept awake for days and starved in an effort to gain a confession.[19] Petruchio's treatment of Kate, while much less severe, still might echo this horror.

A number of modern critics, uncomfortable with a view of a Petruchio as a "slam-bang wife-beating type," argue instead, suggests Robert Heilman, that he is a "generous and affectionate fellow whose basic method is to bring out the best in his fiancée and wife by holding up before her an image both of what she is and what she can become."[20] Marianne L. Novy takes this position, arguing that "play and mutuality may be goals of taming," and that Petruchio's lessons have given Kate "an education in folly [that] has taught her how to live with relative comfort in a patriarchal culture."[21] Anne Barton sees Petruchio "as a man who genuinely prizes Katherine, and, by exploiting an age-old and basic antagonism between the sexes, manoeuvres her into an understanding of his nature and also her own."[22] Ruth Nevo takes Barton's characterization even further, arguing that "only a very clever, very discerning man could bring off a pyschodrama so instructive, liberating and therapeutic as Petruchio's."[23] But I find it hard to perceive Petruchio as therapist/lover or to discover either generosity or affection on the one hand or playfulness on the other in his treatment of Kate. Though the whips he carried on stage in a number of staged versions are certainly not referred to in the text, the abusiveness of his behavior is. Though my discussion of *The Taming of the Shrew* is perhaps unrelenting in my description of Petruchio's behavior, I would add that I do not believe this character, or the entire play, means we can label Shakespeare as "sexist," a term that may be anachronistic to use about a Renaissance dramatist. Also, one can find an entire range of beliefs and behaviors in the characters of Shakespeare's plays, and it is to my thinking incorrect to read any of them as speaking "for" Shakespeare the playwright.

Nonetheless, it is not only Kate's body which is being tamed, but even more disconcerting is the "taming" of her spirit. Another servant [Curtis] describes how Petruchio

> rails, and swears, and rates, that she, poor soul
> Knows not which way to stand, to look, to speak,
> And sits as one new risen from a dream. (4.1.172–74)

By bringing in food and then not allowing her to eat, by bringing her to bed and not allowing her to sleep, Petruchio is refining his cruelty to her by setting up expectations before he crushes them. His telling Kate that something is not what she believes it to be, and forcing her to agree, creates in Kate a belief that her own perceptions do not matter or may even be incorrect. Kate, knowing this is the only way to stop his abuse, agrees to what Petruchio says:

> What you will have it named, even that it is,
> And so it shall be so for Katharine. (4.5.21–22)

But Petruchio then confuses the matter further by telling Kate she is wrong when she agrees with him that an old man they encounter on the road is really a young girl:

> Why, how now, Kate? I hope thou art not mad.
> This is a man, old, wrinkled, faded, withered,
> And not a maiden, as thou sayst he is. (4.5.41–43)

While Novy suggests that in this interchange there is more play going on, where Kate "replaces a language determined by the external world . . . with another determined by her relationship with Petruchio,"[24] I see something very different, and more disturbing, in this interchange. In modern parlance, one might say that Petruchio is "gaslighting" Kate. This term for attempting to manipulate someone so that he or more likely she believes she is going crazy came into use after the Hitchcock film "*Gaslight*" where the Victorian husband, greedy for his wife's wealth, attempts to convince her that she is going mad. Mysterious footsteps, objects that disappear and reappear suddenly, and gaslights that dim and flicker are all part of his plan.[25] Petruchio's constant harangues that what Kate perceives is not accurate might well have the same result. In the same way, while some critics call Kate and Petruchio's interchange on the street where he demands, "Kiss me, Kate," as more play and private language, he is still threatening "Why, let's home again," when she refuses out of a sense of modesty (5.2.135, 140).

In our discussion of *Taming of the Shrew* we have been concentrating on the parallels between Queen Katherine and Kate but I want to complicate the discussion further by suggesting that the Katherine who both studies and presents herself in the modest way of the ideal young woman yet still remains true to herself is also echoed by the other woman of *Shrew*, Kate's sister Bianca. Though in play and film presentations of *Shrew*, Bianca is often shown as a simpering fool who has not an iota of studious intent but only uses her books to flirt, this is not necessarily the Bianca of the text.

While many of Shakespeare's women are literate, and can both read and write—we think of Lady Macbeth reading her husband's letter, or Beatrice writing of her affection for Benedick—there are few characterizations of women studying. One Shakespearean character that definitely presents this in the most tragic of modes is Lavinia whose father Titus Andronicus says of her:

> But thou art deeper read and better skilled;
> Come and take choice of all my library,
> And so beguile thy sorrow . . . (4.1.33–35)

Lavinia, with neither tongue nor hands, manages to point out with her stumps the story of Philomel from Ovid's *Metamorphoses*, a book she obviously knows well, so that she can let her family know how she was ravished and mutilated.

Bianca's love of study has none of these tragic connotations. But though she is presented as the ideal feminine counterpart to the shrewish Kate, she is also from the beginning fascinated by her studies and music:

> My books and instruments shall be my company,
> On them to look and practice by myself. (1.1.82–83)

Her father Baptista recognizes this about her and approves it. He is delighted to accept a "small packet of Greek and Latin books" (2.1.100) for his daughters and says specifically about Bianca:

> And for I know she taketh most delight
> In music, instruments, and poetry,
> Schoolmasters will I keep within my house. (1.1.92–94)

Indeed, her suitor Lucentio disguises himself as her tutor so that he can be near her. Though David Bevington describes the relationship between the two as "superficial" (109) they spend much more time together than most courting couples and Bianca is learned enough that she tells him her feelings for him in Latin. Indeed though often described as "passive" (109) Bianca does inform Lucentio that she is no school boy liable to be whipped if he does not know the correct answer but rather learning for her own pleasure, which may well serve as a warning of how she will act when married:

> I am no breeching scholar in the schools;
> I'll not be tied to hours nor pointed times.
> But learn my lessons as I please myself. (3.1.18–20)

Bianca is an example of the new brand of teaching and learning fostered earlier in the century by Thomas More and Roger Ascham that discouraged use of corporal punishment and encouraged pedagogy that made learning fun and engaging. Bianca so enjoys her studies that she has to be dragged away from them. A servant calls to her:

> Mistress, your father prays you leave your books
> And help to dress your sister's chamber up,
> You know tomorrow is the wedding day. (3.1.80–82)

At the end of the play Petruchio, Lucentio, and Hortensio, recently married to a widow, wager on which of their wives is most obedient, betting on their women as they might upon their dogs or their horses.[26] Like the widow, Bianca does not come when summoned, sending word that she is busy. After Kate comes and wins her husband his bet, she then brings the widow and her sister Bianca back with her. Petruchio demonstrates further how much he has tamed Kate:

> Katharine, that cap of yours becomes you not.
> Off with bauble. Throw it underfoot. (5.2.127–28)

Kate at this moment is silent, but the stage directions inform us "She obeys." On stage Bianca may well show her disapproval of Kate's action even before she speaks. Novy suggests that the cap had become "a fool's toy," and "Bianca's scorn for folly has modulated into a scorn for duty."[27] But we might well wonder about the meaning of duty and reasons for obedience. Patient Griselda was held up as a model of wifely obedience in sixteenth-century England—she also agreed to, as she thought, the death of her children when Count Walter demanded it. Though Lucentio is distressed that he has lost his bet, Bianca's "What a foolish duty call you this?" is certainly a question worth pondering. At Petruchio's urging, Kate's final speech in *Shrew* sounds most similar to Katherine Parr's submission to her kingly husband. Kate tells the other women that

> Thy husband is thy lord, thy life, thy keeper,
> Thy head, thy sovereign . . .
>
> . . .
>
> And craves no other tribute at thy hands
> But love, fair looks, and true obedience—
> Too little payment for so great a debt.

> Such duty as the subject owes the prince
> Even such a woman oweth to her husband;
> And when is froward, peevish, sullen, sour
> And not obedient to his honest will
> What is she but a foul contending rebel
> And graceless traitor to her loving lord?
> I am ashamed that women are so simple
> To offer war where they should kneel for peace,
> Or seek for rule, supremacy, and sway
> When they are bound to serve, love, and obey.
>
> . . . .
>
> Come, come, you forward and unable worms!
> My mind hath been as big as one of yours,
> My heart as great, my reason haply more,
> To bandy word for word and frown for frown;
> But I see our lances are but straws
> Our strength as weak, our weakness past compare,
> That seeming to be most which we indeed least are.
> Then vail your stomachs, for it is no boot,
> And place your hands below your husband's foot,
> In token of which duty, if he please
> My hand is ready; may it do him ease.

Scholars such as Nevill Coghill would argue that Kate is "generously and charmingly" making this speech for Petruchio and "it is a total misconception to suppose that she has been bludgeoned into it."[28] Stephen Bretzius places Coghill in the "revisionist" school, suggesting, "For revisionist readers Kate's final speech simply humors Petruchio."[29] Ruth Nevo maintains "that Kate is in love by act 5 is, I believe, what the play invites us to perceive." Nevo continues, "And indeed she may well be. The man she has married has humour and high spirits, intuition, patience, self-command and masterly intelligence."[30] Novy sees a Kate and Petruchio who have "exclusive dependence on each other." Kate's speech "presents their marriage as a private world, a joke that the rest of the characters miss, a game that excludes all but the two of them."[31] I'm afraid it's a joke that I miss also.

Some scholars would argue for Kate's autonomy and spirited pleasure throughout the play all the way to this last speech. Margie Burns proposes that Kate's final speech succeeds as "intentional though extemporaneous irony, along the lines of Katherine and Petruchio's games playing in Act IV scene v . . . . Like Katharina herself at every point in the play, the speech continuously displays strength and animation."[32] Camille Wells Slights would see the speech in not quite such an ironic turn, but still would read the relationship between Kate and Petruchio as positive. "Petruchio certainly demands that Kate submit to his will, but we know, as she does, that he won't step on her hand."[33] But I am not so sure that Kate's hand, or more importantly her sense of self, is all that safe. The actual Katherine Parr was a far more complex woman than the idealized version of her in Foxe; in some ways both Kate and Bianca are her symbolic daughters. The shadow of this early sixteenth-century queen consort, knowing that the wrong word may lead to her death, stands behind Kate as she makes this speech, and is a troubling reminder to audiences both then and now of what can happen to wives who are not "tamed."

Notes

My deep thanks to my co-editors Jo Carney and Debra Barrett-Graves for their help on this essay. Lena Orlin's great knowledge of Shakespeare was also most helpful. My women in the Renaissance rhetoric study group offered valuable feedback to me. I also wish to thank Linda Shenk for her most insightful comments and Jarrod Brand for his research support. A shorter version of this paper was presented at the Northern California Renaissance Conference at Mills College, Oakland, April 2002. Carolyn Biltoft, Christine Couvillon, Kat Jensen, and Johanna Perry were a wonderful cheering section as I worked on this essay.

1. John Foxe, *The Acts and Monuments of John Foxe*, ed. Stephen Reed Cattley (London: Seeley and W. Burnside, 1838), 5: p. 554. Hereafter cited in the text as Foxe.
2. Susan James, *Kateryn Parr: The Making of a Queen* (Aldershot: Ashgate, 1999), pp. 114, 115.
3. J. J. Scarisbrick, Henry VIII, p. 456.
4. J. J. Scarisbrick, Henry VIII, pp. 479–81.
5. 4.5.6–8. All quotations are from William Shakespeare, *Complete Works*, ed. David Bevington 4th edn. (New York: Harper Collins, 1992).
6. Scarisbrick, *Henry VIII*, p. 481.
7. Sara Mendelson and Patricia Crawford, *Women in Early Modern England* (Oxford: Oxford University Press, 1998), p. 98.
8. "The Law's Resolution of Women's Rights" in *Half Humankind: Contexts and Texts of the Controversy about Women in England, 1540–1640*, ed. Katherine U. Henderson and Barbara F. McManus (Urbana: University of Illinois Press, 1985), p. 79.
9. Ruth Nevo, *Comic Transformations of Shakespeare* (London and New York: Methuen and Co. Ltd., 1980), p. 38.
10. Lynda Boose, "Scolding Brides and Bridling Scolds: Taming the Woman's Unruly Member," in Dana E. Aspinall, ed., *The Taming of the Shrew: Critical Essays* (London and New York: Routledge, 2002), p. 141.

11. Cherubino de Siena, Regole della vita matrimoniale. Bologna, 1888, pp. 12–14 in Frances and Joseph Gies, *Women in the Middle Ages* (New York: Harper, 1978), pp. 46, 48.
12. William Whatlely, *A Bride-bush* (London, 1623), p. 107.
13. Thomas Gouge, *Works* (Whitburn, 1798), pp. 290, 291.
14. As is stated in "The Law's Resolution of Women's Right" in *Half Humankind*, p. 79.
15. Mendelson and Crawford, *Women in Early Modern England*, p. 147.
16. Linda Bamber, *Comic Women, Tragic Men: A Study of Gender and Genre in Shakespeare* (Stanford: Stanford University Press, 1982), p. 32; *Is Shakespeare Still Our Contemporary?*, ed. John Elsom (London and New York: Routledge, 1989), pp. 68–70.
17. Lena Cowen Orlin, "The Performance of Things in *The Taming of the Shrew*," in Aspinal, p. 194.
18. Mendelson and Cawford, *Women in Early Modern England*, p. 140.
19. Keith Thomas, *Religion and the Decline of Magic* (New York: Charles Scribner's Sons, 1971), p. 517.
20. Robert Heilman, "The Taming Untamed, or, The Return of the Shrew," in Aspinal, *The Taming of the Shrew: Critical Essays*, p. 46.
21. Marianne L. Novy, "Patriarchy and Play in *The Taming of the Shrew*" in Harold Bloom, ed., *William Shakespeare's The Taming of the Shrew* (New York: Chelsea House, 1988), pp. 17, 21.
22. *The Riverside Shakespeare*, ed. G. Blakemore Evans (Boston: Houghton Mifflin, 1974), p. 106.
23. Nevo, *Comic Transformations*, 39. Fiona Shaws suggests this was the way Jonathan Miller directed his version of Shrew, having Petruchio "very non-violently disorientate her by not accepting anything she says. Jonathan says that what doctors do with aggressive children. I think he was translating the 'taming' of the shrew into 'therapy,' the realignment of the delinquent." Shaw was not happy with this interpretation. "That's a heavy imposition, because once you commit yourself to that statement, you could go a step further and have Petruchio in a white coat." Carol Rutter, *Clamorous Voices: Shakespeare's Women Today* (London: Women's Press Ltd, 1988), p. 6.
24. Novy, "Patriarchy and Play," in Bloom, *William Shakespeare's* The Taming of the Shrew, p. 19.
25. "As a slang term for subtly trying to drive someone crazy, 'gaslighting' was first noticed by lexicographers around 1956, though the term probably actually appeared as soon as the film (which was enormously popular) did." [www.word-detective.com0710000.html]
26. A point made by Michael Bogdanov in *Is Shakespeare Still Our Contemporary?*, p. 71.
27. Novy, "Patriarchy and Play," in Bloom, *William Shakespeare's* The Taming of the Shrew, pp. 22, 23.
28. Nevil Coghill "The Basis of Shakespearean Comedy," *Essays and Studies* (1950): 11 in Stephen Bretzius, *Shakespeare in Theory: The Postmodern Academy and the Early Modern Theater* (Ann Arbor: University of Michigan

Press, 1997), p. 57. I found Bretzius's discussion of different theoretical approaches to *The Taming of the Shrew* extremely helpful.
29. Bretzius, *Shakespeare in Theory*, p. 59.
30. Nevo, *Comic Transformations*, p. 50.
31. Novy, "Patriarchy and Play," in Bloom, *William Shakespeare's* The Taming of the Shrew, p. 25.
32. Margie Burns, "The Ending of the Shrew," in Aspinal, *The Taming of the Shrew: Critical Essays*, pp. 88, 89.
33. Camille Wells Slights, *Shakespeare's Comic Commonwealths* (Toronto: University of Toronto Press, 1993), p. 52.

Mary Queen of Scots as Suffering Woman: Representations by Mary Stuart and William Wordsworth

Joy Currie

Mary Stuart acceded to the throne of Scotland as an infant in 1542. The Scots sent her to France in 1548 for her safety and education and because she was betrothed to the future King of France. Mary's mother, Mary of Guise, who later began acting as regent in Scotland on her daughter's behalf, died on June 11, 1560, leaving a void in the government. The Protestant Scottish nobles took this opportunity to ban the celebration of the Mass. Francis II, now husband of Mary Stuart and King of France, died six months later, on December 5, 1560. A Catholic Mary Stuart returned to Scotland, a kingdom she hardly knew, on August 19, 1561, with very few people whom she could trust to advise her.

At the same time, Mary's widowhood and active rule in Scotland elicited fears in English Protestants, particularly since she coveted the throne of Elizabeth I.[1] To prevent Mary from forming a stronger alliance with France or another Catholic power, Elizabeth seemed to encourage her to marry Englishman Robert Dudley, to whom she gave the title Earl of Leicester "to make him more suitable as a husband for a queen."[2] Neither William Cecil, Elizabeth's principal secretary, nor the Scots expected the marriage to take place. Mary still hoped for someone of a higher status than Elizabeth's rejected suitor, whom she would not seriously consider, at least not without the promise of being named Elizabeth's heir to the throne of England.[3] In fact, failing to secure a Catholic prince for a husband and ignoring Elizabeth's suggestion, Mary wed Henry Stuart, Lord Darnley, a cousin who was also in line for the crown, on July 29, 1565, thereby perhaps strengthening her own claim.

Mary Queen of Scots Goodrich, S. Griswold. *Lives of Celebrated Women.* New York: John Allen, 1844, p. 308.

Although Mary named Darnley King of Scotland without the consent of her nobles, she soon realized how inadequate he was to help her rule. She came to rely more and more on her Italian secretary David Rizzio for advice and companionship, a relationship the Scottish nobles resented. The nobles obtained Darnley's cooperation in a conspiracy by falsely suggesting that Mary and her secretary were having an affair. On March 9, 1566, they stabbed Rizzio to death in Mary's presence. According to Sir James Melville, Mary knew that the nobles were plotting a rebellion. He had informed her of his fears, but she discounted his talk as "rumours."[4] However, she probably knew nothing about the plans for the attack on Rizzio. Although visibly upset and furious with Darnley for his part in the plot, the day after the murder she controlled her passion and managed to gain his assistance by convincing him of his own danger. With the help of others, they escaped to Dunbar Castle. Mary, who had been pregnant at the time, never forgot the trauma of Rizzio's murder. After the birth of James, she reminded Darnley that she and the unborn child might have been killed.[5]

Early in 1567, many of the same nobles conspired to rid themselves of Darnley, who had betrayed them when he denied prior knowledge of, or complicity in, the Rizzio conspiracy. Mary, now estranged from Darnley, was present at some of the nobles' discussions and insisted that nothing be done that would hurt her reputation or her son's right to inherit the crown,[6] but she did nothing to stop the conspirators. Meanwhile, Darnley, who had heard rumors of a plot against him, believed Mary would do him no harm.[7]

Nevertheless, Mary's subjects later believed she had played a role in Darnley's death.[8] She had convinced him to return to Edinburgh while visiting him in Glasgow in January, perhaps because she feared the Earl of Lennox's influence.[9] On the night of February 8, 1567, Darnley was convalescing at Kirk o'Field, probably from a flare up of syphilis, when the house was blown up. He was strangled while attempting to flee. Mary was attending a wedding celebration and later spent the night at Holyrood. After Darnley's death, she failed to observe the usual forty days of mourning. The trial of James Hepburn, Earl of Bothwell, most likely one of the chief instigators of the plot, became a mockery of justice when Bothwell's entourage intimidated the court into dismissing the case. Public animosity toward Mary increased after her hasty marriage to Bothwell on May 15, 1567. Soon after, the confederate nobles, some of whom had once been Mary's allies, arrested and imprisoned her and forced her to abdicate in July in favor of the infant James. Almost a year later, Mary escaped, raised an army, lost a battle at

Langside on May 13, 1568, and fled to England. Her troubled life in Scotland became the prolog to nineteen years of captivity in England.

Most monarchs of the time distributed some sort of propaganda to encourage the loyalty of their subjects—propaganda that included images conveyed through words, portraits, and the public performances of the monarchs themselves, not unlike the "self-fashioning" that Stephen Greenblatt sees in Renaissance writers.[10] Elizabeth I, among others, saw herself as an actor on a stage with a role that she could manipulate through language to serve her will. As Susan Frye suggests, Elizabeth "believe[d] in an unshakeable relation between the words of the monarch and the monarch herself."[11] Carole Levin describes how Elizabeth manipulated society's gender expectations as "she represented herself and her authority as monarch."[12] Writers represented Mary Stuart in literature from an early age and, depending on the author's politics, James Emerson Phillips points out, variously as "Circe" and "a saint."[13]

I suggest that as part of her "self-fashioning," Mary spoke and wrote from a particular subjectivity, selecting the thoughts and emotions that best reflected the image she desired to project. In her letters and lyric poems, she describes her sorrow, anxiety, and despair. Writing from captivity in England in 1579, she depicts her suffering self as subject and her fame and friends who have abandoned her as objects, placing responsibility for her lingering "sorrow" on their faithlessness: "Et plutôt que changer de mes maux l'aventure / Chacun change pour moi d'humeur et de nature." ["Rather than change my sorrows' destiny, / All change their mood and manner unto me."][14] She portrays herself as a model of Catholic piety and expresses her conviction that she is the lawful Queen of Scotland and rightful Queen of England, as she had done since she and Francis adopted the title and arms of the English monarchy a few months after their marriage in 1558.

Even after Elizabeth had her moved to Fotheringhay Castle for trial in September 1586, and though ill, Mary continued to construct her own image. As Garrett Mattingly observes, although "she had failed repeatedly to learn some of the more important lessons of politics... she had learned how to dominate a scene."[15] When asked to answer the charges brought against her, Mary demanded the respect owed her as an "absolute Queen" and claimed that she was not subject to English law. "She warned [her examiners] therefore to look to their Consciences and to remember that the Theater of the whole World is much wider than the Kingdom of England."[16] Mary's words suggest several ideas: the commonplace of rulership as theater, the very real threat to England from the Catholic powers, and possibly even Christ's admonition: "For what will it profit a man if he shall gain the *whole world*, and loses his own soul?" (emphases added).[17] In spite of her resistance to being tried, on February 8, 1587, she accepted the role of Catholic martyr and calmly submitted to her fate, "willingly bending her steps toward the place of execution," and spending her last few moments requesting that her servants be provided for, consoling them, declaring to the last her innocence, and praying in the manner of her faith.[18]

Two hundred and sixty years later, William Wordsworth began writing poems that depict Mary as a solitary, suffering woman who "laments" her "captivity."[19] Reading Mary's writings alongside Wordsworth's sympathetic portraits reveals similarities between how he perceived her and how she perceived herself or wished to be perceived by others. Both draw on the tradition of the subject as an individual that began during the Renaissance in lyric poetry to create a picture of the Scottish Queen that fits their respective desires. Mary wished to claim her rights as Queen of Scotland, to effect her release from captivity, and to encourage her image as a pious Catholic and martyr for her faith; Wordsworth hoped that his poetry would teach his readers how to love others, replacing his earlier real and fictional subjects of suffering with historical ones, such as Mary Queen of Scots.

Interest in the subject as the agent of fiction grew during the Renaissance. Catherine Belsey traces the development of the subject in drama—the subject who possessed an "imaginary interiority" not previously found in drama as opposed to the "representative" characters of medieval drama.[20] Especially in a soliloquy, the actor presents a unified subject who speaks, what Belsey calls "the subject of the enunciation," that is different from "the subject of the utterance, the subject defined in the speech."[21] This difference or "gap...opens the possibility of glimpsing an identity behind what is said, a silent self anterior to the utterance."[22] Belsey refers to dramatic characters portrayed by the physically present actor, but I believe we can apply similar terms to the narrator of a lyric poem, if we think of the narrator as possibly distinct from the author, as well as different from the object the narrator describes. While an author conveys the experience of the narrative or emotion through a speaker or point of view called the subject, the object of a work is that which the speaker contemplates.

An examination of the subject–object relationship within a work of literature, then, helps us identify "the gap" between the constructed subject—what the poet wants the reader to perceive about a subject—and the actual subject. When her young French husband died, Mary poured out her grief in a poem. She describes how it alters her face: "J'ai au coeur et à l'oeil / Un portrait et image / Qui figure mon deuil / Et mon pâle visage... Si parfois vers ces lieux / Viens à dresser ma vue, / Le doux trait de ses yeux / Je vois en une nue..." ["Deep in my eyes and heart / A portrait has its place / Which shows the world my hurt / In the pallor of my face.... Sometimes in such a place / His image comes to me. / The sweet smile on his face / Up in a cloud I see."][23] Not only does Mary evoke sympathy for her dead husband through the image she sees, by writing and sharing her poetry, she also asks for sympathy for her loss and to be seen herself, giving an early indication of her desire to create a particular image.[24] Joel Fineman describes the sort of two-part subjectivity that Mary's poem suggests—the seeing and the being seen—in his work on Shakespeare's sonnets. He observes that at the same time a subject directs attention outward toward an object, that subject draws attention back toward the self because of his or her thoughts of sympathy or disparagement. While Fineman is "more concerned with the poet's seeing rather than with what he sees,"[25] I am interested in both subjects and objects as constructs in the poems of Mary Stuart and Wordsworth and the reasons for those constructs.

In his work on Wordsworth's autobiographical writing, Paul de Man suggests the impossibility of determining what is true and what is fiction: "We assume that life *produces* the autobiography as an act produces its consequences, but can we not suggest, with equal justice, that the autobiographical project may itself produce and determine the life...?" He asks, then, is not autobiography "something more akin to a fiction?"[26] I suggest that de Man's analysis applies to Mary Stuart. Her life, especially after her imprisonment, was created in a sense through her poetry and letters. Her confinement in England limited her physically to an existence stripped of autonomy and royal authority and dictated that she place her hopes for her freedom, her rule, and her life on her subjective portrayals.

At least on two different occasions, Mary declined to see Elizabeth for political reasons. Elizabeth stipulated that Mary ratify the Treaty of Edinburgh in exchange for safe passage to Scotland through England in 1561. Instead Mary traveled by sea rather than "renounce the title and arms of England," because the treaty "might... nullify her future claim to the English throne."[27] Several scholars suggest that her renewed negotiations for a marriage with the Spanish heir Don Carlos influenced her decision to cancel the meeting with Elizabeth in the summer of 1564. However, Thomas Randolph writes that Mary left Edinburgh to "comfort the Lady of Murray for the loss of her son."[28] Perhaps she gave him this excuse, when in reality she feared jeopardizing a possible marriage with a Catholic prince by meeting with the Protestant Elizabeth.

During her captivity in England, on the other hand, Mary pleaded for an audience in poems and letters to Elizabeth, hoping to convince the English queen in person of her innocence. Mary's possible involvement in Darnley's death made it politically unwise for Elizabeth to see her cousin, and she never conceded to the meeting Mary so passionately desired.[29] In "Sonnet to Queen Elizabeth I of England," written in both French and Italian, Mary candidly expresses her fluctuating emotions of "torment and delight," eventually concluding with the cause of her imprisonment: "Ainsi je suis en souci et en crainte, / Non pas de vous mais quant aux fois à tort / Fortune rompe voile et cordage double." ["Likewise fear and distress fill all my hopes, / Not because of you, but for the times there are / When Fortune doubly strikes on sail and shroud."][30] With herself as subject and her emotions as the primary object, Mary takes the poetic form usually reserved as a vehicle for expressions of praise, love, or sorrow and uses it, in a bit of "self-fashioning," to simultaneously mourn her plight and solicit notice from the one person who can alter her situation. In the final couplet she exonerates her captor and, in Renaissance fashion, blames "the times" and "Fortune" for her circumstances.[31] Similarly, in her 1568 letter to Elizabeth requesting sanctuary, Mary writes: "next to God, I have no hope but in your goodness."[32] In 1574, she asks if she "might go to France or Scotland, things being by you re-established for my honour and safety,"[33] when she most likely feels dismay at Elizabeth's treatment of her. In later letters, her anger became more overt.

Mary sought to ingratiate herself with whomever she thought was most likely to help her. For a time before her first trial in England, she pretended to show interest in the Protestant faith, hoping to gain Elizabeth's sympathy.[34] During most of her captivity, however, she wrote of her fidelity to Catholicism in order to maintain Catholic interest in freeing her and placing her on the English throne and encouraged a belief in her ability to re-establish Catholicism in England through her devotion and her piety. One of her sonnets became a public declaration of her faith when her friend John Leslie, the Bishop of Ross, published it in *Consolations* in 1574, a collection most likely designed to elicit support for Mary's rule in England.[35] In the sonnet, "Lord My God, Receive My Prayer," she asks God to help her to be "Humble et dévot en un corps Chaste étant" ["In a living chaste body, devout and humble"].[36] Later during her captivity (1583) she writes: "Fors seulement de parvenir à Toi, / Pénitament et constante en ma foi"

["Only allow me to draw near to you, / Repentant, constant in my faith and true"].[37] Camden reports that she rejoiced on hearing her sentence, "that she was taken to be an instrument for the reestablishment of Religion in this land."[38] At the end of her last sonnet, "Sonnet Written at Fotheringhay," she affirms her belief that she will receive her "joie infinie" ["eternal bliss"].[39]

In her last letter to Elizabeth, written on December 19, 1586, Mary accepts her sentence of death, but she also writes: "I entreat you not to permit that execution to be done on me without your own knowledge."[40] She feared that false rumors would be spread about her fidelity to Catholicism, so she asked that her servants be allowed to witness the execution. Comforting one of them, her servant Robert Melvin, immediately before her execution, she asked him to "carry this message from me, that I die a true woman to my religion, and like a true Queen of Scotland and France."[41]

Although given to sudden reversals of emotion and bouts of weeping, Mary argued her case at her trial with conviction and eloquence. While incompetent to rule in many respects, she never forgot how to charm a crowd. "She had only to play this last scene well," Garrett Mattingly writes of her execution, to secure herself a lasting place in the hearts of the devout.[42] After mounting the platform on which the block was placed and "as if acknowledging the plaudits of a multitude (though the hall was very still), she turned for the first time to face her audience and, some thought, she smiled."[43] Arrayed in her finest clothing and carrying the accouterments of her faith, she prayed so loudly that her voice covered that of the Protestant Dean of Peterborough, Dr. Fletcher, and "all being present did clearly hear her."[44] She kissed her crucifix and "made herself unready with a kind of gladness."[45] Some chronicles mention the rude manner in which the executioners handled the removal of some of her garments. Others describe her flirtatious good will: she "smilingly said 'Now truly, my lords, I never had two such grooms waiting on me before.'"[46]

Situating the action of "Sonnet Written at Fotheringhay Castle" (1587) at her final dwelling place, Mary writes poignantly of her loss of identity and failure to gain her freedom, her rule, or immunity from English law: "Que suis-je hélas? Et de quoi sert ma vie? / Je ne suis fors qu'un corps privé de coeur" ["Alas what am I? What use has my life? / I am but a body whose heart's worn away"].[47] She points to two essential aspects of human life—the body and the heart (or mind, soul, or spirit), while reflecting on the useless years of her captivity, during which for a long time she courageously or naively believed that her release and restoration were possible. Although Mary's efforts to secure her own release and to regain her kingdom failed, her suffering and her courage and dignity at the end of her life made her the model of the solitary, suffering woman and, as Jayne Elizabeth Lewis says, "the creation of the English-speaking individual" that she became during her lifetime and has remained ever since.[48]

Not surprisingly, since he was influenced by the eighteenth-century tradition of sensibility, Wordsworth writes sympathetically of outcasts about whom he knows or hears. He describes in *The Prelude*, his most autobiographical poem, how Nature taught him concern for others: "images of danger and distress / and suffering, these took deepest hold of me."[49] He eventually came to see it as his duty to instruct his readers, calling poets, he and Coleridge specifically, "joint labourers in the work... Of their redemption... what we have loved / Others will love."[50] Imagination, Wordsworth felt, allows the poet to add "properties" not inherent in an object. Thus, he creates something "like a new existence."[51] He wished to come so close to the feeling of those he describes that he almost blended his "identity" with theirs, "for short spaces of time perhaps, to let himself slip into an entire delusion."[52] Meditating on objects allowed Wordsworth to infuse his poetry with sympathy so as to produce in the reader a "feeling" similar to that initially produced in the writer.

Wordsworth's relationship with the figure of human suffering evolved from his early poems, where he merely depicts them, to the yoking of suffering to morality, to his attempts to avoid the exploitation of human suffering in his verse.[53] Although he wrote less frequently of suffering after 1802, he by no means abandoned it entirely. History and place became the objects of meditation on which he exercised his imagination: "the tragedies of former times" or "what had been here done, and suffered here / Through ages, and was doing, suffering, still."[54] By 1819, he imaginatively explored history by entering the mind of the captive Mary Stuart and, thereby, depicted her historical suffering.

During the nineteenth century, history became a recognized source for poetic inspiration. Arabicus, a contributor to *Gentleman's Magazine*, in a critique of a contemporary production of the drama *Mary Queen of Scots* provides a possible explanation for Wordsworth's representation of Mary: "It is, I believe, generally allowed that the Tragic Muse may be supplied with nobler materials from History than either from Mythology or the invention of the Poet."[55] Alan Liu, among others, suggests that Wordsworth's poems "romanticize" history.[56] Several modern historians describe how the historical past of the British people became a source for political and patriotic rhetoric.[57]

Wordsworth presented Mary in ways similar to many other artists. From her lifetime through the nineteenth century, she played a significant role as a symbol of suffering. Several nineteenth-century women historians cast sympathy toward Mary and blame upon Elizabeth for using deception in her communications to Mary and for keeping her confined when she asked for protection. In giving in to the demands to execute Mary, many believed that Elizabeth had failed in her duty as a monarch and as a Christian to protect her cousin and sister queen. Still, Lucy Aikin would not have her readers be blind to human error in judging others either because of "resentment" or "compassion," since Mary played a role in her own demise.[58] As Jayne Elizabeth Lewis suggests, Mary "is impossible to separate from the ways she has been represented through time."[59]

Mary's poems were reprinted in French and English in *Gentleman's Magazine, Scots Magazine*, and the *Annual Register* during the late eighteenth and early nineteenth centuries. Articles debated her guilt or innocence, but frequently they represented her with sympathy: O. R. describes how Mary changed her subjects' attitude toward her when they saw her tears upon her confinement at Carberry-hill.[60] Wordsworth may have read Mary's poems; he was reading the *Annual Register* and the *Gentleman's Magazine* around the time that some of her poems were printed in these periodicals.[61] He certainly knew her history, having played as a child in one of her places of confinement that is the setting for "Address from the Spirit of Cockermouth Castle,"[62] a poem located just three before "Mary Queen of Scots" in his "Itinerary Poems of 1833."

With her premier place as a tragic figure, Mary was the perfect historical figure through which Wordsworth could express his sympathy for the solitary outcast. Abandoned by her countrymen; and except for a few foolhardy individuals, the Catholics; and even her son, King James VI of Scotland, Mary was truly alone. Two of Wordsworth's poems describe her as a solitary woman within the natural setting. He adopts Mary's subjectivity to imagine how it must feel to be imprisoned with little hope of release. In "Lament of Mary Queen of Scots" (1820), Mary bemoans in rhyme royal her captive state and blames Elizabeth, who breaks the primary Wordsworthian law: "A Woman rules my prison's key; / A sister Queen, against the bent / Of law and holiest *sympathy*..." (50–52, emphasis added).[63] Earlier in this poem, Wordsworth captures the dignity and pride that Mary retained until her death: "... for even here / Can I be proud that jealous fear / Of what I was remains" (47–49).

Wordsworth's "Captivity" (1819) depicts Mary's reliance on her faith for sustenance against despair and waywardness: "Just Heaven, contract the compass of my mind / To fit proportion with my altered state" (9–10). She asks God, in "Lament," to "keep" her "thoughts" "innocent" (55–56). Both of these poems reflect the spiritual focus seen in many of Mary's own poems. To return for a moment to one of them, another verse written in her Book of Hours reveals the length to which she was willing to go to fashion herself as a Catholic martyr—she boldly compares her abandonment by her friends to the rejection of Christ that led to his crucifixion: "En feinte mes amis changent leur bienveillance. / Tout le bien qu'ils me font est désirer ma mort, / Et comme si, mourant, j'étais en défaillance / Dessus mes vêtements ils ont jeté le sort." ["With feigned good will my friends change toward me, / All the good they do me is to wish me dead, / As if, while I lay dying helplessly, / They cast lots for my garments round my bed."][64] Mary's analogy is not without precedent: contemporary chronicles of Richard II's deposition compared him to Christ and Bolingbroke to Pilate.[65] While Wordsworth stops short of giving her a Christ-like quality, he acknowledges her image as a pious woman, as well as an unfortunate, abandoned one. He echoes Mary's cries of loneliness in "Lament," where only the moon and other sufferers show her sympathy. She addresses the moon, which "... did seem / To visit me, and me alone; / Me, unapproached by any friend, / Save those who to my sorrows lend / Tears due unto their own" (19–21). As in her own poetry, here Mary blames her friends, also recognizing the fact that they can console only by contemplating their own suffering.

After his third tour of Scotland, Wordsworth wrote "Mary Queen of Scots Landing at the mouth of the Derwent, Workington" (1835), using a third-person narrator to describe Mary's landing near his birthplace at Cockermouth in Cumberland. The narrator observes that "The Queen drew back the wimple that she wore; / And to the throng, that on the Cumbrian shore / Her landing hailed, how touchingly she bowed!" (2–4). Here Wordsworth re-creates in his subject's actions before the crowd a theatrical gesture reminiscent of the historical Mary's own behavior, evoking her reputed charm.

In most instances, Wordsworth follows history in his depiction of Mary, but he focuses almost exclusively on her subjective experience.[66] Exceptions occur when Mary mentions her jailor and when the third-person narrator breaks in to remind the reader of her ultimate fate with references to "the block." "Wordsworth conceives the past not as a self-contained moment," Peter J. Manning writes, "but as a force that continually generates renewed interpretation in the present," allowing him to move out of the realm of autobiography and into history.[67] It concerned Wordsworth little if objects were in front of him, if he recalled them through memory, or created them through his imagination. For him, time and circumstances disappear, since all are part of one "human nature."[68] He wanted first to please his readers and then to remind them of suffering, not to present literal history.

Wordsworth chose two Renaissance verse forms to write about Mary, the sonnet and rhyme royal, the stanza used in *Mirror for Magistrates* (1559) to recount the downfall of famous men and women in English history. Poets of the Romantic period, while undoubtably influenced by the Renaissance interest in the subject, furthered this interest because of their concern for the individual. De Man connects Wordsworth's "figures of deprivation, maimed men, drowned corpses, blind beggars, children about to die... [with] Wordsworth's own poetic self."[69] The poet's earlier work displays an interest in manipulating the subject so as to include the self, yet by the time he writes about Mary he has moved past the need to inscribe himself within his poetry. He may still desire to attract his readers' attention to himself, as writers do, but his primary emphasis had become the figure of suffering. Mary provided him with that figure and with a character through whom he could continue his efforts to fulfill his role as "labourer" in the "redemption" of those who lack human sympathy. At the same time, his lyrical and narrated portraits add to the rich tapestry that makes up our complex image of the Scottish queen.

Mary needed to write subjectively, since her only role as monarch was her self-constructed role through her writing and her occasional appearances in front of groups of people, most notably her final trial and execution. The identification of the subject in Renaissance literature (and perhaps even in medieval French literature as Michel Zink contends)[70] suggests the possible source for Mary's lyric form of poetry. Zink believes that "literary subjectivity defines literature. The latter truly exists only the moment a text seeks to present itself... as the product of a particular consciousness."[71] He ties the occurrence of subjectivity to the increasing importance placed on the author of a work as a writer of truth. Educated in France, Mary was exposed to works of French and Italian poets, who drew their models from medieval tradition.[72] Thus, she tells her subjective woes in the lyrical mode that portrays a created self that differs from the "subject of the utterance." The depth of feeling in her poetry and letters helps us to understand her better and evokes in us a sympathy that perpetuates our enduring attraction to the myth of Mary conceived and born into existence so many generations ago.

Notes

1. James Emerson Phillips, *Images of a Queen: Mary Stuart in Sixteenth-Century Literature* (Berkeley and Los Angles: University of California Press, 1964), p. 10; Duke of Hamilton, *Mary R: Mary Queen of Scots: The Crucial Years* (Edinburgh and London: Mainstream, 1991), p. 28.
2. William Camden, *History or Annals of England During the Whole Life and Reign of Elizabeth, late Queen thereof. Complete History of England: with the Lives of all the Kings and Queens Thereof* (London: Brab Aylmer, 1706), p. 396; see also Jayne Elizabeth Lewis, *The Trial of Mary Queen of Scots: A Brief History with Documents* (Boston and New York: Bedford/St. Martins, 1999), pp. 9–10, hereafter *Trial*; and Jenny Wormald, *Mary Queen of Scots: A Study in Failure* (London: George Philip, 1988), p. 147, hereafter *Failure*; see also T. F. Henderson, *Mary Queen of Scots: Her Environment and Tragedy*, 2 vols. (1905; reprint, New York: Haskell, 1969), 1: p. 294.
3. Thomas Wright, *Queen Elizabeth and Her Times; a series of original letters*, vol. 1 (London: H Colborn, 1838), pp. 179, 187; and Wallace MacCaffrey, *The Shaping of the Elizabethan Regime* (Princeton: Princeton University Press, 1968), pp. 166, 170.
4. *Memoirs of Sir James Melville of Halhill 1535–1617* (New York: E. P. Dutton, 1930), p. 113.
5. John Maxwell, Baron Herries, *Historical Memoirs of the Reign of Mary Queen of Scots, and a Portion of the Reign of King James the Sixth* (Edinburgh: Abbotsford Club, 1836), p. 79; and Antonia Fraser, *Mary Queen of Scots* (New York: Delacourte, 1969), p. 253.
6. Andrew Lang, *The Mystery of Mary Stuart* (1901; reprint, New York: AMS, 1970), pp. 117–20. See also *Calendar of State Papers, Relating to Mary, Queen of Scots, 1547–1603, preserved in the Public Records Office, the British Museum and elsewhere in England*, eds. Joseph Bain et al., 13 vols. (Edinburgh: H. M. General Register House, 1898–1969), 2: pp. 598–99, hereafter *CSP, Scotland*.
7. Henderson, Appendix C, 2: p. 665.
8. *CSP, Scotland*, 2: 329, 351.
9. Henderson, 2: 664, and Wormald, *Failure*, p. 161.
10. *Renaissance Self-Fashioning: From More to Shakespeare* (Chicago and London: University of Chicago Press, 1980).
11. *Elizabeth I: The Competition for Representation* (New York: Oxford University Press, 1993), p. 4.
12. *The Heart and Stomach of a King: Elizabeth I and the Politics of Sex and Power* (Philadelphia: University of Pennsylvania Press, 1994), p. 1. See also S. P. Cerasano and Marion Wynne-Davies, " 'From Myself, My Other Self I Turned': An Introduction," and Frances Teague, "Queen Elizabeth in Her

Speeches," both in *Gloriana's Face: Women, Public and Private, in the English Renaissance* (Detroit: Wayne State University Press, 1992), pp. 1–24, 63–78.
13. *Images of a Queen*, p. 7.
14. Mary Queen of Scots, from "Verses Written in Her Book of Hours," *Bittersweet within My Heart*, trans. and ed. Robin Bell (London: Pavilion, 1992), pp. 86–87, hereafter *Bittersweet*. All citations of Mary's poetry are from this edition. Page rather than line numbers are given.
15. *The Armada* (1959, Boston: Houghton, 1987), p. 2.
16. Camden, p. 520.
17. In conversation, Stephen M. Buhler suggested the Catholic threat as a possible interpretation of Mary's words; Christ's words are recorded in Mark 8: 36, Geneva Bible. John Durkan reports that no Bibles are listed on the inventory of Mary's library, although she "could have used a plagiarized and Catholicized Genevan one," "The Library of Mary, Queen of Scots," *Mary Stewart: Queen in Three Kingdoms*, ed. Michael Lynch (Oxford: Basil Blackwell, 1988), p. 86.
18. Robert Wyngfield, "A Circumstantial Account of the Execution of Mary Queen of Scots" (1587), reprinted in Lewis, *Trial*, p. 115.
19. Peter Wilfred Stine describes Wordsworth's Mary Queen of Scots as a solitary, "The Changing Image of Mary Queen of Scots in Nineteenth-Century British Literature" (Ph.D. diss., Michigan State University, 1972), p. 16.
20. Belsey, *The Subject of Tragedy: Identity and Difference in Renaissance Drama* (London and New York: Methuen, 1985), p. 18.
21. *Subject of Tragedy*, p. 48.
22. *Subject of Tragedy*, p. 49.
23. *Bittersweet*, pp. 16–19.
24. See Sarah M. Dunnigan, "Scottish Women Writers c. 1560–c. 1650," *A History of Scottish Women's Writing*, ed. Douglas Gifford and Dorothy McMillan (Edinburgh: Edinburgh University Press, 1997), p. 19.
25. *Shakespeare's Perjured Eye: The Invention of Poetic Subjectivity in the Sonnets* (Berkeley and Los Angeles: University of California Press, 1986), pp. 5, 12.
26. "Autobiography as De-Facement," *The Rhetoric of Romanticism* (New York: Columbia University Press, 1984), p. 69.
27. J. E. Neale, *Queen Elizabeth I* (London: Jonathan Cape, 1961), p. 109.
28. *CSP, Scotland*, 2: 65. See also *Calendar of State Papers, Foreign Series, of the reign of Elizabeth*, ed. Joseph Stevenson, 25 vols. (1870; reprint, Nendeln, Liechtenstein: Kraus, 1966), 7: 148.
29. See Sir Francis Knollys's explanation to Mary in [James Anderson], *Collections Relating to the History of Mary Queen of Scotland* (London: James Betlenham, 1727), 4: 53; and Anne Somerset, *Elizabeth I* (London: Weidenfeld and Nicholson, 1991), p. 205.
30. *Bittersweet*, pp. 62, 65.
31. In Renaissance thought, reliance on fortune meant the hope for earthly prosperity rather than a Christian hope in the eternal. See H. David Brumble, *Classical Myths and Legends in the Middle Ages and Renaissance* (Westport, CT: Greenwood, 1998), pp. 123–26.

32. *The Letters of Mary Queen of Scots*, ed. Agnes Strickland (London: Colburn, 1844), 1: p. 66. All letters cited are taken from this edition.
33. *Letters*, 1: p. 260.
34. Fraser, pp. 381–83.
35. See *Bittersweet*, p. 78. See also Phillips, who describes Leslie's work as "a series of Latin poems, purportedly exchanged between Mary and Leslie during his imprisonment" in the Tower. Leslie commends Mary for her piety and fidelity to Catholicism. A French translation of his work was published in 1590, pp. 102, 270, n. 54.
36. *Bittersweet*, pp. 78–79.
37. *Bittersweet*, pp. 98–99.
38. Camden, p. 528.
39. *Bittersweet*, pp. 108–09.
40. *Letters*, 2: 203.
41. Qtd. In Wyngfield, p. 115. See also *CSP, Scotland*, 9: 272.
42. *Armada*, p. 5.
43. *Armada*, p. 2.
44. Adam Blackwood, "The History of Mary Queen of Scots" (1587), reprinted in Lewis, *Trial*, p. 123.
45. Wyngfield, p. 119.
46. *CSP, Scotland*, 9: 275; see also Wyngfield, p. 119.
47. *Bittersweet*, pp. 108–09.
48. *Mary Queen of Scots: Romance and Nation* (London and New York: Routledge, 1998), p. 3.
49. *The Prelude: 1799, 1805, 1850*, ed. Jonathan Wordsworth et al. (New York: Norton, 1979), 8, pp. 211–12. All citations come from the 1805 version.
50. *Prelude*, 13, pp. 439, 441, 444–45.
51. Citations from Wordsworth's prefaces and other prose works are taken from *The Prose Works of William Wordsworth*, ed. W. J. B. Owen and Jane Worthington Smyser, 3 vols. (Oxford: Clarendon, 1974), 3: p. 32.
52. *Prose Works*, 1: 138.
53. See James H. Averill, *Wordsworth and the Poetry of Human Suffering* (Ithaca and London: Cornell University Press, 1980), p. 283; and David Simpson, *Wordsworth's Historical Imagination* (New York and London: Methuen, 1987), especially pp. 160–84.
54. *Prelude*, 8, pp. 782–83.
55. *Gentleman's Magazine*, 59 (1789), p. 697, hereafter *GM*.
56. *Wordsworth: The Sense of History* (Stanford: Stanford University Press, 1989), p. 497.
57. Linda Colley, *Britons: Forging the Nation 1707–1837* (New Haven and London: Yale University Press, 1992); and Gerald Newman, *The Rise of English Nationalism* (New York: St. Martin's, 1987).
58. *Memoirs of the Court of Elizabeth, Queen of England* (London: Ward, Lock, and Tyler, n.d.), p. 366. See also Jane Austen, *The History of England*, ed. Deirdre Le Faye (London: British Library, 1993), p. xxii; Matilda Betham, *A Biographical Dictionary of the Celebrated Women of Every Age and Country* (London: B. Crosby, 1804), p. 310; Mary Hays, *Memoirs of Queens Illustrious and Celebrated* (London: T. and J. Allman, 1821), pp. 415–16.

59. "'The *sorrow* of seeing the Queen': Mary Queen of Scots and the British History of Sensibility, 1707–1789," *Passionate Encounters in a Time of Sensibility*, ed. Maximilian E. Novak and Anne Mellor (Newark: University of Delaware Press, 2000), p. 200.
60. *GM*, 58 (1788), pp. 312–13.
61. See *GM*, 57 (1787), pp. 815, 1178–79; 58 (1788), pp. 63, 160; and Duncan Wu, *Wordsworth's Reading 1770–1799* (Cambridge: Cambridge University Press, 1993), pp. 6, 62. Wordsworth's library contained volumes of the *Annual Register* and may have included vol. 31 (1789), where Mary's poem on the death of Francis appeared. See Chester L. Shaver and Alice C. Shaver, *Wordsworth's Library: A Catalogue* (New York: Garland, 1979), p. 9.
62. David Watson Rannie, *Wordsworth and His Circle* (New York: Putnam's, 1907), p. 25.
63. Except for *The Prelude*, citations from Wordsworth's poetry are taken from *Wordsworth: Poetical Works*, ed. Thomas Hutchinson and Ernest de Selincourt (Oxford and New York: Oxford University Press, 1969). Line numbers are given parenthetically in the text.
64. *Bittersweet*, pp. 90–91.
65. See Ernst H. Kantorowicz, *The King's Two Bodies* (Princeton: Princeton University Press, 1957), p. 38.
66. Peter Stine suggests that writers of the Romantic period "saw Mary as an individual free from any specific historical context," p. ix.
67. "Cleansing the Images: Wordsworth, Rome, and the Rise of Historicism," *Texas Studies in Literature and Language*, 33 (1991), p. 288.
68. *Prelude*, 8, p. 761.
69. "Autobiography," p. 73.
70. *The Invention of Literary Subjectivity*, 1985, trans. David Sices (Baltimore and London: John Hopkins University Press, 1999), pp. 10–11.
71. *Subjectivity*, p. 4.
72. The Duke of Hamilton writes that Ronsard, Mary's one-time tutor, "was one of the best, and probably the most prolific poets of the French Renaissance," p. 62, n. 3; see also Durkan, especially pp. 78–90.

Re-imagining a Renaissance Queen: Catherine of Aragon among the Victorians

Georgianna Ziegler

During the first few years of her reign, from 1837 to 1839, the young Queen Victoria spent hours discussing English literature, history, and politics with her senior statesman, Lord Melbourne. She recorded these conversations in some detail in her diaries, thus giving us a window into the developing mind of a young woman whose schooling had been above the standards for a female of the period, but hardly scholarly. Several times, Lord M., as she called him, touched on the personalities around the time of Henry VIII, including Henry's first queen, Catherine of Aragon.[1] Victoria recounts Lord M. as saying that Catherine was always troubled by the fact that her first marriage to Prince Arthur depended on the "inhuman murder" of the Earl of Warwick—"that Catherine felt this all along and observed that it dwelt upon her and 'that it did not go well with her in the world' for this reason."[2] On a later occasion when Lord Melbourne declared that "we owed the Reformation" to Henry VIII, Victoria writes, "I said his motives for that were not the best; but Lord M. said that didn't signify. Talked of Henry VIII Lord M. said, 'Those women bothered him so.' I observed he had ill-treated Catherine of Aragon so. 'That was his conscience,' said Lord M. funnily; 'he thought he was living in a state of concubinage, not of marriage'" (2: 158). Finally, the next year when Victoria is twenty, they launch again into a discussion of Henry VIII and his wives, following a production of *Henry V*, and again, Victoria defends Catherine of Aragon: "And poor Catherine of Aragon he ill-used, I said; 'He got tired of her,' said Lord M., 'she was a sad, groaning, moaning woman,' which made me laugh" (2: 218). Though Victoria laughs, the

Griffith. She is asleep: good wench, let's sit down quiet,
For fear we wake her.

Act IV. Scene II.

Henry VIII, Act IV, scene ii in Cassell's *Illustrated Shakespeare*
By permission of the Folger Shakespeare Library.

growth of her independent opinion becomes evident over the course of the three years chronicled here, as evidenced in her willingness to speak her own mind in defence of Henry's first queen.[3]

In at least one of these conversations, they touch on Anne of Cleves, Jane Seymour and Katherine Parr as well, but it is striking that Victoria always returns to Catherine of Aragon, focusing on how she was "ill-used" by Henry. Though young and innocent about some aspects of life, Victoria was certainly aware of the profligacy of her own uncles and the relief with which England welcomed her ascent to the throne in 1837. Wary of trading the dominance of her mother for the dominance of a husband, she may also have pitied Catherine for her ill-usage as a pawn in the hands of men: her father, her father-in-law, and her husband. But as Margaret Homans has pointed out, marriage in Victoria's time also provided the only acceptable "independence" that women could achieve,[4] and Victoria's own ultimately successful marriage with Prince Albert created an image of family and home that came to dominate the public view of monarchy in the period. The numerous representations of the couple "helped to disseminate a complex picture of royalty's superordinary domesticity, to publicize the monarchy as middle-class and its female identity as unthreateningly subjugated and yet somehow still reassuringly sovereign" (19). Such a view of domesticated female sovereignty, as I shall show, also influenced the depiction, during the nineteenth century, of Henry VIII's first queen.

The whole notion of "queenship"—of what a queen should be in her personal character and public persona—was re-defined during the Victorian age. Initially on the accession of Victoria, as Nicola Watson has shown, the country looked back to the reign of their most eminent female sovereign, Elizabeth I, romanticizing the age and seeing it as the beginning of the modern era from whence flowed religious toleration, British imperialism, manliness, chivalry, scientific advancement, and the like.[5] Eventually, however, this positive reception of the Virgin Queen was complicated by an aversion to what was seen as her un-feminine character (refusing to marry and bear children, the lack of the "softer" qualities of a woman), her control over personal political power, and the coarse manners of her age (a favorite excuse given by Shakespearean editors for the Bard's bawdiness). The ambiguities surrounding Elizabeth are well summarized by Louisa Costello in the Introduction to her 1844 *Memoirs of Eminent Englishwomen*:

> When all her grandeur of intellect, her promptness, wisdom, and resolution, are considered, this blemish [vanity] on her *manly* qualities ought

to be looked upon with indulgence, if it does not altogether redeem her reputation, for it was the only *female* trait she allowed to appear. Tenderness, softness, pity, and forgiveness, were unknown to her mind, and, but for her vanity, she would have been scarcely woman or human.... Although her character can never be popular with her sex, still Englishwomen are indebted to Queen Elizabeth's best qualities for a new era in their existence... she had involuntarily bestowed great benefits on her fellow females by proving of what importance they could be.[6]

The image of Victoria was then constructed against this darker image of her predecessor; while Elizabeth proved that a woman could rule successfully, Victoria proved that a woman could do so without compromising what were considered the traits of her sex: domestic, feminine, wifely, motherly. Summing up the two queens from "a woman's point of view," the author of an article in *Victoria Magazine* of June 1864 writes:

> Two queens, belonging to two as different types of womanhood... yet both stamping their own individuality... on the whole era through which they move.... Elizabeth, with her masculine intellect, her iron will, ... her stately court... and the utter blank of her domestic life...; Victoria, gifted with moderate not commanding talent, who if not born a Queen might have been much like an ordinary gentlewoman; refined, accomplished, wise, and good: in everything essentially womanly, and carrying through life a woman's best amulet, the power of loving nobly, deeply, and faithfully.[7]

As Victoria's reign progressed, she became so domesticated and "middle class" that it was important to re-establish a sense of mythic queenly power to her image. This she achieved in part by withholding herself from public view for years after the death of Albert, while carefully constructing and controlling the images of herself that were circulated to the public.[8] But her regal image was also articulated in the important essay by John Ruskin, "Of Queens Gardens," part of his popular book, *Sesame and Lilies* (1865).[9] As Sharon Weltman has convincingly argued, Ruskin takes Coventry Patmore's "Angel in the House" figure and makes her a queen, symbolically expanding the walls of her home into a mythic realm where she is the wise and moral center, prepared to guide men, with "power to heal, to redeem, to guide, and to guard."[10] The operative word here is "guide": in Ruskin's view, the sexes have equal but complementary powers; men determine action but women give it moral direction. There is an implicit comparison with Victoria's method of ruling: "in a constitutional monarchy, the queen's legal powers are sharply restricted, but remain symbolically and politically significant. Victoria used her position to affect domestic affairs and foreign policy all the time" (Weltman 1997, 117). Ruskin's essay mythologizes and expands this role, heightening Victoria's position and raising the power of all other women (Weltman 1997, 117).

The nineteenth-century view of female sovereignty is thus conflicted. While on the one hand it domesticates the powers of the actual sovereign by making her appear more familiarly middle-class as wife and mother, on the other hand it glorifies the position of the middle-class woman, giving her moral direction over the affairs of men so that in Ruskin's terms, she becomes queen of her own home. Though Catherine of Aragon was not technically a queen regnant, as was Victoria, nevertheless she was crowned in a splendid and festive double coronation with Henry VIII, making her queen consort, and when Henry went to France in 1513 to fight as an ally of the Emperor Maximillian, he left Catherine at home as his regent.[11] In their presentations of Catherine, however, historians throughout the nineteenth century tend to emphasize the domestic side of her life and the strong moral stance that she maintained, in the face of overwhelming pressures from church and state to renounce her position. Furthermore, as I shall show, there are nuanced differences among the historical accounts, in part determined by the gender of the author. I shall also argue that the reception of the character of Catherine of Aragon in productions of Shakespeare's play *King Henry VIII* during the period reflect the growth of opinion toward domesticated queenship.

I

"The throne itself, with but few exceptions, secures not woman from the peculiar disadvantages that have hitherto attended her sex." Thus writes Mary Hays in the preface to her *Memoirs of Queens Illustrious and Celebrated*, London, 1821.[12] Hays was one of a group of early nineteenth-century women writers following on Hannah More and Mary Wollstonecraft, who "advocat[ed] the revolutionary idea that women must think as well as feel," and who would criticize men as well as women for intellectual and moral failure.[13] In her preface, while asserting "the powers and capacity of woman for rational and moral advancement," Hays laments the current state of education for women that trains them "for adornment rather than for use" (vi–vii). Her biographical entry for Catherine of Aragon emphasizes the queen's intellectual attainments; in the first sentence she describes the queen as "distinguished for her learning and piety," and the last two paragraphs emphasize her devotion to literature and the esteem in which she was held by Erasmus and Vives (133, 141–42). Hays asserts that "by her personal and mental qualifications," Catherine "acquired a great ascendency, for nearly twenty years, over the affections of the king" (134).

Hays's contemporary, Elizabeth Ogilvy Benger, goes further in her *Memoirs of the Life of Anne Boleyn* (first published 1821). She describes Catherine as "a queen lovely in person and in mind, of exemplary prudence and virtue, and truly gentle and feminine in her manners." With her "considerable learning," Catherine "cordially co-operated in [Henry's] liberal patronage of literature."[14] She speaks of the gross immorality of the city and court during Henry VIII's time, modified only by the "purer morals and more decorous manners" of the Reformation, a trend that she sees beginning in Sir Thomas More's family, and ushering in a time when "female cultivation ceased to be rare when learning became the badge of a superior station" (36). In spite of Catherine's Catholicism, Benger evidently sees her as fitting into this later Reform trend of cultivated women, for she describes her "feminine reserve" and mildness as offsetting the frivolity of Henry, who, she feels, nevertheless "approved the reformation which, both by precept and example, ... [Catherine] sought to introduce in female manners" (152). "Unhappily for Catharine, as her beauty declined, her gravity increased; and though celebrated for her learning, she appears not to have possessed those companionable talents which enliven domestic retirement. It is the misfortune of the female sex, that superior moral qualities, though necessary to ensure esteem, are not sufficient to preserve affection..." (152). While, as we saw, Hays deplored the emphasis on female beauty to the detriment of intellectual and moral education, Benger sees that women need both in order to maintain their influence over men. For Hays and Benger, the contrast with their own queen Caroline must have been painfully evident. Surely, the disgust with which Benger describes the "venality, perfidy, and corruption" of Henry VIII's period owes something to the corruption of the contemporary court of George IV, whose mistreated queen Caroline, having just been tried for adultery and acquitted, died in 1821, the year these two memoirs of queens were published.[15]

Hays, who knew Mary Wollstonecraft, and Benger, who was a friend of Lady Caroline Lamb, belonged to the generation of women who grew out of the eighteenth-century bluestockings and were advancing women's intellectual development, just as the child was born who would become Queen Victoria, a woman not "celebrated for her learning," but whose "superior moral qualities" and "companionable talents" would restore the tarnished image of queenship.

Memoirs and literary biography, along with straight history, written for a broad range of audiences, became ever more popular as the nineteenth century advanced. Biographical dictionaries of famous women, such as that by Hays, multiplied on both sides of the Atlantic, and helped to inject a female perspective into the dominant view of history as *"man's business."* Couching their histories as "lives" or "memoirs," authorized women to enter the masculine realm of historical discourse.[16] The first serious work in this genre was *Lives of the Queens of England* by Agnes and Elizabeth Strickland (12 vols., 1840–48). In an age when women were not admitted to university, the Stricklands learned paleography and read original English and continental documents, relying on the generosity of antiquarians and members of the gentry for access to public institutions, such as the British Library, and to private collections (Preface: x).[17] Though their aim, as stated by Agnes, was "without reservation or one-sided views, to bring forward every thing that tends to display character in its true light" (viii), in fact their depiction of Catherine of Aragon is consistently sympathetic, emphasizing her intelligence and political engagement with more detail than Hays or Benger. They describe Catherine's upbringing by her mother, Isabel of Spain, "the most learned princess in Europe," who instructed her daughters herself and provided them "with tutors of great literary attainments" (64). Erasmus dedicated his treatise on "Christian Matrimony" to Catherine "and always cited her as an example to her sex," giving "a brilliant list of the great and virtuous men, who were patronised at the English court when Katharine presided as queen of Henry VIII" (93). Though ironically Erasmus held the marriage of Henry and Catherine as an example of " 'united wedlock'," asking, " 'Where can a wife be found better matched with the best of husbands?' ", the Stricklands remark: "The conduct of a man is almost invariably influenced by the moral qualities of the woman who has his heart in her keeping. ... can we believe that women of equal worth had his [Henry's] moral guidance in the meridian and decline of life?"(93). They stress Henry's reliance on Catherine when he went to fight in France, entrusting her "with the highest powers that had ever yet been bestowed on a female regent in England"(81), and note that "while queen Katharine retained her place and influence, the career of improvement commenced, which has ever since continued to progress in this country" (89).

Writing ten years into Queen Victoria's reign, the Stricklands "emphasize a sense of a female tradition, of a succession of empowered women and a feminized version of the concept of descent" (Melman 13). While their statement about Catherine's influence as regent is exaggerated, nevertheless they depict her as virtuous and pious but also full of queenly authority and an "accurate [judge] of character" (Strickland 109). Their final judgment privileges her integrity and firmness above her more womanly qualities: "The grand abilities of Katharine of Arragon, her unstained integrity of word and action, united with intrepid firmness, commanded even from her enemies that deep respect, which her sweetness, benevolence, and other saintly virtues, would not have obtained, unsupported by these high queenly qualities" (121).

In stark contrast to the work of the Stricklands is the four-volume *History of Two Queens: Catherine of Aragon; Anne Boleyn* by William Hepworth Dixon that appeared about thirty years later in 1873–74.[18] For Dixon, the past is another country into which we must try to enter, and he sees each queen "as a type of what was best and worst in the revolt from Rome" so that "her human nature is forgotten in the cause for which she stood."[19] In redrawing that human nature, however, Dixon's interpretation of the historical facts of Catherine's life is often diametrically opposed to that of the Stricklands. He stresses the influence of Isabel of Castille's cruelty, violence, and ardent Catholicism on Catherine rather than her learning. Instead of mentioning her Latin education, Dixon describes Catherine as "eating angel bread, ... lisping endless prayers, ... dancing with her ladies, and ... talking with her teacher," as well as seeing the Inquisition burn piles of books and people "beneath her lattice ledge" (1: 248). Dixon sees Catherine as an agent of the Catholic church when she marries Arthur and again when she marries Henry, in spite of his scruples. Though he admits that she "assumed the conduct of her own affairs" in the difficult transition between marriages (2: 234), the second marriage itself was "a test and an appeal," waiting for its outcome on her production of an heir (3: 9). And while the Stricklands write that Catherine "identified herself with the interests of England in all things, as if she had been a native-born queen" (92), Dixon says that she saw her "foremost duty" lying with Spain, not with England (3: 52).

In words that seem inspired by Shakespeare's *Taming of the Shrew*, Dixon shows Catherine as at first pleasing to Henry, never "lovelier ... than when he heard her battling in imperious language for her nephew Charles.... She failed to change his purpose; yet he liked his councillors to see that Kate—his own brave Kate—was every inch a Queen" (3: 332). Eventually, "old and sad," "living a proud and joyless life," she drifts apart from Henry who finds new interest in the talented and intelligent Anne Boleyn (3: 370). The Stricklands admit and describe the ascetic routine of her life, but temper it by indicating that she "delighted in conversation of a lively cast," and especially took pleasure in the company of Sir Thomas More (92). In her last retreat at Kimbolton, Dixon writes that Catherine "had chosen to regard herself as being a prisoner and a martyr of her Church," though in fact she was neither (4: 241). Dixon's whole view is colored by his obvious distaste for Catholicism, and while evoking the sights and sounds of early modern Spain and England with the gusto of a traveler (which he was), Dixon is unable to distance himself from his own prejudices. Rather than seeing Catherine's self-agency as an intelligent woman, Dixon judges her as the victim of her own intransigence.

Coming somewhere between the Stricklands and Dixon, both chronologically and philosophically, are the more general histories by Froude and Cassell, both published in 1856. In his *History of England from the Fall of Wolsey to the Death of Elizabeth*, Froude recognizes the distance of the past, but unlike Dixon, he cannot "stand amidst the conflicts out of which they came and into which they merged" (Dixon, vii). For Froude, the gulf between the period of Henry VIII and his own time is too vast; "they cannot come to us, and our imagination can but feebly penetrate to them" (51).[20] Aware of his own point of view, Froude knows that he reads the divorce of Henry and Catherine differently than it was read in its own time. Then, the divorce seemed "right and necessary"; now, it appears "an act of enormous wickedness." "In the sixteenth century, Queen Catherine was an obstacle to the establishment of the kingdom, an incentive to treasonable hopes. In the nineteenth, she is an outraged and injured wife, the victim of a false husband's fickle appetite"(94).

Froude cannot understand Catherine's decision not to enter a cloister, saying, "It is not for us to dictate the conduct which a woman smarting under injuries so cruel ought to have pursued" (137). Reacting with the sensibilities of the Victorian gentleman he is, Froude decides that "the explanation of her conduct lies...in regions into which it is neither easy nor well to penetrate...in a vast drama of passion which had been enacted behind the scenes" (129–30). Ultimately, he sees the weakness lying within Catherine, in her "wilfulness," inferring that the fault of an injured wife must be a blemish in herself (455–56). In this judgment he foreshadows that of Dixon, as we have seen.

The image of Catherine as Victorian wife forms the basis for her depiction by William Howitt in Cassell's *Illustrated History of England*. With sales of 250,000 copies, this was one of the most popular books of the mid-Victorian period, geared to a more general audience than Froude's history. Howitt's description of Catherine at the time of her marriage to Henry might be applied to any nineteenth-century bride: "very agreeable in person... [and] distinguished for the excellence of her disposition and the spotless purity and modesty of her life" (117).[21] But onto this figure he also maps something of the character and demeanor of Queen Victoria. He describes the meeting between the English and French monarchs at the Field of the Cloth of Gold as though it were the occasion in 1855 involving a visit of Victoria and Albert to the Emperor Napoleon III and the Empress Eugenie: "The two queens, amiable and serious women, from the first showed a far greater confidence in each other, which seemed to grow into a real regard" (150).[22] When Catherine is visited by Wolsey and the papal legate, Howitt describes her as "calm, but firm," and after quoting the lengthy speech she makes in court to King Henry, Howitt calls it an "admirable speech, as confounding by its home truths and plain common sense, as it was affecting by its genuine pathos" (190, 191), thus evoking familiar traits for which Victoria herself was praised.[23] And his final evaluation of Catherine as a woman who had borne her afflictions "with a dignity, a firmness, a wisdom, and a gentleness, which won her universal respect and admiration" (221) might have been written about Victoria as well.[24]

I have tried to suggest the ways in which these several historical writers have weighed and interpreted the queen's position and actions during the major episodes of her life: her marriage to Henry; her brief regency; Henry's interest in Ann Boleyn and concern about the legality of his marriage; the trial with Wolsey and Campeggio, the papal legate, and their subsequent visit to try to persuade Catherine to the divorce; Catherine's refusal to endorse the document relegating her to "princess dowager"; and her retreat and death at Kimbolton. Most of these episodes also occur in Shakespeare's play *King Henry VIII*, which was given two prominent productions during the period when these historians were at work.

II

In his review of the Charles Kean production of *Henry VIII*, the critic John Oxenford wrote in the *London Times* of May 21, 1855: "Mrs. Charles Kean, reappearing after an absence from the stage which had been misconstrued into retirement, appeared as the Queen. Her performance in this character is still remembered. The tragic intensity, the majesty of bearing, and the solemnly impressive dignity of Mrs. Siddons were not there, but the character had much truth to nature and infinite pathos." He goes on, like many Victorians, to praise in particular her death scene—a scene treated quite differently by the Kemble/Siddons production earlier in the century. I want to suggest that the nineteenth century's conflicted image of Catherine of Aragon is finally epitomized in the differing interpretations of these two actresses, Sarah Kemble Siddons and Ellen Tree Kean. Before considering the stage tradition, however, I want also to complicate the notion of change by considering briefly the commentary by critics of Shakespeare writing about his heroines.

As early as 1817 when images of Siddons's majestic Catherine were quite fresh, William Hazlitt wrote a contrasting estimation of Shakespeare's heroine: "The character of Queen Katherine is the most perfect delineation of matronly dignity, sweetness, and resignation, that can be conceived. Her appeals to the protection of the king, her remonstrances to the cardinals, her conversations with her women, shew a noble and generous spirit accompanied with the utmost gentleness of nature."[25] The key words here are "matronly," "sweetness," "resignation," "generous," and "gentleness"; all attributes particularly associated with the feminine. In his view, Hazlitt is similar to his contemporary Elizabeth Benger, writing about Catherine in her *Memoirs of the Life of Anne Boleyn* (1821). Benger, as we saw, uses terms such as "lovely in person," "exemplary prudence," "gentle and feminine"; the difference is that Benger, writing about a real queen, also highlights her "considerable learning" (5). This distinctly feminized Catherine, however, appears throughout the century in works on Shakespeare's heroines that continue to downplay her intellect in favor of her virtues. The most prominent and most frequently reproduced of these responses appears in Anna Jameson's *Characteristics of Women* (1832).

In her Introduction, Jameson says that she chose Shakespeare's heroines, rather than historical women, as figures to portray the moral qualities of women, for "women are illustrious in history, not from what they have been in themselves, but generally in proportion to the mischief they have done or caused," while Shakespeare's characters, "combine history and real life; they are complete individuals, whose hearts and souls are laid open before us."[26] Nevertheless, she cannot ignore historical figures, since so many of Shakespeare's plays are based on them, so she treats them in the last section of her book. It does not mock "the serious sorrows of real life" to represent them on the stage in tragedies, she writes, "but it adds infinitely to the moral effect as a subject of contemplation and a lesson of conduct" (210). In her commentary on the great historic women, then, Jameson looks for the woman behind the figure. When laying out the historical Catherine of Aragon, Jameson describes her as having "no dazzling qualities of mind, and no striking advantages of person," but as someone whose "natural turn of... mind was simple, serious, and domestic, and all the impulses of her heart kindly and benevolent" (297). Though written before Victoria's ascent to the throne, these words create an image remarkably similar to the Catherine/Victoria conflation in Cassell's *Illustrated History* almost thirty years later. What Shakespeare does with the historical figure Catherine, Jameson finds remarkable: she is "the triumph of Shakespeare's genius and wisdom" because he has stripped her of the pomp of a queen, and "dispensed with all the usual sources of poetical interest, as youth, beauty, grace... commanding intellect," to depict a woman who is primarily "distinguished by *truth*" (303). This virtue is her moral core.[27]

Subsequent writers on Shakespeare's heroines dilute Jameson's remarks so that Catherine's domestic virtues are even more privileged, or they omit her altogether, as do Helena Faucit Martin and Mary Cowden Clarke. Henrietta Lea Palmer in *The Stratford Gallery; or the Shakspeare Sisterhood* (1859), puts aside the historic elements of her character—"her overweening pride of birth" from her Castilian ancestry, and "her austere and narrow-minded bigotry"—to praise "her quiet, domestic virtues, conjugal devotion, simple tastes, and genuine piety,"[28] a reprise of Howitt's estimation of the historic Catherine's "excellence of... disposition and the spotless purity and modesty of her life" (Howitt, 2: 117). The commentator in *The Heroines of Shakspeare* (1883) declares, "The Queen is introduced as the loving, faithful, and obedient wife" who "becomes the victim" of Wolsey's jealousy. During the trial scene, "she nobly pleads her own cause, as a woman and wife," and finally dies a "faithful but unfortunate woman," similar to Froude's "outraged and injured wife."[29] While nineteenth-century British commentators on Shakespeare, then, were fairly consistent in delineating Catherine as virtuous wife, the actual stage presentation of her character changed from majestic to domestic during the century, as epitomized in the performances of Sarah Siddons and Ellen Kean.

Siddons first performed Queen Katherine at Drury Lane in November of 1788 to great acclaim, with a reprise of the role in 1792–96, followed by a revival at Covent Garden in 1806, and subsequent performances and "readings" in later years, including one for Queen Charlotte, the royal princesses and other members of the court in 1813.[30] Looking back from the 1830s, Thomas Campbell was able to write: "in the history of all female performance on the British stage, there is no specific tradition of any excellence at all approaching to hers as *Queen Katharine*" (237). Allowing for the prejudice of a biographer, there is yet no doubt that any subsequent actress had to take account of Siddons's delineation of the role. The terms used by Oxenford to describe her—"tragic intensity," "majesty of bearing," "impressive dignity"—are repeated by others including the novelist Maria Edgeworth, who heard Siddons at one of her readings and described her "composure," "dignity," "suppressed feeling," and matronly tenderness.[31] Siddons's reading of Katherine, thus, I would argue, is similar to that put forth by Mary Hays and the Stricklands. Hays, we remember, stressed Catherine's mental as well as personal qualifications, affirming that "the character of the queen was decided, her temper firm, her claims were just, and she resolved to maintain them," adding the feelings of a mother to those of a wife (135), while the Stricklands applauded her "integrity," "intrepid firmness," and "innate grandeur of soul" (121).

Siddons's majesty and grandeur are evident in the painting of her in the trial scene (Act II. scene v) by George Harlow, ca. 1816. The work was begun as a portrait of Siddons, but Harlow enlarged it to show the entire scene with her Kemble brothers as Wolsey and Cromwell. Nevertheless, the focal point of the painting is Siddons herself in a black ermine-trimmed dress, facing us, the viewers, while she accusingly points her right arm at Wolsey across the picture plane, leaving Henry VIII lost in the shadows. This painting was reproduced and circulated through many engravings, and the bust of Siddons was extracted and presented by itself in engraved format. John Kemble's direction of the scene gave full scope to Siddons. The original stage directions indicate that the queen is already in the room, and rises from her chair to come and kneel before the king when she is called. Kemble has her *enter* the room when she is called, and as she enters, "all stand up and bow to her—they continue standing till the Queen rises from the Cushion" (MS note, p. 31) which Guildford has placed for her. She rises just before saying, "Alas, sir, / In what have I offended you?" (2.4.16–17).[32] Making an entrance and receiving the ovation of the courtiers enhances her dignity and respect. James Boaden recalled that after Wolsey's insult, "the commanding air, look, and tone, with which she called up her enemy, excited a delightful astonishment."[33] Bell, Boaden and others remark on a bit of stage business instituted by Siddons. Campeius rises when Katherine says "Lord Cardinal," but "'she turns from him impatiently; then makes a sweet bow of apology, but dignified. Then to Wolsey, turned and looking *from* him, with her hand pointing back to him, in a voice of thunder, "to *you* I speak."'" (Bell quoted in Parsons, 129). The impact of her presence in this scene was so grand, that

Boaden says when she left the stage, "it was in truth quite time to break up the council," as the audience was not paying attention to the other actors (2: 265).³⁴

Siddons thus played Katherine as a woman of dignity and majesty, reproducing on stage the Shakespearean character most pleasing to herself and to Dr. Samuel Johnson, who thought that Katherine was the best thing in the play, and even best among Shakespeare's characters.³⁵ Such a commanding figure, however, was difficult to reproduce, and fortunately for Ellen Kean, whose physique was less imposing than that of Sarah Siddons, the tide had turned by mid-century, and a different kind of Katherine was expected, the one who was seen as injured wife, accepting her afflictions with dignity, an interpretation closer to that of the Shakespeare commentators.³⁶ The change may be documented in the histories and in the pictorial tradition as well, for this is the Catherine of Froude and Cassell's *Illustrated History* and of genre painters following Harlow.

Thirty years after Harlow, Henry Nelson O'Neil painted the trial scene in 1848, calling it "Catherine of Arragon Appealing to Henry VIII." Catherine no longer dominates the canvas with her strident gesture as in Harlow's trial scene; instead, O'Neil shows her a dark-clad figure, kneeling at the foot of Henry's throne, her clasped hands raised in appeal. The pocket with handkerchief hanging at her side gives a domestic touch to her figure. The episode was reproduced by William Theed in 1854 as a bas-relief for the Palace of Westminster, and as an illustration to Cassell's *History*, but as the century progressed, the courtroom scenes gave way to depictions of Queen Katherine's dream—her vision of angels before death. O'Neil painted this scene in 1853 and 1878, with a version by Henry Le Jeune in 1857, and various illustrations scattered in Shakespeare editions.³⁷

When, in his 1855 historic spectacle of *Henry VIII*, Charles Kean re-instituted the angelic vision as part of the death scene, he was catering to a Victorian audience who took morbid delight in such scenes, and had wept at the deaths of Little Nell and Paul Dombey, among countless others.³⁸ While Siddons was commended for the naturalistic way in which she indicated the nervous discomfort of the ill, Ellen Kean was praised for the beauty of her "attitude" or pose. The *Times* reviewer, John Oxenford, dwelt at length on this scene, noting how, "half rising from her couch, she follows with her eyes the departing forms [angels]," and declares that she "might serve as a study for some picture of a saint's ecstasy" (169). A drawing of this scene was featured in the press as a representation of the play, and the effect was so striking on viewers, that several first-hand accounts comment specifically on the vision. Queen Victoria, who loved spectacle, noted in her diary: "Queen Katherine's dream, with the angels descending on a sunbeam, waving palm branches and holding out to her a crown of the same" (quoted in Rowell, 56). The true impact of the scene, however, is best ascertained from the account made by Lewis Carroll in *his* diary. Kean's *Henry VIII* was the first staged production of Shakespeare ever seen by the young Carroll, who writes:

> But oh, that exquisite vision of Queen Catherine! I almost held my breath to watch: the illusion is perfect, and I felt as if in a dream all the time it lasted ... the column of sunbeams shone down upon the sleeping queen, and gradually down it floated a troop of angelic forms, transparent, and carrying palm branches ... they waved these over the sleeping queen, with oh! such a sad and solemn grace.... She in an ecstasy raises her arms towards them, and to sweet slow music they vanish as marvellously as they came. Then the profound silence of the audience burst at once into a rapture of applause; but even that scarcely marred the effect of the beautiful sad waking words of the Queen, '*Spirits of peace, where are ye?*' I never ... felt so inclined to shed tears at anything fictitious, save perhaps at that poetical gem of Dickens, the death of little Paul.[39]

A dutiful Anglican with the mind of a logician, Carroll is nevertheless caught up in the spectacle of viewing the ecstasy of a dying Catholic queen. Imbued with the scepticism of the age, and inclining toward Christian humanism, Victorians held conflicted views of heaven and of the Christian doctrine of immortality, though they sought a certain comfort in death scenes, because such events were so frequently part of their own family life. Three important elements of such occasions were "the last words of the dying," "deathbed visions," and a comforter, "usually a woman ... often described as angelic."[40] Shakespeare's play offers all three with Catherine's words about her husband, daughter Mary, and faithful companions; her vision of angels; and her waiting-woman, Patience, though it is Catherine herself who takes on saintly qualities, rather than the aptly-named Patience. When O'Neil turned to painting this scene in 1878, he showed Catherine lying back on a large pillow in a chair like a Victorian invalid, her eyes closed, hands raised with palms up as she sees the vision of angels in a white light before her.

While Catherine's Catholicism was important to the historian Dixon, it was evidently not an issue to the majority of the audiences who attended the hundred or so performances of the Kean production. What they saw was a good, true, and faithful woman who, spurned by her husband, died a holy but lonely death. The anonymous theater reviewer in *The Athenaeum* for May 19, 1855 suggested with hindsight a harmonious rationale for the various spectacles that made up the performance. Monarchs and people alike, he wrote, were caught up in a controlling destiny that created chaos with their lives so that the new order of "the great period of the Reformation" could begin: "The principle of impending change overrides all. It is a season of revolution, and fortune rules in all spiritual places. In the midst of the sufferings, the faultless *Katharine*, both in her elevation and decline, is the type of greatness—true and just in her power, resigned, religious and forgiving in her fall. All the elements of a perfect majesty are in her combined, and she presents to the mind the very model of womanhood in her highest gifts and graces" (593). Here we have a nineteenth-century mind retroactively reading its understanding of rational change onto the sixteenth century, and seeing in the earlier queen the best qualities of his own Victoria. The fact that Kean's production was played against the background of tactical mistakes, human suffering, and horrors that comprised the Crimean War gives added weight to the "season of revolution" and the rule of fortune. The subtext suggested by the review is that change and crises occur, but in the larger scheme of things, in a well-ordered and civilized society led by an enlightened monarch, progress, rather than chaos, is the result.[41] Catherine *is* Victoria, combining "all the elements of a perfect majesty" with "the very model of womanhood."

Notes

1. I have mainly adopted the spelling of Catherine's name used by modern historians. When referring to Shakespeare's play, *Henry VIII* or quoting from nineteenth-century sources, I use the spellings preferred by those writers.
2. Queen Victoria, *The Girlhood of Queen Victoria*, ed. R. B. B. Esher, vol. 1 (New York: Longmans; London: Murray, 1912), p. 267. Referred to as *Diaries*.
3. Victoria's strong opinions about Catherine of Aragon are represented earlier in two notebooks on the queens of England that she compiled between about 1834 and 1837. She describes Catherine of Aragon as "irreproachable," while "Anne Boleyn is 'extremely beautiful, and accomplished, but inconsiderate.'" Quoted in Lynne Vallone, *Becoming Victoria* (New Haven: Yale University Press, 2001), p. 120; and n. 125, p. 224.
4. Margaret Homans, *Royal Representations: Queen Victoria and British Culture, 1837–1876* (Chicago: University of Chicago Press, 1998), p. 16.
5. Nicola J. Watson, "Gloriana Victoriana: Victoria and the cultural memory of Elizabeth I," in *Remaking Queen Victoria*, ed. Margaret Homans and Adrienne Munich (Cambridge: Cambridge University Press, 1997), pp. 79–81.

6. Louisa Stuart Costello, *Memoirs of Eminent Englishwomen* (London: Bentley, 1844), pp. iii–vi.
7. [Anonymous], "Elizabeth and Victoria. From a Woman's Point of View," *The Victoria Magazine*, 3 (June 1864), p. 99.
8. On Victoria's creation of a self-image, see Homans, *Royal Representations*.
9. See John Ruskin, "Of Queens Gardens," in *Sesame and Lilies* (London: Smith, Elder, 1865; reprint London: Allen, 1904), pp. 87–143.
10. Sharon A. Weltman, "'Be no more housewives, but queens': Queen Victoria and Ruskin's domestic mythology," in *Remaking Queen Victoria*, pp. 111, 117–18. Ruskin, 132. See also Sharon A. Weltman, *Ruskin's Mythic Queen: Gender Subversion in Victorian Culture* (Athens: Ohio University Press, 1998), chapter 5.
11. Albert's exact position in relation to Queen Victoria was conflicted throughout his lifetime. See Stanley Weintraub, *Victoria: An Intimate Biography* (New York: Dutton, 1988), chapters 6 and 7.
12. Mary Hays, *Memoirs of Queens Illustrious and Celebrated* (London: Allman, 1821), p. vi.
13. Anne K. Mellor, *Romanticism and Gender* (New York: Routledge, 1993), pp. 40–41.
14. Elizabeth Ogilvy Benger, *Memoirs of the Life of Anne Boleyn, Queen of Henry VIII*, 3rd edn. (London: Longman, 1827), p. 5.
15. During Caroline's trial for adultery in the autumn of 1820, her attorney, Henry Brougham arguing in her defense, compared the efforts of George IV "to make out a case against the Queen to the efforts of King Henry VIII to secure...his divorce from Queen Catherine of Aragon." Caroline herself, when she signed a protest against the Parliamentary Bill containing the divorce clause, wrote "'Caroline Regina'—adding aloud, 'Regina in spite of him.'" (Flora Fraser, *The Unruly Queen: The Life of Queen Caroline* [London: Macmillan, 1997], pp. 436, 444). Similarly, Queen Catherine crossed out the words "princess dowager" on the documents sent to her by Henry.
16. Rohan Amanda Maitzen, *Gender, Genre, and Victorian Historical Writing* (New York: Garland, 1998), pp. 33, 35. Maitzen points out that "the didactic, public role of the historian was not one easily appropriated by women; during the nineteenth century the past came to be seen as the key to the present, particularly the political present—and this was *man's* business" (p. 33). See also Billie Melman, "Gender, History and Memory: The Invention of Women's Past in the Nineteenth and Early Twentieth Centuries," *History and Memory*, 5 (1993), pp. 5–41.
17. All references are to Vol. 4 of *Lives of the Queens of England*, new edn., 12 vols. in 6 (Phila.: Lea and Blanchard, 1847–59).
18. Dixon was editor of the *Athenaeum*. The DNB characterizes his histories as popular if not entirely accurate.
19. William Hepworth Dixon, *History of Two Queens. I. Catharine of Aragon. II. Anne Boleyn*, 2nd edn., vol. 1 (London: Hurst and Blackett, 1873), p. vii.
20. James A. Froude, *History of England from the Fall of Wolsey to the Death of Elizabeth*, 12 vols. (London: Parker, 1856–70). All references are to vol. 1 (1856).

21. John F. Smith and William Howitt, *John Cassell's Illustrated History of England*, 8 vols. in 5 (London: W. Kent, 1857–64). All references are to vol. 2.
22. Compare, for example, Victoria's statement in a letter dated May 1, 1855 to her uncle the King of the Belgians: "I am sure you would be charmed with the Empress; it is not such great beauty, but such grace, elegance, sweetness, and *nature*." Queen Victoria, *The Letters of Queen Victoria*, ed. Arthur Christopher Benson and Viscount Esher, vol. 3 (New York: Longmans, 1907), p. 154.
23. See for example the statement in Robert Wilson, ed., *The Life and Times of Queen Victoria*, 4 vols. paginated continuously (London: Casell; New York: Carter, 1901) summing up "the Queen's life-work": "several of her statesmen gave testimony to her shrewdness and commonsense in political matters" (p. 947).
24. One memorial tribute to Victoria described her as passing all other queens "in nobility and grandeur and thoroughness of character." T. De Witt Talmage, "Her Throne Near to God," in Charles Morris, *The Life of Queen Victoria and the Story of Her Reign* (Phila.: Winston, ca. 1901), p. 529.
25. William Hazlitt, *Characters of Shakespeare's Plays* (London: Reynell for Hunter, 1817), p. 237.
26. Quotations are from Anna Jameson, *Characteristics of Women, Moral, Poetical, and Historical* (Boston: Phillips, 1854), pp. xviii–xix.
27. The actress Fanny Kemble in an article on Queen Catherine and Wolsey sees pride as the main characteristic of each; hers pride of birth, his of power. Frances Anne Kemble, "Notes on the Characters of Queen Katharine and Cardinal Wolsey in Shakespeare's Play of Henry VIII," *Lippincott's Magazine*, 16 (1875), p. 685.
28. Henrietta Lee Palmer, *The Stratford Gallery; or the Shakespeare Sisterhood* (New York: Appleton, 1859), p. 238.
29. *Heroines of Shakspeare* (London and New York: London Printing, ca. 1883). This book is not paginated. The commentary on Katherine is found on the page preceding her portrait by J. W. Wright as engraved by H. W. Mote, originally appearing in Charles Heath's second set of portraits of Shakespearean heroines, 1848.
30. See Siddons's letter describing the event to her friend Mrs. Fitz Hugh, January 26, 1813 as printed in Thomas Campbell, *Life of Mrs. Siddons* (1839; reprint New York: Blom, 1972), pp. 348–51.
31. See Edgeworth's letter also reproduced in Campbell, p. 353. Siddons's biographer, Mrs. Parsons, remarks that when she assumed the role of Katherine, "we first feel conscious of her increasing suitability for forceful and magnanimous, in contradistinction to tender and dependent, characters" (Florence M. W. Parsons, *The Incomparable Siddons* [London: Methuen, 1909], p. 128).
32. Citations from the play are to the New Cambridge Edition by John Margeson (Cambridge University Press, 1990). Kemble's notes are from his 1804 printed edition of *King Henry The Eighth*, the annotated copy in the Folger Library, reproduced in *John Philip Kemble Promptbooks*, ed. Charles H. Shattuck, vol. 4 (Charlottesville: University of Virginia Press for the

Folger Shakespeare Library, 1974). In having the Queen enter when called, Kemble is evidently following an eighteenth-century practice, which changed again in the nineteenth century (as with Kean). For a discussion of the staging of this scene, see W. Moelwyn Merchant, *Shakespeare and the Artist* (London: Oxford University Press, 1959), chapter 13.

33. James Boaden, *Memoirs of Mrs. Siddons*, vol. 2 (London: H. Colburn, 1827), p. 264.
34. Merchant notes that Kemble's focus on the dramatic tension between Katherine and Wolsey seems a more faithful reproduction of Shakespeare's plan for the scene, than the more diffused staging by Kean (pp. 201–02).
35. Boswell gives an account (from Kemble) of Siddons's visit to Dr. Johnson in October of 1783, during which Johnson "particularly asked her which of Shakspeare's characters she was most pleased with. Upon her answering that she thought the character of Queen Catherine, in Henry the Eighth, the most natural:—'I think so too, Madam' (said he)..." (James Boswell, *Boswell's Life of Johnson*, ed. George Birkbeck Hill and L. F. Powell, vol. 4 (Oxford: Clarendon Press, 1934), p. 242. His own estimation of Catherine's character appears in his notes to the play: "The meek sorrows and virtuous distress of Catherine have furnished some scenes which may be justly numbered among the greatest efforts of tragedy." (Samuel Johnson, *Johnson on Shakespeare*, ed. Arthur Sherbo, "The Yale Edition of the Works of Samuel Johnson," vol. 8 [New Haven: Yale University Press, 1968], p. 657). Perhaps he would have been disappointed in Siddons's interpretation, which was hardly "meek."
36. In spite of foregrounding the womanly pathos of Katherine, Kean kept the traditional cut of lines 135–38 in Act II, scene iv, where Henry VIII praises Katherine's "rare qualities, sweet gentleness... meekness saint-like, wife-like government," etc. Probably this decision was in the total interest of shortening the verbal in the interest of the visual.
37. The Trial scene was painted by Westall in 1790, Harlow in 1817, and Cattermole in 1827, then picked up again at century's end by John L. Pott in 1880 and Edward Austin Abbey in 1900. Fuseli painted the vision in 1781 and Westall portrayed Catherine's death without the vision in 1796. Not surprisingly, William Blake found the vision particularly compelling as a subject and produced four drawings, dating from around 1807–09 (*Shakespeare in Art: Paintings, Drawings, and Engravings devoted to Shakespearean Subjects* [London: Arts Council, 1964], pp. 21–22). See the listing of nineteenth-century British history paintings in Roy Strong, *"And when did you last see your father?" The Victorian Painter and British History* (London: Thames & Hudson, 1978).
38. Dickens's *Old Curiosity Shop* appeared in 1841 and his *Dombey and Son* in 1847–48. Andrew Sanders thinks that Dickens may have been influenced by productions of *Henry VIII* (Andrew Sanders, *Charles Dickens, Resurrectionist* [New York: St. Martin's, 1982], pp. 21–22), but a full-scale representation of Catherine's vision was not staged until Kean in 1855 (George C. D. Odell, *Shakespeare from Betterton to Irving*, vol. 2 [New York: Scribner's, 1920], p. 336).

39. Lewis Carroll, *Lewis Carroll's Diaries*, ed. Edward Wakeling, vol. 1 (Luton: Lewis Carroll Society, 1993), pp. 105–06.
40. Michael Wheeler, *Death and the Future Life in Victorian Literature and Theology* (New York: Cambridge University Press, 1990), pp. 30–31.
41. Three days after this theater review appeared, on May 22, 1855 Victoria wrote to her uncle, the King of the Belgians, "The state of affairs is uncomfortable and complicated just now, but our course is *straight*; we *cannot* come to any peace unless we have such guarantees by *decided* limitation of the Fleet, which would secure us against Russian preponderance for the future" (*Letters*, 3, p. 161). A few days later she wrote in her journal that she had spoken with Colonel Jeffrys about conditions in the Crimea: "He described the misery, the suffering, the total lack of everything, the sickness etc., and in no way exaggerated by other accounts I have seen" (quoted in Weintraub, p. 242).

THE WOMAN IN BLACK: THE IMAGE OF CATHERINE DE MEDICI FROM MARLOWE TO *QUEEN MARGOT*

Elaine Kruse

The *Discours Merveilleux de la Vie... de Catherine de Medicis*[1] [The Marvelous Discourse of the Life of Catherine de Medici], a tract published in 1574 anonymously, but attributed to Henri Estienne, was brought out in an English edition in 1693. The preface began: "no greater injury can be done to Posterity, than to bury in Oblivion the cursed Memory of those, whose Ambitious Designs for Rule and Empire have been managed with such Furious Lusts, that they have not stuck, in their pursuit of them, to commit the basest Villanies."[2] Thus, one hundred years after the death of Catherine de Medici, the Black Legend of the wicked Italian Queen surfaced again as an English tract in which John Wyat, the publisher, warned "to attain her ambitious Designs with Masculine thoughts, exchanged the imperfections of her Sex."[3] The Black Legend, the "cursed Memory" of Catherine de Medici, began as an attempt to bring down the regency of the Queen Mother, using anti-Italian and misogynist arguments about how unnatural it was to have a Queen.[4] Reading the Black Legend carefully over time, we can detect the gender codes of the period in which the myth is revived.

Catherine de Medici ruled in sixteenth-century France, first as Queen, the wife of King Henri II (1547–59), then, after his untimely death, as Queen Mother during the reigns of her sons François II (1559–60), Charles IX (1560–74), and Henri III (1574–89), and as Queen Regent when her son Charles IX was a minor (1560–63) and when the future Henri III was returning from being the King of Poland (1574–75), the time of the original tract. Struggling to maintain the crown for her sons during religious and civil strife, Catherine became the lightning rod for dissension and calumny.

The focus of the legend, the Saint Bartholomew's Day Massacre, occurred in the context of the 1572 wedding of Marguerite de Valois, Catherine's daughter and sister to the reigning Charles IX, to Henri de Bourbon, King of Navarre, and scion of the Protestant branch of the royal family. Catherine had tried unsuccessfully to end religious warring through arranged truces, such as the Peace of St. Germain (1570). The marriage was her plan to unite the two factions and calm the passions of years of atrocities on both sides. Among the Protestants in Paris for the wedding was Gaspard de Coligny, lord of Chatillon and Admiral of France, a prominent Protestant leader and bitter enemy of the Catholic Guise family. On Friday morning, August 22, four days after the wedding, an assassination attempt against Coligny miscarried when he bent over to adjust his shoe as a shot was fired from a window, wounding him. Tensions escalated between the three major parties: Catholic, Protestant (known as Huguenots), and crown, with rumblings of Huguenot retaliation against the parties responsible. On Saturday night, a royal order went out to murder the wounded Coligny and other leading Protestants before trouble erupted. The ensuing massacre spread to the streets of Paris, a rabidly Catholic city, and ultimately to provincial towns, resulting in the deaths of thousands of Huguenots.

Following the massacre, Protestant polemics proclaimed that Catherine was malevolent to the core, the wicked Queen who masterminded the massacre, poisoned her enemies, taught her children Machiavellian political strategies, and corrupted their morals. What could be explained as religious rancor, misogyny, and xenophobia in the sixteenth century has been transmuted through tracts, plays, histories, novels, and films into the full-blown popular image of the Queen as evil incarnate.

Anonymous political tracts poured out their venom in the wake of the St. Bartholomew's Day Massacre. The original Black Legend, as recounted by Estienne, began with her supposed bourgeois Italian lineage: "Catherine de Medici is Italian and Florentine. Amongst the nations, Italy takes the prize for cunning and shrewdness; in Italy, Tuscany; and in Tuscany, the city of Florence.... Now when a person without a conscience has the art of deception, as often seen in that country, imagine how much evil you can expect. And besides, Catherine comes from the house of Medici."[5] Even more damning was the fact that she was the daughter of the man to whom Machiavelli had dedicated *The Prince*. Supposedly she regarded *The Prince* as her Bible, using it to instruct her children, and her son, Henri III, carried it constantly in his pocket. According to her detractors, she deliberately corrupted her children, introducing them to Italian sexual perversions and encouraging them to be cruel through cock fights and other nasty court diversions. The legend took on witch imagery, claiming that it was foretold at her birth that she would bring calamity to whatever family she married into. She supposedly turned to magic in order to become pregnant after ten years of barrenness. She was charged with poisoning the older brother of her husband, the heir to the throne, in order to bring her husband to power and later poisoning Henri de Navarre's mother before the wedding. According to the legend, she had planned the massacre in advance and arranged the marriage of Marguerite and Henri de Navarre deliberately to bring Protestant leaders to Paris for the slaughter. The witch image culminated with Catherine leading her son by the hand to gloat over the mutilated body of Coligny in the street. The fact that Catherine chose to wear black following her husband's death rather than the traditional French customary white for mourning adds to the witch image in future representations, whether drawings or cinematography.[6]

The legend began as a concerted effort to attack the regency of the Queen Mother after the death of Charles IX in 1574, serving as propaganda for her son Alençon, as well as a rallying cry for Huguenots and what Robert Kingdon terms "Malcontent Catholics."[7] But the legend took on nuances to fit the political context of each successive era.

In 1592, Queen Elizabeth ruled over an England traumatized by the recent threat of the Spanish Armada and Catholic conspiracies, while anxious over the succession question. Echoes of anti-papal sentiment reverberate in Christopher Marlowe's play *The Massacre at Paris*, which appeared approximately twenty years after the massacre.[8] Although the protagonist is the Duc de Guise, a Machiavellian aspirant to the throne and dedicated Papist, Catherine appears throughout as his ally. Marlowe apparently knew the legend both from the Protestant tracts and from the Huguenot refugees in Canterbury during his childhood.[9] His play starts with the massacre but then telescopes history through the assassinations of Henri de Guise and Henri III in 1589, events he knew through his own secret service in France and recent reports.[10]

Marlowe introduces Catherine's perfidy in Act I, scene i with an aside referring to the marriage of Henri de Navarre and Margaret: "Which I'll dissolve with blood and cruelty."[11] Catherine willingly sacrifices her own son, Charles IX, for the papal cause led by Guise. Guise explains:

> The Mother Queen works wonders for my sake,
> And in my love entombs the hope of France
> Rifling the bowels of her treasury,
> To supply my wants and necessity[12]

Together she and Guise plan the slaughter of the Huguenots:

> My noble son, and princely Duke of Guise,
> Now have we got the fatal, straggling deer
> Within the compass of a deadly toil,
> And as we late decreed, we may perform.[13]

Catherine seems to be deliberately contrasted with Elizabeth, England's legitimate sovereign, as she seeks illegitimate power, no matter what the cost for the hereditary line. When Charles IX regrets the slaughter, she hints that she will poison him:

> For Catherine must have her will in France.
> As I do live, so surely shall he die,
> And Henry then shall wear the diadem;
> And, if he grudge or cross his mother's will,
> I'll disinherit him and all the rest;
> For I'll rule France, but they shall wear the crown,
> And, if they storm, I then may pull them down.[14]

When Henri III does not follow her lead, she threatens:

> Tush man, let me alone with him,
> To work the way to bring this thing to pass;
> And, if he do deny what I do say,
> I'll dispatch him with his brother presently,
> And then shall Monsieur wear the diadem.
> Tush, all shall die unless I have my will:
> For while she lives, Catherine will be queen.[15]

Treading carefully, Marlowe seems to denigrate one Queen, Catherine de Medici, while praising his own. Henri de Navarre, the leader of the Protestant forces and himself the next legitimate heir, promises:

> And with the Queen of England join my force,
> To beat the papal Monarch from our lands[16]

Alençon, the French prince Elizabeth had courted, plays no role. Marlowe must have known of the fate of John Stubbs, who dared to criticize the possible marriage of Alençon and Elizabeth in a 1579 pamphlet, *The Discoverie of a Gaping Gulf whereinto England is like to be swallowed*, and was sentenced to have his right hand cut off.[17] But, as Penny Roberts points out, Marlowe "highlights the dangers of a weak monarchy, of relying on favourites, of allowing nobles too much influence, of disposing of your enemies by dubious means, and of an insecure succession—all of which would have had resonance in England during Elizabeth's last years."[18] Catherine's "bad mother" image may have served to undermine

Elizabeth's use of "mother" as her self-representation to her people. Indeed, even though the Duc de Guise was the central Machiavellian figure, the legend of Catherine, the wicked queen, could have worked to Elizabeth's detriment.

During the reign of Louis XIV in seventeenth-century France the legend revived in both France and England. Madame de la Fayette published anonymously what some have called "the first novel in the contemporary sense of the word."[19] *La Princesse de Cleves* (1678) detailed the psychological conflict of a young married woman passionately in love with a man at Henri II's court in 1559. Her struggle is set against that of Catherine de Medici, Diane de Poitiers, and Mary Stuart, Catherine's daughter-in-law. Despite the readily available positive sources about Catherine, Madame de la Fayette chose to draw on Mezeray and other negative "histories" to stress Catherine's dissimulation, pent-up hostility, and ultimate vengeance on her enemies.[20] Catherine hides her hatred of Diane till Henri's death, then exiles her from court; promotes an image of austere virtue while trying to establish a liaison with the Vidame de Chartres; then believing herself betrayed by Chartres with Mary Stuart, she arranges his execution at Amboise, chases Mary back to Scotland after the death of François II, and forges a new alliance with the Cardinal de Lorraine. The novel, while seemingly historically accurate, was, in fact, laced with fictions, including not only the Princesse de Clèves and her husband, but also the "execution" at Amboise, as Chartres actually died years later. Madame de Lafayette utilized a sixteenth-century story as a vehicle to comment on the social mores of seventeenth-century court life and to present a pessimistic portrayal of human nature, and in the process, perpetuated the Black Legend surrounding Catherine de Medici.

The combination of gender and politics may have played into the editing of the original tract by John Wyat, the publisher of the English *Discourse* in 1693. He titled Estienne's tract *The History of the Life of Katherine de Medicis Queen Mother and Regent of France or The Exact Pattern of the Present French King's Policy*. Overtly, the comparison was being made between the policies of Catherine and those of Louis XIV, who had revoked the Edict of Nantes in 1685, resulting in the persecution and exodus of Huguenots from France. Wyat's summation reads: "She was a person of unlimited Ambition and Pride, who from the Commotions she often raised, and composed together, with the Jealousies and Enmities that for thirty years raged between the Nobles, made the Advantage of centering in her self, in that publick Calamity, the whole Authority of the Gouvernement; and to attain her ambitious

Designs with Masculine thoughts, exchanged the Imperfections of her Sex."[21]

William III and Mary II were reigning in England in 1693. Under the Regency Act of 1690, Mary exercised royal power in both her name and William's whenever the king was away, but he always had the final say and sole exercise of power on his return. Because William was frequently at war, Mary reigned alone during four regencies, a total thirty-two months in four years. Was Wyat using the Black Legend to foment anxiety over a woman in power? I would argue exactly the opposite: that he was using Catherine's image to bolster that of his Queen. Wyat explains that he has drawn excerpts from the French sources, but that he is directly addressing the perfidy of Louis XIV in plotting the assassination of William III, as evidenced in the recent trial and execution of Grandvall. An earlier pamphlet, *Reflections upon the Late Horrid Conspiracy*, dealing directly with the assassination plot, had questioned whether any such "horrid deed" had ever been done before.[22] Wyat responded with the Black Legend, suggesting that the current French king was following the same pattern. In *Reflections upon the Late Horrid Conspiracy* the author had gone to great pains to exculpate the former James II, Mary's father, from conceiving and planning the assassination, laying the blame directly on Louis XIV.[23] Wyat, a Nonconformist printer, was thus supporting Mary, known for her stand on religious toleration.[24] In contrast to the scheming Catherine, Mary made a point of submission to her husband, William, and was a religious model for her people. She proved to be intelligent, responsible, and loyal when, according to Lois Schwoerer, "England faced enormous problems of war, naval mismanagement, treason or suspicion of treason at the highest reaches of government, and the possibility of invasion and counter-revolution, all exacerbated by the growing unpopularity of the Dutch king."[25] The image of Catherine as "a person of unlimited Ambition," "centering in her self all the Authority of Gouvernement," "with Masculine Thoughts" served as the counterfoil to the beloved Queen Mary, whose only ambition was to serve well in her husband's stead.

Voltaire played a similar game as he tried to publish an epic poem, the *Henriade*, attacking religious intolerance and absolute power in France through the story of the massacre. Voltaire had explained to his English readers, "Both tragedy and comedy are a lively picture of the passions of mankind; the ambition of a monarch is represented in Tragedy."[26] The Regency government and the Catholic censors refused to authorize it in France of the 1720s, so he dedicated it to Queen Caroline in England, who, like Elizabeth, (who) protected Henri de

Navarre, is "not only...the Protectress of all Arts and Sciences, but...the Best Judge of them."[27] In contrast, Catherine, the ambitious Queen, spread dissension:

> Her Husband dying in his Prime of Life,
> Free course to her Ambition left; each Son
> Deliver'd from her Tutelage became
> Her Foe as fast as He without Her reign'd.
> Confusion, Jealousy, about the Throne
> Her Hand, ill-fated, with Division sow'd,
> Incessantly opposing by her Craft
> The Guise's to the Condé's, France to France.[28]

While cleverly contrasting her to Queen Elizabeth, he paints a picture of illicit power and civil war:

> Charles, more a Child, enjoy'd the Name of King,
> But Medicis alone possess's the Pow'r,
> And made the Nation tremble; to secure
> Her Rule, She purpos'd to be Tutress still,
> And in eternal Childhood keep the King.
> In Discord's Hands She put the flaming Brand,
> And by a Hundred Battles kept the Throne.
> To wrath the Rival Sects She wrought, and War
> As fierce, as Civil always is, ensu'd.[29]

Catherine planned the massacre in the context of the wedding of Marguerite and Henri de Navarre. As Voltaire explained in *An Essay upon the civil wars of France*: "She feared no other Enemies but Jeanne d'Albret (Henry of Navarre's mother), Coligny, and the Protestants: She thought one Blow could destroy them all, and fix her own Power for ever."[30] She greeted her future son-in-law with tears and open arms. His fears were lulled by her dissimulation, which she has taught her sons:

> The King by Medicis's Lessons form'd
> Of Fraud and Perjury the Practice knew.
> Murder She made familiar to his Heart,
> And, as to Cruelty his Nature bent,
> Her cruel Counsels He with Pleasure heard;
> Apt Scholar in her execrable School.
> The better to conceal th' accurs'd Design[31]

But Charles IX's death is linked to feelings of remorse:

> With Horror Charles was on a sudden seiz'd,
> Remorse succeeded Rage, and rent his Soul.
> The fatal Culture of his tender Years
> Went far his easy Nature to corrupt,

> But had not stifled that tremendous Voice,
> Which startles Kings, and frights them on the Throne.
> His Mother's Maxims on his Mind imprest,
> He was not harden'd in his Crimes, like Her.[32]

Thus, the Black Legend of a cruel, dissimulating, ambitious, and fractious pretender to power, contrasting good Queen Elizabeth of England with the wicked Queen Catherine in France, served Voltaire's purposes to castigate religious intolerance and arbitrary power.

The Black Legend revived in the late eighteenth century, first indirectly and later directly aimed at destroying Marie Antoinette. In 1783, Marie Genevieve Charlotte Thiroux d'Arconville published a *History of François II* in which she viciously attacked Catherine: "a woman without character, combined all the weaknesses and vices of every type... using them as needed for her insatiable ambition and satisfaction." She continued in that vein to suggest that Catherine flitted endlessly between opposing factions and was "irresolute, false, inconstant, and coldly cruel."[33] Clearly, this was a veiled attack on the present queen. Pamphlets and books compared Marie to Catherine, Messalina, and other queens tainted by tales of murder.[34] Louise Keralio's extended study, *The Crimes of the Queens of France from the beginning of the monarchy until Marie Antoinette*, attacked the queens one by one, emphasizing their dissimulation, suggesting that Marie, like Catherine, said one thing in public and carried on a vicious campaign in private.[35] Catherine was charged with setting up an inquisition-style *chambre ardente*, carrying on bloody persecutions even while she was governing in her husband's stead while he was at war. Keralio played on the theme of licentiousness, claiming Catherine surrounded herself with a band of young beautiful women to seduce men and carry on Sappho-like lesbian activities, and charging that she taught her sons every Italian sexual perversion. Her daughter Marguerite carried on an incestuous relationship with her brother Anjou, and was known for her promiscuity.[36] Similar charges of corruption and nymphomania were being directed at Marie-Antoinette.

Satiric pamphlets linked Catherine and Marie Antoinette as part of the vitriolic campaign to desacralize the monarchy. In *Antoinette d'Autriche, ou Dialogue entre Catherine de Médicis et Frédégonde, Reines de France, aux enfers (Antoinette of Austria, or a Dialogue between Catherine de Médicis and Frédégonde, Queens of France, in Hell)*[37] Fredegonde tells Catherine that their misdeeds are nothing compared to those of Marie. She defends Catherine as a clever political leader who lived at a time of religious strife and finally had to act, even though the massacre was really to eliminate those who challenged her authority. Catherine admits, "Medicis is still the most barbaric of women," but Fredegonde replies that Marie intends to slaughter all those who attend the Estates-General. This use of the legend to blacken the image of Marie Antoinette is repeated in *Catherine de Médicis dans le cabinet de Marie-Antoinette, à Saint Cloud (Catherine de Médicis in the chamber of Marie Antoinette at Saint Cloud)*.[38] Marie complains that she owes all her misfortunes to her husband who should have stood up to the people at the first sign of revolt. Catherine agrees, decrying his weakness, saying that in her day the sword or poison would have punished him; "all was ready for Charles if he had not supported my orders, even if he were my son." Marie praises Catherine: "You have shown that women are capable of governing an empire as despots." Catherine suggests Marie blow up the assembly or kill her husband. If she killed the deputies, her husband, "your cowardly spouse, might keep you from enjoying your victory." She would have to get rid of Monsieur (the King's brother), as well. "Don't watch these atrocities; it's only natural after so many injuries to want to bathe leisurely in the blood of your guilty subjects."

The Queen as evil influence was reinforced in a public setting by Marie-Joseph Chenier's play *Charles IX*, first performed on November 4, 1789, four months after the fall of the Bastille, despite the objections of the king's censor and the leadership of the Comèdie Française.[39] The legend was evoked from the outset with Henri de Navarre suspecting his mother had been poisoned and Coligny regretting the "Medici" influence, the "poisoned breath" surrounding Charles IX from the cradle. The reluctant king struggled against Catherine's argument that the massacre was necessary, and revoked the order, only to find that the executions had begun. "You have ruined me! I dare to ask: is it you who reigns?"[40] The play was a huge success, to the great distress of the establishment. The young duc d'Orleans, only sixteen, the future Louis Philippe, was present. He recalled: "It had an electrifying effect. Each line brought on stomping of feet. The room filled with a huge cry and the play continued amidst frantic applause. It was intoxicating."[41] The audience roared as L'Hôpital, who represented the ousted minister Necker, tried to defend the people against the influence of the manipulative Queen and the vacillating King, representing Marie Antoinette and Louis XVI. Danton prophesied, "If Figaro killed the nobility, *Charles IX* will kill the royalty."[42] After twenty-three performances, the play was taken off the repertoire. Only a mob-backed confrontation at the theater reinstated it a year later.

This tie between Marie Antoinette and earlier queens became overt in her trial in 1793. The charge against her read: "In the fashion of Messaline, Brunehilde, Fredegonde and Medicis, who qualify as former queens of France, and whose names are so odious that they ought to be effaced from the annals of history, Marie Antoinette...has been the scourge of France and a blood-sucker of the French."[43] The Black Legend was used to destroy Marie Antoinette. Marie Antoinette was attacked for political reasons, with the charges carrying the same weight of misogyny. Between the lines lay the fear of women exercising power, whether it was overtly political or through their lives as wives and mothers.

In the first half of the nineteenth century, French writers were heavily influenced by the writings of Sir Walter Scott and the themes of romanticism, along with the recent past of the French Revolution. Seeking a romantic historical period to focus on, Prosper Mérimée, Honoré de Balzac, and Alexandre Dumas hearkened back to the Renaissance and particularly the religious wars of the sixteenth century. The politics of the reign of Charles X, which would end in the Revolution of 1830, augmented this interest. Article Five of the Charter of 1814 had granted religious freedom, but established Roman Catholicism as the state religion. In 1828, a debate raged in the Chamber of Deputies over a proposed organization of primary instruction, designed to cull out Protestant and other non-Catholic teachers. As a result, many plays and books came out on the massacre in the following years.[44]

Perhaps the most perceptive comment about nineteenth-century writings was that of the novelist Honoré de Balzac when he wrote, "In every age where there is a great battle between the masses and those in power, the people have created an ogre figure."[45] Prosper Mérimée published his *Chronique du règne de Charles IX (Chronicle of the Reign of Charles IX)* in 1829. Mérimée, one of the most outspoken anti-religious authors of his time, discounted the massacre and viewed it as a popular insurrection, a logical outcome of religious enthusiasm.[46] "As for me, I am firmly convinced that the massacre was not premeditated and I can only conjecture that the opposite opinion was adopted by others who had decided to represent Catherine as a truly wicked woman, but one of the most adept politicians of her century."[47] He might well have been referring to Balzac, who perpetuated the legend while championing Catherine as a "Robespierre in skirts," driven to murder for the good of the state.

Balzac, a legitimist, wrote his first novel about Catherine in 1828, but post-dated it to 1830. Entitled *Les Deux Rêves (The Two Dreams)*, the novella is set at a dinner party in the late 1780s attended by

Beaumarchais, Lavoisier, Robespierre, and Marat, among others. Robespierre recounts a dream in which Catherine appears to him as a ghost and justifies the massacre as "necessary," driven not by passion but by the needs of the state: "Do you think I acted out of hatred, that I only breathe vengeance and fury? I was as calm and cold as reason itself. I condemned the Huguenots without pity, but without passion; they were only the rotten oranges in my basket. The Queen of England would have done the same thing to the Catholics if they were seditious."[48]

In his *Letters on Paris* on December 30, 1830 he wrote: "Catherine de Medici is a grand image of Christianity and of Kings." But in 1836 when Balzac published the second novel, *La Confidence des Ruggieri (The secrets of the Ruggieri)*, he focused on the astrologers at Catherine's court. Drawing on the calumnies of the *Discours* and other Protestant pamphlets recently published in the 1835 *Archives Curieuses de l'Histoire de France*, Balzac depicted Catherine as driven by "domination and superstition." He justified her reliance on astrologers, alchemists, and soothsayers, decried by the Protestant writers as witchcraft, as valid sources of valuable predictions. She was fighting, not for religion, but in order to subdue the nobles who threatened the crown. Her son, Charles IX, was terrified of her: "My mother is the cause of all the troubles here. In three months I will either be dead or the *de facto* King."[49] The third novel, *Le Martyr Calviniste*, published in 1842, continued the theme of her insatiable ambition, charging that she let her eldest son, François II, die, by refusing to allow the skilled physician Amboise Paré to lance his ear infection and save his life, in order to take power from the Guises. Her children were merely her pawns; her own rule was all important. Contradicting himself, he defended Catherine in the *Introduction* he wrote for the 1842 edition of the three novels, called *On Catherine de Médicis*.

> Catherine de Médicis... saved the crown of France; she maintained royal authority under circumstances where more than one great prince would have succumbed. With men like the Guises and the house of Bourbon heading up factious and ambitious parties... it required the use of rare qualities, the most precious gifts of men of state.... Thus, whoever examines the history of the sixteenth century in France will see that Catherine de Médicis was like a great king... this exceptional princess who had none of the weaknesses of her sex, who lived chastely in the midst of one of the most galant courts of Europe, and who, despite the lack of money, built monuments to make up for the losses caused by the Calvinists to the body politic.... All power, legitimate or illegitimate, must defend itself when attacked.[50]

A bold statement, but Catherine was neither the heroine, nor the focus of the novels. Instead of relying on the facts, as he had set out to do, he repeated all of the calumnies of the *Discours*. He maligned her reputation while arguing her absolute government was valid because the unity of the state was threatened by religious divisions.

On the other side of the political fence, Alexandre Dumas, père, a Republican, had written a hit play in 1829, *Henri III et son cour*. In the 1840s he may have been stoking the anti-monarchical, anti-court resentment growing in the French populace against the entrenched interests when he wrote the novel *La Reine Margot* and followed it up two years later, in 1847, with a play by the same name.[51] Jo Burr Margadant's argument that the Orleanists failed to develop a popular royal family image may be reflected in Dumas's depiction of the scheming of Catherine de Medici and the willingness of Charles IX to sacrifice others for the sake of the family honor, both in the massacre and in the death warrant for La Mole.[52] Dumas may also be responding to the ideological struggle of the 1840s over the proper role of women. Catherine represented the nefarious outcome of a woman in power while Marguerite represented the loyal wife and sacrificial lover.

La Reine Margot (Queen Margot) begins with the wedding day of Henri and Marguerite; it ends with the death of Charles IX, the murder of Henri's mistress, and the revelation by René, Catherine's astrologer, of Henri's future as King of France. Dumas developed several Romantic themes: the love of two couples: Marguerite and La Mole and Henri and Charlotte de Sauve, the diabolical machinations of Catherine de Medici, and the male bonding of La Mole and Coconnas. Dumas uses the Black Legend of Catherine as the villain, "that soul so full of darkness and mystery,"[53] to contrast with the romantic figure of Marguerite, the heroine. Catherine is cold, calculating, and determined to keep Henri de Navarre from inheriting the throne. She relies on René, her perfumer and source of poisons, to aid her through poisoning the gloves of Jeanne d'Albret, the lip balm of Madame de Sauve, and the falconry book given to Henri de Navarre. Although she intends to eliminate Henri through ingesting poison when he licks his fingers to turn the pages of the book, instead it results in the slow, painful death of her own son, Charles IX. Catherine uses the hunting book as evidence to execute La Mole for the poisoning, eliminating another Huguenot leader, but also the beloved of Margot, as Marguerite is called in the novel. Thus, the Black Legend is embellished with more murders, reiterating the dangers of a powerful woman.

In the novel, Dumas presents a heroic picture of both Margot and Henri. Since Henri, who becomes Henri IV, is the most beloved of the

French kings, Dumas was playing into the sympathies of his audience. The same was true of his repetition of the Black Legend. Nicola Sutherland, the leading historian in attacking the Black Legend, wrote "The legend of her wickedness reached its apex in the nineteenth century. It depicted her as cold, cruel, calculating, treacherous and evil. She was a monster of selfish ambition who sacrificed all who stood in her way to the satisfaction of her all-consuming desire for power."[54] This is certainly true in Dumas's novel, where Catherine is malevolent, carrying out poisonings against her enemies and urging her sons on to mayhem.

The legend of Catherine de Medici as the Wicked Italian Queen originally was designed to undermine her role as Queen Mother before the return of Henri III from Poland. In the years that followed it was used whenever women had power: warning Elizabeth I of the perils of favorites, supporting Mary when William was abroad, and in seventeenth- and eighteenth-century France undermining the monarchy through links with "devious" women. In the early nineteenth century it seems to have served to raise doubts about the royal "family." After the demise of the monarchy, the legend was used to reinforce the misogyny directed against women's power. The positive image of the nineteenth century was the submissive wife and mother. Representations of Catherine warned of the powerful woman and the infamous Bad Mother. Reading the Black Legend over time reminds us to beware: it may poison your mind.

Notes

1. Henri Estienne. *Discours Merveilleux de la Vie, Actions, et Departmens de la Reyne Catherine de Médicis, Mère*...in M. L. Cimber and F. Danjou, *Archives Curieuses de l'Histoire de France*. 1re serie, tome 9 (Paris: Beauvais, 1836).
2. *The History of the Life of Katherine de Medicis Queen Mother and Regent of France or The Exact Pattern of the Present French King's Policy*, trans. John Wyat (London: John Wyat at the Rose in St. Paul's Churchyard, 1693), Preface.
3. *The History*, p. 95.
4. Nicola Mary Sutherland, *Catherine de Medici and the Ancien Régime* (London: Historical Association, 1966) and Robert Kingdon, *Myths about the St. Bartholomew's Day Massacres, 1572–76* (Cambridge, MA: Harvard University Press, 1988).
5. *The History of the Life*, trans. John Wyat, p. 5.
6. Robert J. Knecht, *Catherine de' Medici* (New York: Addison Wesley Longman Inc., 1998), p. 58.
7. Robert M. Kingdon, *Myths About the St. Bartholomew's Day Massacres, 1572–76* (Cambridge: Harvard University Press, 1988), pp. 20–211.
8. Douglas Cole, *Suffering and Evil in the Plays of Christopher Marlowe* (Princeton: Princeton University Press, 1962).

9. A. D. Wright and Virginia F. Stern, *In Search of Christopher Marlowe* (New York: Vanguard Press, 1965), p. 35; Andrew M. Kirk, *The Mirror of Confusion: The Representation of French History in English Renaissance Drama* (New York and London: Garland Publishing, 1996), p. 90.
10. Roger Sales, *Christopher Marlowe* (London: Macmillan, 1991), pp. 10, 37.
11. Christopher Marlowe, *The Massacre at Paris* in *The Complete Plays*, ed. J. B. Steane (London: Penguin Classics, 1986), pp. 535–84.
12. Marlowe, *The Massacre at Paris*, p. 543.
13. Marlowe, p. 546.
14. Marlowe, pp. 557–58.
15. Marlowe, p. 562.
16. Marlowe, p. 568.
17. Carole Levin, *'The Heart and Stomach of a King': Elizabeth I and the Politics of Sex and Power* (Philadelphia: University of Pennsylvania Press, 1994), pp. 61–62.
18. Penny Roberts, "Marlowe's *The Massacre at Paris*: a historical perspective," *Renaissance Studies*, 9, no. 4 (1995), pp. 430–41.
19. Terence Dawson, "Catherine de Médicis and *La Princesse de Cleves*," *Seventeenth Century French Studies* (1992), 14, p. 191.
20. Janet Letts, *Legendary Lives in La Princesse de Clèves* (Charlottesville: Rockwood Press, 1998), pp. 67–71, 229–30.
21. *The History of the Life*, p. 95.
22. *Reflections Upon the Late Horrid Conspiracy Contrived by Some of the French Court to Morther His Majesty in Flanders: And for Which Monsieur Grandvall, one of the Assassins, was Executed* (London: Richard Baldwin, 1692).
23. *Reflections*, pp. 6–25.
24. Henry R. Plomer, *A Dictionary of the Printers and Booksellers who were at Work in England, Scotland and Ireland from 1668 to 1725*, ed. Arundell Esdaile (London: Oxford University Press, 1922) in *British Biographical Archive* II (Microfiche edition, London: K.G. Saur, 1991), p. 106.
25. Lois G. Schwoerer, "The Queen as Regent and Patron," in *The Age of William III and Mary II: Power, Politics and Patronage 1688–1702*, ed. Robert P. Maccubbin and Martha Hamilton-Phillips (College of William and Mary in Virginia, 1989), p. 222.
26. Voltaire, *A Discourse on Tragedy, with Reflections on the English and French Drama (published with An Essay upon the Civil Wars of France)* (London: N. Prevost and Comp., 1731), p. 21.
27. Voltaire, *Henriade, An Epick poem in ten cantos, translated from the French into English blank verse to which are now added, the argument to each canto, and large notes historical and critical* (London: C. Davis, 1732), p. v.
28. Voltaire, *Henriade*, p. 28.
29. Voltaire, *Henriade*, pp. 29–30.
30. Voltaire, *The History of the Civil Wars in France upon which the Henriade is grounded* (London: N. Prevost & Comp, 1731).
31. Voltaire, *Henriade*, p. 34.
32. Voltaire, *Henriade*, p. 34.
33. Marie Genevieve Charlotte Thiroux d'Arconville, *Histoire de Francois II* (Paris: Chez Belin, 1783), p. 47.

34. *Essai historique sur la vie de Marie Antoinette* (1789) and others cited by Lynn Hunt, *The Family Romance of the French Revolution* (Berkeley: University of California Press, 1992), pp. 104–11.
35. Published under the name of Louis Prudhomme, but attributed to Louise-Félicité Gunement de Keralio Robert (Paris: Révolutions de Paris, 1791).
36. Louise Keralio, *Les Crimes des reines de France, depuis le commencement de la monarchie jusqu'à Marie-Antoinette* (Paris: Révolutions de Paris, 1791), pp. 263, 266, 277–78, 327–29, 336–39.
37. Published anonymously in London in 1789.
38. Anonymous (Paris: Imprimerie Royale, no date, but probably 1791).
39. Daniel Hamiche, *Le Théâtre et la Révolution: La Lutte de Classes au Théâtre en 1789 et en 1793* (Paris: UGE, 1973); Jacques Boncompain, "Théâtre et Formation des Consciences: L'Example de Charles IX," *Révue d'Histoire du Théâtre*, 41:1 (1989), pp. 44–48.
40. Marie-Joseph de Chenier, *Charles IX: tragedie en cinq actes* (Paris: Les Bons Livres, 1870), pp. 3, 5, 36.
41. *Souvenirs et notes de M. Lebrun*, cited in Bruno Villien, "Talma Pendant la Révolution," *Révue de la Société d'histoire du Théâtre*, 1 (1989), p. 38.
42. Jacques Boncompain, "Theatre et formation des consciences: L'Exemple de Charles IX," *Revue d'histoire du theater*, 1 (1989), p. 46.
43. Charles Ostyn, "Le proces de Marie Antoinette," *La Revolution Francaise*, 6 (1884), pp. 646–64 contains the complete transcription of the trial.
44. Nicole Cazauran, *Catherine de Médicis et son temps dans la Comedie Humaine* (Lille: Université de Lille, 1977), pp. 48–9. Cazauran provides a detailed study of Balzac's inconsistencies in dealing with Catherine.
45. Honore de Balzac, *Sur Catherine de Médicis*, Introduction, in *Oeuvres Complètes*, vol. 20 (Chambery: La Société des Études Balzaciennes, 1961), p. 70.
46. Frank Paul Bowman, *Prosper Mérimée: Heroism, Pessimism, and Irony* (Berkeley: University of California Press, 1962), p. 29.
47. Prosper Mérimée, *Chronique du Règne de Charles IX*. Preface (Paris: Charpentier, 1865), p. 6.
48. *Les Deux Rêves* in Honoré de Balzac, *Oeuvres Complètes*, vol. 20 (Chambery: Imprimeries Réunies, 1961), p. 390.
49. *La Confidence des Ruggieri*, p. 327 in Balzac, *Oeuvres Complètes*.
50. Honoré de Balzac, *Sur Catherine de Médicis* in *Oeuvres Completes*, vol. 15 (Paris: Grapinhot, 1967), pp. 471–72.
51. Fernande Basson, *Dumas Père et l'Histoire: A Propos de la piece "La Reine Margot,"* *Revue d'Histoire du Théâtre*, 39:4 (1987).
52. Jo Burr Margadant, "The Duchesse de Berry and Royalist Political Culture in Postrevolutionary France," in *The New Biography: Performing Femininity in Nineteenth-Century France*, ed. Jo Burr Margadant (Berkeley: University of California Press, 2000), pp. 33–71.
53. Alexandre Dumas, *La Reine Margot*, ed. David Coward (Oxford: Oxford University Press, 1997), p. 12.
54. Nicola Mary Sutherland, *Princes, Politics, and Religion, 1547–1589* (London: Hambledon Press, 1984), p. 247.

Anne Boleyn in History, Drama, and Film

Retha M. Warnicke

Anne Boleyn, the second consort of Henry VIII, holds a controversial place in historical accounts and dramatic representations largely because her marriage to Henry VIII ushered in the English Reformation. Scholars agree that the king withdrew from the Roman Catholic communion because Pope Clement VII refused to annul his marriage with Catherine of Aragon, the aunt of Emperor Charles V. Henry sought an annulment on the grounds that his union with Catherine, his brother's widow, which he claimed violated divine law, was the cause of the deaths of their male infants. Henry secretly wed the pregnant Anne in January 1533; that spring, by authority of the recently passed Statute of Appeals, Thomas Cranmer, archbishop of Canterbury, annulled the king's first marriage and validated the second one. In June, Anne was crowned queen and in September her daughter Elizabeth was born. Less than three years later, in January 1536, she miscarried a male fetus.

The following May, a royal commission convicted her of having committed adultery with five members of the king's privy chamber including her brother, George, Lord Rochford; Cranmer annulled her marriage to Henry, and a Calais swordsman beheaded her. Two recent biographers, E. W. Ives and I, agree about her innocence but disagree about the reasons for her death. Relying on the letters of Eustace Chapuys, the resident Imperial-Spanish ambassador, who had friendly ties with Queen Catherine, Ives maintains that a court faction led by Thomas Cromwell, the king's principal secretary, worked for Anne's ruin because she had been interfering with his attempts to negotiate an alliance with her enemy, and Catherine's nephew, Emperor Charles. Cromwell used Henry's lust for Jane Seymour to manipulate him into

Anne Boleyn by an unknown artist
By courtesy of the National Portrait Gallery.

assenting to Anne's death. By contrast, I argue that only some catastrophic event, such as the birth of a deformed fetus, which contemporaries interpreted as one of God's ways of punishing its parents for a heinous sin, would have led Henry to admit that five men had cuckolded him. He hoped, I further argue, to cast doubt on the fetus's paternity and believed that the accused had committed adultery with Anne.[1]

Dramatists have also disagreed about how to interpret her life. As Agnes Strickland remarked, "Prejudice, on the one hand, has converted her faults into virtues, and on the other, transformed even her charms into deformity and described her as a monster."[2] In 1612–13, William Shakespeare, undoubtedly influenced by the martyrologist John Foxe's moving description of Anne, portrayed her as an innocent object of the affections of the king, who hoped to realize his desires for a male heir in her.[3] In his poetic drama about the queen in 1682, John Banks followed Shakespeare's lead concerning her innocence.[4]

In the nineteenth century, three authors, two Englishmen and an American, published poetic dramas about Anne.[5] The one by the Reverend Henry Montague Grover in 1826, which was never performed, and the other by Tom Taylor, which was featured at the Haymarket in 1876–77, confirmed her to be innocent of political ambition and adultery.[6] In 1849–50, George H. Boker, an American playwright, wrote a transitional piece that, unlike the others, characterizes her as a manipulative, ambitious woman who achieves redemption at the end of her life. Like Grover's, it was never produced.[7]

Developments in the field of history in the late nineteenth century influenced twentieth-century interpretations of the Tudors. As historical studies became increasingly housed in male-dominated, scientifically oriented universities, they ceased to be the province of part-time amateurs. Assuming that facts speak for themselves, these academicians quoted "undigested" excerpts from early modern secondary works and archival evidence, mostly failing to allow for the biases of the authors whose evidence they validated.[8] Consequently, Catholic writings, especially Nicholas Sander's study of the Reformation and Chapuys's letters, became important sources of information about Anne Boleyn.

In his Latin book published posthumously in 1585, Sander, a Catholic priest, described Anne as a tall, witchlike creature with a wen on her throat, a protruding tooth, and six fingers. Rendered into English and published in 1877, it was followed in print seven years later by Paul Friedmann's two-volume biography of Anne that depended greatly on Chapuys's dispatches. In his correspondence, which had begun appearing in an English calendar in 1879, the ambassador accused Anne of bewitching Henry.[9] Contemporaneously, the *Letters and Papers, Foreign and Domestic, of the Reign of Henry VIII* also contained translated, albeit, abridged versions of Chapuys's dispatches.[10] The Victorians published no new Protestant documents to counter Catholic charges about

Anne's manipulative role or to substantiate Foxe's claim that her death lay shrouded in mystery. Ironically, while his "Martyrs" was exerting a decreasing influence on views of Anne, his work was continuing to direct general Reformation studies.

The impact of these Catholic writings can be seen in three modern films or videos that dealt with Anne. Although in 1933 Lajos Biro and Arthur Wimperis gave her only a tiny role in *The Private Life of Henry VIII*, they do have the king refer to her as ambitious. Maxwell Anderson's 1948 verse drama, *Anne of the Thousand Days*, which was adapted into a film in 1969, and Rosemary Anne Sisson's and Nick McCarty's 1970 pieces in the BBC production, *The Six Wives of Henry VIII*, elaborate upon her ambitious ways.[11]

This essay will examine the changing representations of Anne Boleyn. It will compare and contrast how early modern and modern writers differ in their interpretations of her relationship to Henry and Jane Seymour and her attitude toward her daughter. It will demonstrate that the Sander–Chapuys witch has replaced the Foxe–Shakespeare innocent in modern media forms. Ironically, even some revivals of Shakespeare's play represent her in this negative mode. Essentially, modern writers have transferred the role of the innocent and religious wife from Anne Boleyn to Jane Seymour.

A major theme of Shakespeare's *Henry VIII* is the king's struggle to secure his dynasty. This episodic play is held together by the challenges Shakespeare presents to the political power of four figures, Edward, duke of Buckingham, Queen Catherine, Thomas, Cardinal Wolsey, and Cranmer. The script builds toward a triumphant ending in which Henry, confident of his dynasty's future, protects the archbishop who facilitated the marriage to Anne that providentially will prove fruitful through Elizabeth.[12]

In essays on this play, Linda McJ. Micheli, Kim H. Noling, and Jo Eldridge Carney agree that Shakespeare's focus was on Henry's desires rather than on the women, although the dialogue and action serve to define expectations about queenship.[13] It is not a feminist play, for the king remains in charge of the destiny of both his subjects and wives. An occasional misogynist remark can also be found, as for example, Lord Sands's reference to women's garrulity (1.4.43–44).[14]

In a play on words, Carney remarks: "As far as the presentation of the queens is concerned, there is only one issue: the issue is issue."[15] Throughout his drama, Shakespeare associates Anne's attractiveness with her probable fertility. Compliant and untarnished by ambition, the ribald words of Lord Sands and the Old Lady seem to highlight her innocence rather than to besmirch her character. When the Lord Chamberlain announces that the king has raised Anne to the peerage, he claims that "Beauty and honour" are "mingled" in her (2.3.75–80).

Anne does not draw attention to herself. At Wolsey's festivities, after she is forbidden to sit with her ladies, Sands is seated beside her. When the king discovers her sitting silently, he selects her as his dance partner. Shakespeare may have invented the above-cited scene with the Old Lady to provide Anne an opportunity to deny harboring royal ambitions.[16] After she learns of Anne's ennoblement, the Old Lady laments her own futile search for rewards and complains that Anne has had her "mouth fill'd up before it was opened" (2.3.87–88). Modern critics often emphasize the Old Lady's lewd words about Anne's future rather than her remark that Anne has never sought political advancement.[17]

As the coronation scene makes clear, Anne complies with Henry's wishes. Without expressing a desire to become queen, she takes on the expected female roles of consort and motherhood. The play avoids her disgrace in its vindication of her marriage by the birth of Elizabeth, for only a lady without blemish could become the mother of such a great queen.

This interpretation depends on a reading of the Arden edition of the play. Clearly, an actress could develop these scenes with totally different meanings. As Micheli points out, Anne speaks at length in only one scene and elsewhere she is presented "almost exclusively through visual means."[18] In fact, from the late nineteenth century, perhaps influenced by Friedmann's biography of her, directors have often instructed actresses playing Anne to appear ambitious and flirtatious. In Hugh Richmond's book on this play, he examines an important, but controversial, early twentieth-century version of Anne, as acted by Linda Cowan in Herbert Beerbohm Tree's production in 1910. In the dance scene, Cowan played Anne as a coquettish flirt intent upon attracting the king: She was, according to Richmond, "made frivolous to serve as a foil" to the "wronged" Catherine of Aragon.[19]

The modern production of *Henry VIII*, which is probably the most well known, is the BBC video of 1979 that the Shakespeare Association of America rated as the best version of Shakespeare in its series of his plays. As Anne, Barbara Kellerman seems to play her basically as I have interpreted her from the Arden edition. At Wolsey's festivities, she smiles compliantly, but when the king, acted by John Stride, escorts her to the banquet, she looks concerned rather than victorious. It is interesting how through close-ups the video intensifies her presence in these scenes. To highlight her innocence, the video shows her combing her hair, which hangs loose, a sign of virginity, as she prepares for the coronation. No stage directions call for this action or for her appearance outside the procession itself.

Afterward Anne does not reappear, but the audience remains aware of her presence off stage. The drama ends with Cranmer's providential speech at Elizabeth's christening, predicting that she will be "the happiness of England" and will die a "virgin" with the entire "world" mourning her. Afterwards, the king, who participates in the ceremony, turns to London's Lord Mayor and his "brethren":

> Ye must all see the queen, and she must thank ye,
> She will be sick else. This day, no man think
> 'Has business at his house; for all shall say:
> This little one shall make it Holy-day. (5.5.75–76)

It can be conjectured that in the Restoration revivals of this play the actresses, like Kellerman later, played Anne as lacking in ambition. It is unfortunate that, as Hugh Richmond points out, there was a "lack of recorded appreciation of the women's parts" in those productions.[20] Their success could have influenced the writing of John Banks's 1682 poetic drama, *Vertue Betray'd: Or, Anna Bullen*. Little is known about Banks; he was probably born in 1650 and died in 1704. A member of the New Inn, he wrote the first of his seven tragedies in 1677. His source for *Vertue Betray'd* was Marie-Catherine Le Jumel de Barneville, Comtesse d'Aulnoy's *The Secret Novels of Queen Elizabeth*, a French romance that was printed in English in 1680.[21]

This study of Banks's play relies on Diane Dreher's 1981 facsimile of its first edition. Although it has lacked scholarly interest since 1981, it was well received when it was produced and became somewhat popular. By the end of the eighteenth century, it had gone through fifteen editions and many revivals.[22]

Anne appears as a virtuous woman who is betrayed by others' ambition. The "plight of innocent young lovers victimized by corruption and political intrigue was a favorite theme for Banks," and it is one of two major themes in *Vertue Betray'd*. It opens with Wolsey, whose lifetime is extended and who is an "evil caricature of the Catholic Church," conspiring with the king's ex-mistress, Elizabeth Blount, to ruin Anne, identified here as a Lutheran.[23] As Anne prepares for her "unwelcome coronation" (1.1), she reveals that she wed the king only after her relatives deceived her into believing that her real love, Henry Percy, was secretly married. In the meantime, Wolsey introduces the king to Jane Seymour, who does not appear in the play (2.1). After Henry becomes attracted to Jane, the love letters that Anne's brother, Lord Rochford, sent to Blount, which she now claims were addressed to Anne, lead to Rochford's and the queen's downfall (4.1). In her prophetic speech at the end of the play, with Elizabeth in her arms, Anne predicts about the papacy:

> That holy Tryant...
> Thou shalt destroy, and quite unloose his Bonds,
> And lay the Monster trembling at thy Feet.
> When this shall come to pass, the World shall see
> Thy Mothers Innocence reviv'd in thee. (5.1)

This dialogue highlights the second, important theme of the play—its anti-Catholicism. While Anne supports the Lutheran cause, Wolsey seems to represent the Borgia Pope Alexander VI. The audience in 1682 was probably receptive to this theme because of fears about a trumped-up Popish Plot to assassinate King Charles II, which had only recently been brought to a close.[24]

The dialogue makes it clear that Banks meant to emphasize Anne's lack of interest in achieving political power. If the Restoration theater could successfully portray Anne as an innocent but compliant lady, so could have the earlier Jacobean theater that also had contemporary reasons for honoring the mother of Queen Elizabeth, the namesake of James I's daughter who married the Lutheran Frederick of Palatine in 1613.[25] This theme of Anne's innocence was continued in the nineteenth-century work of two English playwrights, Grover and Taylor.

Grover, who was born in 1791, became a solicitor in 1816, received his L. L. B. in 1830 at Peterhouse, Cambridge, and was appointed rector of Hitcham Buckinghamshire in 1833. Because of frail health, he subsequently lived in seclusion and, before his death in 1866, had written several miscellaneous pieces on a variety of topics. He composed his only play, which was published in 1826, before taking holy orders.[26]

Far from being the aggressor in her relationship with the king, Grover has her remark how "small the worth" (1.2) is of she whom the king now favors, although she does also question Catherine's failure to submit to his pleasure. Except for this one criticism, Anne's dialogue has only rueful references to Catherine. As she prepares for her coronation, for example, she says:

> Absolved from reproach; since, being fated
> To this estate and Catherine declared
> Unjustly crown'd, I do but tread the way
> Heav'n hath appointed. Yea, and by Heav'n's grace,

Will I devoutly tread the paths he points.
Hence then, ye clam'rous yearnings of my soul
Which would too deeply study Catherine's woe. (2.4)

While Banks has Blount as villainess, Grover casts Jane, Lady Rochford, who befriends Jane Seymour, in that role. Encouraged by Rochford, Jane at first accepts the king's advances, but she soon questions whether any "ground of controversy" exists for divorcing Anne (4.1). Finally, she insists she cannot be "worthy" of his love while he is married, a resistance that signals the queen's downfall (4.3). In the next scene an attendant reports to Anne that Thomas, duke of Norfolk, has informed the king that she favors Sir Francis Weston, one of her alleged lovers who is later executed. After Anne is imprisoned in the Tower, accused of adultery with three men, her brother, Weston, and Mark Smeaton, a musician, Jane receives the king's attentions once again. The imprisoned queen reminds Cranmer of her innocence and thanks him for his comforting words. She laments that she might have been unkind to the child of poor Catherine and her last thoughts are of her daughter, Elizabeth, for whom she says a mother's prayer.

Grover thus justifies Anne's marriage to Henry because Catherine was "unjustly crown'd" and depicts Anne as an innocent, who is a devoted mother to Elizabeth and rues her predecessor's treatment. Grover's Jane Seymour, on the other hand, also projects innocence because she refuses Henry's attentions until after Anne is charged with adultery. The play is about women who fall victim to a lustful man, who as king has the power to destroy them.

In contrast to Grover, Tom Taylor, who lived from 1817 to 1880, was one of the most popular playwrights of his day. Having earned a B.A. and an M.A. at Trinity College, Cambridge, by 1842, he attended the Inner Temple and was called to the bar in 1846. After holding various positions, he turned to drama, writing over seventy pieces that were produced in the theatre between 1840 and 1880. Winston Tolles has condemned his play about Anne because of its "inferior verse," its great length, and boring script, which seems like a "dramatic version of an illustrated textbook."[27]

It probably reminded Tolles of a textbook because it has a large, generally valid cast of characters, including even Ambassador Chapuys. Although his dispatches had not yet been published, Taylor apparently had access to English state papers that referenced Chapuys, whose role here is to conspire with Lady Rochford to destroy Anne.[28] As in Grover's earlier play, Anne remains generally innocent of ambition, even forcing Henry to wait for years until her love for him conquers her scruples.

Taylor's Jane Seymour, however, unlike Grover's, aggressively pursues Henry. She arranges to be at the "chestnut walk," her favorite meeting place, where she knows he will find her (4.1).

Even though Anne, who discovers them together, believes that she was justified in marrying him, she remarks to Margaret Wyatt:

> Who knows how cruel man can be to woman
> When he is wearied of her? Now it comes,
> The thought of that poor Queen whose place I took,
> As she [Jane] takes mine. (4.1)

When Margaret protests that Anne "had full warrant" for "There was no marriage bond between them," Anne responds:

> And yet thought of her misery should have stayed me.
> No, No, twas too much love, and some ambition. (4.1)

Following historical accounts, the five alleged lovers and Anne die. Until the end of her life, she denies her guilt and her last thoughts are of her daughter. To Margaret, she says:

> Farewell, dear friend! Be mother to my babe.
> Tell her I blessed her with my dying breath. (5.1)

The third nineteenth-century author of a play about Anne was an American, George H. Boker, who was born in 1823 in Philadelphia, attended Princeton University, and died in 1890. He composed nine of his eleven plays between 1848 and 1857, and next to playwright Francesca da Rimini he is now acknowledged as the best American playwright of the century. His study of Anne was never produced, for theatrical companies in both the United States and Great Britain rejected it. As Thomas Kitts remarks, "In an age that valued melodrama," it "does not have enough action." Furthermore, since Boker looked for models in Elizabethan drama, he was out of step with his society's literary nationalism and even felt it necessary to defend himself from the claim that he was a mere imitator of Shakespeare. His major source was Strickland's biography from which he borrowed heavily for some of Anne's speeches.[29]

Boker's play begins with Anne as the queen of a corrupt court headed by an immoral monarch, who is a slave to the "curse of kings," his "pampered appetites" (3.2). She is far from innocent because she, along with her ambitious contemporaries, is guilty of having destroyed others on her ascent to power. Her victims are Catherine of Aragon, Cardinal

Wolsey, Sir Thomas More, and Bishop John Fisher. Although some believe she bewitched Henry (1.1), she identifies him as the "copartner of her guilt and shame" (2.1).

While Boker presents her as an ambitious member of a corrupt court, he still has her lobbying for "Our faithful Protestants in Germany" (1.3) and appearing surprised to learn that "not two years as queen" she has a competitor in Jane Seymour, who seeks to win Henry's love with the comment, "What mercy showed she to poor Katharine?" (2.1). In this play as in the others of this century, Rochford figures as the villainess; she provides the king with the names of six alleged lovers, adding to the list Sir Thomas Wyatt, who is pardoned (3.3).

The play's major theme is the transformation of Anne's character, for she realizes as Oliver H. Evans points out, that "her fall is in part a test of her strength and in part a punishment for the suffering she inflicted."[30] In fact, she achieves a dignified and heroic status, and awaiting death in the Tower laments:

> O Wolsey, Wolsey!
> I, whose ambitious footstep thrust aside
> Your tottering age—I, who with crafty toil
> Climbed to the seat of patient Katharine—
> Feel every pang which I tortured you!
> My power is gone; another cunning maid
> Plays o'er my part of heartless Treachery
> O More and Fisher—blood, blood!—save my wits. (5.2)

She declines the hope of pardon if she will "offer no obstruction" to a divorce, for she refuses to "stamp the bastard" on her daughter's "brow" (5.2). Choosing death, she claims that Henry "crowns my innocence with martyrdom" (2.1).[31]

Boker's view of her as redeemed at her death serves as a transition between the other nineteenth-century plays that treat her as politically innocent and the twentieth-century drama that depict her as an ambitious plotter. Important to the depiction of the modern Anne are Sander's history and Chapuys's correspondence, both of which described her as a witch.

In contrast to their increasingly negative influence on Anne's dramatic character, Chapuys's dispatches began to have a benign effect on Jane Seymour's image. In March 1536, for example, two months before Anne's death, he reported that Jane had returned some gifts to the king who was attempting to woo her with presents.[32] Once queen, as she was kind to her stepdaughter, Mary, the child of Catherine of Aragon,

Chapuys usually referred to her favorably.[33] He failed, however, to allege as did a French diplomat that she was opposed to the dissolution of the monasteries or to claim as did Martin Luther that she was an enemy to the gospel.[34] Writers began to interpret these French and German remarks to mean that she was devoted to Roman Catholicism.

The first of the three screenplays or films to be examined here is Biro's and Wimperis's *The Private Life of Henry VIII*, which was produced in England in 1932. A Hungarian who was born in Vienna in 1880 and who died in 1948, Biro published thirty volumes of plays, novels, and short stories. When talking pictures arrived, he turned to cinema, and his screenplays include "Catherine the Great," which was also a collaboration with Wimperis, a dramatic author and lyricist. Born in London in 1876, Wimperis, who died in 1953, wrote many pieces including a number of plays adapted from the French.[35]

Their screenplay, which begins with preparations for her execution, has only a small role for Anne, acted by Merle Oberon. The prologue reveals that the king, performed by Charles Laughton as a caricature of majestic power, divorced his first wife because she was "respectable" but that there was an entirely different reason for the second divorce, thus hinting that Anne was not respectable, although viewers later learn that the motive was his desire to wed Jane Seymour.[36] Even the court ladies express disbelief that Anne committed adultery with five men, who remain unnamed and who are said to have confessed under torture. Oberon portrays a mature, sensual Anne, but she is given no opportunity to play the "ambitious" woman described by her husband. Henry goes on to characterize Jane Seymour as a "lovable fool," who seems more concerned with fashionable clothes than with political power. In a fascinating contrast to BBC's Kellerman in Shakespeare's *Henry VIII*, who later combs her loose tresses to signal her virginity, Oberon traps her hair in a hairnet to facilitate her beheading.[37]

The first film featuring Anne was *Anne of the Thousand Days*, a loose adaptation by Bridget Boland and John Hale of Maxwell Anderson's poetic memory drama. Born in 1888 near Atlantic, Pennsylvania, Anderson earned his B.A. at the University of North Dakota at Grand Forks in 1911 and his M.A. in English at Stanford University in 1914. After working as an educator, an editor, and a journalist, he wrote his first full-length play in 1922. Until his death in 1959, he not only composed stage drama but also wrote screenplays. Of his thirty-five plays, thirty-three were produced, twenty-seven of them on broadway.[38]

Anne of the Thousand Days, which opened at the Schubert Theater in New York City in December 1948, was performed 386 times, and although reviews were mixed, it was a commercial success. The original cast included Joyce Redman as Anne and Rex Harrison as the king.[39] Anderson was forced to reveal his sources for the play when an unsuccessful plagiarism suit was filed against him by Francis Hackett, author of *Queen Anne Boleyn: A Novel*.[40] In his response, Anderson confessed that, although he had read Hackett's novel, he had also read Edith Sitwell's *Fanfare for Elizabeth*,[41] Martin Hume's *The Six Wives of Henry VIII*, and other texts.[42]

Since the screenplay differs markedly from the original drama, my comments will be mostly about Hal Wallis's production although contrasts with the printed play will be included. In the film Genevieve Bujold plays Anne and Richard Burton plays Henry as Richard Burton.[43] At its beginning the youthful Anne is in love with Henry Percy, and perhaps in a misguided attempt to highlight her independent, even "liberated" character, Anderson, whose lead is followed by the screenwriters, has her reveal to Percy that she had lost her virginity in England when she was "little."[44] Regardless of what the immediate source for this revelation was, it originated in the work of Sander, who claimed that from her childhood she had indulged in sexual liaisons with several men, including her father. Sander's intent was not only to disparage her but also to discredit her daughter, the queen.

After Henry breaks up her romance with Percy, Anne rebuffs his advances until he promises marriage to ensure that her children will be born legitimate. Thus, Henry's divorce from Catherine has its roots in his lust for Anne rather than in his need for a son, although that need forms the backdrop to the action. After Elizabeth's birth, Anne requires the deaths of all who refuse to swear to support her daughter's succession. As the king tires of Anne, he turns to Jane Seymour who appears only once in the film. While dancing with the king, she is flirtatious and receptive of his attentions but not the initiator of their relationship. The writers decided to omit a scene from Anderson's play in which, recalling Chapuys's rumor, she returns a gift from the king.[45]

After Anne expels Jane from court, Cromwell reveals to her that the people call her "witch queen." Through his machinations, the innocent queen is convicted of adultery. The ultimate sources for the claim that she was a witch and that Cromwell engineered her execution are the writings of Sander and Chapuys. Wishing to marry Seymour, Henry offers exile to his queen if she will only agree to an annulment of their marriage, which will result in Elizabeth's becoming illegitimate. Defiant to the end, Anne proclaims providentially: "Elizabeth shall be a greater queen than any king of yours. She shall rule a greater England than you could ever have built. Yes, my Elizabeth shall be queen and my blood shall have been well spent." This statement is repeated at the end of the film as the audience sees the young Elizabeth walking away.

While Anne's hairstyle in the BBC's *Henry VIII* emphasizes her innocence and in *The Private Life of Henry VIII* focuses attention on her beheading, in the film of Anderson's drama, it has a grander role. Anne assumes greater beauty and vivaciousness, even sensuality, because her auburn tresses, usually uncontained by coverings, are permitted to fall down her back from a tiara or a band on top of her head. To modern audiences this arrangement is more attractive than the Tudor custom of concealing the hair under headdresses, the style adopted for the other actresses in the film. Anderson depicts Anne as bereft of political ambition until after Henry intervenes in her life, but Sisson and McCarty, who are still writing professionally in Great Britain, present a more calculating character that is obviously based on the Sander/Chapuys model.[46] In their pieces, Keith Michell offers a caricature of Henry while Dorothy Tutin plays an ambitious Anne. Choosing to ignore the Percy episode, Sisson describes Anne from the onset as manipulating the king. Recalling an anecdote of Chapuys, who is a character in Sisson's but not in McCarty's screenplay, Anne eavesdrops on conversations between the king and the ambassador.[47] McCarty's dialogue begins after Elizabeth's birth with an estranged Anne and Henry quarreling about his philandering. Then when she miscarries a male fetus, Henry accuses her of bewitching him and his son. Soon Cromwell and Norfolk plot her downfall, aided and abetted by Rochford who resumes the part of villainess that she held in nineteenth-century drama. She provides Cromwell with several names, including that of her own husband, and ultimately all five of the alleged lovers are identified.[48]

As he plots Anne's demise, Cromwell says to Norfolk: "She must not speak. She has cunning words. Else how did she bewitch our King?" Once she is imprisoned, Cranmer holds out the hope of mercy if Anne will confess her guilt since the king wishes to marry Seymour. Facing death, the imprisoned queen refuses to admit to having committed "incest and whoring" with the comment that she will do nothing to harm her daughter.[49]

Jane, the king's next wife, actually has only a small non-speaking role in McCarty's play. Ian Thorne, the author of the BBC drama on Jane, explores the depths of her religious devotion in his play. On the whole, Jane, a quiet woman who has lived at a nunnery, appears receptive to Henry but is neither politically ambitious nor flirtatious.[50] In these three screenwriters' drama, the Victorian Jane and Anne have, in a sense, exchanged places. In the film version of Sisson's and McCarty's screenplays, unconfined hair seems to depict the purity, as young women, of both Catherine and her daughter Mary. For the most part, except during her coronation, the hair of Anne by contrast hangs loose only in private moments. When it is unconfined, Anne appears somewhat less attractive than when she wears the usual Tudor hairstyle. The loose tresses, which are normally not dressed up with a tiara or band on the top of her head, appear slightly disheveled. In a scene in which she combs her hair, her brother takes the implement from her to continue the grooming, an interaction that seems to predict the ruin their kinship will bring down upon them.[51]

Except for Boker's transitional figure, the contrast between the earlier Annes and the twentieth-century Annes is startling. The previous ones never initiate intimate relationships with Henry and remain innocent throughout the marriage; their lives are vindicated by Elizabeth's birth. While Anderson's Anne has to be pressured into a relationship with Henry, she, like her modern counterparts, is ambitious. The influence of Catholic writers can thus be seen in the characterizations of her and also of Seymour, who relinquishes to Anne her flirtatious role in the Taylor/Boker drama. Unlike Taylor, Boker does not depict Anne as innocent of ambition, but unlike the manipulative Annes of modern media, he transforms her into a heroic but tragic figure.

Notes

1. E. W. Ives, *Anne Boleyn* (Oxford: Blackwell, 1968), pp. 49–52, 87, 358–82; Retha M. Warnicke, *The Rise and Fall of Anne Boleyn: Family Politics at the Court of Henry VIII* (Cambridge: Cambridge University Press, 1989), pp. 191–233. See also Warnicke, "Conflicting Rhetoric About Tudor Women: The Example of Queen Anne Boleyn," in *Political Rhetoric, Power, and Renaissance Women*, ed. Carole Levin and Patricia A. Sullivan (Albany, N.Y.: State University of New York Press, 1995), pp. 39–56.
2. Agnes Strickland, *Lives of the Queens of England* (London: Henry Colburn, 1842), 4:157.
3. For citations and his sources, see the Arden Edition of the Works of William Shakespeare, *King Henry VIII*, ed. R. A. Foakes, 3rd edn. (Cambridge, MA.: Harvard University Press, 1957). For the controversy over the play's authorship, see G. R. Proudfoot, "Henry VIII (All is True)," in *Shakespeare: A Bibliographical Guide*, new edn. (Oxford: Clarendon Press, 1990), pp. 381–83; and Hugh M. Richmond, "The Resurrection of an Expired Form," in *Shakespeare's English Histories: A Quest for Form and Genre*, ed. John W. Velz (Binghamton, N.Y.: Medieval and Renaissance Texts and

Studies, 1996, pp. 205–27; John Foxe, *The Ecclesiastical History: Containing the Acts and Monuments* (London: John Day, 1563); Thomas S. Freeman, "Research, Rumour, and Propaganda: Anne Boleyn in Foxe's 'Book of Martyrs,'" *Historical Journal*, 38 (1995), pp. 797–819.
4. John Banks, *Vertue Betray'd: Or, Anna Bullen*, ed. Diane Dreher (Los Angeles: for the William Andrews Clark Memorial Library by the University of California Press, 1981).
5. Two Librettos also appeared: Gaetano Donizetti, *Anna Bolean: Libretto. English and Italian* (New York: Snowden, 1850); and Conway Edwardes, *Anne Boleyn: An Original Historical Burlesque Extravaganza* (London: S. French, 187?).
6. Henry M. Grover, *Anne Boleyn: A Tragedy* (London: Longman, Rees, Orme, Brown and Green, 1826); Tom Taylor, "Anne Boleyn: An Original Historical Play in Five Acts," in *Historical Dramas* (London: Chatto and Windus, 1877), pp. 343–414.
7. George H. Boker, "Anne Boleyn," in *Plays and Poems* (New York: AMC Press Reprint, 1967), pp. 115–236.
8. Robin Winks, *The Historian as Detective: Essays on Evidence* (New York: Harper & Row, 1968), p. 229. For the quotation, see Ira Bruce Nadel, *Biography, Fiction, Fact, and Form* (London: Macmillan, 1984), p. 6.
9. Nicholas Sander, *Rise and Growth of the Anglican Schism*, ed. David Lewis (London: Burns and Oates, 1877), p. 25; Paul Friedmann, *Anne Boleyn: A Chapter of English History 1527–1536* (London: MacMillan, 1884), especially vol. 2; *Calendar of Letters, Despatches, and State Papers, Relating to the Negotiations Between England and Spain*, ed. G. A. Bergenroth, P. de Gayangos, G. Mattingly, M. A. S. Hume, and R. Taylor (New York: Kraus Reprint, 1969), especially vols. 3, 4, 5 (hereafter *CSP Span*).
10. *Letters and Papers, Foreign and Domestic, of the Reign of Henry VIII*, ed. J. S. Brewer, J. Gairdner, and R. H. Brodie (London: His Majesty's Stationery Office, 1862–1932), especially vols. 11, 12 (hereafter *LP*).
11. Lajos Biro and Arthur Wimperis, *The Private Life of Henry VIII*, ed. Ernest Betts (London: Methuen & Co., 1934), scene 48; Maxwell Anderson, *Anne of the Thousand Days* (New York: W. Sloane Assoc., 1948); Rosemary Anne Sisson, "Catherine of Aragon," and Nick McCarty, "Anne Boleyn" in *The Six Wives of Henry VIII*, ed. J. C. Trewin (New York: Frederick Ungar Company, 1971), pp. 1–186.
12. Wolfgang G. Muller, "Shakespeare's Last Image of Royalty: 'Henry VIII,'" in *Henry VIII in History*, ed. Baumann, pp. 232–34.
13. Linda McJ. Micheli, "'Sit By Us:' Visual Imagery and the Two Queens in *Henry VIII*," *Shakespeare Quarterly*, 38 (1987), pp. 452–66; Kim H. Noling, "Grubbing Up the Stock: Dramatizing Queens in *Henry VIII*," *Shakespeare Quarterly*, 39 (1988), pp. 291–306; Jo Eldridge Carney, "Queenship in Shakespeare's *Henry VIII*: The Issue of Issue," in *Political Rhetoric*, ed. Levin and Sullivan, pp. 189–204.
14. Like Noling, I disagree with Hugh M. Richmond, "The Feminism of Shakespeare's *Henry VIII*," *Essays in Literature*, 6 (1979), pp. 11–20.
15. Carney, "Queenship in Shakespeare's *Henry VIII*," p. 205.

16. Noling, "Grubbing up the Stock," p. 298, argues that the scene was invented to "hint at Anne's hidden desires without ever making her fully responsible for them." By contrast, Micheli, "Set By Us," p. 460, notes that Anne disassociates herself from the "sauciness of the Old Lady."
17. Hugh Richmond, *Shakespeare in Performance: King Henry VIII* (Manchester: Manchester University Press, 1994), p. 5; however, Micheli, "Sit By Us," pp. 454–57, notes that Anne was compliant.
18. Micheli, "Sit By Us," p. 454.
19. Richmond, *Henry VIII*, pp. 60–63.
20. Richmond, p. 34.
21. My thanks to John Watson, University of Minnesota, for the reference to Joan DeJean, *Tender Geographies: Origins of the Novel in France* (New York: Columbia University Press, 1991), pp. 127–28, 158, 184.
22. Banks, John, *Vertue Betray'd*, pp. iii–ix. The MLA Bibliography does not have a single entry concerning this play after 1981.
23. Banks, John, pp. iv, vi.
24. Banks, John, pp. vi–vii.
25. In the early nineteenth century, Elizabeth Inchbald thought that Shakespeare's play was actually produced during the reign of Elizabeth. See Cecilia Machesi, ed., *Remarks for the British Theater 1886–1889* (Delmar, N.Y.: Scholars' Facsimiles and Reprints, 1980), p. 4. See also, G. G. Gervinus, *Shakespeare Commentaries*, trans. F. E. Bunnett (London: Smith, Elder, & Co., 1883), pp. 824–25.
26. *Dictionary of National Biography*.
27. Winston Tolles, *Tom Taylor and Victorian Drama* (New York: Colorado University Press, 1940), pp. 220, 238. This was the only time it was performed. Adelaide Neilson played Anne, Miss Carlisle, Jane Seymour, and Charles Harcourt, Henry VIII.
28. *State Papers of Henry VIII* (London: Her Majesty's Commission, 1830–52), I: 597, 740, for example.
29. Oliver H. Evans, *George Henry Boker* (Boston: Twayne Publishers, 1984), pp. 37–38; Thomas M. Kitts, *The Theatrical Life of George Henry Boker: 1823–1890* (New York: Peter Land, 1994), p. 6.
30. Evans, *George Henry Boker*, pp. 37–44.
31. There are references in this play to witchcraft but they are not solely directed at Anne. Lord Rochford, for instance, asks himself if he has been "bewitched" (p. 147).
32. Warnicke, *Anne Boleyn*, p. 208; *LP*, especially 11 and 12.
33. *CSP Span*, 5-ii, No. 70.
34. No contemporary English source in the *LP* even hints that she had strong religious views. See *LP*, 11-ii, Nos. 475, 860, 1250; 12-i, Nos. 892, 1327.
35. Biro and Wimperis, *Private Life of Henry VIII*, pp. vi–vii.
36. Bongartz, "Henry VIII—The Moving Image," p. 320.
37. Biro and Wimperis, *Private Life of Henry VIII*, pp. ix, 5–6, 9, 19–21.
38. Barbara Lee Horn, *Maxwell Anderson: A Research and Production Sourcebook* (Westport, CT.: Greenwood Press, 1996), pp. 1–10.
39. Horn, *Maxwell Anderson*, p. 14.

40. Published by Literary Guild of America in New York, 1939.
41. Published by Macmillan in London in 1946.
42. Hume, *The Wives of Henry the Eighth: And the Parts They Played in History* (New York: Brentanos, 1905?); Horn, *Maxwell Anderson*, p. 9; Alfred S. Shivers, *Maxwell Anderson* (Boston: Twayne Publishers, 1976), pp. 79–80.
43. Bongartz, "Henry VIII—The Moving Image," pp. 318–20.
44. Arthur T. Tees, "Maxwell Anderson's Liberated Women," *North Dakota Quarterly* (Spring 1974), pp. 53–59.
45. Anderson, *Anne of the Thousand Days* (New York: William Sloane Associates, 1948), p. 84.
46. Bongartz, "Henry VIII—The Moving Image," p. 320.
47. Sisson, "Catherine of Aragon," pp. 60, 67, 77, 85; see Warnicke, *Anne Boleyn*, pp. 97–98.
48. McCarty, "Anne Boleyn," pp. 116–17, 122, 135, 138, 148.
49. Ibid., pp. 149, 175–76.
50. Ibid., pp. 135, 169; Ian Thorne, "Jane Seymour."
51. McCarty, "Anne Boleyn," p. 126. See also pp. 49, 87, 152, 175, 183.

Notes on Contributors

Debra Barrett-Graves is Assistant Professor of English at California State University-Hayward. Her articles have appeared in *Shakespeare Yearbook* and in *The Early Drama, Art, and Music Review*. She collaborated with Levin and Carney on an essay collection, *Elizabeth I: Always Her Own Free Woman* (Ashgate, 2003) and she, Carney, and Levin were among the coauthors of *Extraordinary Women of the Medieval and Renaissance World* (Greenwood Publishers, 2000).

Jo Eldridge Carney is Associate Professor of English at The College of New Jersey. She is the editor of *Renaissance and Reformation, 1500–1620* (Greenwood Publishers, 2000), which was chosen by CHOICE as an Outstanding Academic Book. Carney, Barrett-Graves, and Levin were among the authors of *Extraordinary Women of the Medieval and Renaissance World* (Greenwood Publishers, 2000). She also collaborated with Levin and Barrett-Graves on an essay collection, *Elizabeth I: Always Her Own Free Woman* (Ashgate, 2003).

Joy Currie is completing her Ph.D. in Renaissance and Romanticism at the University of Nebraska where she received the Maud Hammond Fling Fellowship. She has twice received the John Robinson Prize for best paper from the English Department and recently published an article in *Medievalia*.

Susan Dunn-Hensley teaches at the University of Kansas where she is completing her Ph.D. in English Renaissance literature; her dissertation is on women healers and witches in early modern drama.

Timothy G. Elston is completing his Ph.D. in History at the University of Nebraska where he has received the Barnes Fellowship to support his dissertation research on Catherine of Aragon. He has published in the area of his speciality, early modern English history.

Matthew C. Hansen is completing his Ph.D. in Renaissance Drama at the University of Nebraska where he holds the Gustav Cobb Fellowship.

He is the coeditor of a special issue of *The Sidney Journal* on Fulke Greville and the author of a study edition of *The Tempest*. In 2002 his essay in this collection received the prize for the best paper in literature presented at the Sixteenth Century Studies Conference the previous year.

Elaine Kruse is Professor and Chair of the History Department at Nebraska Wesleyan University. She has published widely in the field of early modern French history and women's history.

Carole Levin is Willa Cather Professor and Professor of History at the University of Nebraska. Her books include The *Reign of Elizabeth I* (Palgrave, 2002); *The Heart and Stomach of a King* (University of Pennsylvania Press, 1994), and *Extraordinary Women of the Medieval and Renaissance World* (Greenwood Publishers, 2000). Her coauthors on this book included her two coeditors of this volume. She also collaborated with Carney and Barrett-Graves on an essay collection, *Elizabeth I: Always Her Own Free Woman* (Ashgate, 2003).

Karen L. Nelson is Associate Director of the Center for Renaissance and Baroque Studies at the University of Maryland. She coedited *Women, Writing, and the Reproduction of Culture in Tudor and Stuart Britain* (Syracuse University Press, 2000), which won honorable mention from the Society for the Study of Early Modern Women. Her dissertation, *Pastoral Literature and Religious Reform in England 1575–1625*, won the Alice B. Geyer prize in 1999.

Sid Ray, Associate Professor of English at Pace University, is the author of articles on Shakespeare and on medieval and early modern film. She is currently completing a book entitled *Holy Estates: Marital Metaphors and Political Ideology in Shakespeare and his Contemporaries* and coediting a collection entitled *Time Bandits: Representations of the Medieval Hero on Film*.

Judith Richards teaches History at La Trobe University. In recent years, she has written about issues of gender, monarchy, and authority in early modern England. Her various essays, published in Britain, USA, and Australia, on these themes have considered the impact of royal gender on emergent national identity, constitutional thought, political culture, and popular attitudes to monarchy.

Louis Roper is Associate Professor and Acting Chair of History at SUNY/New Paltz where he specializes in the overseas activity of English early modern peoples. He has published articles in *New York History* and *The Historian*. He participated in the seminar on the History of the Atlantic World at Harvard University in 1996.

Kirilka Stavreva is Assistant Professor of English at Cornell College in Mount Vernon, Iowa. Her articles on early modern women and culture have appeared in book collections and journals, such as *The European Legacy* and *The Journal of Medieval and Early Modern Studies*. She is currently completing a book on the representations and cultural significance of unruly, outspoken, and wandering women in Elizabethan and Jacobean England.

Retha Warnicke is Professor of History at Arizona State University where she specializes in early modern England and women's history. Her books include *Women of the English Renaissance and Reformation* (Greenwood Publishers, 1983), *The Rise and Fall of Anne Boleyn* (Cambridge University Press, 1989) and *The Marrying of Anne of Cleves* (Cambridge University Press, 2000).

Georgianna Ziegler is Louis B. Thalheimer Reference Librarian at the Folger Shakespeare Library. She has published widely in the area of Shakespeare and also on Victorian ideas about the Renaissance. Her work has appeared in a variety of edited collections and in such journals as *Shakespeare Quarterly*, *Textual Practices*, and *Shakespeare Studies*.

Index

Abbot, George, Archbishop of
    Canterbury, 50, 51
Actes and Monumentes (Foxe), 7, 27,
    87, 171
Adelman, Janet, 110–11, 116n29
Albert, Prince of England, 205, 206,
    212, 219
Albret, Jeanne d', 229, 234
Alençon, Francis, Duke of, 225, 226
Alexander VI, Pope, 245
Amazons, 6, 117, 130n16, 145, 150
    in Chaucer, 118–21
    in *Midsummer Night's Dream, A*,
        118–21, 123–6, 130n6
    in *Sea Voyage, The*, 118, 124–6
    in *Two Noble Kinsmen, The*, 118,
        121–3, 125–9
Anderson, Maxwell, 242, 249–52
Anna of Denmark, Queen of
    England, 3–5, 50, 57n18, 105
    frivolous, reputation as, 47
    power, establishes own center of,
        48, 49, 51
    Villiers, George, Duke of
        Buckingham and, 45, 46, 49,
        51, 55–6
    Virginia Company and, 45, 46,
        52–5
Annales (Stowe), 87, 90, 91
Anne of Austria, 65
Anne of Cleves, Queen of England,
    3, 205
Anne of the Thousand Days
    (Anderson), 242, 249–51

Anne, Queen of England, 2
*Antoinette d'Autriche, ou Dialogue
    entre Catherine de Médicis et
    Frédégonde, Reines de France, aux
    enfers*, 230
*Archives Curieuses de l'Histoire de
    France*, 233
Arconville, Marie Genevieve
    Charlotte Thiroux d', 230
Arden, Shakespeare editions, 98n22,
    150n23, 243
Arthur, Prince of England, 21, 29,
    83, 203, 210
Ascham, Roger, 182
Aylmer, John, 4, 103–4, 135–7, 143

Balzac, Honoré de, 232–4
Banks, John, 241, 244–6
Barneville, Marie-Catherine Le Jumel
    de, Comtesse d'Aulnoy, 244
Barroll, Leeds, 47, 48
Barthelemy, Gerard, 142
Beaufort, Lady Margaret, 13
Becon, Thomas, 4, 103
Bell, George Joseph, 215
Benger, Mary Ogilvy, 208, 209, 213
Bennett, Judith, 14–15
Berkeley, Sir Maurice, 49, 55
Biro, Lajos, 242, 249
Blackfriars, Court at, 84, 89, 91, 92
Blount, Charles, 19, 20
Blount, Elizabeth, 244, 246
Blount, William, Lord Mountjoy, 13,
    19, 20, 22

Boaden, James, 215, 216
Boker, George H., , 241, 247–8, 252
Boleyn, Anne, Queen of England, 3, 4, 8, 31, 210, 212, 218n3, 239, 240
  accusations of adultery and, 239–41
  in film, 249–52
  in *Henry VIII* (Shakespeare and Fletcher), 242–4
  in 19th Century drama, 245–8
  in *Vertue Betray'd* (Banks), 244–6
Boleyn, George, Lord Rochford, 239, 244–5
Boleyn, Mary, 3
Bonner, Edmund, 38, 39
Book of the City of Ladies, The (Pizan), 117
Bride-bush: Or, A Direction for Married Persons, A (Whately), 122, 141, 178
Brigden, Susan, 28, 38
Brougham, Henry, 219
Buckingham, Edward, Duke of, 242
Bullinger, Heinrich, 133

Calvinists, 67, 68, 135
Camara, Juan Rodriquez de la, 17
Cambridge University, 22
Camden, William, 194
Campbell, Thomas, 214
Campeius, Cardinal, 88, 92, 93, 94
Canterbury Tales (Chaucer), 86, 118, 121
Carleton, Dudley, Lord Carleton and Viscount of Dorchester, 69
Caroline, Queen of England, 208, 219n15, 228
Carr, Robert, Earl of Somerset, 45, 51
Carroll, Lewis, 217
Cassell, John, 211, 214, 216

Catherine de Médicis dans le cabinet de Marie-Antoinette, à Saint Cloud, 231
Catherine de Médicis, On (Balzac), 233–4
Catherine of Aragon, Queen of England, 4, 30, 31, 36, 79, 245–8, 250, 252
  in *Actes and Monumentes* (Foxe), 87, 90, 91
  in *Annales* (Stowe), 87, 90, 91, 93
  Catholicism of, 208, 210, 211
  Henry VIII, marriage to, 2, 3, 27, 28, 29, 239
  Henry VIII (Shakespeare and Fletcher), represented in, 80, 86, 89, 92, 94–7, 242, 243
  education of Mary and, 11–17, 20–2
  Hall's writings on, 87–9, 91
  Holinshed's writings on, 89–90, 93
  painting, "Catherine of Arragon Appealing to Henry VIII," 216
  Patient Griselda, comparisons to, 6, 80–7, 90, 92–6
  Victorian perceptions of, 7, 203–22, 218n3, 219n15, 220n27
Catholicism, 73, 85, 245
  Anne Boleyn as subject of writings, 241, 242, 252
  of Catherine of Aragon, 208, 210, 211
  in England, 1, 2, 3, 33, 37, 38, 64, 66, 86, 87, 190
  in France, 225, 228, 232
  of Henrietta Maria, 62, 63, 74n18
  of Mary I, 27, 34, 39, 103, 135
  Seymour, Jane, rumored of, 249
  spirituali, 37, 42n45

of Stuart, Mary, 135, 187, 191, 194, 196, 197, 200*n*17
of Vives, 23
Catholic League, 68
Cavendish, George, 90, 91
Cecil, Robert, Earl of Salisbury, 48–9, 53
Cecil, William, Lord Burghley, 187
Chapuys, Eustace, 239, 241, 242, 246, 248–51
Charles V, Holy Roman Emperor, 31–3, 210, 239
Charles I, King of England, 3, 5, 6, 46, 47, 51, 61–4, 66–72, 166
Charles II, King of England, 245
Charles IX, King of France, 223–6, 229, 231, 233, 234
Charles X, King of France, 232
Charlotte, Queen of England, 214
Charter of 1814, 232
Chartres, Vidame de, 227
Chaucer, Geoffrey, 84, 86, 118, 120
Chenier, Marie-Joseph, 231
Chettle, Henry, 86, 87
Christen state of matrimonye, The (Bullinger), 133
Christian IV, King of Denmark, 47, 50, 69
Christiani matrimonii instituti (Erasmus), 22
Chronique du règne de Charles IX (Balzac), 232
Civil War, English, 105, 115*n*16
Clement VII, Pope, 239
Coghill, Nevill, 183
Coke, John, Secretary, 71
Coligny, Gaspard de, Lord of Chatillon, 224, 225, 229, 231
Commonwealth of Women, A (D'Urfey), 117
Comodye of Patient and Meeke Grissill, The (Phillip), 86

Company of Grocers, 55
Confidence des Ruggieri, La (Balzac), 233
"Confronting Continuity" (Bennett), 14 –15
Consolations (Leslie), 193
Cope, Sir Walter, 53
Cordoba, Fray Martín Alonso de, 17
Cosins, John, Bishop of Durham, 62
Costa, Milagros Ortega, 22
Counter-blaste to Tobacco, A, 53
Cranmer, Thomas, Archbishop of Canterbury, 3, 33, 239, 242, 244, 246, 251
Cranvelt, Francis, 14
Crawford, Patricia, 105, 115*n*16, 177, 178
Crimean War, 218, 222*n*41
Crimes of the Queens of France from the beginning of the monarchy until Marie Antoinette (Keralio), 230
Cromwell, Sir Oliver, 55
Cromwell, Thomas, Earl of Essex 239, 250, 251
Crucius, John, 20

Dale, Sir Thomas, 53, 54
Danter, John, 80
Danton, Georges Jacques, 231
Darcy, Elizabeth, Lady Savage, 74
de la Warr, Lord Thomas, 53, 55
de Man, Paul, 192, 198
de Vere, Elizabeth, Countess of Derby, 51
de Vere, Susan, Countess of Montgomery, 51
Dekker, Thomas, 86, 87, 91
Deux Rêves, Les (Balzac), 232–3
Devereux, Robert, Second Earl of Essex, 48
Dickens, Charles, 216, 217

Discours, 233, 234
Discourse (Wyat), 227
Discours Merveilleux de la vie...de Catherine de Medicis, 223
Discoverie of a Gaping Gulf whereinto England is like to be swallowed, The (Stubbs), 226
Dixon, William Hepworth, 210, 211, 217
Domesticall Duties, Of (Gouge), 148n1
Dominio Maris, De (Welwood), 51
Don Carlos, son of King Phillip II, 192
Dowling, Maria, 20, 29, 40n18
Drummond, Jean, Countess of Roxborough, 57n18
Duchess of Malfi, The (Webster), 151
Dudley, John, Duke of Northumberland, 33, 37
Dudley, Robert, Earl of Leicester, 187
Dumas, Alexandre, père 232, 234–5
D'Urfey, Thomas, 117
Duwes, Giles, 31, 38

Edict of Nantes, 227
Edinburgh, Treaty of, 192
Education of a Christian Prince, The (Erasmus), 11
Edward VI, King of England, 3, 31–3, 38, 40n4, 40n18, 135
Elizabeth I, Queen of England, 1–4, 34, 68, 102, 104, 136, 152, 173, 190
  birth as vindication of Anne Boleyn, 239, 243–6, 251, 252
  Catherine de Medicis, comparisons with, 225–30, 235
  Protestantism and, 135
  Shakespeare, as model for characters of, 117, 133, 140
  1601 rebellion against, 48
  speech at Tilbury, 104
  Stuart, Mary and, 187, 192–4, 196
  Victorian perceptions of, 205, 206
Elizabeth of Bohemia, 5–6, 61, 62, 64, 68–73, 144
Ellesmere, Thomas Egerton, Lord Chancellor, 51
Elton, G. R., 27, 28
Erasmus, Desiderius, 11–13, 15, 19, 20, 22, 29, 30, 38, 209
Erskine, John, Earl of Mar, 47, 49
eruditione nobelium puellarum, De (Geraldino), 13
Essay upon the civil wars of France, An (Voltaire), 229
Estienne, Henri, 223, 224, 227
Eugenie, Empress of France, 212
Evans, Oliver H., 248
Exemplary Lives...of the Nine Most Worthy Women (Heywood), 117

Ferdinand of Aragon, King of Spain, 22, 29, 35
First Blast of the Trumpet against the Monstrous Regiment of Women (Knox), 103, 134
Fisher, Bishop John, 38, 248
fitable and necessary doctrine for every Christian man, A (Bonner), 39
Fitzroy, Henry, Duke of Richmond, 21
Fletcher, John, 117
  Henry VIII (with Shakespeare), 6, 80, 86, 89–97, 98n22, 204, 207, 212–14, 216–17, 221n34, 242–4, 249, 251
  Humorous Lieutenant, The (with Massinger), 151
  Sea Voyage, The, 6, 118, 124–9
  Two Noble Kinsmen, The (with Shakespeare), 6, 118, 121–6

Flodden, battle of, 30
Forrest, William, 6, 80–7, 90, 91, 93, 96
Fortescue, John, 137
Foxe, John, 7, 27, 37, 39, 87, 90, 91, 171–4, 176, 184, 241, 242
Francis II, King of France, 187, 223, 227, 233
Frederick Henry of Nassau, Prince of Orange, 69
Frederick V, Elector Palatine, 61, 62, 68, 69, 73, 144, 245
Froude, James A., 211, 214, 216

Gardiner, Samuel Rawson, 46, 56, 57n18
Gardiner, Stephen, Bishop of Winchester, 173, 174, 176
Garland of Good Will, The (Deloney), 86
Gentleman's Magazine, 195, 196
George IV, King of England, 208, 219n15
Golden Age Restored, The (Jonson), 51
Goodman, Christopher, 4, 103
Goodrich, S. Griswald, 188
Gouge, Thomas, 178
Greenblatt, Stephen, 152, 190
Gresley, George, 67
Grey, Lady Jane, 3, 32, 33, 37
Grover, Reverend Henry Montague, 241, 245, 246
Guise, Henri, Duke of, 225–7
Gustavus Aldolphus II, King of Sweden, 69

Hackett, Francis, 250
Hakluyt, Richard, 52
Hale, John, 249
Hall, Edward, 87–91
Hamilton, Marchioness of, 74n19
Hamor, Ralph, 53, 54
Hapsburg Empire, 62, 68, 70–3

Harborowe for Faithful and Trewe Subjectes (Aylmer), 4, 103–4, 135
Harlow, George, 215, 216
Harrington, Sir John, 55
Haryngton, John, 33
Haughton, William, 86, 87
Hay, Lady Lucy, Countess of Carlisle, 67
Hay, Sir James, Earl of Carlisle, 69
Hays, Mary, 207–9, 215
Hazlitt, William, 213
Henriade (Voltaire), 228
Henrietta Maria, Queen of England, 3, 4, 5–6, 61–69, 71, 73, 74n18, 74n19
Henri II, King of France, 223, 227
Henri III, King of France (previously Duke of Anjou), 223–6, 230, 235
Henri III et son cour (Dumas père), 234
Henri III, King of Navarre, later Henri IV, King of France, 224, 225, 266, 228–9, 234
Henry IV, King of Castile, 35
Henry I, King of England, 103
Henry VII, King of England, 13, 36, 83
Henry VIII, King of England, 32, 33, 37, 135, 147, 147n1
  Anne Boleyn, marriage to, 239–42, 246, 248, 252
  Catherine of Aragon, marriage to, 2, 22, 27, 29, 207–12, 219n15
  Henry VIII (Shakespeare and Fletcher), depiction in, 243
  Katherine Parr, marriage to, 7, 171–4, 176
  Mary I, and education of, 11–15, 19, 21, 28

Henry VIII, King of England – *continued*
  Patient Griselda story, comparison with Walter in, 80–2, 87, 88
  Queen Victoria's perceptions of, 203
Henry, Prince of England, son of James I, 47, 48, 56
Hepburn, James, Earl of Bothwell, 101, 189
Herbert, William, Earl of Pembroke, 49–51, 53–55
History of England from the Fall of Wolsey to the Death of Elizabeth (Froude), 211
History of François II (Arconville), 230
History of Grisild the Seconde, The (Forrest), 80, 86, 87
History of the Life of Katherine de Medicis Queen Mother and Regent of France, The or The Exact Pattern of the Present French King's Policy (Estienne), 227
History of Two Queens: Catherine of Aragon; Anne Boleyn (Dixon), 210
Holinshed, Raphael, 87, 89, 90, 93, 98, 98*n*27
Home, George, Earl of Dunbar, 49
How Superior Powers ought to be obeyd (Goodman), 103
Howard, Charles, Earl of Nottingham, 51
Howard, Frances, 51
Howard, Henry, Earl of Northampton, 49, 51
Howard, Katherine, Queen of England, 3
Howard, Mary, née Sidney, Countess of Pembroke, 47
Howard, Thomas, Duke of Norfolk, 51

Howard, Thomas, Earl of Suffolk, 51, 55
Howitt, William, 211, 212, 214
Huguenots, 224, 225, 227, 233, 234
Humanism, 11, 12, 13, 15, 17, 20, 28, 29, 30, 37, 38
humble suplicacioun unto God for the restoring of his holye woorde unto the churche of England, An (Becon), 103
Hume, Martin, 250

Illustrated History of England (Cassell), 211, 214, 216
Institutione Feminae Christianae, De (Vives), 12, 14–19, 21, 22, 30, 80, 85
Introductorie for to learne to speke Frenche Trewely, An (Duwes), 38
Isabella of Castile, Queen of Spain, 2, 11, 13, 17, 22, 29, 30, 35, 136, 209, 210

James I, King of England, 52, 57*n*22, 104, 121, 137, 165, 166, 189, 196
  Anna of Denmark (wife) and, 3, 56
  Elizabeth of Bohemia (daughter) and, 68, 69, 70, 144, 245
  factions within his court, 47–50
  head/body metaphor and, 133, 143, 148*n*1, 149*n*14, 150*n*24
  Villiers, Duke of Buckingham and, 45, 46, 51
James II, King of England, 228
Jardin de las nobles doncellas (Cordoba), 17
Johnson, Dr. Samuel, 216, 221*n*35
Jones, Inigo, 45
Jonson, Ben, 45, 51, 166
Journal of Women's Studies, 14

Juan, Prince of Spain, son of Ferdinand and Isabella, 13

Kean, Charles, 212, 216–18, 221n34, 221n36
Kean, Ellen Tree, 212–14, 216
Kellerman, Barbara, 243, 244, 249
Kemble, John, 213, 215, 221n32, 221n34
Kingdon, Robert, 225
Kitts, Thomas, 247
Knight's Tale, The (Chaucer), 118, 121
Knox, John, 3, 4, 103, 134–8, 141, 143, 147

L'Isle, Viscount, 55
Lamb, Lady Caroline, 208
Lamb, Mary Ellen, 163, 168n20
Lamb, William, Viscount of Melbourne, 203
Lapotaire, Jane, 94, 95
Le Jeune, Henry, 216
Leland, John, 14
Leon, Fray Luis de, 22
Leslie, John, Bishop of Ross, 193, 201n35
Letters and Papers, Foreign and Domestic, of the Reign of Henry VIII, 241
Letters on Paris (Balzac), 233
Levin, Carole, 104, 135, 190
Lewalski, Barbara, 47, 48
Lewis, Jayne Elizabeth, 195, 196
Liber de monstruosis hominibus (Thomas of Cantimpre), 149n16
Libero Arbitrio, De (Erasmus), 30
libro de las virtuosas y claras mugeres, El (Luna), 17
Life of Wolsey (Cavendish), 90
Linacre, Thomas, 13, 14, 20, 21
Liu, Alan, 195

Lives (Plutarch), 118
Lives of Celebrated Women (Goodrich), 188
Lives of the Queens of England (Strickland), 209, 210
Loach, Jennifer, 38
Loades, David M., 13, 21, 28, 80
Lorraine, Cardinal de, 227
Louis Philippe, King of France, 231
Louis XIII, King of France, 63, 65, 66, 72
Louis XIV, King of France, 227, 228
Louis XVI, King of France, 231
Luna, Alvaro de, 17
Luther, Martin, 17, 249
Lutherans, 42, 50, 68–9, 244, 245

Machiavelli, 224
Macray, Rev. W. D., 80
Manning, Peter J., 198
Marcus, Leah, 104
Margadant, Jo Burr, 234
Margaret of Austria, 72
Margaret of the Cross, 72
Maria, Holy Roman Empress, 72
Marie-Antoinette, Queen of France, 230–2
Marie d'Medici, Queen of France, 63, 65, 66, 72
Marlowe, Christopher, 8, 225, 226
Martin, Helena Faucit, 214
Martyr, Peter, 30
Martyr Calvaniste, Le (Balzac), 233
Mary, Dowager Queen of France, 13
Mary I, Queen of England, 2, 3, 5, 6, 80–2, 85, 88, 102, 103, 136, 217, 248, 252
  Catholicism of, 4, 27, 37–9
  education of, 11, 13–17, 19–21, 28, 30, 38
  History of Grisild the Second (Forrest) dedicated to, 80–2, 96

Mary I, Queen of England – *continued*
   Philip II of Spain, marriage to, 33–6, 115n6
Mary II, Queen of England, 2, 8, 228, 235
Mary of Guise, 102, 136, 187
Mary Queen of Scots, 195
Massacre at Paris, The (Marlowe), 225
Massinger, Philip, 151
Matilda, Queen of England, 103
Mattingly, Garrett, 15, 21, 81, 190, 194
Maximilian of Bavaria, 68
Maximillian, Holy Roman Emperor, 207
McCarty, Nick, 242, 251, 252
Medici, Catherine de, 3, 4, 7–8, 102
   Black Legend of, 223–5, 227–l9, 233–5
   Marie Antoinette, compared with 230–2
   Marlowe's depiction of, 223, 225–7
   Princesse de Cleves, La, depiction in, 227
   Queen Margot, depiction in, 223
   Voltaire's writings on, 228–30
Melville, Sir James, 189
Memoirs of Eminent Englishwomen (Costello), 205–6
Memoirs of Queens Illustrious and Celebrated (Hays), 207
Memoirs of the Life of Anne Boleyn (Benger), 208, 213
Mendelson, Sara, 105, 177, 178
Metamorphoses (Ovid), 118, 164, 181
Metrical Versions of Some Psalms (Forrest), 80
Middleton, Thomas, 151
Montague, Richard, 62, 74n18
More, Hannah, 207

More, Sir Thomas, 12, 17–19, 21, 182, 208, 211
Mullaney, Steven, 111

Napoleon III, Emperor of France, 212
Nethersole, Francis, 70–3
Neville, Richard, Earl of Warwick, 203
Nevo, Ruth, 177, 183
New Ballad of the Marigolde (Forrest), 80
Noreña, Carlos, 18
Norfolk, Thomas Duke of, 246, 251
Notestein, Wallace, 46
Novy, Marianne L, 179, 180, 182

O'Neil, Henry Nelson, 216, 217
Opechecanough, 54, 55, 58n28
"Oration consolatorye to Queen Mary, An" (Forrest), 80
Orleanists, 234
Orleans, Duke of, 88
Overbury, Sir Thomas, 51
Ovid, 18, 120, 164, 181
Oxenford, John, 212, 215, 216
Oxford University, 12, 14, 22, 29

Pace, Richard, 13, 14
Palmer, Henriette Lea, 214
Paraphrase on St. John's Gospel (Erasmus), 22
Paré, Amboise, 233
Parliament, 3, 66, 70, 115n6, 133, 147n1, 150n24, 219
Parr, Katherine, Queen of England, 3, 4, 7, 171–6, 180, 182, 184, 205
Parr, William, 173
Patient Griselda, 6, 19, 28, 29, 80, 81, 84, 86, 87, 95, 96, 98n22, 182
Patterson, Annabel, 90, 91, 98n27

Paul IV, Pope, 37
Peace of Augsburg (1555), 28
Penna, Lucas de, 137
Percy, Henry, 244, 250
Percy, Henry, Earl of
 Northumberland, 55
perfecta casada, La (Leon), 22
Philip II, King of Spain, 28, 33, 34,
 37, 115n6, 143
Philip III, King of Spain, 50
Phillip, John, 86, 87
Phillips, James Emerson, 190, 201n35
Pizan, Christine de, 117
Pleasant Comodie of Patient Grissill
 (Chettle, Dekker, and
 Haughton), 86, 91, 94
Pliny, 138
Plutarch, 19, 120
Plymouth Company, 52
Pocahontas, 5, 45, 46, 52–5, 58n30
Poitiers, Diane de, 227
Pole, Reginald, 37–9, 42n45
Politics, The (Aristotle), 147n1
Powhatan, 52, 54, 58n28
Princesse de Cleves La (Fayette), 227
Prinne, William, 67
Private Life of Henry VIII, The
 screenplay (Lajos and
 Wimperis), 242, 249, 251
Protestantism, 39, 50, 69, 70, 72, 73,
 80, 91, 104, 135
 of Edward VI, 31, 40n4
 of Elizabeth I, 103
 in England, 1, 3, 27, 33, 37, 38,
  86, 87
 in France, 232, 233
 Stuart, Mary and, 193
 see also Calvanism, Huguenots,
  Lutherans, Puritanism
Protestant Union, 69
Puckering, Sir Thomas, 67
Puritanism, 62, 122
Pynson, Richard, 14

Queen Anne Boleyn: A Novel
 (Hackett), 250

Raleigh, Sir Walter, 50, 55, 130n16
Ratione Studii Puerilis, De (Vives),
 14, 16, 19–22, 85
Reflections upon the Late Horrid
 Conspiracy, 228
Reformation, English, 33, 203, 208,
 218, 239, 241, 242
Regency Act of 1690, 228
Reine Margot, La (Dumas père),
 234–35
"Reprinting Tudor History: The Case
 of Catherine of Aragon"
 (Travitsky), 79
Restoration, 244, 245
Revolution of 1830, 232
Revolution, French, 232
Rich, Penelope, 47, 50
Richard II, King of England, 197
Richelieu, Cardinal, 63
Richmond, Hugh, 243, 244
Ridgeway, Sir Thomas, 49
Riverside Shakespeare, The, 150n23
Rizzio, David, 101, 189
Roaring Girl, The, 87
Roberts, Penny, 226
Rochford, Lady Jane, 246, 248, 251
Roe, Sir Thomas, 69–72
Rolfe, John, 5, 45, 46, 52–5
Rowley, Samuel, 171
Rudyerd, Sir Benjamin, 49, 50
Ruskin, John, 206
Russell, Francis, Earl of Bedford, 55
Russell, Lucy, Countess of Bedford,
 47, 50

Saint Bartholomew's Day Massacre,
 224, 229, 231–3
St. Germain, Peace of, 224
Sanders, Nicholas, 241, 242, 248,
 250, 251

Sandys, Sir Edwin, 49–51, 55
Scarisbrick, J. J, 173, 176
Scots Magazine, 196
Scott, Sir Walter, 232
Secret Novels of Queen Elizabeth, The (Barneville), 244
Sesame and Lilies (Ruskin), 206, 207
Seymour, Jane, Queen of England, 3, 205, 239, 242, 244, 246–52
Seymour, Thomas, 173
Shakespeare, William, 117, 192, 205
  Antony and Cleopatra, 115n5, 142
  Cymbeline, 6, 7, 102, 110, 112–14, 151, 154, 156–7
  Hamlet, 6, 102, 109–14, 116n29
  Henry VIII (with Fletcher), 6, 80, 86, 89–97, 98n22, 204, 207, 212–14, 216–17, 221n34, 242–4, 249, 251
  Henry V, 94, 203
  Henry VI, Part 1, 153
  Henry VI, Part 2, 153
  Macbeth, 7, 151, 154–9, 168n20, 181
  Midsummer Night's Dream, A, 6, 118–21, 130n6
  Much Ado About Nothing, 181
  Othello, 7, 133, 134, 137–44, 150n23
  Richard III, 153–4
  Taming of the Shrew, The, 7, 98n22, 171, 173, 174, 176–80, 182–4, 210
  Tempest, The, 7, 53, 127, 133, 134, 137, 143–7, 150n23, 151, 162–5
  Titus Andronicus, 6, 102, 105–110, 114, 181
  Two Noble Kinsmen, The (with Fletcher), 6, 118, 121–6

Winter's Tale, The, 7, 98n22, 151, 159–62
Siddons, Sarah Kemble, 212–16, 220n31, 221n35
Sidney, Sir Philip, 50
Sisson, Rosemary Anne, 242, 251, 252
Sitwell, Edith, 250
Six Wives of Henry VIII, The (BBC production), 242
Six Wives of Henry VIII, The (Hume), 250
Smith, John, 52, 54, 58n30
Smyth, John, 16
Sommers, Alan, 107
Spanish Armada, 225
spirituali, 37, 41n45
Stafford, Thomas, 37
Statute of Appeals, 239
Stowe, John, 87, 90, 91, 93
Stratford Gallery, The; or the Shakespeare Sisterhood (Palmer), 214
Strickland, Agnes and Elizabeth, 209–11, 215, 241
Stride, John, 243
Strode, Sir William, 49
Stuart, Esmé, Earl of Lennox, 189
Stuart, Henry, Lord Darnley, 101, 187, 189
Stuart, Lodovick, Duke of Lennox, 49
Stuart, Mary, Queen of Scotland, 2, 3, 4, 101, 102, 227
  captivity in England, 190, 191, 193
  Catholicism of, 187, 190–1, 193, 194
  Hepburn, James, Earl of Bothwell and, 189
  poetry, self-representation in, 7, 193, 190–2 194, 196–9

Stuart, Henry, Lord Darnley and, 187, 189
Wordsworth's poetry and, 192, 195–8

Taylor, Tom, 241, 245–7, 252
The Prince (Machiavelli), 224
Theed, William, 216
Thirty Years War, 71
Thomas of Cantimpre, 149n16
Travels of Sir John Mandeville, The (Mandeville), 134, 138, 145, 150n28
Tree, Herbert Beerbohm, 243
Trémoille, Charlotte de la, Duchess of Thours, 69
Trew Law of Free Monarchies, The (James I), 149n14
triunfo de la donas, El (Camara), 17
True Discourse of the Present Estate of Virginia, A (Hamor), 53
True Relation of the State of Virginia, A (Rolfe), 54

Urban VIII, Pope, 63, 72

Valois, Marguerite de, 224, 225, 229, 230, 234
Vertue Betray'd: Or, Anna Bullen (Banks), 244–6
Victoria, Queen of England, 7, 203, 205–9, 212, 214, 217, 218, 218n3, 219n11, 220n22
Victoria Magazine, 206
Villa Sancta, Alphonso de, 14
Villiers, George, Earl of Buckingham, 45–7, 51, 55, 64, 65, 69, 70, 74n19

Villiers, Mary, Countess of Buckingham, 67, 74n18
Virginia Company, 5, 45–6, 52, 53, 55, 58n26
Vision of Desire, A (Jones and Jonson), 45
Vives, Juan Luis, 5, 11–23, 30, 80, 85
Voltaire, 228–30

Watson, Foster, 15, 20
Watson, Nicholas, 205
Webster, John, 151
Weston, Sir Francis, 246
Whately, William, 122, 141, 178
When You See Me, You Know Me (Rowley), 171
White Devil, The (Webster), 151
White Mountain, Battle of, 68
William III, King of England, 228, 235
William of Lyndwood, 137
Wimperis, Arthur, 242, 249
Witch, The (Middleton), 151
Witchcraft, 2, 151–66
Wittkower, Rudolf, 149n16
Wollstonecraft, Mary, 207, 208
Wolsey, Cardinal Thomas, 3, 12, 88–90, 92–4, 212, 214, 220n27, 242–5, 248
Wordsworth, William, 7, 191, 192, 195–8
Wotton, Nicholas, 33–4
Wriothesley, Thomas, Earl of Southampton, 49–51, 55, 176
Wyat, John, 8, 223, 227, 228
Wyatt uprising, 37
Wyatt, Sir Thomas, 14, 248

SHE WHO IS FIT FOR PURPOSE

All rights reserved.

No part of this book can be reproduced in any form or by written, electronic or mechanical, including photocopying, recording, or by any information retrieval system without written permission by the author.

Printed in Great Britain

Although every precaution has been taken in the preparation of this book, the publisher and author assume no responsibility for errors or omissions. Neither is any liability assumed for damages resulting from the use of information contained herein.

Bible translations used: ESV, NKJV, NLT

A catalogue record for this book is available from the British Library

ISBN 978-1-8383486-1-8

Published by WritershouseConsultancy
www.writershouseconsultancy.com

ACKNOWLEDGMENT

I would like to thank my Heavenly Father who placed this book in my heart to write in 2015. You walked with me as I lived out the pages of this book and used it to bring so much healing to me, as I believe it will bring to every young girl and woman that picks up this book to read. Thank You for trusting me with this task and providing the provision to transform what was once a vision into a reality. Thank You for every woman and destiny helper You thoughtfully picked to support me in this process of writing and publishing; I am grateful.

And to you that has chosen to take the time to read this book, thank you! What you hold in your hands is the documentation of a journey that ultimately leads to emancipation, not just to be known and kept between Christ and I, but you and every single girl and woman that must know that emancipation belongs to them too.

CONTENTS

Acknowledgment v

PURPOSE
Chapter 1: Good News 1
Chapter 2: My journey 7
Chapter 3: Identity 33
Chapter 4: Purpose 41

FITNESS & WELL-BEING
Chapter 5: Well-being & Mental Health 47
Chapter 6: Food 59
Chapter 7: Fitness 79
Chapter 8: Social Media 89
Chapter 9: Sexual Objectification 107

INNER BEAUTY
Chapter 10: Comparison 119
Chapter 11: Perfectionism 127
Chapter 12: Is Your Body Your Golden Calf 137
Chapter 13: My Journey with the Holy Spirit 145

Bibliography 157

CHAPTER 1
Good News

Receiving good news is great isn't it? It tends to make you feel overwhelmed with joy and excitement! When I receive good news, I walk around with an extra spring in my step, and if things aren't going right in my life at the time, it gives me a boost of hope.

Good news can benefit us in such powerful ways, whether spiritually, mentally, psychologically or physically. With the state the world is in right now and negative reports echoing across the globe, hearing good news is something we could all do with more often.

As much as being a recipient of positive news is good, it's equally important to be a vehicle to which uplifting information is shared. Spreading great news that you've heard or experienced can change the lives of others for the better, forever.

Having encountered life-transforming news a few years ago, I cannot help but share, in the hopes that it would transform you as it did me. Some may wonder, what type of information, story or report could be that good that it carries the power to change a life forever?

Well, for many years of my life I kept hearing about this 'good news', but I was too broken, had a hardened heart that was full of perversion, pain and pride that I dismissed anyone trying to share what I later came to realise was worthy of hearing and receiving as truth. And, by now, some may know what this good news is, but for the benefit of those that may still be unaware, I'm excited to share that the life-transforming news is Jesus Christ.

The mystery of being fully God, yet fully man; Jesus Christ gave His life for you and me so that we could be reconciled back to God and receive eternal life. Doesn't that sound like good news to you? Knowing instead of paying the price for our wrong actions, someone came along and decided to take our place. And what makes this news even more remarkable, is this incredible act of love isn't limited to a select few, but for the entire world. Yes, you read correctly! Without having known Him, Christ decided to die for all (Romans 5:8).

This sacrificial love of Christ that I have come to know and understand knows no bounds. Regardless of promiscuity or how unattractive you may feel, His love covers you. No matter how worthless and inadequate you count yourself to be, His love counts that out. Perhaps you've messed up countless times, feel lost, depressed, or experienced deep hurt as a child - whatever your current or past situation is, the overwhelming love of Christ overshadows that too. And there's more to this marvellous news! Christ is a restorer of hope, a Healer and the One whose power is made perfect in our weakness (2 Corinthians 12:9). He is able to forgive, transform and is the pathway to everlasting life - and in all of this, there are no works that we can do to be deserving of such a grand gift, because all that's required of us, is faith.

It took a while for me to understand the depths of such a sacrifice, but by faith, accepting the love of Christ and what

He did for me on the cross, my life truly changed for the better. Where eternal damnation should be the outcome, He gave life (1 John 4:9). He didn't wait for me or you to change before loving us, as some people would; Instead, having the full knowledge of every sin we would ever commit, He willingly bore the brunt, died on the cross and rose on the third day - defeating sin and death forever! (1 Corinthians 15:4).

I also battled with understanding God's love for me because it didn't feel tangible. However, His supernatural power brought me to understand His love for me in a way that I can only describe as unique. Unique because it seemed tailor-fit just for me. Jesus causes me to laugh randomly in the middle of crying my eyes out, and He demonstrates His love for me through friends, family and various other ways! His pursuit to showcase His love for me is truly astounding.

I recall fear being used as a tactic to scare me into giving my life to Jesus, and maybe you've experienced that too? Where you are forcefully guilt-tripped by all the bad things that would happen to you if you didn't give your life Christ. However, hearing this caused me to run further away from Christ, because I felt like I didn't measure up, which instead pushed me back towards a sinful lifestyle. Now, the truth is, hell is indeed real and is the final destination for those who do not believe, confess and accept Jesus Christ as their Lord and Saviour, but we need not be fearful of drawing nearer to Him. After all, having taken our place, He has provided a way of escape from the fiery pit and allowed us to live a life full of abundance (John 10:10). We no longer have to depend on ourselves but can seek help from the Holy Spirit promised to us by Jesus, if we choose to love Him and keep His commands (John 14:15-17).

My hope is that as you journey through this book, you would experience the love of Christ and begin to invite Him into your heart. What you may think is your best life at this very moment, or even your worst, doesn't compare to what He, who is able to do exceedingly and abundantly above all you could ever think or imagine, can provide (Ephesians 3:20).

CHAPTER 2
My Journey

On Saturday 3rd October 1992, I, Carla Zanika Cordelia Mark-Thompson, was born with a great destiny to discover and explore. As I look back at my baby pictures, I see a beautiful little girl and wonder how she later became a broken soul filled with self-hatred who would soon label herself as spoiled goods.

I recall some great memories from my childhood, where I lived with my parents, my older sister and my older brother, and our traditions. Friday nights we spent eating out, Saturday's were for grocery shopping at Asda, with the evenings watching

Gladiators. Sunday's arouse visions of my mum cooking up a Sunday roast and the smell of freshly laundered school uniform prepped for the week ahead. I also cannot forget the family holidays to America, Greece and Spain.

Although grateful for these unforgettable warm memories, as an adult, armed with the ability to discern between healthy and dysfunctional environments, I trace back and realise the cracks in my upbringing that at the time seemed normal, but later led to my brokenness. Some of those cracks stemming from the relationship I had with my parents. Which, between the two, contributed to my self-esteem, how I functioned as a growing child and the behaviours that began emerging in my own life. After all, the home is the first classroom for children, and our impressionable hearts make for fertile ground to learn behaviours and form mindsets, whether good or bad. In the case of the beautiful little girl in the picture, many of those behaviours and mindsets fell on the latter.

My father was a hard-working man who would toil day and night, sometimes seven days a week, and I admired his drive to succeed. He took pride in his appearance, was financially healthy, drove fancy cars and wouldn't hold back where it concerned providing for me materially. Gifts were his love language to me. I recall around the age of six, asking for a

Rabbit, and I was picked up from school, taken straight to a pet shop and bought a Rabbit. As I got older, shopping sprees were the norm and money was given whenever I asked for it. And although it was great having a lot of stuff, I longed for a meaningful bond and quality time that the lavishing of gifts couldn't make up for.

The truth is, my father had his own set of struggles, and in a bid to avoid confronting them, he threw himself into overworking, indulging in porn, drugs, women and alcohol abuse as a coping mechanism. And whilst I cannot count it as a means to justify the neglect I felt from his emotional unavailability, as I grew, it did drive me towards compassion and, ultimately, forgiveness.

As an adult, I've come to understand and agree that you can only do your best with what you know, and leaving issues unresolved will result in them resurfacing in other areas. So, for my father, torments from his past affected his ability to thrive as a parent dedicated to protecting and providing a healthy atmosphere where I could grow. From the tender age of five, I witnessed his battle with alcohol, would come across pornographic material that was carelessly left around and would often feel abandoned when he would go missing for periods. It was later discovered those moments 'away' were spent with other women resulting in a sister outside of my immediate household. Processing everything I was exposed to as a child was extremely difficult; Hearing the arguments, seeing my mother cry, and nights spent crying myself from the confusing and unbearable pain. Struggling to trust his word from the many times I had been let down caused me to feel insecure. I felt rejected and abandoned by my father - and by the age of six, the relationship between my parents ended for good.

The end of their relationship, however, marked the beginning of my life spiralling out of control. What should have been innocent fun-filled, nurturing years as a child was instead a catapulting into adulthood way before my time. I had developed a taste of porn and would seek to look at the naked women on page three in the newspapers. By the time I reached primary school, I was masturbating, and harmless child games became perverted in nature. I was engaging in sexual acts with several girls and boys the same age as me - and I had not reached the age of nine at this stage.

My parents never taught me anything about sex, the safe or appropriate age to engage in it. I had picked up an idea of it based on what I had been exposed to and explored it with very little understanding of what I was doing. When I got caught engaging in a sexual act by my sister, she informed my mother - who was immensely angered by what I had done. I was punished by beating, and I recall my mother stopping the car we were travelling in to beat me all over again. It was never a thought to correct me in an educative way that brought redemption. Instead, I felt shame, was condemned and told I would go to hell for the things I had done. This missed opportunity to steer me right led me to go further down the road to brokenness.

My mother and I didn't have the best relationship, but as I got older, I realise she was the best mum she could be with what she had and knew. Like a closed book, impossible to read - it was difficult to determine her mood. I often felt like my mother's internalised battles were projected on to me, as I became the object of her anger and frustrations. When I got into trouble, she would beat me with a wooden spoon. I understand this may be an acceptable method in some cultures - but to me, it was more harmful than corrective. Unsavoury memories of running late for school and not finding my school skirt resulted in a bloodshot eye from the impact of a wooden spoon being thrown at me by my mother. I was blamed and told to lie at school and the hospital about the true nature of how I got injured.

I was also to blame for my mother's financial debt; and made to feel like I was behaving self-centered; she would say things like "not everything is about you", when I wanted to gather the family to celebrate my GCSE results. While others could bond with their mothers and have girly chats, I didn't have this. Instead, I found myself trying to navigate life as a young girl going into pubescent years without parental guidance. My father wouldn't willingly offer financial support to help my mother raise me, so my mother worked two jobs to help carry the responsibility of raising children and household bills. There was undoubtedly a strain on the relationship between my mother and I. Showing affection or saying 'I love you' felt unnatural over time.

Perhaps her childhood, life experiences and burdens she carried put a strain on her ability to be emotionally available for me. Was it a cycle? Did she go through, as a child, what I was going through as a child with her? Because, I couldn't understand why my mother wasn't an affirming voice to my forming mindset, why we never discussed sensitive topics and why I was constantly blamed and scolded for things that weren't my fault.

As an early developer, I recall starting my period around the age of nine and shocked when I began to bleed, that I hid all of my knickers and didn't tell anyone. Eventually, my mother found some of them and instead of educating me about the changes my body was going through, I was told off. Why was I punished and made to feel dirty when nature was taking its course with my body? After all, no one had told me what a period was or what to do when it starts, so how could I respond to the change in a better way? In the end, my sister sat me down to explain what a menstrual cycle was, even though embarrassment had already set in.

The criticism and verbal abuse continued, and I recall when I had tried on a pair of shorts that turned out to be too small and how furious my mother became. She screamed at me to take them off because I dressed like a 'Lolita'! For those unaware, Lolita is a movie about a professor and his inappropriate infatuation and sexual relationship with a young adolescent girl - described as a nymphet. I don't think my mother understood how the harmful comments were constantly shattering my self-worth & confidence. The seeds of rejection were so frequently sown into the fibre of my being, making it extremely difficult to value and see myself worthy of respect and love.

If I'm honest, it wasn't solely at the hands of my parents, as I was treated differently by my father's mother and sister too.

My aunt would blow hot and cold with me. I would be blanked by my grandmother entirely when visiting her house occasionally and would often be compared to her other grandchildren. One day I finally plucked up the courage to ask my aunt why they treated me differently. It turned out she felt my father took care of my older sister that shared the same mother as me, while neglecting my other sisters, resulting in my grandmother and aunt having to pick up the pieces. The bitterness shown towards me seemed crazy because, firstly, I was a child and secondly, the father they felt my two sisters were missing out on wasn't the father they assumed him to be.

As time went on and my self-esteem continued to diminish, I longed to feel wanted. At the age of ten, having had various sexual encounters before this age - I decided I wanted a boyfriend. After my efforts to gain male attention failed, I went to a friend, and she introduced me to her neighbour, who agreed to be my 'boyfriend'. He was two years older than me and had just started secondary school. We would hang around together in the neighbourhood, and on one occasion when we were hugging, he placed his hand on my private area, and I remember moving his hand, feeling weird. I guess as much as I craved attention, to be loved and to belong, I wasn't fully committed or mature enough to pursue sexual endeavours wholeheartedly. This 'relationship' didn't last long after that, as he broke up with me and said he never liked me anyway and only agreed because my friend told him to.

Heartbroken, at the tender age of ten, over a boy! When I should have been busy playing, being carefree. I documented this experience in my diary and hid it under my pillow, thinking no one would find it. To my embarrassment, my brother and his friend discovered it and informed my mother. Once again, no redirection, just a telling off. From then on, I spent a lot of time in my bedroom because of the shame I felt; eventually, my brother consoled me and said I shouldn't feel ashamed. It was comforting to feel as though someone cared about my feelings, but it was just a tiny droplet of positive affirmation in the ocean of negative feelings towards myself that had swelled over the years. And so, my encounters with boys continued. Everything that I had experienced in the earlier years of my childhood played a huge part in the destructive path I walked down into my teenage and young adult years.

As I entered secondary school, I became self-conscious about my appearance, which followed me into my twenties. I was always entertaining a boy and was never content being single. I allowed myself to be used, touched and kissed on, only to be dumped right after as if I was rubbish. And although I wasn't sexually active until a few years later, I was a young girl who didn't know her worth, had no ounce of self-respect and would jump from boyfriend to boyfriend. The immediate discarding of me from these continued failed 'relationships' reinforced the mindset that I indeed was worthless.

It came to the point that I wanted to be anyone but myself, and the desire to be noticed deepened. During my early secondary school years, I often used MSN Messenger to message friends, which could've opened me up to online predators. On one occasion, a random man I had been speaking to online asked me to send him some pictures. I was afraid of what he would think of my appearance, so I sent a picture of someone else instead. He was pleased with what he thought I looked like, and this left me wondering what he would think about my true identity, so I sent a real picture of me and told him it was of my friend to see what he would say. He said the photo was ugly, which further shattered my confidence and reaffirmed why I feared disclosing how I honestly looked in the first place. He continued to request images, but this time of my body and I complied, but only sent a headless shot of my bra covered breasts. In exchange, he sent an image of his private area and thankfully, despite my craving for attention, love and affection, we never met in person.

As I approached the final months of being fourteen years old, I was unaware that I was about to step into a traumatic eight-year battle with my mental well-being and body image. The familiar trigger, being told I wasn't pretty by a boy at school. Although hearing this wasn't new to my ears, this time, it was different. It instantly set off an obsession to want to change my appearance. Consequently, I began to research ways to lose weight, watch what I was eating with more caution and engage in excessive amounts of exercise."

A few months later, by the age of fifteen, I entered into what I would say was my first 'official' relationship. If my past and current patterns were anything to go by, this relationship was filled to the brim with dysfunction too. There were red flags from the beginning when my boyfriend, only a few months apart in age, randomly ended things with me within the first couple of weeks because his uncle died (which I later found out was a lie) and then returned a week or so later and asked me back out. Unbeknown to us, we headed towards an on and off relationship fuelled by co-dependency, insecurity, emotional and psychological abuse for the next four years. When things went from bad to worse, I got more serious with dieting, started counting calories and developed an eating and body dysmorphic disorder.

We lost our virginity to one another. I believed I would be with him forever, not necessarily out of love, but because he would tell me I would never find anyone like him if we ever broke up. Perhaps, because he had a budding career as a footballer, I found his words to be true? Maybe I felt he was the catch, making me lucky to have him? The reality of our relationship was different from the scenarios and reasons I may have had.

He was extremely jealous and would get angry when I had to do my coursework because I couldn't speak to him. He would get envious when I would spend time with my friends and blackmail me by threatening to tell my mother that we had sex, if he didn't get his way. This relationship didn't fill the void I felt where it concerned being loved; instead, it heightened my lack of self-worth and abandonment issues. I would walk on eggshells every day trying to avoid upsetting him. Regardless of me treading carefully, he had a habit of finding a reason to break up with me almost every two weeks for different reasons. At times, it was because he woke up in a bad mood and other times because I disgusted him! He would even go as far as to break up and say 'only joking', and I would experience such anxiety off the back of it. It was like a cruel game of Russian Roulette with my heart, yet I couldn't walk away. To deal with the breakups, I would go out partying and get heavily intoxicated, but once the high was over and I left the club, I would experience a comedown and feel depressed.

I knew the relationship I had with my boyfriend was not healthy, but it was like an addiction I could not shake off. I would feel shame and embarrassed whenever we got back together, over our four-year relationship. I would even lie about where I was going if I had plans to meet him, yet I'd get back with him all the same. It was not long before he decided it was one of those days he did not feel like being with me again, and it just so happened I had purchased tickets for us to visit the London Aquarium. He was not concerned about the efforts made or my heartache for that matter, and I ended up going alone. Tears were flowing down my face as I stood watching the sharks swim around the tank, and all I wanted was him. I had become accustomed to the toxicity of our relationship that being apart felt too hard to bear.

Eventually, my boyfriend and I got back together, the dysfunction continued, and I began to feel isolated as he became more controlling. I was not allowed to have any male friends, I hardly spent time with my female friends, and he would regularly check my phone. As broken as I was to allow myself to continue accepting the ill-treatment, it begged the question: how broken was my boyfriend to behave in the way he did towards me? Hurt people, hurt people, so the saying goes. I may even add that broken people break others down, if not first fixed themselves - it's a vicious cycle.

Looking back on the various events that had taken place in my life before I even turned twenty did not leave me with much hope. It seemed everywhere I went, I attracted negative attention. I remember travelling home by bus one evening from my boyfriend's house and was met by a group of men on the top deck, one of which deemed it appropriate to grope my bum as I left the bus. What was alarming about this is they all laughed. Nobody considered how I felt at that moment; violated, dirty and shamed. I began to cry because, throughout my life, I felt that nobody truly cared for me. That there was no safe place to pour out and process my hurts. The times I would journal, the details were shared by prying eyes without my permission. If I did open up about my pain, somehow, I was to blame. This mindset crippled me into silence, and I never told my boyfriend what had happened to me on my journey home that night.

The relationship with my boyfriend finally came to an end when I was nineteen, but the toxic behaviour continued. He would stalk my house and send abusive text messages, so I changed my phone number. The reality of being single tormented me, and I was determined never to go back. But to move forward with my life, I sought another relationship instead, but this time with a woman. I felt this would act as a repellent to my ex and cause him to be less threatened as it wasn't another man. And while it did ward him off successfully, it failed to fill my emptiness. I knew I wasn't gay or even bisexual, yet found myself in lesbians night clubs on a desperate mission to be seen and to fulfil the lust and desires I had to be with someone. In my attempts to be rid of my ex's memories, I didn't allow myself to heal from the emotional and psychological abuse I endured; Instead, I was right back looking for a man to take his place. It did not take long; in fact, does it ever take long to find something bad? 'Good things take time', is another saying that comes to mind. However, in that season of my life, good things seemed few and far between because, it was only a few weeks later that I met another man and entered into another dysfunctional situation.

He was relatively well known, a drug dealer, had a big build, and I felt somewhat important and safe with him until it quickly became evident that I was not. There was no commitment towards me; I was just one of the many girls he was having sex with at the time. He believed he was kind to me because my cab fare to and from his house was paid for by him, but the reality was he was controlling and manipulative.

Speaking to other men was strictly prohibited for me, but he could talk freely to women. He felt no way to display his freedom to do as he pleased, as he would openly share his lusts for other women. After what I went through in my previous relationship, deep down, I knew I deserved better than this, yet having a functional, healthy relationship seemed so far out of reach that I continued to settle with the crumbs of poisonous affection I was getting.

My heart and soul deeply desired love—a redemptive love, a love that was patient and genuinely kind. Even though I was still young, it felt like an eternity had passed in my years of suffering. What I was searching for was never going to be found in any man, woman, any nightclub or at the bottom of any alcohol bottle. I had a God-sized void that nothing else could fill and I began to seek after Him. I had an idea about God and believed He existed, having grown up Catholic, completing four of the seven sacraments. However, as an adult, I restarted my spiritual journey via the Pentecostal Church.

I thought I was well on my way to recovery and waving my past goodbye when I began searching for God, but I quickly realised the emotional turbulence wasn't over yet. I still bore the scars of emotional and psychological abuse and found myself back in the arms of yet another man. On this occasion, he was a 'God-fearing' man who attended Church - however, I met him in a nightclub. He dressed sophisticated, drove an expensive car, but was highly secretive about his life. He was not interested in committing himself to an exclusive relationship and would frequently lie, disappear for periods and then pop back up as if nothing happened.

Compared to what I had experienced in previous relationships, I thought this one was an upgrade due to the fact that we went on dates. However, in hindsight, those moments spent together always ended up in hotels where we would have sex, so it was not any better. Eventually, things came to an end when the consequence of unprotected sex caught up with me. I discovered I was seven weeks pregnant and was not prepared for it at all. I thought I had taken the proper precautions with the morning-after pill, but it had not worked.

How could I possibly become a mother? I wasn't ready, I was emotionally shattered, and life was still seemingly treating me unfair. Would I now fail as a parent and go on to raise a broken child? It was a lot to take in, and at this point, I felt abortion was the only route to take. The father to be agreed and was in no way interested in keeping our unborn child anyway. To further add to my pregnancy's disapproval, my mother and sister also encouraged me to abort, as they felt I couldn't cope with having a child at twenty years old. Truth be told, I lacked understanding of the severity of abortion, until I saw my baby on the monitor during a scan at the clinic. I wept at the idea of ridding myself of my unborn child, who did not ask to be born. I was conflicted within myself and was scared to go against those who encouraged me to continue the procedure. I knew I was not living right before God, but found myself praying, asking for peace and clarity in my choice before I returned to the clinic. By the following day, I had such an indescribable peace and decided I would keep my baby.

The father was furious that I had changed my mind and did not want to talk to me, but I just knew it was the right choice whether he or anyone else approved. Sure, I was a university student and working part-time, but I began making plans on preparing for my baby. I had even chosen the name Lily for a daughter or Ishmael for a son and recall that name being opposed by a friend, as Ishmael in the bible was not the 'chosen one'.

As time went on and I became more and more used to the idea of becoming a mother, I began spotting light blood while I was at work. Not wanting to risk anything, I took myself to A&E, and when I arrived and spoke to the doctors, they advised that if the bleeding progressed, I could potentially miscarry. By the following day, my biggest fear was confirmed; I was losing my baby. Heartbroken, I called the father to inform him, to which he sounded happy and relieved. I could not understand why God would give me peace in my decision to keep the baby, yet knowing I would lose it. I was so hurt and cried so many tears - yet, that was the day God made a promise to me that was as clear as day and brought me so much hope. That promise was 'Carla, I have better for you.' So, even though I was physically going through it alone, the strength that was carrying me was God - and thankfully so.

I looked for comfort from my mother during this season. But she showed no compassion when learning of my miscarriage. Instead, found it as an opportunity to shout at me that I should have known better than to have unprotected sex and that I was not thinking about catching sexually transmitted diseases.

And while I cannot deny the truth in her statement, at that moment, all I wanted was to know everything would be okay and to feel loved. It also dawned on me that even though I had grown in age, I still felt like the beautiful little girl in the picture who wanted to be held and reassured by her parents. However, the reality was there was no refuge to find in my mother, so I tried to remain hopeful in the promise God had spoken to me; that there was better for me. Conversely, judging by my actions following on from my miscarriage, I clearly did not believe it.

The non-committed sexual relationships continued, and the men I would end up with were always comfortable, almost eager to vocalise their negative perceptions about me. I was good enough for sex, but I wasn't 'marriage material', and I was 'ghetto' because I was black. It was as if I was a magnet for expressed hatred. In a desperate bid to repel what I seemed to attract continually, I deemed it a good idea to try treating men how they treated me. Perhaps, if I gave them a taste of their own medicine, it would somehow turn down the noise of disrespect and increase the volume of worthiness. I became determined to be respected, but my attempts to instil fear, treat unfairly and make the guy I was now seeing feel less than, backfired and I ended up in the trap I set for him.

At this point, I was becoming increasingly exhausted with how things were turning out with the guys I kept meeting and decided to give online dating a try. It seemed more of an attractive idea when a friend shared how she had successfully managed to go on dates and receive gifts with no strings attached. To further broaden my chances of experiencing the same success, I opted for both men and women. I would admit, it did feel somewhat strange having a bi-sexual profile, as I did not have a natural desire to be with a woman. Consequently, I ended up removing the option from my profile and stuck to heterosexual dating instead. It was not long before I started to feel empowered by all the attention I was garnering online. This virtual experience was proving a 'hit' as I received 100s of messages from men, and for once, I felt like I was in a position of power to choose who I wanted to entertain or date. Finally, I felt adored, beautiful and wanted.

There was a particular guy I met online, and we seemed to click. We invested a lot of time just speaking to each other, and I formed quite an attachment to the idea of being in a relationship with him until we met in person. For some reason, things felt off. The sparks from our internet interaction just weren't there, but I could not face the reality of being alone. I selfishly went along with the relationship to fill the void I had been carrying for years. Soon after, things went from digital delight to physical plight as the relationship turned sour. We would often fight, and there was a lack of trust on his part. Often, he would accuse me of seeing other men and would check my phone. I found myself crossing the limits to what I could manage with alcohol, and I recall buying a bottle of Vodka on New Year's Eve and heading to a nightclub to drink and dance my sorrows away, but what I planned as a means to a temporary end, was the beginning of a new dawn in my life. Sure, I completely embarrassed myself that night by falling over, exposing myself and throwing up, but I like to look back at this moment as the last kicks of a dying horse - as unbeknown to me, there was undoubtedly a death taking place.

When I got home that night, I remember crying out to God for forgiveness for my behaviour. It seemed random for me to do this, as I had never felt convicted about any of my actions being wrong, but rather a result of everything terrible people had done to me. The convictions did not stop there though. I no longer desired to go out partying anymore, instead found myself extremely focused and determined to get the best possible grades at university. My boyfriend continued to frequent the nightclubs, and we slowly grew apart. My perception of life was changing in a way that I could not explain, and marriage was one of them. I had never seen marriage modelled, and thought it was just a piece of paper with no significant meaning or value, yet I found myself pondering on the true meaning of it.

My boyfriend was strongly opposed to the idea of holy matrimony, however, something in me wasn't discouraged this time around. I began to be hopeful and believe marriage was something for me, even if it was not with him and found myself deeply convicted the next time we slept together. The feeling of filth and dirt consumed me. It was not a feeling directed at myself this time, but rather towards the act of sex, specifically outside of marriage. Sin was showing up on my radar even though, at the time, I did not have a name for what was coming to my attention - I just knew I was growing increasingly aware of its presence in my life and wanted no part of it.

I went from wanting to always be with a man to avoiding being intimately touched by my boyfriend and rejoicing when it was time for him to go home. I could feel the tug of war for who would sit on the throne of my heart, and I wanted it to be God. Although the battle was not a straight path to triumph, more and more, I tried to acknowledge God in my day to day life. I would pray and sometimes attend Catholic Church but would still engage in aspects of my 'wildlife', because I found the standard to which I should live too restricting and difficult to obtain. I did not understand God's grace and the fact I couldn't fix myself or work towards earning His love. Not being used to receiving something for nothing, I honestly could not grasp the gift God was extending to me. He wanted a relationship with me, which essentially cost me nothing but cost Him His life - it was mind-blowing and difficult to fathom.

The years I had spent in darkness, sinking in the quicksand of pain, shame, rejection, and self-hatred, were on the brink of becoming a thing of the past. I only had to stop fighting in my own power, which was only destroying me further and be still and trust that He indeed is God, the redeemer of my soul and, like He had promised, had better for me.

On Saturday 16th May 2015, I did a 10k charity walk called 'walking out of the darkness' and looking back was a foreshadow of what I was about to do. I had plans to attend the Catholic church the following day, when a dear friend of mine invited me to her church service. I accepted the invitation and turned away from Catholicism. When Sunday came, I drove to meet my friend, and suddenly became very unsettled and called her crying uncontrollably. A deep wave of conviction troubled me, and I could not shake it. I felt such a strong urge to break up with my boyfriend immediately, and while I was anxious, the expectation for the better days ahead spurred me on.

I wanted whatever God had for me. No longer did I want to accept the way life had been for me so far. I was tired of identifying myself as an emotionally battered woman, tormented by emptiness. As a result, I gave up working in tandem with the enemy of my soul and surrendered my life to

God. On Sunday 17th May 2015, I walked into that church service as the beautiful but broken little girl in the picture and left her at the altar, re-emerging as the young woman, made in the image of God, determined to live a life for Jesus Christ.

CHAPTER 3
Identity

Who are you? A question that would often give me heart palpitations, bring my thought processes to a halt, and blow tumbleweed through my mind. It was a question that had such an effect on me due to there being a time when I had no clue who I was. So, responding with confidence was always a daunting task. I've thankfully come to understand that knowing who you are and whose you are is fundamental to walking in our true identity.

Realising through scripture in Psalm 139:14 that God

thoughtfully and uniquely created us, likewise from Genesis 1:27 that we were made in His image, means you and I have a purpose; we have the capacity to demonstrate and reflect His glory in the earth. God has designed every aspect of our being with intent. From the shade of our skin to the number of hairs on our head. From the talents and gifts we possess, to the fingerprints intrinsically mapped out on our hands. No part of us is a mistake or by chance. In fact, God describes everything that He created as 'very good' (Genesis 1:31) and understanding this blessing brings great relief to the very question that once had me perplexed.

One of my favourite scriptures is Ephesians 2:10 states, "For we are God's masterpiece. He has created us anew in Christ Jesus, so we can do the good things He planned for us long ago." It is God's plan for us to know that He created us as an exquisite work of art. His desire for us is to be spiritually transformed in Christ, so we can truly walk in the extraordinary life that He knowingly planned for us before we were born. Not knowing who we are (in Christ) causes us to function outside of God's intended purpose and plans for us, because identity and purpose go hand in hand.

A well-known quote by the late Evangelist and Minister Dr Myles Munroe states, "When purpose is not known, abuse is inevitable." While at first, the term abuse may not come to mind when navigating life outside of God's plans for us, but when the realisation of how precious we are in God's sight comes, we can begin to recognise that anything outside of His intended purpose is abuse. For example, not knowing your value can open you up to accept being treated in ways below your true worth. Aside from this one example, the effects of misplaced identity are seen throughout the world. Beauty standards, relationships and marriage all viewed through a tainted lens, which causes one to pursue and live according to the world's standards and not God's. From season to season and trend to trend, the ideologies of the world change, making it an unobtainable goal to reach. Whereas, God's opinion on His creation as a whole remains the same; there is safety and protection in this.

Knowing who you are in Christ lessens the chances of succumbing to pressures to go with the flows and pulls of the world. Similarly, finding your identity in Christ reduces the likelihood of falling into the 'pleasing people' trap or holding the opinions of others above God's sovereign word. People-pleasing is not just about wanting to make people happy; it is a part of a far deeper issue to do with your self-worth. Some of the behaviours that may occur in someone who desires to please others includes, the tendency to say yes to everything and anything people ask you to do, even if you know you cannot do it or know that it is wrong. They may attempt to be like others to feel accepted. They may agree with what others say even if they do not agree, or find themselves doing things for the approval or praise of others.

The bible says, "The fear of man brings a snare, but whoever trusts in the Lord is safe" (Proverbs 29:25). When your identity is rooted in what God says about you, His opinion is your safe place. What others say about you will be like water off of a duck's back and no longer will you fear people's disapproval or rejection. That's one of the beauties of knowing who you are in Christ; it allows you to be free. Rejection cannot hold you bound.

As you read in the previous chapters, rejection was the root of my issues and whilst living in that space, lies constantly tormented me. I was blind and did not know the truth. Thankfully, the power and love of God broke me out of that cage, opened my eyes and set me free. My mind began to be renewed through His word. Through this renewal of mind and discovery of my true identity, I loved myself with the God kind of love and was empowered to love others in this way too.

In Matthew 22:37, Jesus makes it clear that "You must love the Lord your God with all your heart, all your soul, and all your mind", He then goes on to say in verse 39, "A second is equally important: Love your neighbour as yourself". To go back in time, I recall when I was 11 years old, I had just started secondary school and found it easy to make friends and was quite popular. At this age, I became more conscious of my appearance, and although I did not necessarily feel insecure, my insecurities were beginning to manifest. I remember sitting at the lunch table with a group of girls, and I suggested that we all cast votes on who was the prettiest around the table. I knew I wanted to target and put another girl in the group down, who I thought would get the lowest votes from my perspective. At 11 years old, I had just bullied someone, unaware of the severity of my actions. I do not justify my behaviour, but now I understand that I put her down to elevate myself. I did not realise the rejection and self-hatred that was growing inside of me was what I was now projecting onto others. If I had known God's love and what it meant to love God with all my heart, I would had been able to understand how to love myself and therefore love others correctly.

I have experienced being on both sides of the fence. The perpetrator and the victim; neither of them being God's purpose for any of us. I have been the popular girl who everyone thought had it all together and the girl who felt like the oddball, an outsider and insignificant in a crowded place.

Knowing my identity and worth in Christ was crucial for me to be free from such confusion and mess. I have since become so passionate about women knowing who they are because I believe that it would save many from painful experiences, from hurting others and themselves. Walking around in confusion and lacking true identity robs you of the life God intended and means one walks around with a false identity.

If you, like me, have found yourself questioning who you are, you can find out who you are and who you belong to by reading the truth about what God says about you. God is for you, loves you and wants you to be free from the lies that you have believed about yourself and the hurtful things people have said about you. Christ desires for you to be free from the need for constant approval from people because He loves and accepts you. While we unfortunately have an adversary, the devil, who roams to and fro, looking for who he can destroy, we thankfully have a victorious God who has won that battle and defeated the enemy of our soul.

My prayer for you is that you would no longer look at yourself through a distorted lens and that you would come to know and understand that you were created for a great purpose. I pray that you will learn and believe that your life has meaning and that God Himself blessed you with life and can satisfy your every need. I pray for a renewal and transformation to take place over your mind and that the truth of God's word stands. In His truth alone, may you know that you are His chosen vessel to be used for good things here on earth, because you are fearfully and wonderfully made in His image, for His glory. Amen.

CHAPTER 4
Purpose

The average lifespan of a human being is 79 years; that is 28,835 days in total. While some will make it to see 79 years old or even beyond, the reality is that many will not. Although, I pray that you and I will live long and meaningful lives by the grace of God.

Knowing our days are numbered on this earth, and none of us discerning the exact moment when our time is done, means we cannot afford to waste any of the days we are gifted with.

So, a question I pose to you as you read: Do you know why

you were placed here on earth? Can you genuinely say that you know what your purpose in life is? If you do, what are you doing about it? If you don't, I also ask you what are you doing about it? Being on borrowed time means we cannot afford to, 'kind of think' we know why we are here, live life aimlessly, just going with the flow or even live day-to-day trying to figure out life for ourselves, especially when we don't have to.

How are you stewarding your time here on earth?

Something that I found terrifying was imagining on the day that I die, God playing back the video of the life I chose to live and then playing a video of the life that He had planned for me to live, and it is not only different, but so much better. It frightened me because many of us do not realise that the One who created us has the blueprint for our lives, and without seeking His guidance, we will always live below our potential and walk in the wrong purpose. It would also mean that we are unknowingly robbing others of having the opportunity to access God's gifts and talents bestowed upon us. Your purpose is not what you do, i.e. your job/career, but what God gives you. Your purpose is to glorify God and make His name known through all you do.

We will all be held accountable for everything that we have been called to do and how we utilised our time here on earth.

This is why I feel so strongly about the importance of knowing your purpose. If we want to live a fulfilling, meaningful, and purposeful life, we must seek understanding, wisdom, and guidance from God.

As defined in the dictionary, the word purpose is: 'the reason for which something is done or created or for which something exists.' At various moments in my life, I often pondered on my existence and wondered why I was created. I then realised that I was not wired to figure out my purpose for myself and that the answer I was looking for was as clear as day in God's word. Did you know that before you were conceived, God had thought about you and had already set your purpose in place (Jeremiah 1:5)?

> "'For I know the plans I have for you,' says the Lord. 'They are plans for good and not for disaster, to give you a future and a hope.'"
>
> (Jeremiah 29:11)

God's plans for our lives are far better than we could imagine, and we can rest in the security of following God's plan rather than our own.

If you were trying to get to a particular destination and weren't sure how you would get there, would you attempt to find your way by walking down different roads, prolonging your journey, or would you choose to use a GPS to get you there instead? Now I don't know about you, but I would opt to use a GPS to get me to my destination, because nobody has (well, at least not me) time to be wasted on getting lost. This analogy is how it is with God. He is like our GPS helping us reach our destination to fulfil our purpose, and without Him, we are bound to get lost.

God is the Alpha and Omega, which means He is the Beginning and the End (Revelations 22:13). He knows everything and has every day of our lives written in His scrolls (Psalms 139:16), which means He knew the day you would enter the world, and He knows the exact day you will leave the world, and every single detail in between. Therefore, placing our trust in His hands to lead us through life will bring security and comfort, because you know you are in safe hands, no matter what hurdles we come across.

Not only is knowing your purpose important, but fulfilling it is just as important, and a part of this means it is crucial to take care of your health. I like to use an analogy: Think of your body as a car, God as the GPS, and your purpose as the destination you need to travel to. Imagine a car is driving along the road, it is filled with the wrong fuel, it is dented, rusting and has flattening tyres. It begins to slow down and eventually breaks down and is not able to reach the destination. That could happen to many of us if we do not fill our bodies with the right foods (fuel). We only have one life and one body to get through life with, and without good health, we could potentially be the stumbling block that gets in the way of how and whether we reach our destination to fulfilling our purpose; which is preventable if care is taken with stewarding the body God has blessed us with.

God cares about every area of our lives. This means He cares about the condition of our body, our mind and our spirit. Therefore, we have a duty to take good care of our bodies to fulfil our purpose.

CHAPTER 5
Well-being & Mental Health

Well-being can be defined as good general health, happiness, living with a sense of purpose and high life satisfaction. It is beneficial to look at well-being from a holistic viewpoint, which means to take into account its multifaceted make-up of several interdependent dimensions that affect your overall well-being as a whole.

These dimensions are spiritual, psychological & emotional, social, economic, vocational, intellectual and physical.

Well-being is something that I believe is crucial and extremely important for us all to understand. In doing so, we will position ourselves to be proactive and intentional about managing our well-being adequately. The result of doing this, means we enable ourselves to do all that is within our ability to take good care of ourselves, so we can function optimally in our everyday lives.

Let's take a quick look at the dimensions of well-being and what they consist of:

Spiritual
Spiritual well-being focuses on feeling connected to God and having a sense of meaning, peace and purpose in life.

Psychological & Emotional
Psychological and emotional well-being focuses on your mental health. This is based on the way you think, how life affects you, your ability to cope with life, how you engage with others, the choices you make and how you feel.

Social
Social well-being is based on the fact that we are designed to be relational beings with a natural desire to connect with others to establish good and healthy relationships. It also focuses on having a sense of belonging within a community and contributing to society.

Economical

Economic well-being is based on financial security and the ability to financially manage basic needs such as food, clothing, housing etc., whilst also having discipline and control over everyday expenses.

Vocational

Vocational well-being is based on feeling content and fulfilled within your working life and balancing this with day-to-day life.

Intellectual

Intellectual well-being focuses on engaging with mentally stimulating activities that enable the expansion of knowledge, skills, and creativity.

Physical

Physical well-being focuses on taking care of your physical body to help prevent disease and health complications by staying active and eating well.

For the sake of what I aim to convey throughout this book, I'm going to hone into three aspects of well-being mentioned above; spiritual, physical and psychological & emotional, and look at how these three interlink.

The link between Spiritual, Physical & Physiological Well-being

Over time I have come to see, experience and understand the strong link between spiritual, mental and physical well-being. Whilst I believe it is essential to highlight all the dimensions of well-being when examining your overall health, I will only delve into three over the next few chapters and share why I believe they so powerfully interconnect. One thing I think is incredible and so beautiful is that God cares about our whole being. He sees and cares about the nights you have cried yourself to sleep. He desires to help you with your emotional state. He cares about your mind, the condition of your spirit, and your physical body.

Psychological & Emotional Wellbeing

Having good mental health is vital because it can significantly impact all aspects of your life, and it plays a role in helping you function well day-to-day. Poor mental health has detrimental effects on how you operate emotionally and how you connect with people. It can affect your productivity and your ability to cope with everyday stresses in life. Mental illness can affect you at any point in your life. Sadly, one in four adults and one in ten children experience mental illness (NHS, n.d.).

Research has found that three in four mental illnesses start in childhood; 75% of mental illnesses start before a child reaches their 18th birthday, while 50% of mental health problems in adult life (excluding dementia) take root before the age of 15 (MQ Mental Health, 2017).

Your quality of life and even how long you live can be influenced by poor mental health. People with severe and prolonged mental illness are at risk of dying on average 15 to 20 years earlier than those without a mental health issue (Pharmaceutical Services Negotiating Committee, n.d.).

Unfortunately, in many cases, people completely lose hope, which is why suicide is a leading cause of death in young men and women aged 20-34 in the UK. The latest figures from the Office of National Statistics reveal that the number of young suicides each year is greater than it has been for the past ten years. In 2015, 1,660 young people under 35 years took their own lives; 103 more than in 2014 and 58 more than the previous highest recorded figure (1,631 in 2011) (MQ Mental Health, 2017).

It is devastating that so many lives are affected by mental illness, and it is something close to my heart as I have been there. I have been through seasons where I wished I was dead. I have felt hopeless and fought many battles in my mind. But, if it wasn't for Jesus Christ and His saving grace, I'm not sure if I would be here today, and I'll explain why.

For many years of my life, I have battled with different trials with mental health. I would look in the mirror and feel so ugly and repulsed. Having my picture or video taken or seeing photos or videos of myself began to give me anxiety. They would often lead me into depressive and suicidal states because of how ugly I felt.

I believed the issue was my face. I didn't see myself as created in the image of God - instead, when I looked in the mirror, I saw a monster. I thought I was fat, hated my eyes, and thought that losing weight would change this. I was fifteen years old at the time, and I went on a calorie-restricted strict diet in which I would rigorously calculate calories and exercised excessively. Unfortunately, I became so obsessed with dieting that I developed Bulimia.

People with Bulimia go through periods where they eat a lot of food in very short amounts of time (binge eating) and then make themselves sick, use laxatives or do excessive exercise, or a combination of these to try to stop themselves from gaining weight (NHS, 2010). Men and women of any age can have Bulimia, but it is most common in young women and typically starts in the mid to late teens. In my case, I would be so hungry from all the exercise I was doing, and the restriction I placed on my food intake, that I would end up binging and then feeling guilty. This would result in me going to the toilet to make myself sick. I remember an occasion where I had some friends over and we had a take-away. I pretended that I needed the bathroom, but I was going to the bathroom to throw up all the food.

Over 1.6 million people in the UK are estimated to be directly affected by eating disorders (Anorexia Bulimia Care, n.d.). This figure is based on those seeking help or receiving treatment, which means that the number of people suffering is higher.

I was good at hiding my condition, and it is a tendency Bulimia sufferers have. Consequentially, many people did not realise what I was going through. Various symptoms aren't always easy to spot, but eventually, people noticed I had lost a lot of weight. Some of the symptoms of Bulimia are binge eating, fear of putting on weight, mood changes, being critical of weight and body shape, making yourself vomit, using laxative and engaging in excessive exercise. Bulimia can also cause very negative health implications such as fits and muscle spasms, heart, kidney and bowel problems, bone issues such as osteoporosis, dental problems and fatigue.

I developed safety behaviours that were responses used to help prevent fears from coming true. That made me feel more comfortable in situations that made me anxious.

I only felt comfortable taking my picture, as I could take it at an angle that made me feel safe. Putting an image of myself up as my display picture gave me anxiety because of what I thought people would think. I often hid behind my hair by always having a fringe of some sort that would not overexpose my face, making me feel less vulnerable. I often sought reassurance from my cousin before putting up a photo or distorted the image with filters, bringing me some form of comfort. I had instances where I would do a full face of make-up only to take it all off and re-do the whole thing because I just felt like I looked awful. I would often avoid looking in mirrors or reflective surfaces, mainly if anyone was around. Before leaving the house, I would repeatedly check my reflection in a specific mirror that I felt safe using. I was not too fond of bright lights because I felt extremely exposed and felt like my flaws were highlighted. I had social anxiety and was always paranoid around people. My heart would race, and I would get hot and clammy, thinking that people were looking at me and thinking about how ugly I was or judging me in their mind. I struggled to accept genuine compliments because I believed that people complimented me out of pity for my confessed unattractiveness.

I was so obsessed with my appearance that my whole life revolved around it, and it affected my mood and emotions heavily. In some cases, I would cancel plans at the very last minute because of a meltdown and wouldn't be able to leave the house. For over ten years of my childhood to early adult years, I went through this thinking that I was crazy because it felt like no one understood that what I was experiencing was real. Going to the doctors was a challenge. I would be told my feelings were linked to my monthly cycle, and all I needed to do was take Evening Primrose to help manage my hormones.

I knew I wasn't making up how I was feeling, and it became exhausting because these feelings would consume my everyday life. It wasn't until I went back to the doctors in desperation two years later that I cried and begged for her to try and understand that I desperately needed help. I was then referred to a Psychiatrist at a Social Anxiety Unit to have an assessment. I finally discovered that I had been experiencing a medical term known as Body Dysmorphic Disorder (BDD), which is an anxiety disorder related to your body image. Some of the key signs of this mental health disorder are having obsessive worries about your perceived physical appearance that are hardly noticeable to others. Another sign is compulsive routines such as plucking hair, picking skin or repeatedly checking mirrors due to worrying about your appearance. It is a mental illness that is closely related to Obsessive Compulsive Disorder.

I went through many years not understanding why I constantly felt so bad about myself. No amount of 'self-love' ritual, self-help book or standing in the mirror convincing myself of my beauty brought a lasting change. I needed psychological help, but most importantly, I needed Jesus. I always wondered why it felt like I was so alone in my battle as my symptoms were always brushed off as vanity or hormonal. It is estimated that approximately 0.5-0.7% of the UK population have BDD (Ocdaction, n.d.). Surveys have put BDD at about 2% of the population and is often associated with fears of rejection or humiliation (Body Dysmorphic Disorder Foundation, n.d.). BDD is recognised as a hidden disorder as many people are too ashamed to reveal that this is their main problem.

After discovering I was suffering from BDD, I took Cognitive Behavioural Therapy (CBT) for 12 weeks. Every case of BDD is different. I chose not to take any medication as I was afraid of the side effects of taking them for a prolonged period. Successively, I sought counselling which helped me confront many of my wounds that were beginning to surface.

As I reflect on my life so far and thankful God has brought me through, I always tell people that I would never want to go back to my teenage years because those were some of the most painful and darkest years of my life. Waking up feeling like there was a dark force over me, and no matter what I did, I couldn't shake it. So, while some would love to relive their teenage years, I would never opt to relive that season again. I remember the day I told God that I wish no one else could feel how I felt then because it was that bad.

It has burdened me to help encourage young women who may be experiencing the darkness I did off the back of what I went through. So, to you who may be blind to the beauty others see in you, to you who looks in the mirror and hates what you see. To you, that may be feeling like your dark days seem like they are getting darker, and to you, that feels like things couldn't possibly get better; I am here to tell you and encourage you that brighter days are coming, and there is freedom in Christ from this oppression.

I know what it is like to feel trapped in overwhelming negative thoughts. I can relate to being captive. I recognise the lie that says there's no way out and what it's like to be scared to discover the real you. I once felt like surrendering my life to Jesus was a huge risk because I lacked trust, but He never fails. Accepting His guidance, seeking psychological aid and getting connected to a church community to support me on my journey helped me overcome the False, Evidence, Appearing, Real (FEAR).

On the other side of stepping out in faith is freedom. The freedom I pray you'll receive, and the freedom Christ desires to give. Is it easy? No, but is it worth it? Yes! Your invitation to true freedom awaits.

CHAPTER 6
Food

According to online reports, the average person consumes about 35 tons of food during a lifetime (Express, 2013). To help visualise how much a ton is, it is about the weight of two horses! As a food lover and someone who enjoys the places and people food brings to remembrance, discovering this makes me more mindful of the foods I consume.

Food is something that can bring back sweet memories of our childhood. It has the power to unify and connect us across cultures and generations and a way that some mothers express their love towards their family (The Well Co., n.d.). I remember meals being an avenue for my family to gather together over holiday seasons to overindulge in our favourite traditional dishes.

Food has become a pathway to pleasure and careers. Some people host 'mukbangs', which translates to 'eating broadcast' whereby the person consumes a gluttonous amount of food for viewing entertainment. Where others create a stream of revenue, travelling the world, tasting and reviewing different foods.

A good meal can turn a frown upside down after a bad day, be a source of comfort during challenging times, or a 'fix' for boredom. If there is one thing we can agree on, food has both the power to uplift our moods and nourish our bodies, as well as make us more susceptible to disease, whereby sending us to an early grave.

If you ask anyone that knows me well, they can confirm how much I love food! But as you have read in the previous chapters, it was not always this way, having had my fair share of battles in this area. I went from being obsessed with counting calories, depriving myself of eating, which later developed into an eating disorder, to going on a crazy quest to increase my calorie intake to attain the 'thick girl/tight waist curvy look'. Meals and snacks consisted of sugary cereals with full-fat milk.

Weight gain shakes made using vanilla ice cream and full-fat milk. In addition, I would drink cans of Nurishment, scoff down bags of potatoes and any other carbohydrates I could get my hands on. Still, when I gained the weight, I had not arrived at the utopia of self-love, acceptance and contentment I longed for. Even though all the unhealthy eating did cause my bum, hips and breasts to inflate, it also came with an enlarged stomach and chubbier face. This made me more self-conscious.

Food is there for us to enjoy and nourish our bodies daily. However, the food choices we make today affect our tomorrow and future. So why is it necessary to be conscious of the foods we choose to consume? I believe in understanding the why; it is essential to go back to the basics of food and its benefits.

First and foremost, we need food to stay alive! It is one of our basic needs, and without any food for an extended period, we would die of starvation. Food provides us with nutrients essential for energy to move, grow, and helps with the adequate functioning of our bodies like breathing and digestion. In addition, it helps keep us warm, repairs our bodies, and keeps our immune systems strong. Understanding what food we need to consume will help us reap even more of the benefits.

The National Health Services (NHS) provides an insight into a healthy balanced diet within a guide titled "The Eatwell Guide". It seems pretty simple when you think about it; fruit, vegetables and carbohydrates should make up the bulk of our intake. The rest of our food intake should consist of protein, dairy, vitamins, minerals, unsaturated fats and foods high in fat. In addition, salt and sugar should be consumed less often and in small amounts. Lastly, staying hydrated by drinking 6-8 cups of water a day should not be overlooked (NHS, 2019).

Fruits and Vegetables

Fruits and vegetables contain fibre, often associated with a lower risk of heart disease, strokes, type-2 diabetes, and bowel cancer. Fibre also helps you feel fuller and aids with digestion and constipation. Fruits and vegetables are naturally low in fat and contain many of the essential vitamins and minerals that our bodies need. We are further encouraged to consume five portions of fruit and veg in their array of colours per day to really tap into their nutritional benefits. What we should also keep in mind when eating fruits is the high level of naturally occurring sugars, so it is best to be wise with our overall consumption.

Carbohydrates

Often carbs are seen as the evil food group, but the benefits depend on the type, quantity, and quality of the carb that we consume, such as fruit, vegetables, pulses, and starchy foods. Carbohydrates are the body's main sources of energy; they fuel our ability to move around and exercise as well, helping us with our breathing. Suppose the carbohydrate consumed is of good quality. In that case, they can contain essential nutrients like vitamin B, iron, calcium and fibre. This promotes excellent health benefits, such as good bowel movements, reductions in cholesterol levels, cardiovascular disease, bowel cancer and type-2 diabetes. However, the potential issues of not consuming enough carbs mean you may not get enough of the nutrients that you need.

Furthermore, reducing your carb intake and increasing the amount of protein and fats you consume can potentially pose health problems like heart disease. In all of this, balance is key! Make a choice to choose unrefined (wholegrain) and high fibre carbs and avoid refined (processed) carbs like sugary cereals, white flour, noodles etc., as there is little to no fibre or nutritional benefit.

Protein

Protein is an essential part of a healthy diet. Its purpose is necessary for the growth, repair and maintenance of good health of the body, and it provides the body with energy.

Beans, pulses, fish, eggs, meat and tofu are some forms of protein that contain iron for healthy red blood cells, which help to carry oxygen to the body's tissues. B vitamins, particularly B12, help maintain a healthy nervous system. Zinc, which is important for the immune system, magnesium, an essential component of all cells and soluble fibre, help to reduce blood cholesterol levels and improve blood sugar levels. It is better to consume proteins with a lower fat content like lean meat, i.e. skinless chicken and turkey breasts. Plant-based protein sources like chickpeas, spirulina, legumes, tofu and nuts, rather than processed meats or excessive amounts of red meat (often linked to heart disease, colorectal cancer and type 2 diabetes), are also better protein options.

Dairy
Dairy foods such as cheese, yoghurt, milk and butter help with dental health, improve bones and provide vitamins like B12, A and D. They also contain calcium which helps to promote strong bones and protein that contain essential amino acids. There are dairy-free alternatives that can give you the same nutritional benefits that dairy products provide. You can get calcium from plant-based products like soy, almond milk, hemp milk, coconut milk, and rice milk. Calcium can also come from tofu, pulses, vegetables like broccoli, cabbage and

okra. Things like nuts, soy-based products, spirulina, quinoa and pulses are all sources of protein that give the same benefits as consuming dairy products.

Vitamin B12 in dairy products help with the essential functioning of the nervous system and helps the body process protein and fat into a usable source of energy. You can also get B12 from fortified cereals, yeast flakes, liver, salmon, trout, clams, or you can take a supplement.

Vitamin A in dairy foods are essential for maintaining healthy skin, hair and eyesight. Still, you can also get this from cod liver oil, eggs, orange and yellow coloured fruits and vegetables and dark green vegetables like spinach.

Vitamin D is essential for bone and tooth development, but you also get this from the sun, supplements and food such as almond milk, oranges, mushrooms and items fortified with vitamin D, like cereals and soy yoghurt.

Fats

Fat in small amounts is an essential part of having a healthy and balanced diet. It provides essential fatty acids that the body cannot make itself and helps vitamins that are fat-soluble like vitamin A, D and E that can only be absorbed with the help of fats. Fats also provide energy, cell growth, support in protecting our organs, aid in keeping our body warm and assistance in producing hormones. However, we need to be conscious of the fats we choose to consume, as some are more harmful than others. Unhealthy fats can cause serious health problems such as heart disease, strokes, high blood pressure, certain cancers, sleep apnea, osteoarthritis, fatty liver and fatty kidney disease. Fats that have the potential to cause serious health problems are saturated fats and trans fats.

Ideally, we should avoid trans fats entirely as they can raise blood cholesterol, cause type-2 diabetes, obesity, increase infertility in women and the risk of developing heart disease. Trans fats contain hydrogenated fats, which are liquid vegetable oils made creamy when manufacturers convert some of the unsaturated fats into saturated ones through a process called hydrogenation (Rehagen, 2021). These fats can be found in commercially baked goods like pies, crackers, crisps, biscuits, cakes, pastries, frozen pizzas, microwave popcorn, vegetable shortening, margarine, fried chicken, French fries, and doughnuts, to list a few.

Other fats to consume sparingly are saturated fats, which increase cholesterol, clog up arteries, and increase heart disease and stroke risk. Foods high in saturated fats are full-fat dairy products like cheese, milkshakes, cream, ice cream, animal fats like ghee, butter and lard, palm oil and coconut oil. Processed meats such as sausages, burgers, bacon, kebabs, dark meats like beef, lamb, pork, fatty cuts of meat, cured meat like chorizo, pepperoni and pancetta also contain high saturated fats, along with chocolate, chocolate spreads, biscuits and cakes.

It is best to avoid or cut back on trans fats and saturated fat and steer more towards unsaturated fats within your diet. Unsaturated fats are better, and they are found in foods like oily fish such as salmon, mackerel and trout, avocados, nuts, seeds, and olives.

When cooking, using avocado oil, which can be used for dressings and cooking at high temperatures, is healthier. Sunflower oil (in moderation; as it contains omega 6, which can produce inflammation in the body) is excellent, as it has vitamin E and can be heated to high temperatures. Oils like extra virgin olive oil, walnut oil, flax oil are great unsaturated fats, but they have a low smoke point. Thus, it is best to use them on low heat or just for dressings. When heated at high temperatures, these oils release toxic fumes and free radicals, which are incredibly harmful to your body.

Salt

Salt and sodium are often used interchangeably; however, they are not the same thing. Sodium is a mineral found in salt, which is what the body needs. Salt is a naturally occurring compound that consists of sodium and chloride. Table salt is a common salt found in people's kitchens that derive from natural salt, but is refined; it is not natural salt. The body needs dietary salt for adequate functioning of muscles, a healthy nervous system, and to help to balance fluid in the body. Having the right amount of salt is important as problems can occur if you have too much or too little. Sodium deficiency can result in low blood pressure, dehydration, cramps, headaches, water retention, weakness and confusion. If it is severely deficient, it can lead to seizures and can be fatal in extreme cases. Too much sodium, on the other hand, can cause high blood pressure, which can lead to heart disease and strokes. Foods high in salt are anchovies, bacon, cheese, gravy granules, smoked meat, and fish. Soy sauce, stock cubes, yeast extract, bread products such as crumpets, bagels and ciabatta, pasta sauces, crisps, pizza, ready meals, soup, sandwiches, sausages, and tomato ketchup are also high in salt, along with mayonnaise, and breakfast cereals.

To the human body, salt is essential for body functioning. Sodium is a crucial element that help maintain cellular balance, circulation, and blood sugar levels. Sodium is one of the minerals primarily responsible for maintaining your electrolytes. Common electrolytes include sodium, potassium, calcium, and bicarbonate. Without adequate sodium, your brain would not be able to send necessary electrical impulses to the rest of your body to function correctly.

Just as the body requires the right amount of sodium for proper function, consuming too much salt can be considered unhealthy. Higher salt intakes are known to increase blood pressure and water retention. Elevated sodium levels cause the body to hold on to water to keep the serum sodium concentration from increasing beyond certain limits. It is considered a protective response, and your body is working to maintain balance. Excess sodium tends to cause an elevation in blood pressure, so doctors recommend that people with hypertension reduce or eliminate salt intake (Leal, 2021). You can purchase various salts like the commonly used table salt, kosher salt, sea salts like lack Sea, Celtic, French (fleur de sel), or Hawaiian sea salt and Himalayan salt.

Sugar

It comes in many forms such as sucrose, glucose, fructose, lactose, treacle, syrup, high fructose corn syrup, caramel, maltose, hydrolysed and honey.

Glucose is an essential sugar that your body needs to survive; it is a simple sugar that is an important energy source required for all cells and organs in your body. Foods naturally high in glucose are honey, agave, dried fruit, fruit juices and sweetcorn. Other foods like sauces, salad dressings, pies, fizzy drinks, sweets, cakes and biscuits all have added sugar in them. Foods that have added sugar and glucose are also known as free sugars and should be avoided. Overeating sugar can cause tooth decay and lead to weight gain. This can lead towards an increased chance of health issues like heart disease, type-2 diabetes and some types of cancers.

Vitamins & Minerals

Vitamins and minerals are essential substances that our bodies need to develop and function normally. The known vitamins include A, C, D, E, K, and the B vitamins: thiamin (B1), riboflavin (B2), niacin (B3), pantothenic acid (B5), pyridoxal (B6), cobalamin (B12), biotin (B7), and folate/folic acid (B9) (NIH, 2018). Several minerals are essential for health: calcium, phosphorus, potassium, sodium, chloride, magnesium, iron, zinc, iodine, sulfur, cobalt, copper, fluoride, manganese, and selenium (NIH, 2018). You can get these vitamins and minerals by eating a healthy diet, but where you cannot get enough of these vitamins or minerals, supplements are available (Help Guide, n.d.). There are at least 30 vitamins, minerals, and dietary components that your body needs, but cannot manufacture on its own in sufficient amounts.

Water

Water plays a significant role in the human body, making up approximately 60 per cent (Migala, 2020). Water serves many essential purposes in the body. It is vital to constantly stay hydrated through the fluid and foods that we consume. Our bodies lose water through digestion, sweating and breathing. Your water intake is dependent on your climate, the amount that you exercise and many other factors. Water helps rid the body of toxins through perspiration, defecation and urination. It also aids digestion, prevents the body from becoming dehydrated and protects the tissue. In addition, water acts as a lubricant and cushion for joints, and keeps the skin looking fresh and supple. If sufficient water is not consumed, dehydration, fatigue, a weakened immune system and dry skin can occur.

The whole purpose of including a food chapter is to recognize that our bodies are gifts from God. We only get one body that will carry us around for the set number of days that God has placed us here on earth. We cannot go to the shop and purchase a replacement when it runs down. But, we do have the power to do all we can, to ensure we take care of our precious bodies in the best way possible.

Proactive vs Reactive

We all have the power and free will to make choices.

To be proactive is to act in anticipation of future problems; it also refers to taking actions and making changes rather than allowing things to unfold before you, which is reactive. We can choose to be proactive about taking care of our bodies, by eating the right food or be reactive when making unhealthy choices, by responding when illness strikes. But in being reactive, this may be too late! I do not know about you, but I think it is best to be proactive and make the right choices now, rather than regret the choices made later. "In every single thing you do, you are choosing a direction. Your life is a product of choices."– Dr Kathleen Hall.

Food and Mental Health

What we put in our bodies can affect our mental and emotional wellbeing (Mental Health Foundation, 2017). Depression is one of the most common mental illnesses (Beata Lewis MD, 2018). Several extensive studies have linked the intake of certain nutrients with a reported prevalence of different types of depression. Nutrition plays a significant role in our ability to regulate psychological and emotional wellbeing. Deficiencies in key vitamins and minerals can compromise optimal brain functioning and increase stress and anxiety levels. Research shows that certain foods affect powerful mood-modifying brain chemicals called neurotransmitters (Speaking of Women's Health, n.d.). These neurotransmitters are made from the foods we eat and are present in higher concentrations after meals than between them; this is not to rule out any other causes of depression, but to highlight that nutrition in effect can play a role. For example, vitamin deficiencies such as B12, B5, B1 and folate, which all come under B-complex vitamins, are crucial for mental and emotional wellbeing. We can get these vitamins from food as the body does not store them, yet they are destroyed by alcohol, refined sugars, nicotine, and caffeine (NHS, n.d.).

The purpose of this is to emphasise that a balanced diet is vital for both physical and mental health. Aside from food being something we can enjoy, its primary purpose is to aid our survival and fuel our bodies. The problems begin to arise when we start to abuse food or use it as a coping mechanism. It is essential to think about why we use food as a form of comfort, why we eat to make us feel better when we feel down, why we turn to food when we feel stressed, or why we sometimes avoid food and the thought of it creates anxiety.

Underneath battling with food, by comfort eating and calorie obsessions, were unaddressed wounds. I was using food as a coping mechanism to adverse effects. The truth is food will never provide true comfort, relief from stress or the peace we seek; only Jesus can do that. I could eat and eat and eat, but deep down, I would never be satisfied; it just put me in an unhealthy relationship with food. I was never reaching for anything nutritious to help positively, but I made food choices that ultimately had a counterproductive effect on my physical body and contributed to my poor mental health; it was self-sabotage.

When we look at what self-sabotage is (a destructive form of behaviour, defined as actively or passively taking steps to prevent yourself from reaching a goal or target), we can look over our choices to see if this behaviour is unknowingly present. For example, knowing that eating fried food every day can cause heart disease that already runs in your family, but still choosing to eat it every day is self-sabotage. Continuing to dig into that packet of cookies when the doctors have informed you that you need to cut down on your sugar intake; otherwise, there will be detrimental consequences is also a form of self-sabotage.

Whether the revelation of our purpose here on earth is realised, it does not negate the fact that we all have one, and to an extent, control whether we live to walk out that purpose out or not. So, how we take care of ourselves is a crucial part! We have been called to be fruitful and multiply (Genesis 1:28), and the food we put in our bodies can affect our reproductive system. Think about it; if you are unfit, overweight, underweight, or ill due to improper nutrition, how will you be able to run around after your children, play with them or be around to see them grow up if you are not well enough?

Your body is a temple of the Holy Spirit (1 Corinthians 6:9). This means that God dwells within you. You wouldn't eagerly dump a whole bunch of trash in a sacred place, so why would you do that to your body? You are valuable and have a destiny that no one else on this planet has. You are needed, so be encouraged to be in the best position to not only be spiritually available for God's use but physically available too.

Let me make it clear. I am not in any way stating you cannot eat that chocolate bar you like. I'm saying you do not need to go on and eat the second or third bar in one seating or eat it every single day. We have been given a spirit of self-discipline (2 Timothy 1:7 NIV) to control our feelings and overcome our weaknesses. This means we have the power to say no when tempted to pop open that bag of pork scratchings or order that second double cheeseburger. Know your limits and ask yourself if what you are eating is because you are genuinely hungry or eating for the sake of it. Ask yourself if it will nourish your body or if it will leave you feeling sluggish. In all of your eating, a healthy, nutritious balance is the ultimate goal.

I do not believe or even encourage diets as they are often associated with temporal changes that are not sustainable, but healthy eating ties in with the lifestyle you create. Treat yourself now and then, but eat to function well and keep God and the purpose He has given you at the forefront of your mind.

Heavenly Father,

I thank you for your daughter and the beautiful body that you have gifted her. Lord, I pray that you help her to understand that her body is a temple of your Holy Spirit. May she grow in knowledge and understanding of how to nourish and nurture her body so that she would function in the beautiful way that you intended for her. Lord, I pray that you would free her from any challenges she may be facing with food and that she would experience comfort in your unfailing love that is enough to bring her more satisfaction than any food can, in Jesus name, Amen.

CHAPTER 7
Fitness

I have always loved fitness, despite my former poor eating habits. I believe this influence came from my dad and my elder brother, who were gym fanatics.

As a child, I enjoyed going swimming weekly and achieved many badges until I reached about ten and began to go through puberty. I found it embarrassing, being an early developer and experiencing periods, that I was eventually put off swimming lessons. Going through so many bodily changes at such a young was a lot to deal with. I became a bit self-conscious and as a result my love for swimming started to dwindle Going through so many bodily changes at such a young age was a lot to deal with, and I became a bit self-conscious, so much so my love for swimming started to dwindle. I started worrying about my hair getting wet, becoming extra frizzy and looking unkempt for the rest of the day. Eventually, I forgot my swimming abilities, because I cared more about my appearance than retaining a life skill.

Despite this, I was more into athletics, and I would look forward to every sports day throughout primary and secondary school. Running was my thing! I remember winning the cross country race in year eight and competing in the eight-hundred-meter race and winning! My endurance was pretty good during my teenage years; I could run long distances well.

My preference for the type of fitness I enjoyed changed over time, and my brother became my inspiration for trying out weight lifting. I remember the days he would bring his friends to the house and play music while doing a workout session. Thinking about those moments, they were a sight to see! A full-blown gym session on the landing in my mum's house. My brother had a bench, pull up bar, barbell, dumbbells and all sorts. As I matured into my teenage years, he often encouraged me to join him in charity runs and go jogging with him, which was fun. He passed down some of his old weights to me, and to this present day, weight lifting is my favourite form of training.

My gym journey began at sixteen when I was battling with my body and developed bulimia. It has since become a significant part of my lifestyle and almost feels like a second home. If I'm not at work, home or church, you can be sure to find me at the gym. Even though I was a frequent gym head, I was not always comfortable being there. I would often stick to cardio machines that were easy to navigate, because I did not want to look clueless trying to figure out the other equipment. I would try to avoid working out in front of men and mirrors as body dysmorphia raged within me. It came to a point where the level of discomfort and anxiousness increased that I began to pay £55 per month from my student finance to use a private gym! But I could not escape the feeling, so I moved to an all women's gym in Central London. I felt safer and free to experiment with new exercises, but then faced the problem of the weights not being heavy enough to progress. So, it was time to conjure up the courage and switch gyms again if I was to continue on my fitness journey.

To my horror, the new gym was crowded with 'mandem' who would often stare at other women and made us feel like we were kebabs on a rotisserie grill. It made me feel more awkward, but I was determined to push past it, because while I did not know what I was doing or how to train my body to yield better results, I enjoyed working out.

There was something about seeing the human body's transformation when working out that had me fascinated. The before and after pictures piqued my interest, and I loved watching programmes like The Biggest Loser. I also was a big fan of bodybuilder and influential fitness professional Simeon Panda and admired how he trained. But, unfortunately, I didn't know of many black females within the fitness industry, so most of my 'know-how' concerning fitness training came from videos I would watch of male bodybuilders. The investment into my fitness journey began to pay dividends beyond my physique as people approached me for tips. I wanted women to experience the joy and empowerment I felt with getting into shape and later studied to become a qualified personal trainer.

Before receiving my qualification, I took a bold step out of my comfort zone and competed in a beauty pageant! Not because I believed I was pageant worthy, but to push myself to overcome the fear of what people thought of me, and to my surprise, I made it as a contestant. I was the biggest girl in the competition against slender modelesque women and while I did not win or make it to the top 5, mounting that stage was a powerful moment not just for me but for anyone who may have felt like I did. Now armed with a little more confidence, I was encouraged to enter a second time a couple of years later and vowed to get myself in the best possible physical shape.

It was 2016, and I was working as a receptionist at Fitness First while working towards my personal trainer qualification. During this time, I networked a lot with personal trainers, made new connections, learned new skills and grew in confidence, that I increased my training to 4 days a week. Finding out that I had gotten to the finals to be a contestant in the pageant was exciting and fuelled my motivation to work out even harder. Through discipline, clean eating and consistent training, I went from a size 14 to a size 10 in 5 months, and from not making it to the top 5 to winning second place, all by the grace of God.

Now a qualified personal trainer and a woman with more self-confidence, I began to train female-only clients to help them become more confident with using gym equipment and how to train their bodies. It was a blessing and it caused me to look back at all the challenges I went through as literal training for the position I was now in, because many of my clients were either facing or had gone through body image issues or lacked confidence. So, while I was a personal trainer to them, I was able to offer compassion and a level of counsel, having overcome in those areas myself. God put me in a position to empathise, encourage and empower other women, and it brings Romans 8:28 to mind that says: "And we know that all things work together for good to those who love God, to those who are called according to *His* purpose". My past hurts have purpose and are working for good!

However, one thing that was not always working out good were my motives behind training, which I will discuss in later chapters. What I will say for now is that the Lord convicted me, and I had to take some time to step out of the fitness industry and away from all social media platforms to deal with unresolved identity issues that I did not even realise I had. I needed inward refining and to rebrand my personal training business before I would teach others again.

If you recall from the previous chapter, I spoke about the importance of food and how we can either benefit or hinder ourselves by what we choose to eat. I believe exercising goes hand in hand with eating well and, in tandem, glorifies and honours God.

Exercise is defined as an activity requiring physical effort to sustain or improve health and fitness. It involves engaging in physical activity that encourages the increase of heart rate beyond resting levels, many of which do not require the gym if that is not your thing. As you may have gathered, my favourite training style is weight lifting and functional training, which may not be for everyone. However, activities such as brisk walking, cycling, and swimming, or team sports like basketball, football, or even gardening, amongst other things, can get your heart rate up.

The **NHS** (National Health Service) recommends that we should aim to be active daily instead of doing diddly squat, as I like to say. In more detail, 150 minutes of moderate-intensity activity a week or 75 minutes of vigorous-intensity exercise a week is recommended (Bupa, n.d.). Exercise is beneficial at every age in your life and should be considered a part of your lifestyle. If you are not already exercising, here are some reasons why you should consider getting active:

Exercise improves your muscular and cardiorespiratory fitness. Improves bone health, reduces the risk of high blood pressure, coronary heart disease, stroke, type-2 diabetes and some cancers. It also helps reduce the risk of obesity, anxiety, depression, and helps with other mental health problems and boosts your mood. Let us not forget that you reap the aesthetic benefits too! So after reading this, why wouldn't you want to work out!

A major wake up call for me was looking at my family history and the illnesses that have run through generations, from heart disease, high blood pressure, strokes, diabetes and cancer. However, I refuse to repeat history, and I declare that it is not my portion in the mighty name of Jesus! I realised I am getting older, and everything I do with my body will affect me later on, if not immediately. It goes back to the proactive and reactive concept that I touched on. I believe I am a generational curse breaker, and these illnesses will not come near me, but imagine if I was screaming that all day whilst scoffing down a kebab, snoozing my alarm and making all the excuses in the world. I want to be different and have a different outcome from my family by doing what is within my power to change.

Statistically, people from a Black African and Caribbean heritage are at higher risk of diabetes and stroke than their white counterparts. But through diet and exercise, these statistics have a chance at changing. High blood pressure is also more common among black Caribbean people than any other ethnic group. Now I do not claim this for myself or anyone from this background, but these are the statistics put forward by the Stroke Association, so it seems evident that we must be proactive about our health (Stroke Association, n.d.).

Of course, we all have a choice whether to take it on board or not, but there are consequences to living a lifestyle that involves little to no exercise. Without keeping active, you can become more breathless as you do activities. Your body becomes deconditioned, which means that your muscles weaken and lose bulk, including the muscles you need for breathing. If you add inactivity to a poor diet, you risk developing one of the aforementioned associated illnesses. I say all of that merely to implore you to exercise. After all, there is potentially a lot more to lose if you don't.

Your body and all its functions are a gift from God. Make the decision today to take better care of it. If you struggle with staying motivated to exercise or tempted to eat unhealthy foods, there is nothing we cannot ask God to help us overcome.

Dear Father,
Thank you for blessing your daughter with a body that she can glorify you with. Thank you for the opportunity that she has today to reflect on how she nourishes and takes care of it. I pray that you would be the motivation and drive behind her staying in shape. Please remove any condemnation she may

have towards the way she treated her body. I ask that you would renew her mind and give her a desire to live on purpose and choose to exercise, that she may reap the benefits and that you may ultimately get the glory.
In Jesus name, Amen.

CHAPTER 8
Social Media

Does Bebo, Piczo, Myspace or MSN Messenger ring a bell? If you are a 90's baby like me, you may be familiar with these social platforms. However, back then, social media was not like it is now, where you can become a viral sensation for popping pimples, having a big butt or being an in-demand influencer based on your #OOTD (Outfit of the Day). Instead, I recall social media being an innocent time of posting pictures for fun, and the extent of our cyber worries only reached how many "luvs" you received on Bebo.

I have a love and hate relationship with social media. I think many would agree that these digital platforms can change your life for good when used wisely, but can also be a tool with the potential to destroy you. One of those not so pleasant seasons came in 2010 when I decided to step away from my social platforms due to jealousy from a mentally abusive partner. It wasn't until 2015 that I began to engage online again, and in this same season emerged Carla Lotus, a brand idea given to me by God.

Carla Lotus is a concept the Lord blessed me with when I committed my life to Him. The Lotus flower, a significant symbol to my brand, is a remarkable flower that grows in the dirtiest of waters. Yet, despite the conditions, beautiful flowers bloom, rise and float on the surface - much like my life.
Prior to establishing my brand, the Lord revealed that He would use me to help and encourage women. However, to walk in my purpose and help these women, it would require me to come out of hiding.

Being Hidden By God
Over time, I have realised that being hidden can come in two forms: you can hide away yourself, or God can hide you. The latter I perceive to be a blessing because being hidden by God is loaded with benefits. Whether it is for protection, a time of healing, pruning, refining, growth or intimacy, it always works out for the best. A season of hiding came for me in 2019, which

was the ugliest, painful, yet beautifully refining year during my walk-in Christ! It was a season where I attempted to wrestle with God (which is never a good idea), because of a lack of patience. I felt like my life was not how it should be, so out of frustration started to give God a helping hand, as I did not understand the blessing of being hidden by God nor how His plans for me would unfold.

The Martha Moment

I kept pushing to build my business. I had just started back on YouTube and was regularly posting content on Instagram. However, I battled with thoughts of being behind in life and felt a lot of pressure to be successful, and as a result, I would feel anxious about taking a step back from creating content in fear of becoming a 'failure'.

During this battle, I was simultaneously juggling multiple positions; working a 9-5, part of a counselling ministry, mentoring two teenagers, shepherding ten women, serving on the youth ministry team, trying to keep up with my strenuous gym routine and dealing with my father being in and out of the hospital due to his alcohol addiction. I was constantly on the go and eventually experienced burnout, to the extent I gave up serving in the church and trying to pour into others, because I had run dry. I slowly stopped with my business pursuits, lost hope, had multiple breakdowns and became suicidal. I had let go of my old ways, but life did not seem to be yielding better results, so I rebelled as my faith dampened and saw death as a better option because my desire to live had waned.

You see, I had completely missed the point! I was caught up in myself and idolised my dreams while trying to win God's and other people's approval of me, rather than submitting to God's will. It took me a few months to completely let go, rest in God and go back into hiding. When I did, I found that there was transformation, affirmation, strategy, healing and peace waiting for me. It was a time where my foundations and identity in Christ were being corrected and re-laid. I also became convicted about specific types of content that I put out on social media and became aware of my responsibility to lead by example, by upholding the standards of God in a standardless world. Being hidden by God and away from social media meant I would no longer contaminate anyone or pour from an empty cup. It allowed me to break away from the pressure to post. And while consistency is a good form of discipline to practice, I now understood the value of sharing content that carries substance.

So, my encouragement to you is to be obedient to the voice of

God. If He wants to keep you hidden for a season, trust that it is for a greater reason, that may not immediately make sense.

Social Media Fasts

Fasting from social media is beneficial and something that I would encourage others to try and do at some point. There are several reasons to abstain from social media from time to time. Some of them being; to escape the comparison trap, to alleviate the pressure to post, to enjoy better sleep but most importantly, to be present in the now, refocus and spend more time in the presence of God. Social media fasts have helped me stay in my lane and focus more specifically on my calling and goals. It may be easier to step away from social media if you do not run a business via these platforms, but if you do, having a strict allocated time to engage with your online community can also be beneficial.

Hiding Ourselves

The other form of hiding is when we deliberately or unconsciously do things to become obscure. Whether that be hiding away entirely or keeping parts of ourselves that we do not want anyone to see thoroughly tucked away.
I've come to understand that when we hide and shrink ourselves, it can be a defence mechanism to make ourselves

feel safe and be out of sight of people's disapproval or the fear of not being accepted by others as we are.

Personally, for me, being seen by people was something that gave me anxiety at one stage. I would often hide because I was afraid of people becoming aware of what I hated about myself. One of my biggest fears was someone confirming everything that I hated about myself because, in my mind, that would have meant that my negative thoughts were true. Thinking this way led me to adapt safety behaviours to help me feel safe, i.e. avoiding mirrors, avoiding being filmed or photographed, and even avoiding certain hairstyles that showed my whole face. Thankfully I can laugh about this now and thank God for who I am, for healing me and shutting down the lies I once believed because the thought of using my hair as some cloaking device out of fear lets me know the devil is a liar!

My time away from social media lasted five years; I battled with Body Dysmorphic Disorder and Bulimia for two of those years. While I was still very fragile for three of the years, I had gone through therapy and was finally healing when I came to Christ at the end of those five years. It was very apparent that my hiding in God season was over when the Lord put me on national daytime TV to share my story of BDD. I felt anxious that day because I was scared of being scrutinised by people and potentially confirming what I had thought about myself for so many years. To add to that, it was also the first time a lot of people, especially my parents, would learn of everything that I had been going through. I did not immediately realise this opportunity to share my story on national television shamed the devil and glorified God. I was a baby Christian, having been saved for two weeks at this point, but I believe this moment was a catalyst for the days that followed. I no longer lived in secrecy about battling with my image, and more beautifully, it allowed many other people who watched the interview to see that they were not alone and that there was hope.

Knowing the impact my experience carried vividly reminded me of Matthew 5:16, which says, "In the same way, let your light shine before others, that they may see your good deeds and glorify your Father in heaven". If I chose to dim my light that day and live in fear of the possibility of scrutinising people, the opportunity to glorify God would have been missed, and those in need would not have received hope or understanding of their symptoms. The fear of man is real, but God and His undefeatable power can rescue us from the lies and hurt that sometimes grip us in life.

I have learned that people will love you one day and then

desire to cancel you the next day. So, it goes back to knowing who you are and whose you are; otherwise, if you are building yourself up based on the opinion of others, you will be building your identity on the sand and end up sinking. Why not be built up with a strong foundation in Jesus Christ, whose opinion will never change and who loves you not just on one day but every day? Whose opinion matters the most to you? Is it a human's or God's opinion?

Depending on which answer you give, it may just show you whose approval you are seeking after. And let me not get started on social media followers! As you would have learned about me so far, rejection was something I battled with for so long. So, being unfollowed was something I would take personally. It would offend and hurt me as I would make it about me and question my worth if my following went down. I can only imagine the level of pride that could have risen if I gained a high follower count without first being refined and dealing with deep-rooted issues. My followers did drop through my deliverance and time away, but I refused to allow it to make me come back and prove myself or rush getting back on to look like I was doing something before the right time and season permitted. I have also had to ensure I never allowed any of my platforms or success to cause me to think that I am better than anyone who has fewer followers than me or any less than anyone who has more followers than me. It is saddening how easy and often people measure the value and success of another based on their number of followers. When in reality, when life is all said and done, will it even matter? No! Because no one is getting into heaven based on how many followers we have.

Shame

Oftentimes shame can be a part of the root cause of why we hide away from people. Brene Brown states in her book, The Gifts of Imperfection, "Shame is basically the fear of being unlovable" (Brown, 2010, p.39). She then goes on to say that "Shame is the intensely painful feeling or experience of believing that we are flawed and therefore unworthy of love and belonging" (Brown, 2010, p.39). As humans, we all have something in common, and that is the basic need for love. Wanting to be accepted and received by others is something we all experience.

An example I can share is the anxiousness I would feel when posting on YouTube. My heart would race every single time as my thoughts flooded with what people would say, but I would shut down the noise with the word of God and make His voice louder. Shame does not come from God; Romans 5:8 states, "but God demonstrates His own love for us in this:

While we were still sinners, Christ died for us". This verse tells me that God still loved us enough to send His son to die for us despite the wrongs that we have done. So, we need not shrink back or feel unworthy of love because God loves us and always will, and even if others do not love us, that is okay because His children's names are known in heaven regardless.

Vulnerability

Being present on social media requires a level of vulnerability, which refers to the state of being exposed to the possibility of attack, harm, either physically or emotionally. Being yourself means being vulnerable, it means taking that risk and not holding back. It means being brave and ready to face whatever comes along the way despite how you may feel at the time. It is easy to avoid this by pretending to be someone else, but pretending robs others of experiencing your authenticity and connecting with the person God created you to be. I now understand why this should not be wasted.

I have found every time I have been vulnerable, it has empowered me because I took the risk and survived each time with the safety and guidance of the Holy Spirit, and it made me stronger. I also found that anything the Holy Spirit led me to share presented a relatable "me too" connection with other individuals that had experienced similar things. In this, they gained some hope in knowing they were not the only ones and that there is light at the end of the tunnel. Of course, you do not have to share everything or be vulnerable with everyone on or offline. I truly believe the Holy Spirit is a great leader in helping you know what to share and what to keep for yourself.

Nowadays, everybody and their cat are on social media! It is said that 3.1 billion people are on social media as of 2021, so can you imagine how much that number will increase over the years to come (Karsay, Knoll and Matthes, 2017). When considering how many people use social media, there must be some good reasons right? Social media is a great way to connect with friends and like-minded individuals, and it gives a platform for people to express and share their creativity with others. Furthermore, it is a fantastic way to spread the gospel worldwide, highlight social awareness, keep updated with world news, and laugh and scroll through memes. There are, however, always two sides to a coin. Although I can admit that social media has its pros, it would be unrealistic not to point out that it also has its cons.

Social Media as A Distraction

A distraction is something that stops you from focusing on something else. Timelines on Instagram are endless, and at points, I would find myself saying, "Okay, I'm just going to check my DM's", then before I know it, I have completely forgotten why I had initially signed in.

It is also a massive distraction from the reality that we live in; it is almost like an alternative world plastered with people living their quote on quote 'best lives'. It can be a golden gateway to covetousness and comparison, especially if you are discontent with any area of your life. Although social media allows us to express who we are, it also allows us to become characters that are a part of this alternative world.

One of the reasons I knew I had to write this book was because I wanted to show you how easy it can be to think that the only way things can be great for you and work out well, is to do what everyone else is doing. So when I stepped out to pursue the vision the Lord gave me, to help women build confidence and show them how to nurture their bodies through fitness, it started with pure motives. However, as time went on, I believe that I began to get distracted and slowly become influenced by the sexual objectification of the fitness industry and unintentionally encourage the continuity of social standards of body image.

Photoshopped Bodies, Filters & Angles!
It is easy and sometimes subconscious to compare yourself to

someone you have seen on social media or aspire to be like someone simply from what they post. The alarming thing about this is that there is a high percentage of what you compare yourself to that isn't even real. In turn, many find themselves aspiring to something unattainable.

Knowing your angles in photos is great, and I know the ones that look super cute and work for me, but I also know which of them I used to show off my figure blatantly. That is not to say that I should have been hiding my body and just taken pictures of my face only. But again, my motivation behind why I thought it would have been a good idea to post certain pictures was not pure.

Filters can be fun to use, and I used to love the flower headband on Snapchat and the dog filter that every girl used obsessively whilst miming a song! Besides the fun aspect of using filters, there were so many that would slim down your face and facial features, smooth and blend out blemishes, lighten your skin tone or alter your facial features in some way, shape or form. I found that I would put a filter on simply because it made me look cute, but I also found myself doing it because I did not want to be seen in a particular state. Filters on social media platforms have their downside, and becoming reliant on using them may indicate insecurity. I'm not against filters and think using them in moderation is perfectly fine. But again, for me, it comes down to my motives. It is not always going to be this deep for everyone, but I will always check my heart before editing or posting anything. Ask yourself truthfully; are you using the filter because it accentuates and compliments your photo? Are you using it because you cannot stand any picture of yourself without a filter and do not think you look good enough without one? I don't know about you, but the thought of always having to filter and edit images could create a vicious cycle that only makes you feel worse about yourself and reinforces negative self-beliefs. And in all seriousness, all the likes in the world won't help that.

The 'ideal' body is very subjective; different cultures, standards, and trends significantly affect this. For example, in Mauritania, which is in West Africa, women are put through a practice called leblouh which is intensive force-feeding. This practice is observed because of a belief that the fatter a woman is, the more beautiful she is because her size symbolises her husband's wealth and is physical proof that he has enough riches to feed her well. In contrast, the western standards of beauty and the ideal body image of being super skinny with big breasts and a thigh gap is seen as the perfect prototype. However, I don't know if it is just me, but the trend that perhaps I've witnessed on a whole different level is the slim waist, thick thighs, with a big bottom to match. Although this is commonly the natural physique of a black women's body, we have seen celebrities like J-Lo, Kim Kardashian and Nicki Minaj bring more attention to being curvy.

A few years ago, unless you had Kim K money or your genes set up that way, no matter how many squats you did, that body standard was unattainable. But today, surgery is a lot easier to access, and we are seeing more and more young women, in particular on social media who are influencers and models flexing their BBL's (Brazilian Butt Lifts). I do not aim to cast shame; however, many celebrities and influencers are not always honest about their bodies. Many have falsely claimed to have achieved their shape using slimming teas, wearing waist trainers and working out, which is highly misleading if they went under the knife. I fell for this big-time during my time of being obsessed with gaining weight. My motivation was video vixens who had surgery, so what was I hoping to achieve? Something that was not even real! When I realised why I was chasing this body, it made me realise the perception I had of myself needed work.

The thing with surgery is that one may decide to get it done, but if the reason behind it is from a wounded place, it may be better to work on that instead. We frequently see that physically changing the body does not always change what is going on mentally. The result can lead to additional surgery to modify the body further because happiness has not been attained. I believe what tends to be overlooked is the real source of the problem, not the body; instead, it is the mind. To add to this, we cannot forget the dangers that come with surgeries like excessive blood loss, bruising, stretch marks, infection, blood clots, cardiac and pulmonary complications, deep vein thrombosis and death.

It is vital to remember to work with the body that God has gifted you with and understand that we are all built differently. How our bodies respond to exercise and nutrition will indeed differ, and that is okay! Through my personal training skills, I never sell people dreams about doing a 30-day challenge to grow a booty because, first and foremost, it won't work for everyone as we all have different genes. Some girls can lift 10x their body weight and still won't grow a bum, but should anyone care? Be confident with what you have got; it does not make you any less or more of a woman, nor does it reduce or heighten your position as a daughter of God. It can be hard when the 'perfect body image' is plastered around, but be determined to renew your mind. Fill it with the truth of God's word and remember your worth is not based on your physical appearance.

May I also break it to you that waist trainers are a waste of time in my humble opinion! I would not recommend buying one or even putting the one you may already own back on. The results are temporary, and if you wear them over a long period, you can cause health problems. The safest advice I can give is to clean up your diet and exercise regularly. Your body can be in its best shape and remain healthy through better eating habits and working out. Just keep the motives in check!

CHAPTER 9
Sexual Objectification

Having read about the journey I have had with my body in earlier chapters, you may have gathered that I did not always view my body as a temple of the Holy Spirit or something that God took His time to create. Not only did I despise my physical appearance, but I grew up not knowing my worth or value, thus allowing my body to be used in a manner contrary to the way God intended for it to be used. Being exposed to sex at an early age and experiencing relationships solely built on sex brought a lot of attention to my body from both men and women. At the time, allowing men to use and view my body whenever and however they pleased did not seem that abnormal because of the early exposure. So, walking down the street and having men notice my bum then do a U-turn to talk to me did not shock me, rather helped fuel the notion that my body was an object and the basis that I was deemed worthy of attention.

Objectification can be described as referring to someone as less than human or literally an object. I find it a destructive, dehumanising and demeaning act as it seeks to reduce a person's worth. Sexual objectification, on the other hand, uses a person as a mere object of sexual desire, and over time I began to ponder the effects these acts had on my own and other women's lives.

Finding someone physically attractive is natural for any human being. I'll go further to add that within a marriage, aside from Christ being the foundation, I think being sexually attractive to your spouse is of importance. However, when it comes to wanting someone just for their body and nothing else but for your selfish desires, we see the manifestation of lust and sexual objectification; there is no substance. Sexual objectification is not a new concept, but now more than ever, it is something I see every day, to the point of desensitisation. Seeing scantily clad women day in day out in all manner of provocative ways will have that effect.

As a result of objectification, I began to experience self-objectification and admittedly confess to viewing myself as an object first and a human being second. Self-objectification occurs when you evaluate yourself based on your appearance because that is the way others view you. It can provoke shame, appearance anxiety, depression and eating disorders. I have experienced all of these. I continuously wanted to adapt my body in the hopes of one day becoming 'enough', which was an endless rat race.

I was blind; I would purposefully have my breasts lifted and squashed together to accentuate their size and show cleavage, as well as posing specifically to show off my curves. The motive, in my mind, was to look sexy and show off all that I had. Deep down, however, it was a result of being used to attract attention because of my body, not my personality or character. The men I drew in would not want anything more than to have me as a sex buddy. I did not know who I was, so I ascribed to unconsciously being a sexual object. When I gave my life to Christ, I became convicted about things I would wear and how I presented myself. However, it was not until 2019 when the Lord showed me I was wearing a dead person's garment (the deceased person being the old me that died in

2015 when I renounced my old way of life) and why I was still wearing those clothes. Was I attached and unable to let go of the attention I received as the old Carla? I know better now and that I truly am more than my body. I came to understand my position as a daughter of Christ, as a respectable woman with a unique personality and character. Reflecting this in my outfit choices had to match up.

Something that burdens my heart in the present day is the hypersexualisation of young girls. With life moving fast and sex being introduced to the younger generation in extremely unhealthy settings, these innocent girls are growing up before their time. The scary thing about it, is hypersexualisation over time becomes 'normal'. In today's society, sexual material such as softcore porn is easily accessible and even imposed on young girls. Soft porn refers to pornography that shows or describes sex in a non-violent, vulgar manner or detailed way. Still, whether it is softcore or hardcore, it is detrimental and should be avoided as a whole.

I took steps to guard myself against being desensitised and unfollowed a popular clothing brand, because of the images of half-naked women posing in suggestive manners. I get they want to sell their products, but it is far too sexual! It is this type of content these young girls consume every day subconsciously and consciously. I can only imagine the influence it has on their impressionable minds.

To many, it may seem harmless, but it sends out the wrong message that the more you reveal your body, the more attention you will get and the more famous you become. It is dangerously wrong. Social media platforms like Instagram, Twitter, Tik Tok and Snapchat are platforms many young girls use daily. If their eye gates aren't flooded with sexual content, they are potentially vulnerable to online predators. According to the NSPCC, in 2019 over 5,000 online grooming offences were recorded over 18 months and there was a 200% rise in recorded instances in the use of Instagram to target and abuse children over the same period (NSPCC, 2019). These statistics are shocking, and I cannot help but think of the trauma, shame and brokenness that follows such events, as these young girls are unknowingly preyed upon by these predators.

We can also see how sexual objectification plays out throughout society; in advertisements, video games, magazines, movies, music videos, social media, television programmes and reality TV shows. An example is the 'headless woman', where images or videos, only the body would be displayed or marketed and purposely not revealing the face, which plays into the toxic idea of women being nothing more than their body.

Some forms and experiences of sexual objectification can be easily identifiable, but others are not always that easy to recognise. Some women do not realise that they are sexually objectified because they've become desensitised and, as a result, subconsciously accept it as normal behaviour. Women who have also experienced sexual trauma, come from a broken home, have father issues, emotional wounds and lack identity, or self-worth may display signs of their trauma through overly sexual behaviour.

Some women may feel that dressing provocatively is honourable because their self-esteem and security have unfortunately been attached to what they wear. However, it does not help the battle, when the glamourisation of being overtly sexual, promiscuous through language, clothing, imagery and music is not only socially acceptable, but championed as a sense of women empowerment. The truth is a woman's body is something we ought to praise God for because we come in many shapes, sizes, shades and have the miraculous ability to bring forth children from our wombs; amongst many other amazing things.

I think both men and women fail to realise the psychological harm sexual objectification can cause. The more a woman is on the receiving end of sexual objectification, the more her view is distorted. Thus, she unknowingly comes into false agreement about her value, resulting in self-objectification, and a vicious cycle begins.

I once had very low self-esteem, so I would crave attention and affirmation from people to fill my void. Therefore, anytime someone noticed me, whether genuine and harmless or vulgar and demeaning, the attention gave me a temporary boost. Of course, I'm not saying compliments and kind words shouldn't make you feel good, but in my case, if no one acknowledged me or complimented me, I would question myself and feel empty.

I can recall a time I overheard a boy passing a comment about me to his friend by saying something along the lines of 'I would sleep with that'. Looking back, I shake my head at the audacity of being referred to as 'that'. But I shake my head more at myself because although I knew that he was behaving disrespectfully, a part of me sadly liked the fact that a boy would want me in that way.

Over the years, as the Holy Spirit worked on my mind and sharpened my discernment. Red alarm bells started going off in my head when He made me aware of flattery, which refers to excessive and insincere praise given especially to further one's interest. In my case, flattery worked as I never believed in or saw myself as beautiful. So, whenever someone else complimented me, it gave me a sense of validation. With this, it was as if men with impure intentions could smell my vulnerabilities and insecurities and would rope me in with their showers of flattery.

Through my journey of walking with Christ and allowing Him to shed off old layers and destroy lies I believed about myself, I have now seen that I do not need anyone to tell me I am beautiful, because I have a Heavenly Father who accepts me and affirms my beauty through His word. Now, when approached with flattery, I already know what God told me and how I now feel about myself. Consequently, regardless of what they may think, I am beautiful whether they acknowledge me or not.

Sexual Objectification on Social Media

According to the APA, the media found that girls are depicted sexually more often than boys, dressed in revealing clothing and bodily postures or facial expressions that imply sexual readiness. And if you were to scroll through your social timelines, would you agree?

Sexual Objectification through History and in Today's Society

Back in 2012, I used to learn a lot from watching male bodybuilding videos. I found the fitness industry generally male saturated, and it was not common to find feminine looking women who lifted weights. When I created my Instagram account in 2015, I began to see and be inspired by women like Mankofit, Get Bodied By J, Scola and Brittney Babe, who were gorgeous and strong women that had a large and growing audience. However, there were women online that I admired that had the typical hourglass figures and took the odd gym picture here and there. Still, from what I remember, there was not a flood of half-naked women and booty building programmes and random influencers promoting fitness products that do not work out like there is now. I got to the point of unfollowing certain pages filled with bikini or tiny outfit workouts, which I felt were turning exercises into something sexual or making claims to have worked out, but had gotten BBL's (Brazilian Butt Lifts).

According to a study published by The American Journal of Psychiatry, social media has "amplified age-old pressures for teenage girls to conform to certain sexualised narratives" (Swift and Gould, 2021). Women talk less after thinking about being sexually objectified, experience more shame, and perform worse on cognitive tasks (Heflick, 2016). Such objectification from others also increases focus on one's appearance, which has been found to do (or relate to) a whole host of negative things among women.

Ephesians 2:10 in the NKJV translation says, "For we are His workmanship" while the NLT translation says, "For we are God's masterpiece". Workmanship referring to the degree of skill of which something is made, and masterpiece refers to a work of outstanding artistry; both words interlink. I often meditate on this scripture, and it is a powerful reminder that God skillfully and thoughtfully created you and I. He made us with emotions, personality, and the ability to think and reason, which is the opposite of objectification. So, if there is one thing I want to use this opportunity to encourage you as you read, it is that you are not a spit roast or a slab of meat to satisfy anyone's degrading sexual appetite.

Dear Lord,

Thank You for your daughter. I pray that you grant her the understanding that she is not of this world and is just passing through. Thank You that she is a new creation, and her mind is renewed in You. I ask that by the power of Your word, Your daughter experiences transformation. May she reject the standards of this world that feed her lies about her body. Empower her to believe that she is more than enough and requires no validation from any human. Increase her faith to know she is acknowledged, valued and loved by You, from the moment she rises in the morning until she safely rests in You at night, in Jesus name, Amen.

CHAPTER 10
Comparison

Comparison is the thief of joy and how I know it so well! How often have we, as women, compared ourselves to one another? If I speak for myself, I indeed have fallen into this pit hole of a trap time and time again. Playing the comparison game either gave me a five-second high (which may I add was never a good thing, as it was a form of arrogance which I will get into later), or most of the time, it left me feeling like I was not enough.

Comparison is defined as analysing the similarities and differences between two things or people.

Examples of comparison are:

"Ugh! Her waist is much smaller than mine, and my waist is so wide."

"I am much prettier than her", "she is so beautiful, and I am ugly compared to her."

"She's married, and I'm not; she must have more value than I do."

The way I would frequently compare myself to other women was in the area of physical appearance. Just above, I gave a few examples to show how comparison can enforce a sense of inferiority and superiority. Whether you verbalise such comparisons or mentally think about these things in your mind, both are counterproductive and open the door to many problems. Envy and haughtiness are some of those problems, and let's not sugar coat these ugly things and call a spade a spade; better still, a sin a sin.

Envy

To be envious is to wish that you had something that another person possesses. It can also be referred to as covetousness. I have undoubtedly fallen short and have been envious of others before. The sad thing about envy is it reveals a level of discontentment and drains you of contentment in Christ, while welcoming idolatry. Whenever I found myself being envious, it showed me that I was under a pretence that I lacked something when, in fact, I was internally saying Christ was not enough for me to make me complete or content. I would go as far as to call it a direct insult to God, who created me in His image, that He was somehow not creative enough.

Not dealing with the root issue could find you trying to be someone you are not or chasing after things you think will make you happier or more attractive because someone else has it. In reality, all you are doing is setting yourself up to take a ride on a very vicious and toxic cycle. For example, being envious of someone can lead to you devaluing them by making petty criticisms, belittling qualities of a person you may believe other people admire about them. This behaviour is a form of defence, due to the fear of feeling inadequate, but ultimately it is destructive.

The truth is, even if you did attain what you envied a person for, you would find very quickly that it does not remedy the void. Before long, you'll move on to the next thing to try and make yourself feel better.

Haughtiness

Haughtiness is defined as the appearance or quality of being arrogantly superior and disdainful, which I legitimately shivered at as I studied the meaning. I found it sobering during my learning about this word, that God showed me how I behaved haughtily. I may not have spoken out loud, but my thoughts were evidence.

I would sometimes go for a workout at the gym and find myself comparing my body to other girls' bodies, and in particular their bums. I would estimate that my bum was bigger than theirs, so I looked better than them. This made me feel that I had some form of superiority over them. But, again, it is that thing of putting someone down to elevate yourself.

Proverbs 16:18 says, "Pride goes before destruction, and a haughty spirit before a fall". Listen! I (once again) had to repent and ask God to forgive and help me deal with this wretched trait. I was walking in dangerous waters with this arrogant attitude, and it is clear that a haughty spirit only leads to a negative end.

Looking back, I can see how that was rooted in insecurity and a wrong perspective of identity. I had internalised that a 'big bum' and a 'body' was what defined me. I would often wait for someone to say something and compliment me on the size of my bum, because that is all that people would notice about me or comment on (both male and female). When people did not see or say something about the size of my bum, I would tend to conclude that perhaps it was not that big, and I would re-evaluate my value, which is extremely shallow and sad.

Comparison encourages low self-esteem and is always a losing game because we are all different. If we took the time to ponder on the fact that we are all one of a kind, we would find that comparison is pointless. It is like comparing a pear to a melon; yes, both are fruits, but they are uniquely different in appearance and taste. We must begin to own and embrace every aspect of ourselves, instead of striving to be like another human, as we run away from who we are when we do this.

Over time, I began to analyse where my value came from, because if my sense of worth came from how I measured up to others, I would be living a miserable and unstable life.

Repeating the opening sentence to this chapter, where I stated that comparison is the thief of all joy, is a fact, point, blank, period.

Comparing causes you to overvalue what someone else has and consequently devalue what you have. It is essential to actively remember that just because someone looks different to you or has something you do not have, does not mean that they are more blessed or better. As I have grown and developed, I have learned to recognise and quickly eliminate any hint of comparison that attempts to creep in.

A scripture that comes to mind that I like to refer to comes from 2 Corinthians 10:5, which says, "casting down arguments and every high thing that exalts itself against the knowledge of God, bringing every thought into captivity to the obedience of Christ". I find capturing those thoughts of comparison and casting them down instead of letting them run wild effectively keeps my identity secure. From an authority standpoint, those thoughts do not have power over me unless I allow them to.

I also found that being vulnerable and honest with God and confessing envious emotions, when I have given the power to the thoughts, allowed me to be free from such views and feelings. Lovingly, God always showed me where the ideas stemmed from and would help me to overcome them. Colossians 2:10, says "So you also are complete through your union with Christ, who is the head over every ruler and authority", which always reminds me that I am complete in Christ and speaking this truth over myself silences comparison.

In Genesis 1:26, God says, "Let Us make man in Our image, according to Our likeness". God created us to be a reflection of His glory. I find this genuinely mind-blowing and the reason why I believe the only One we should look to is Him.

I want to add that being a believer of Jesus Christ means we have an enemy, the devil who deeply hates us with a perfect hatred and has a plan to do all he can to make us miserable. John 10:10 confirms this by saying, "The thief comes only to steal and kill and destroy; I have come that they may have life, and have it to the full". Christ is our only hope and safe place to live out our lives as we should. Therefore, we must strive to have our thoughts aligned to what God says about us. We should seek to love, honour, and glorify God with every part of our bodies and thank Him for His skill and divine ability in creating us. Understand that regardless of the enemy's lies, what society tells you or what bullies have called you, God does not make trash. I love how beautifully 1 Timothy 4:4 puts it, "Since everything God created is good, we should not reject any of it but receive it with thanks". Everything that God created is good, including you and I.

There is power in giving God thanks. It enables us to turn our focus towards God and shift our focus away from how bad we may feel about ourselves and push us into seeing how God sees us. I also found that looking in the mirror and being thankful that my body functions correctly made me more grateful. For example, I would say, "Thank You Lord that I have two eyes to see out of, thank You Lord for giving me two legs to walk with". When you express gratitude to God, you realise just how blessed you are because He made no mistake with you.

CHAPTER 11
Perfectionism

At the end of 2017, I decided to revisit therapy after facing challenging times, which caused unconfronted traumas to resurface. My grandad passed away, and my father suffered a stroke off the back of his battle with drug and alcohol addiction. I found myself in a vulnerable place and knew I needed help. In counselling, I discovered so much about myself that helped me move forward. One of which, was that I was a perfectionist.

I struggled a lot with being unnecessarily defensive because I could not handle criticism, even when it was constructive. For me, being defensive was a protective measure I would take when I felt attacked. It was difficult for me to accept being critiqued because, deep down, it felt like it was confirming lies whispered to me by the enemy that I was not good enough. It also felt like my negative perspective of myself must be true, instead of looking at criticism as a way to get better and improve. Looking back, I think my defensive behaviour was also something that went hand in hand with me being a perfectionist.

Perfection is a personality trait and characteristic defined as the refusal to accept any standard short of being perfect; meaning being without any form of fault whatsoever. It is also having the belief that you genuinely think you can achieve through your own effort.

Some may say that perfectionism can be a good thing because it can help to increase your pursuit of success. However, I beg to differ for the simple fact that perfectionism can be more detrimental to your mental health, lead to defeating thoughts and make succeeding in your goals harder.

I never understood how toxic the perfectionism trait was until it was gently pointed out to me by my counsellor, and I saw how much of a hindrance it was having on my life. Perfectionism is driven by the internal pressure to avoid being judged and feeling shamed. It can lead you to set unrealistic and high expectations for yourself and affect the lens you view others from too. The outcome of this is that you become overly critical about yourself and excessively critical of others and are very quick to find faults and flaws in others. Not only does this cause a cycle of self-sabotaging, but it can also sabotage relationships and cause pain to others.

Perfectionism has many causes; it can come from a frequent fear of the disapproval of others, feeling inadequate and insecure, having parents that are perfectionists or that showed disapproval of you if you achieved anything less than 'perfect'. Having mental health issues like anxiety or Obsessive Compulsive Disorder has been linked to perfectionism too, but not all people diagnosed with OCD are perfectionists.

Some common indicators and traits of perfectionism are:

Having a fear of failure

This is one of the main traits of perfectionism because it tends to tie your identity to your results. Thus, the fear comes from achieving anything less than being perfect. To you this means you have automatically failed and at all costs will do anything to avoid this fear coming true. The issue with this is it can lead to repeatedly putting things off or until the last minute.

Procrastination

Where there is procrastination, you can guarantee perfectionism is lurking around. Procrastination is detrimental to productivity because all you will do is worry about things not being perfect, which means you either do not start or you end up slowing your progress down and becoming stagnant.

Defense

Receiving constructive criticism is a challenge for you because you find it is painful and not what you want to hear.

Results-driven

Instead of enjoying the process of growing and developing whilst achieving your goal or result, all you can think about is the result and the need to avoid the dreaded thought of failure.

Highly critical

You are highly critical, judgmental and hard on yourself. As a result, you tend to spot mistakes and imperfections and stay focused on these, rather than the good things.

Low self-esteem

You are self-critical, have a negative view of yourself, and isolate yourself, leading to loneliness. Your critical nature also plays a part in pushing others away, reinforcing your low self-esteem.

Depressed by unmet goals

You beat yourself up and wallow in negative feelings when your high expectations are not met.

Perfectionism affected me in various ways. You could have called me Miss 'I will do it tomorrow' aka Miss procrastinator. I should not make a joke of it because procrastination is a form of pride. I was assuming that I had tomorrow to do what I knew I needed to do. A verse that slaps me up, down and across my face comes from James 4:14, which says, "Come now, you who say, 'Today or tomorrow we will go into such and such town and spend a year there and make a profit' - Yet you do not know what tomorrow will bring. What is your life? For you are a mist that appears for a little time and then vanishes". Ouch! This is nothing but straight facts. I have procrastinated because I feared failing. I feared the confirmation that I was not good enough if I could not achieve something and realised I made excuses. Although some 'excuses' I do not see as actual excuses in a procrastinating sense, such as waiting until God gives the green light and going through a process before stepping out to do anything. The unacceptable reasons are the, "I need to wait until I'm this first or I can only do that when I have done this first. In essence, the "I need to wait until I am perfect" excuses, which if I continued with this mindset, I would have been living a very stagnant life.

Perfectionism hindered me from sharing the talents that God placed within me to help and encourage others. I was afraid of being vulnerable, which meant baring it all and just being myself, hence the anxiety when posting a video or picture online. Looking back, I can see how it linked to my experience of Body Dysmorphic Disorder, because I consistently saw flaws when I looked in the mirror. I found it very hard to like any other feature as I was obsessed with everything I believed was wrong. It is such an ugly entanglement of issues that can end up destroying your life if not dealt with at the root.

Until this day, I remember my counsellor's words, who told me that there is gold in the journey. I learnt that I could no longer wait until I had arrived at the end of my destination (being the perfect Carla) to share with others. Being a perfectionist is conditional, which means if you do not achieve what you are aiming for, you are not good enough and you are bad. So, I would nit-pick at things, find imperfections that no one else could see, and annoy myself so much because I would remain stuck on the not so perfect things and disregard the good things. I also recognised that because I was so highly critical of myself, I was overly critical of others, which meant I found it hard to extend grace or even give people chances before I cut them off. On a funny note, the Lord knows I had to deal with that mainly because I want to be married one day. Although I have standards, I'm not trying to be the image of that woman that turned into a skeleton covered in cobwebs whilst sitting on a bench waiting for the perfect man (who does not exist)!

There is a Difference Between Perfectionism and Excellence

God is a God of excellence and we are made in His image. There is therefore nothing wrong with wanting to be excellent and do things excellently; however, that does not mean being perfect. Excellence means the desire to attain something of a high standard by doing and being the best that we can be. In comparison to perfectionism, which is driven by the fear of failure and achieving less than perfect, excellence does not sabotage one's self-esteem as it focuses on the process of achievement rather than the outcome.

It is the same reason why I had particular battles in my walk with God, because I was trying to attain this perfect Christian girl image. I fell into the trap that I could earn God's love by trying my best to be perfect so He could love me more. I would try to keep a faultless image and be more like those who were more spiritually mature than I was and who I looked at through a 'perfect' lens. First of all, the only One I should have been pursuing to be like is Christ, because He is the perfect One. Secondly, it is impossible to earn God's love because He first loved us. Thirdly, my efforts were only welcoming condemnation into my life and allowing the devil to have a field day when I kept getting things wrong and falling short. Finally, perfectionism causes you to focus on the end rather than on the journey you are going through.

In all of this, I understood that I could not skip my process and accepted that perfectionism was an issue and a trait that stemmed from a deeper-rooted problem, which was the rejection I have spoken on throughout these chapters. Dealing with that root, which began from childhood, was essential to obtaining healing from the emotional and psychological wounds I endured by my parents. I realised that it is okay to not have it all together and that some choices we make along this journey of life might not always be the best. We may hit bumps along the way but know that each one of us are recipients of His grace. God is not expecting perfection from us after He has healed us from something, nor is He never expecting us to not need comfort and healing again. He understands our imperfections and that is why we desperately need Him so much.

Take comfort in knowing *"that He who began a good work in you will bring it to completion at the day of Jesus Christ"* - Philippians 1:6.

CHAPTER 12
Is Your Body Your Golden Calf?

There are two different extremes that we can fall into regarding how we treat our bodies. Either not taking care of ourselves or taking care of ourselves to excessive levels; both of which can cause lasting damage in the long term.

Idolatry is defined as "the worship of an idol or cult image, being a physical image, such as a statue, or a person in place of God". In other words, idolatry is anything that you choose to place before your relationship with God.

God clearly states that we must not have any other gods except for Himself (Exodus 20:3), and we also find that the first and greatest command is that we are to love the Lord our God with all our heart, with all our soul, and with all our mind (Matthew 22:37). The Lord is jealous of us with godly jealousy (2 Corinthians 11:2), and we provoke Him to jealousy when we begin to replace Him with someone or something else. Now I would like to clarify that His jealousy is not the sinful type of jealousy rooted in covetousness, which is the strong desire to have something that belongs to someone else. His jealousy is godly and righteous, meaning He is provoked to godly jealousy when someone or something takes something that rightfully belongs to Him. God loves you so much that He paid a high price for you, and you can take comfort in knowing that you belong to Him.

The word adoption is defined as the action or fact of legally taking another's child and bringing it up as one's own. Your decision to accept Christ as your Lord and Saviour meant that you became God's child through the spirit of adoption, and you now belong to Him (Galatians 4:5). The high price that He paid was sending His only begotten Son to die for your sins, guilt and condemnation, so why would you ever want to put anyone or anything else before Him? We can find ourselves slipping into sin by worshipping other gods and also giving greater priority and place in our lives to anything other than Christ. The frightening thing is that sometimes we do not even realise that we are doing it because idolatry can take many forms!

Exodus chapter 32 reminds me of how a lack of contentment and putting your complete trust in anything other than God can lead you on destructive and dangerous paths. If you think about all that God did for the Israelites, from setting them free from slavery in Egypt and reading of their complaints and lack of trust in where He was taking them - the children of Israel experienced incredible levels of God's goodness. Yet, they ended up in idolatry by worshipping a golden calf and even dared to exclaim, "O Israel, these are the gods who brought you out of the land of Egypt"?!? Crazy huh?

What if I told you that you could have a golden calf in your life?

Some ways that idolatry can be the golden calf in your life and manifest can be, for example, allowing fear to stop you from obeying what the Lord instructs, therefore placing your fears, personal desires and comfort above the Lord. It can manifest in choosing Netflix over your prayer time, choosing to stay in a relationship with someone that you know the Lord told you to leave, choosing to spend more time on your phone instead of being in the presence of God. Idolatry can manifest in obsessing over success, money, social media, your image, even your belly can be an idol!

I'll be honest, when I realised how easy it could be to slip into the sin that is idolatry, it made me realise that I need not be ignorant to the schemes of the enemy to get so consumed with all of these things. Subsequently, I share this with you and pray you can stay on guard and ask God to continually check and reveal your heart's state.

The Lord made me sit and reflect on my motives behind why I went to the gym. Although I have always been into fitness, like I shared with you at the start of the book, my reasons behind why I went so hard to work out, gradually became ironically unhealthy and quite toxic. The Lord has been walking with me on my journey of becoming secure in my identity in Him. He showed me what was in my heart in regards to my body and working out. The Lord told me that I still had a false sense of identity and that my identity was caught up in my physical appearance, which was a snare. He said, "This isn't who Carla is…Your identity is NOT found in your physical appearance." It was bittersweet hearing this; I found it painful because I genuinely thought I was finally okay with my body image, and yet I was grateful because I knew God had revealed this to me to bring further healing and security in who He says I am.

The Lord also showed me that my body was an idol when He led me to fast and I was resisting the instruction because I became anxious about losing weight, losing my curves and being a 'bag of bones'. It is important to note that you can dislike your body, and it can still be an idol, especially if you obsess over it and let your dislikes take over your life and hinder your relationship with God. Being more concerned with the changes that could happen to my body over being obedient to God showed me there was something wrong. I would feel anxious and worry over losing weight from fasting and battled with the thought that I would not be able to work out. I became bothered about the possibility that people may begin to notice my weight loss and start to point out how skinny I had gotten. I had to repent. I knew I needed to ask God for His forgiveness because I was willing to disobey and choose my body image over Him.

Your Idols Will Always Fail You in The End

"Lest Satan should take advantage of us; for we are not ignorant of his devices" - 2 Corinthians 2:11. Idolatry is one of the devil's devices that he uses to turn us away from God, and as you have seen from my experience, it can come from the things you least expect. The thing is every idol that we chose to replace God with comes with a false sense of security. Imagine if I continued to place confidence in my body, and God forbid I became physically disfigured? My body would no longer provide me with security, and because I depend on it to define a part of who I am, I would be left in a broken, insecure and hopeless place.

The process of God helping me understand and become secure in my identity meant things within me that tainted my true identity would always come to the surface. And that is why it is so important to know your identity in Christ and allow God's truth to be the foundation of who you are because He is consistent, never changing and never fails. Once I began to affirm myself in God's word, I found myself accepting and adapting to the way my body would change when I fasted because whether I am skinny, curvy or whatever else, it will never change how God sees me. In the eyes of God, I will always be beautiful and who I am is not based on my body.

Eventually, I stopped getting anxious about missing a couple of days in the gym to fast and started taking days off if I knew my body needed rest.

Gluttony

Gluttony is defined as habitual greed or excess in eating. I have to be honest, I have been a glutton. Sometimes, I would find myself already full, but still get a second and third helping of food, knowing that I did not need to eat anymore. I knew this because each time I was a glutton, I ended up with a potbelly, stomach ache, and it was always painful to breathe correctly because my stomach was so full. There is a difference between being super hungry and needing to refuel your body and just eating for the sake of eating when you know you do not need to eat anything else. Gluttony has some consequences, as not only does it can make you feel sick, it can lead to obesity and ultimately counts as sin.

CHAPTER 13
My Journey with the Holy Spirit

In 2015, I knew I would one day become an author and the journey to fulfil this began that same year in July, with the plan to publish my debut title by July 2016.

Many are the plans in a man's heart, but it is the LORD's purpose that prevails - Proverbs 19:21

I did not realise that it would take almost six years for this book to be written. You reading my story is a testament to the faithfulness of God, to whom all praise is due! The woman I was in 2015, fresh into the Christian faith at the age of twenty-two, is not the same woman I am today. I had my plans, but God's plans for me went forth. I can genuinely say I am thankful for that, because He knew what He was doing and why.

According to my schedule, my book was to be published in 2016, but evidently, that did not happen. Three years later, in 2019, I told myself that I was not finishing the year without completing the manuscript, and instead of printing a paperback book, I decided I wanted to change it into an eBook. I was rushing the process and wrote to write. Nothing was flowing from a place of authenticity, but a place of pride because being busy made me feel like I was somebody, and God was not at the centre of my writing process. It was not long before I sensed a big red stop sign to pause; specifically on how I was writing my story because the reality was, I was not ready to publish the book. I was still going through pruning and refinement, and releasing the book any sooner would have lacked God's approval and ultimately would have been a disobedient move to make. And so, I waited.

In July 2019, I began a journal titled "Lord, who am I?" to document my journey on seeking God regarding my identity.

I was determined to seek Him to find out who I was, because I was still battling some things.

A Season of Beautifying

On Sunday, 29th September 2019, I received a prophecy that I am still in awe of today, because it gave context to what I had been going through and what was to come. Part of it I can share with you, is that God was processing, beautifying, adorning and dressing me for my destiny and future.

Upon reflection, I thought about beauty and its subjectiveness, because everyone views beauty differently.

The dictionary definition of beauty is: "A combination of qualities, such as shape, colour, or form, that pleases the aesthetic senses, especially the sight".

With God, beauty is more than outward appearance when it concerns us as humans. He cares more about our inner beauty and the condition of our soul. A person can be physically beautiful but can, for example, have a terrible attitude and unrefined character, making them seem less attractive. What is the point of only working on your outward appearance and neglecting your soul? External beauty may fade, but inner beauty is what lasts. I am not saying we should ignore our bodies; after all, nurturing our bodies the right way is part of the inspiration as to why I wrote this book. However, I am saying do not rely on your outward beauty to get you through life. Instead, aim to develop substance by working inwardly too, which is a lesson I have been taught and still perfecting.

Things Began to Change

On Sunday 6th October 2019, to be blunt, I was fed up and wanted to die. I had just celebrated my birthday and the Lord highlighted some cracks in my relationship with Him that affected my identity. At this point, I was over it and wanted to give up! It was tiring to realise there was still residue because I had overcome so much. However, God revealed a few open doors that I was unaware of and a cycle of dysfunction I was still in. The battle to understand God's love for me was ongoing and distorted how I viewed Him as a loving Father. I wanted to want God's love more than I wanted a man's love, but I still struggled with this area of my life, and I remember feeling very low the weekend after my birthday party.

I Felt Empty

What put the nail in the coffin was being triggered by a guy who was sending me mixed signals. It was on that Sunday that I could not deal with the apprehension of not knowing where I stood with him anymore and decided to nip it in the bud there and then. When I approached him about it, he told me he did not see me like that. It felt like a blow to the stomach! I had secretly thought I was not good enough for him, and he was out of my league, so it felt like confirmation of my thoughts. At that point, I abruptly ended the conversation, cut off all possible forms of contact, and emotionally broke down. I had had enough of everything and recalled texting a friend saying that I would kill myself if I never feared God and going to hell!

The next day was Monday 7th October 2019, and my church was doing a 3-day fast. A couple of weeks prior, I received a prophetic word that I was to live a lifestyle of fasting and was in the process of being beautified and dressed for my future. As encouraging as this prophecy was, I questioned the whole fasting thing. However, I chose obedience and made the sacrifice to fast, and it was a day I can never forget. I was tired, desperate for help and begged God to fix me. I wailed, screamed and cried so much in a way I did not know was humanly possible. I had been mentally tormented all year and experienced numerous occasions where I believed it was better to be dead. I never realised from that day onwards that things were about to break off of me. The only way I can describe what happened, is that it was as if I had entered into a three-day spiritual surgery. I was delivered.

The Holy Spirit took me on a journey and showed me how I had made my body an idol. He showed me the false sense of identity I had, which became entangled in my physical appearance. To date, at times, I have to pull down the feelings of shame, guilt and condemning thoughts about my body because, as a Christian woman, I felt having a curvy figure made my body too sexual and would encourage lust even when dressed modestly. I often thought that if I were skinnier with less shape, I would be deemed more holy and pure. I lacked the understanding that purity and modesty are a condition of the heart and expressed in how we conduct our lives. As a result of this mindset, my response of shrinking myself in Church and around those I fellowshipped with was an exterior display of my inner questioning of why God created me the way He did.

Lovingly, God responded to my silent musings with, "This isn't who Carla is". He showed me from inception that my fitness journey had the wrong motives, and part of my self-worth was attached to having a curvy body, which led me to repent. He helped me to understand that I could no longer teach fitness from ignorance and a damaged perspective. As I journaled in this season, I received the revelation that I have been gifted to minister to women through fitness. Not to solely help them achieve a perky bum, washboard abs or reinforce the pursuit to attain unrealistic body goals, but a responsibility to teach women to look after their bodies for the sake of glorifying God. I was encouraged and empowered by the Holy Spirit to live what I teach. That meant being delivered before I can be adequately equipped to help others.

Walking out my calling was never going to work doing things my way, so I surrendered to His ways and let go of the areas of my life that I had still been holding on to. I was determined to stop delaying my destiny and desired to build my fitness brand the way God saw fit, no pun intended. Upon releasing my thoughts, plans and expectations into God's hands, it was as if the gavel dropped and every weight and pain from my past was sentenced to death. Over three days, I experienced a miraculous shift and have never been the same since!

I meditated on 2 Corinthians 5:17, which says, "Therefore if anyone is in Christ, he is a new creation; old things passed away; behold, new things have come". It is a verse of scripture etched in my memory from the day I was baptised, but something about it was different in this season of my life.

Having the correct understanding of scripture is crucial to activate and declare it over your life. I was now in a position to genuinely speak this word over myself, because the old things were gone, and I had become a new creation in Christ, and no one can tell me otherwise!

Becoming new in Christ means to die to your former self, and I'm reminded of the scripture that says, "If fully you cling to your life, you will lose it; but if you give up your life for Me, you will find it" from Matthew 10:39. When I think of a portion of my life and the struggles I went through, I realise holding onto my life, my ideologies and every other dead weight were killing me, but the moment I gave it all up and trusted God, I found myself and felt alive. But it does not stop there; when you give up your old ways, it's vital not to resuscitate and bring them back to life. For me, this meant adjusting my gym clothes and other items I owned, along with erasing some of my Instagram posts. This decision came as a conviction, and one I did squint at initially. Still, understanding that God always has my best interests at heart, I did not object but instead appreciated the reminder and encouragement to walk in my newness of life.

These life changes may seem minor, 'not that deep' or laughable to some, but I'll use this opportunity to insert that just because you have won the battle in an area, does not mean it is ok or wise to visit the area battleground. So, if you need to throw out some outfits for the sake of continuing to walk in freedom, do it! Or, if you need to refrain from being on social media entirely, again, I say do it because only you and the Holy Spirit know the depths of the challenges that have been overcome. Additionally, having empowerment from the Holy Spirit is an invaluable source of help, because trying to modify your behaviour or decisions in your own power is futile.

Galatians 3:3 says, "How foolish can you be? After starting your new lives in the Spirit, why are you now trying to become perfect by your own human effort?" I share this verse to say I have lived out every chapter of this book, and God allowed me to experience deliverance and healing throughout this writing process. Having submitted to His direction and taking responsibility for being intentional about my healing, I am now ready to help others. Writing this book allowed me to reflect on where I have come from and reinforced who and whose I am. If I had released this before its time, it would have been a selfishly written eBook with no substance.

Along the way, I have experienced ridicule, mocking and discouragement from people who believed I had fallen off from building my brand. However, what they fail to realise is the vision is bigger than fitness and this book. What God has brought me through and started with me, He will surely bring to completion, and that is a promise. You are reading the words of a woman, committed to Christ, committed to serving and bringing glory to His name. I may not know in every season what that will look like, but I am excited to continue on my journey with the Holy Spirit, and my prayer for you is that if you are yet to give your life to Christ or perhaps want to rededicate your life to Him, you can say this prayer below and begin to live the abundant life God has for you.

Prayer:

Lord, I recognise my need for You and all of the ways I have sinned and fallen short of Your standard. Help me to live a life that is aligned to Your truth and pleasing in Your sight. Forgive me for every way that I have lived outside Your will for me, and I invite Your Holy Spirit to live in me. I believe You died that I may live and that You rose again on the third day. Be Lord of My life and empower me to love You as you deeply love me, in Jesus name, Amen.

Bibliography

Anorexia Bulimia Care (n.d.), *About Eating Disorder: Statistics*, Anorexia Bulimia Care, viewed on 19 May 2021, Available at: https://www.anorexiabulimiacare.org.uk/about/statistics

Beata Lewis MD (2018), *Is Nutritional Deficiency Causing your depression?*, Beata Lewis MD, viewed on 22 May 2021, Available at: https://www.beatalewismd.com/blog/is-nutritional-deficiency-causing-your-depression

Body Dysmorphic Disorder Foundation (n.d.), *How Common is BDD?*, BDDF, viewed on 19 May 2021, Available at: https://bddfoundation.org/information/frequently-asked-questions/how-common-is-bdd/

Brown, B. (2010), *The Gifts Of Imperfection:Let Go Of Who You Think You're Supposed To Be And Embrace Who You Are*, USA: Hazelden, pp.39.

Bupa (n.d.), *Benefits of Exercise*, Bupa, viewed on 20 May 2021, Available at: <https://www.bupa.co.uk/health-information/exercise-fitness/benefits-of-exercise>.

Express (2019), *Average human grows 590 miles of hair and eats 35 tons of food...AMAZING human stats*, Express, viewed on 20 May 2021, Available at: https://www.express.co.uk/news/weird/437344/Average-human-grows-590-miles-of-hair-and-eats-35-tons-of-food-AMAZING-human-stats

Heflick (2016), *How Frequent Is Sexual Objectification?*, Phychology Today, viewed on 16 May 2021, Available at: https://www.psychologytoday.com/gb/blog/the-big-questions/201609/how-frequent-is-sexual-objectification

Help Guide (n.d.), *A Harvard Health article: Vitamins and Minerals*, Help Guide, viewed on 19 June 2021, Available at: https://www.helpguide.org/harvard/vitamins-and-minerals.htm

Karsay K., Knoll J. and Matthes J. (2017), *Sexualizing Media Use and Self-Objectification: A Meta-Analysis*, SAGE Journals, viewed on 17 May 2021, Available at: https://journals.sagepub.com/doi/full/10.1177/0361684317743019

Leal D. (2021), *Choose the Healthiest Salt for Your Kitchen*, Verywellfit, viewed on 15 July 2021, Available at: https://www.verywellfit.com/what-kind-of-salt-is-healthiest-4157937

Mental Health Foundation (2017), *Food for thought: Mental health and nutrition briefing*, Mental Health Foundation, viewed on 22 May 2021, Available at: https://www.mentalhealth.org.uk/sites/default/files/food-for-thought-mental-health-nutrition-briefing-march-2017.pdf

Migala (2020), *7 Health Benefits of Water Backed by Scientific Research*, Everyday Health, viewed on 22 May 2021, Available at: https://www.everydayhealth.com/water-health/water-body-health.aspx

MQ Mental Health (2017), *12 statistics to get you thinking about mental health in young people*, MQ Mental Health 2017, viewed on 15 May 2021, Available at: https://www.mqmentalhealth.orsg/posts/12-statistics

NHS (2019), *The Eatwell Guide*, NHS, viewed on 22 May 2021, Available at: https://www.nhs.uk/live-well/eat-well/the-eatwell-guide/

NHS (2020), *Overview - Bulimia*, NHS, viewed on 17 May 2021, Available at: https://www.nhs.uk/mental-health/conditions/bulimia/overview/

NHS (n.d.), *About Mental Health*, NHS, viewed on 15 May 2021, Available at: https://www.england.nhs.uk/mental-health/about/

NHS (n.d.), *Vitamins*, NHS Camden & Islington NHS Foundation Trust, viewed on 22 May 2021, Available at: https://www.candi.nhs.uk/wellbeing/vitamins

NIH (2018), *Vitamins and Minerals*, National Centre for Complementary and Integrative Health, viewed on 19 June 2021, Available at: https://www.nccih.nih.gov/health/vitamins-and-minerals

NSPCC (2019), *Over 5000 online grooming offenses recorded in 18 months*, viewed 20 June 2021, Available at: https://www.nspcc.org.uk/about-us/news-opinion/2019/over-5000-grooming-offences-recorded-18-months/

Ocdaction (n.d.), *Body Dysmorphic Disorder*, Ocdaction, viewed on 19 May 2021, Available at: https://www.ocdaction.org.uk/support-info/related-disorders/body-dysmorphia

Pharmaceutical Services Negotiating Committee (n.d.), *Essential facts, stats and quotes relating to mental health*, PSNC, viewed on 17 May 2021, Available at: https://psnc.org.uk/services-commissioning/mental-health/

Rehagen T. (2021), *Do Your Part to Lower Your Cholesterol*, WebMD, viewed on 20 June 2021, Available at: https://www.webmd.com/cholesterol-management/cholesterol-lifestyle-changes

Speaking of Women's Health (n.d.), *What We Eat Affects How We Feel*, Speaking of Women's Health, viewed on 23 May 2021, Available at: https://speakingofwomenshealth.com/health-library/what-we-eat-affects-how-we-feel

Stroke Association (n.d.), *Reducing your Risk*, Stroke Association, viewed on 20 May 2021, Available at: https://www.stroke.org.uk/sites/default/files/reducing_your_risk_black_african_and_black_caribbean_people.pdf

Swift J. and Gould H. (2021), *Not An Object: On Sexualization and Exploitation of Women and Girls*, Unicef USA, viewed on 17 May 2021, Available at: https://www.unicefusa.org/stories/not-object-sexualization-and-exploitation-women-and-girls/30366

The Well Co. (n.d.), *What Is Food Culture And How Does It Impact Health?*, The Well Co., viewed on 20 May 2021, Available at: https://www.thewellessentials.com/blog/what-is-food-culture-and-what-does-it-have-to-do-with-our-health